Contents

Called to Full Unity

Documents on Anglican-Roman Catholic Relations 1966-1983

Joseph W. Witmer
J. Robert Wright
Editors

Bishops' Committee for Ecumenical and
Interreligious Affairs
National Conference of Catholic Bishops

Ecumenical Office
Executive Council of the Episcopal Church

Published by the
Office of Publishing and Promotion Services
United States Catholic Conference

To further the Anglican–Roman Catholic dialogue, to increase knowledge of and contacts between our Churches, and to make available statements of church leaders and theologically agreed statements, Joseph W. Witmer, of the Bishops' Committee for Ecumenical and Interreligious Affairs Secretariat, and J. Robert Wright, Theological Consultant to the Ecumenical Office of the Episcopal Church, have assembled these documents. *Called to Full Unity* is authorized for publication by the undersigned.

> Monsignor Daniel F. Hoye
> General Secretary
> NCCB/USCC

Permission to print the various documents in this publication has been obtained from the following sources:

> *One in Christ*, Turvey Abbey, England
> Commission for Christian Unity, Scottish Conference of (Roman Catholic) Bishops
> Episcopal Diocesan Ecumenical Officers/National Association of (Roman Catholic) Diocesan Ecumenical Officers
> Archbishop Coggan, Archbishop Ramsey, Archbishop Runcie—Archbishops of Canterbury—for their addresses
> Archbishop Runcie, "Rome and Canterbury" (Lenten Address of March 11, 1981) reprinted from *Windows onto God* with the permission of The Society for Promoting Christian Knowledge
> Canon Van Culin, for the Lambeth Documentation
> Other documents have been taken from *Information Services*, the publication of the Vatican Secretariat for Promoting Christian Unity

First Printing, March 1986
Second Printing, October 1999

ISBN 1-55586-937-8

On this eve of Pentecost, we turn again in prayer to Jesus, the Good Shepherd, who promised to ask the Father to give us another Advocate to be with us for ever, the Spirit of truth (cf. Jn 14:16), to lead us TO THE FULL UNITY TO WHICH HE CALLS US. Confident in the power of this same Holy Spirit, we commit ourselves anew to the task of working for unity with firm faith, renewed hope, and ever deeper love.

Common Declaration of Pope John Paul II and the Archbishop of Canterbury, May 29, 1982, no. 7

Introduction

Twenty years may be considered a short or long period of time, depending upon one's perspective. The period is commonly reckoned to be a generation in human affairs, including the life of the Church. There are both sobering and encouraging dimensions in the recognition that ecumenical dialogue between the Episcopal and Roman Catholic Churches, by an officially appointed commission in the United States, has now gone on for a generation.

The first five years the commission met, beginning in 1965, the excitement stimulated by, and the expectation many persons derived from, the Second Vatican Council filled the air. Press releases were not only issued after meetings, reporters sought them; and spokesmen for the commission were eagerly interviewed and questioned by members of the media. The most commonly put question was a variation of how long it would take for the two Churches to get together, or, at the least, when might sacramental Communion be exercised between the two Churches. In the euphoria of the time, some thought five or ten years would bring the latter goal about.

Twenty years have now elapsed since the first meeting of the National Commission in Washington, D.C., and the official canonical relation of the two Churches is no different than it was in 1965. That fact is a disappointment to many, and the fact of continuing separation should be a disappointment to all. While, from the institutional point of view, nothing of major significance has happened in the intervening twenty years, from a theological and attitudinal point of view, many exciting things have happened. Some setbacks have occurred here and there, and some new difficulties—for example, the ordination of women—have appeared. In spite of such occurrences, however, important theological agreement and convergence have been uncovered in the precise areas that are historically responsible for the separation of the Anglican Communion and the Roman Catholic Church. Indicative of such agreement and convergence is the adoption by the 66th General Convention of the Episcopal Church of the Agreed Statements of the International Commission on *Eucharistic Doctrine* and *Ministry and Ordination* as "a statement of the faith of this Church in the matters concerned. . . ."

Significant agreements and statements have not been made just by the National Commission in the United States and by the International Commission; important developments have occurred in other areas of the world also. So it is that, in presenting this collection of documents, a number of items from other countries are included. All of the documents in this collection have been previously published, but not many of our readers will have ready access to the variety of periodicals and publications within which the contents of this volume are found.

The documents are presented in chronological order, but, of course, more documentation is omitted than included. People may be surprised or disappointed by the contents presented. Decisions on the contents of this volume were made by the informal consensus of present members of ARC, based on their understanding and use of the large amount of ecumenical material available to them. We believe a fair representation of what has been going on between and within the two Churches during the last twenty years can be found in these pages.

We hope the easy accessibility of the material here presented will help a larger number of persons better understand evolving relations between the Churches, and we are confident the reader will discern within these pages the Spirit stirring the Churches. The one God, who sent his one Son into the world, wants his one Church to be visibly discernible in the world, as was his Son. Some steps of the recent journey of the pilgrim Church are here described. We think the direction is the one God desires for his people, and we pray that by his Spirit and grace not only will the road be clear but the progress will be constant. May His will be done.

†Raymond W. Lessard
Bishop of Savannah

†Arthur A. Vogel
Bishop of West Missouri

The Common Declaration by Pope Paul VI and the Archbishop of Canterbury

Rome, Saint Paul Without-the-Walls

24 March 1966

In this city of Rome, from which Saint Augustine was sent by Saint Gregory to England and there founded the cathedral see of Canterbury, towards which the eyes of all Anglicans now turn as the centre of their Christian Communion, His Holiness Pope Paul VI and His Grace Michael Ramsey, Archbishop of Canterbury, representing the Anglican Communion, have met to exchange fraternal greetings.

At the conclusion of their meeting they give thanks to Almighty God Who by the action of the Holy Spirit has in these latter years created a new atmosphere of Christian fellowship between the Roman Catholic Church and the Churches of the Anglican Communion.

This encounter of the 23 March 1966 marks a new stage in the development of fraternal relations, based upon Christian charity, and of sincere efforts to remove the causes of conflict and to re-establish unity.

In willing obedience to the command of Christ who bade His disciples love one another, they declare that, with His help, they wish to leave in the hands of the God of mercy all that in the past has been opposed to this precept of charity, and that they make their own the mind of the Apostle which he expressed in these words: 'Forgetting those things which are behind, and reaching forth unto those things which are before, I press towards the mark for the prize of the high calling of God in Christ Jesus' (Phil. 3. 13–14).

They affirm their desire that all those Christians who belong to these two Communions may be animated by these same sentiments of respect, esteem and fraternal love, and in order to help these develop to the full, they intend to inaugurate between the Roman Catholic Church and the Anglican Communion a serious dialogue which, founded on the Gospels and on the ancient common traditions, may lead to that unity in truth, for which Christ prayed.

The dialogue should include not only theological matters such as Scripture, Tradition and Liturgy, but also matters of practical difficulty felt on either side. His Holiness the Pope and His Grace the Archbishop of Canterbury are, indeed, aware that serious obstacles stand in the way of a restoration of complete communion of faith and sacramental life; nevertheless, they are of one mind in their determination to promote responsible contacts between their Communions in all those spheres of Church life where collaboration is likely to lead to a greater understanding and a deeper charity, and to strive in common to find solutions for all the great problems that face those who believe in Christ in the world of today.

Through such collaboration, by the Grace of God the Father and in the light of the Holy Spirit, may the prayer of Our Lord Jesus Christ for unity among His disciples be brought nearer to fulfilment, and with progress towards unity may there be a strengthening of peace in the world, the peace that only He can grant who gives 'the peace that passeth all understanding', together with the blessing of Almighty God, Father, Son and Holy Spirit, that it may abide with all men for ever.

†Michael Cantuariensis   Paulus PP. VI

ARC IV Statement
on the Eucharist

The *Statement on the Eucharist*, issued at ARC's fourth meeting (May 1967), suitably opens this collection, for it has proven to be singularly important in subsequent Anglican-Roman Catholic discussions. One of the first decisions made by the young commission in the United States was to define the Church as a "eucharistic fellowship," and that insight has been a central theme of the International Commission in its later work. The fact that baptismal union with Christ is fulfilled and perfected in eucharistic living is basic to understanding the communal nature of the Church, the ministry of the Church, and the exercise of authority within the Church, as the International Commission has explicated those topics in its Agreed Statements.

For the Episcopal Church, teaching on this subject is now governed by the answer of the Catechism in its new (1979) *Book of Common Prayer*. To the question, "Why is the Eucharist called a sacrifice?" comes the answer, "Because the Eucharist, the Church's sacrifice of praise and thanksgiving, is the way by which the sacrifice of Christ is made present, and in which he unites us to his one offering of himself" (p. 859).

"Since the time of the Reformation, the doctrine of Eucharistic sacrifice has been considered a major obstacle to the reconciliation of the Anglican Communion and the Roman Catholic Church. It is the conviction of our commission that this is no longer true.

"We have made a careful study of the documents of the Second Vatican Council, the Lambeth Conference Report of 1958, the 1949 statement of faith and order of the Protestant Episcopal Church in the U.S. and other statements of the contemporary position of both our Churches. From these statements it is clear to us that the findings of modern biblical, theological and liturgical studies have transcended many of the polemical formulations of an earlier period.

"We believe that it is of utmost importance for the clergy and laity of our two Churches to acknowledge their substantial identity in this area of Eucharistic doctrine and to build upon it as they go forward in dialogue. Whatever doctrinal disagreements may remain between our churches, the understanding of the sacrificial nature (of the Eucharistic) is not among them.

"Here is an effort to sum up the consensus at which we have arrived:

"The Church is the Body of Christ and is built up by the Word through the Eucharist.

"Baptism is the entrance into the Eucharistic community. In the Holy Eucharist, Christians are united with Christ as the fulfillment and perfection of their baptismal union with Him.

"In the Lord's Supper, we participate at the same time in Christ's death, Resurrection and Ascension; the Christian community is thus transformed in grace, and the pledge of future glory is given to us.

"Our communion with Christ in the Holy Eucharist is also communion with one another. Such union is achieved through the Holy Spirit.

"Christian people participating in Christ's priesthood through Baptism and Confirmation are meant to be a living sacrifice to God. That sacrifice finds its fullest expression in the Eucharistic offering of the priesthood of the people of God. Such sacramental offering of the whole people is made possible through the special action of the ministerial priest who is empowered by his ordination to make present Christ's sacrifice for His people.

"The sacrifice of the Holy Eucharist is not just the sacrifice of the Cross, but the sacrifice of Christ's whole life of obedience to the Father, which culminated in His death on the Cross and His glorious Resurrection. We offer nothing we have not first received; because of our incorporation into Christ at Baptism, He offers us in Himself to the Father."

Milwaukee, Wisconsin—May 29, 1967

The Malta Report

Report of the Anglican/Roman Catholic
Joint Preparatory Commission
After Meeting at Gazzada
(9 to 13 January 1967),
Huntercombe Manor
(31 August to 4 September 1967),
and Malta
(30 December 1967 to 3 January 1968)

This seminal document for Anglican-Roman Catholic
relations was produced in 1967 during the course of three meetings
held by the Anglican-Roman Catholic Joint Preparatory Commission.
The Malta Report identified three areas of apparent doctrinal disagreement: ecclesiology, ordained ministry, and authority. It called for
the study of two topics causing critical pastoral concern: moral theology and the theology of marriage and mixed marriage. The report
made general recommendations for practical cooperation. Finally, the
document proposed that a Permanent Joint Anglican-Roman Catholic
International Commission be established that would be "responsible
for the oversight of Roman Catholic-Anglican relations."

I

1. The visit of the Archbishop of Canterbury to Pope Paul VI in
March 1966, and their decision to constitute an Anglican/Roman Catholic Joint Preparatory Commission, marked a new stage in relations
between our two Churches. The three meetings of the Commission,
held during 1967 at Gazzada, Huntercombe, and in Malta, were characterized not only by a spirit of charity and frankness, but also by a
growing sense of urgency, penitence, thankfulness, and purpose: of
urgency, in response to the pressure of God's will, apprehended as
well in the processes of history and the aspirations and achievements
of men in his world as in the life, worship, witness, and service of
his Church; of penitence, in the conviction of our shared responsibility for cherishing animosities and prejudices which for four hundred
years have kept us apart, and prevented our attempting to understand or resolve our differences; of thankfulness for the measure of
unity which through baptism into Christ we already share, and for
our recent growth towards greater unity and mutual understanding;
of purpose, in our determination that the work begun in us by God

7

shall be brought by his grace, to fulfilment in the restoration of his peace to his Church and his world.

2.   The members of the Commission have completed the preparatory work committed to them by compiling this report which they submit for their consideration to His Holiness the Pope and His Grace the Archbishop. The Decree on Ecumenism recognizes that among the Western Communions separated from the Roman See the Churches of the Anglican Communion 'hold a special place'. We hope in humility that our work may so help to further reconciliation between Anglicans and Roman Catholics as also to promote the wider unity of all Christians in their common Lord. We share the hope and prayer expressed in the common declaration issued by the Pope and the Archbishop after their meeting that 'a serious dialogue founded on the Gospels and on the ancient common traditions may lead to that unity in truth for which Christ prayed'.

3.   We record with great thankfulness our common faith in God our Father, in our Lord Jesus Christ, and in the Holy Spirit; our common baptism in the one Church of God; our sharing of the holy Scriptures, of the Apostles' and Nicene Creeds, the Chalcedonian definition, and the teaching of the Fathers; our common Christian inheritance for many centuries with its living traditions of liturgy, theology, spirituality, Church order, and mission.

4.   Divergences since the sixteenth century have arisen not so much from the substance of this inheritance as from our separate ways of receiving it. They derive from our experience of its value and power, from our interpretation of its meaning and authority, from our formulation of its content, from our theological elaboration of what it implies, and from our understanding of the manner in which the Church should keep and teach the Faith. Further study is needed to distinguish between those differences which are merely apparent, and those which are real and require serious examination.

5.   We agree that revealed Truth is given in holy Scripture and formulated in dogmatic definitions through thought-forms and language which are historically conditioned. We are encouraged by the growing agreement of theologians in our two Communions on methods of interpreting this historical transmission of revelation. We should examine further and together both the way in which we assent to and apprehend dogmatic truths and the legitimate means of understanding and interpreting them theologically. Although we agree that doctrinal comprehensiveness must have its limits, we believe that diversity has an intrinsic value when used creatively rather than destructively.

6.   In considering these questions within the context of the present situation of our two Communions, we propose particularly as matter for dialogue the following possible convergences of lines of thought: first, between the traditional Anglican distinction of internal and external communion and the distinction drawn by the Vatican Council between full and partial communion; secondly, between the Anglican distinction of fundamentals from non-fundamentals and the distinction implied by the Vatican Council's references to a 'hierarchy of truths' (Decree on Ecumenism, 11), to the difference between 'revealed truths' and 'the manner in which they are formulated' (Pastoral Constitution on the Church in the Modern World, 62), and to diversities in theological tradition being often 'complementary rather than conflicting' (Decree on Ecumenism, 17).

II

7. We recommend that the second stage in our growing together begin with an official and explicit affirmation of mutual recognition from the highest authorities of each Communion. It would acknowledge that both Communions are at one in the faith that the Church is founded upon the revelation of God the Father, made known to us in the Person and work of Jesus Christ, who is present through the Holy Spirit in the Scriptures and his Church, and is the only Mediator between God and Man, the ultimate Authority for all our doctrine. Each accepts the basic truths set forth in the ecumenical Creeds and the common tradition of the ancient Church, although neither Communion is tied to a positive acceptance of all the beliefs and devotional practices of the other.

8. In every region where each Communion has a hierarchy, we propose an annual joint meeting of either the whole or some considerable representation of the two hierarchies.

9. In the same circumstances we further recommend:

(a) Constant consultation between committees concerned with pastoral and evangelistic problems including, where appropriate, the appointment of joint committees.

(b) Agreements for joint use of churches and other ecclesiastical buildings, both existing and to be built, wherever such use is helpful for one or other of the two Communions.

(c) Agreements to share facilities for theological education, with the hope that all future priests of each Communion should have attended some course taught by a professor of the other Communion. Arrangements should also be made where possible for temporary exchange of students.

(d) Collaboration in projects and institutions of theological scholarship to be warmly encouraged.

10. Prayer in common has been recommended by the Decree on Ecumenism and provisions for this common worship are to be found in the *Directory* (para. 56). We urge that they be implemented.

11. Our similar liturgical and spiritual traditions make extensive sharing possible and desirable; for example, in noneucharistic services, the exploration of new forms of worship, and retreats in common. Religious orders of similar inspiration in the two Communions are urged to develop a special relationship.

12. Our closeness in the field of sacramental belief leads us further to recommend that on occasion the exchange of preachers for the homily during the celebration of the Eucharist be also permitted, without prejudice to the more general regulations contained in the *Directory*.

13. Since our liturgies are closely related by reason of their common source, the ferment of liturgical renewal and reform now engaging both our Communions provides an unprecedented opportunity for collaboration. We should co-operate, and not take unilateral action, in any significant changes in the seasons and major holy days of the Christian Year; and we should experiment together in the development of a common eucharistic lectionary. A matter of special urgency in view of the advanced stage of liturgical revision in both Communions is that we reach agreement on the vernacular forms of those prayers, hymns, and responses which our people share in common in their respective liturgies. (A list of these texts is appended.) We recommend that this be taken up without delay.

We are gratified that collaboration in this work has been initiated by the exchange of observers and consultants in many of our respective liturgical commissions. Especially in matters concerning the vernacular, we recommend that representatives of our two Communions (not excluding other Christian bodies with similar liturgical concerns) be associated on a basis of equality both in international and in national and regional committees assigned this responsibility.

14. We believe that joint or parallel statements from our Church leaders at international, national, and local level on urgent human issues can provide a valuable form of Christian witness.

15. In the field of missionary strategy and activity ecumenical understanding is both uniquely valuable and particularly difficult. Very little has hitherto been attempted in this field between our two Communions and, while our other recommendations of course apply to the young Churches and mission areas, we propose further the institution at international level of an official joint consultation to consider the difficulties involved and the co-operation which should be undertaken.

16. The increasing number of mixed marriages points to the need for a thorough investigation of the doctrine of marriage in its sacramental dimension, its ethical demands, its canonical status, and its pastoral implications. It is hoped that the work of the Joint Commission on Marriage will be promptly initiated and vigorously pursued, and that its recommendations will help to alleviate some of the difficulties caused by mixed marriages, to indicate acceptable changes in Church regulations, and to provide safeguards against the dangers which threaten to undermine family life in our time.

III

17. We cannot envisage in detail what may be the issues and demands of the final stage in our quest for the full, organic unity of our two Communions. We know only that we must be constant in prayer for the grace of the Holy Spirit in order that we may be open to his guidance and judgement, and receptive to each other's faith and understanding. There remain fundamental theological and moral questions between us where we need immediately to seek together for reconciling answers. In this search we cannot escape the witness of our history; but we cannot resolve our differences by mere reconsideration of, and judgement upon, the past. We must press on in confident faith that new light will be given us to lead us to our goal.
18. The fulfilment of our aim is far from imminent. In these circumstances the question of accepting some measure of sacramental intercommunion apart from full visible unity is being raised on every side. In the minds of many Christians no issue is today more urgent. We cannot ignore this, but equally we cannot sanction changes touching the very heart of Church life, eucharistic communion, without being certain that such changes would be truly Christian. Such certainty cannot be reached without more and careful study of the theology implied.
19. We are agreed that among the conditions required for intercommunion are both a true sharing in faith and the mutual recognition of ministry. The latter presents a particular difficulty in regard to Anglican Orders according to the traditional judgement of the Roman Church. We believe that the present growing together of our two Communions and the needs of the future require of us a very serious consideration of this question in the light of modern theology. The theology of the ministry forms part of the theology of the Church and must be considered as such. It is only when sufficient agreement has been reached as to the nature of the priesthood and the meaning to be attached in this context to the word 'validity' that we could proceed, working always jointly, to the application of this doctrine to the Anglican ministry of today. We would wish to re-examine historical events and past documents only to the extent that they can throw light upon the facts of the present situation.
20. In addition, a serious theological examination should be jointly undertaken on the nature of authority with particular reference to its bearing on the interpretation of the historic faith to which both our Communions are committed. Real or apparent differences between

us come to the surface in such matters as the unity and indefectibility of the Church and its teaching authority, the Petrine primacy, infallibility, and Mariological definitions.

21. In continuation of the work done by our Commission, we recommend that it be replaced by a Permanent Joint Commission responsible (in co-operation with the Secretariat for Promoting Christian Unity and the Church of England Council on Foreign Relations in association with the Anglican Executive Officer) for the oversight of Roman Catholic/Anglican relations, and the co-ordination of future work undertaken together by our two Communions.

22. We also recommend the constitution of two joint subcommissions, responsible to the Permanent Commission, to undertake two urgent and important tasks:

> ONE to examine the question of intercommunion, and the related matters of Church and Ministry;
> THE OTHER to examine the question of authority, its nature, exercise, and implications.

We consider it important that adequate money, secretarial assistance, and research facilities should be given to the Commission and its subcommissions in order that their members may do their work with thoroughness and efficiency.

23. We also recommend joint study of moral theology to determine similarities and differences in our teaching and practice in this field.

24. In concluding our Report we cannot do better than quote the words of those by whom we were commissioned, and to whom, with respect, we now submit it:

> In willing obedience to the command of Christ Who bade His disciples love one another, they declare that, with His help, they wish to leave in the hands of the God of mercy all that in the past has been opposed to this precept of charity, and that they make their own the mind of the Apostle which he expressed in these words: 'Forgetting those things which are behind, and reaching forth unto those things which are before, I press towards the mark for the prize of the high calling of God in Christ Jesus' (Phil. 3.13–14).

The Common Declaration by
Pope Paul VI and the Archbishop
of Canterbury
24 March 1966

Malta, 2 January 1968

Appendix

Some Common Liturgical Forms[1]

A. The Lord's Prayer
The Apostles' and Nicene Creeds
The Salutation, Responses
The Gloria Patri
The Kyrie
The Gloria in excelsis
The Sursum corda, Sanctus, and Benedictus qui venit
The Agnus Dei

B. The Te Deum
The Canticles: Benedictus, Magnificat, and Nunc Dimittis

C. The Psalter

Anglican/Roman Catholic Joint Preparatory Commission

List of Members[2]

Roman Catholic Church
The Most Rev. Charles Helmsing, Bishop of Kansas City—St Joseph
(JOINT CHAIRMAN)
The Most Rev. J. G. M. Willebrands, titular Bishop of Mauriana
The Most Rev. William Z. Gomes, Bishop of Poona
The Right Rev. Langton D. Fox, titular Bishop of Maura
The Right Rev. Christopher Butler, O.S.B., titular Bishop of
    Nova Barbara
The Rev. Louis Bouyer
The Rev. Father George Tavard, A.A.
The Rev. Michael Richards
The Rev. Father John Keating, C.S.P.
The Rev. Adrian Hastings
The Rev. Camillus Hay, O.F.M.
The Very Rev. Canon W. A. Purdy

Anglican Communion
The Right Rev. J. R. H. Moorman, Bishop of Ripon
(JOINT CHAIRMAN)

---

1. Except for the Psalter, agreed texts of almost all of these will now be found in *Prayers We Have In Common*.
2. As given in the Malta Report, of which this is part.

The Right Rev. W. G. H. Simon, Bishop of Llandaff[3]
The Right Rev. C. H. W. de Soysa, Bishop of Colombo
The Right Rev. E. G. Knapp-Fisher, Bishop of Pretoria
The Right Rev. H. R. McAdoo, Bishop of Ossory, Ferns, and Leighlin
The Rev. Canon James Atkinson
The Rev. Canon Eric Kemp
The Rev. Professor Howard E. Root
The Rev. Dr. Massey H. Shepherd Jr.
The Rev. Professor Eugene R. Fairweather
The Rev. Professor Albert T. Mollegen
The Rev. Canon John Findlow
The Rev. Canon John R. Satterthwaite

---

3. Unfortunately unable to attend the third meeting.

Letter from His Eminence Augustin Cardinal Bea to His Grace the Archbishop of Canterbury

10 June 1968

Secretariat for Promoting
Christian Unity

Vatican City,
10 June 1968

Your Grace,

It is with heartfelt joy that I am sending to you the personal letter of the Holy Father in which he expresses his satisfaction and gratitude for the work of the Anglican-Roman Catholic Joint Preparatory Commission, which after its sessions held during 1967 at Gazzada, Huntercombe, and in Malta, has completed the preparatory work committed to its members by compiling at its last session a report which makes concrete proposals for the continuation of the work done by the Commission. Despite our diversities we have some truths in common, which are very important and oblige us to travel the road towards unity.

His Holiness has charged me to explain more in detail, how this continuation, on the basis of the work already done should further be planned:

We approve the idea and agree that further studies be made on the points related in the report:

(a) on a common declaration of faith between Catholics and Anglicans;

(b) on liturgical problems of common concern for the Roman Catholic Church and the Anglican Communion;

(c) on the possibility of co-ordinate action through joint or parallel statements on urgent human issues at international, national, and local level;

(d) on the problems and difficulties which arise in the field of missionary strategy and activity of the Church, and the possibility of co-operation;

(e) on the theological and pastoral problems of the doctrine of marriage and the difficulties caused by mixed marriages;

(f) on the ecclesiological principles of the Roman Catholic Church and the Anglican Communion in connection with the problem of sacramental intercommunion;

(g) on the theology of the Church and the theology of the ministry in connection with the nature of the priesthood and the application of this doctrine to the Anglican ministry of today;

(h) on the nature of authority in the Church and its concrete form in the teaching authority, in the Petrine primacy, etc.;

(i) on problems of moral theology;

(j) on the application of practical directions given in the Decree of the Second Vatican Council on Ecumenism and in the Directory issued by our Secretariat for Promoting Christian Unity.

Moreover we approve certain practical recommendations made in the report such as:

(a) periodical joint meetings in regions where both the Roman Catholic Church and the Anglican Communion have a hierarchy of either the whole or some considerable representation of the two hierarchies;

(b) consultations on pastoral problems of evangelization in the modern world;

(c) common prayers, according to the rules of the Directory issued by our Secretariat for Promoting Christian Unity;

(d) development under the direction of the respective Superiors of a special relationship between religious orders of similar inspiration in the two communions.

Other practical recommendations, however, such as agreements for joint use of churches, and agreements to share facilities for theological education and temporary exchange of students require further investigation and especially consultation with the appropriate authorities (the episcopal conferences and the competent authority in Rome).

In order to assure the continuation of the work done by the Anglican-Roman Catholic Joint Preparatory Commission and to carry out the proposals for further studies and activities, we accept the recommendations made by the Commission:

(a) that the Commission be replaced by a Joint Commission responsible for the oversight of Roman Catholic-Anglican relations, and the co-ordination of future work undertaken together by the Roman Catholic Church and the Anglican Communion;

(b) the constitution of joint sub-commissions, responsible to the Joint Commission, which are necessary for the execution of the programme if approved by the authorities on both sides;

(c) the Secretariat for Promoting Christian Unity and the Church of England Council on Foreign Relations in association with the Anglican Executive Officer should study the methods and con-

crete ways in which the practical recommendations, as far as they
have been approved on both sides, can be realized.

Concerning the question of the publication of *The Malta Report*,
we believe it is better not to give the report for publication to the
press. In some of its phrases, the formulation seems not quite clear
and exact. Its publication through the press might create the impression that the report represents more than a report of a preparatory
commission and even create among the Bishops of the Church the
impression that the Report has been already approved by the competent authorities in all its details and that it was communicated to
them for implementation. But in fact we are still at a phase of study
and for the present moment we prefer that further steps be taken
after careful study and with approval of the official authorities on
both sides. Of course we do not intend to prevent Your Grace from
communicating the content of the report to the members of the Lambeth Conference, if you would think this advisable in order to have
their reactions and their proposals for the continuation of the dialogue
and the co-operation.

I express my sincere hope that with the support of the prayers
of all the faithful through the grace of God the Churches may be led
by him who is the way, the truth, and the life, to the unity in the
Holy Spirit, "That there may be one visible Church of God, a Church
truly universal and sent forth to the whole world that the world may
be converted to the Gospel and so be saved, to the glory of God"
(*Decree on Ecumenism*, 1).

With a warm and heartfelt greeting in the name of our common
Lord and with a renewal of my personal pledge of prayers for the
guidance of the Holy Spirit in your momentous labours this summer,

I remain,
Yours devotedly in Christ,

(signed) Augustin Cardinal Bea
†J. G. M. Willebrands

Lambeth Conference 1968
Section Report

This was the first Lambeth Conference to have observers present from other Churches and the first to open its plenary sessions to the press. Noteworthy in the report excerpted here, which was welcomed in an official resolution of the conference, is the theology of episcopal *collegiality* (this may be the first use of this word by a Lambeth Conference) and the balanced but friendly remarks on the papacy (a slight advance over statements of previous conferences). The first draft was even more positive in its attitude toward the papal see, and it has been suggested that the appearance of *Humanae Vitae*, at this very time (July 29, 1968), had a less than positive effect. For further information, see *Episcopalians and Roman Catholics: Can They Ever Get Together?*, editors Herbert J. Ryan, SJ, and J. Robert Wright (Denville, N.J., 1972), pp. 150-151; *Herder Correspondence* 6:1 (January 1969): 27; and Edward R. Welles II, *The Happy Disciple* (Manset, Maine, 1975), pp. 157-167.

Relations with the Roman Catholic Church

In the "Common Declaration", signed in Rome on 24 March 1966, the Pope and the Archbishop of Canterbury gave thanks to Almighty God for the new atmosphere of Christian fellowship now existing between the two Churches, and declared their intention of inaugurating "a serious dialogue which, founded on the Gospels and on the ancient common traditions, may lead to that unity in truth, for which Christ prayed." This dialogue, they declared, was to include "not only theological matters such as Scripture, Tradition and Liturgy, but also matters of practical difficulty felt on either side."

It was as a result of this Declaration that a Joint Preparatory Commission was set up; and the Section received with gratitude the report issued as a result of the three meetings of that Commission.

Essential to such meetings is the spirit in which they are undertaken. For our part we recognize in penitence that many of our past attitudes and actions have contributed to our unhappy divisions and that there are still many things in us for which we must ask the forgiveness of God and of our fellow Christians. Yet we are thankful for the many signs of renewal of the spirit of unity in ourselves and in others.

Together with the Roman Catholic Church we confess our faith in God, Father, Son, and Holy Spirit, as witnessed by the holy Scriptures, the Apostles' and Nicene Creeds, and by the teaching of the Fathers of the early Church. We have one baptism and recognize many common features in our heritage. At the same time substantial divergences exist, many of which have arisen since the sixteenth century, in such matters as the unity and indefectibility of the Church and its teaching authority, the Petrine primacy, infallibility, and Mariological definitions, as well as in some moral problems. These matters will require serious study so that they may be carefully identified and, under the guidance of the Spirit, resolved. This task must be undertaken in the light of the challenge to the whole Church of God presented by the modern world, and in the context of the mission of the Church throughout the world and to all sorts and conditions of men.

Signs of Progress

Relations between Anglicans and Roman Catholics are progressing in various ways and to varying degrees in many places. Examples include common services of prayer and thanksgiving, the joint use of churches, the exchange of preachers, co-operation in theological education, and meetings of official commissions and informal groups. With due regard to individual consciences, we endorse and encourage these developments where local circumstances permit the avoidance of misunderstanding.

We rejoice that the new attitude towards Scripture, expressed in the Constitution on Divine Revelation, has led to cooperation in biblical studies and in the work of the United Bible Societies.

Liturgical renewal and reform represent a field where co-operation is urgent. Unilateral action in regard to the liturgical year and the vernacular forms used by our people is to be avoided.

The Christian witness being given by our clergy and laity in many urgent human issues, in many cases in close association with Roman Catholics, claims our support and our prayers. Where such witness may be strengthened by joint or parallel statements by church leaders, these should be issued.

We welcome the increasing signs of mutual recognition, not least in practical acts on both sides, of the reality of Anglican and Roman Catholic ministry in the whole Body of Christ on earth.

A Permanent Joint Commission

We recommend the setting up of a Permanent Joint Commission, our delegation to be chosen by the Lambeth Consultative Body or its successor and to be representative of the Anglican Communion as a whole. This commission or its subcommissions should consider the question of intercommunion in the context of a true sharing in faith and the mutual recognition of ministry, and should also consider in the light of the new biblical scholarship the orders of both Churches and the theology of ministry which forms part of the theology of the Church and can only be considered as such. The hope for the future lies in a fresh and broader approach to the understanding of apostolic succession and of the priestly office. On this line we look for a new joint appraisal of church orders.

Conversations between Anglicans and Roman Catholics should be conducted with due regard to the multiplicity of conversations also in progress with other Churches. In them all we propose to hold fast the principles of Catholic truth as we have been given to understand them, though we realize that, in renewed obedience to the Holy Spirit, we must at all times be willing to go forward adventurously.

Reports of Anglican/Roman Catholic conversations in the several provinces should be made available to members of the Permanent Joint Commission, and information on all these matters circulated by it throughout our communion.

Mixed Marriages

We are aware of the suffering which may arise from marriages in which one partner is an Anglican and the other a Roman Catholic, but welcome the fact that a Joint Commission on the Theology of Marriage and its Application to Mixed Marriages has been set up. The preliminary discussions of this joint commission have shown that the two Churches are close to one another in acknowledging that Holy Matrimony has a sacramental nature, although this is somewhat differently expressed in our respective formularies.

We welcome a suggestion from the (Roman Catholic) Third World Congress for the Lay Apostolate that Anglican priests should be acceptable as the official ministerial witnesses required by the Roman Catholic Church.

We note that the same Congress has asked that the responsibility for the Christian education of the children of a mixed marriage should be regarded as the responsibility of both parents who share in the grace of the marriage sacrament, and note that this is endorsed by the Declaration on Religious Liberty of Vatican II, which states: "Parents . . . have the right to determine, in accordance with their own religious beliefs, the kind of religious education that their children are to receive."

We also welcome the movement towards joint pastoral care of all concerned both before and after marriage by the clergy of the two Churches. Such joint pastoral care is an expression of the theology of Holy Matrimony which both Churches share.

Episcopacy, Collegiality, Papacy

The Anglican tradition has always regarded *episcopacy* as an essential part of its Catholic inheritance. We would regard it as an extension of the apostolic office and function both in time and space, and, moreover, we regard the transmission of apostolic power and responsibility as an activity of the college of bishops and never as a result of isolated action by any individual bishop.

In the discharge of his episcopal responsibility, the bishop is the guardian of the faith, the father of his people, and the driving force of mission in his area.

Traditionally the bishop is father in God to the clergy and laity of a territorial diocese, and part of his vocation is to represent the Catholic Church in his diocese and, conversely, to represent his diocese within the councils of the wider Church.

While we have no wish to diminish the importance of this traditional pattern, the demands of a new age suggest the wisdom of also consecrating bishops without territorial jurisdiction but with pastoral responsibility, directly or indirectly, for special groups such as the armed forces, industry, and particular areas of concern within the mission of the Church. This principle would simply be the extension of the widespread current practice of appointing suffragans, auxiliaries, and assistants. We submit that all such bishops, by virtue of their consecration as bishops in the Church of God, should have their due place in episcopal councils throughout the world.

The principle underlying *collegiality* is that the apostolic calling, responsibility, and authority are an inheritance given to the whole body or college of bishops. Every individual bishop has therefore a responsibility both as a member of this college and as chief pastor in his diocese. In the latter capacity he exercises direct oversight over the people committed to his charge. In the former he shares with his brother bishops throughout the world a concern for the wellbeing of the whole Church.

Within the college of bishops it is evident that there must be a president. In the Anglican Communion this position is at present held by the occupant of the historic see of Canterbury, who enjoys a primacy of honour, not of jurisdiction. This primacy is found to involve, in a particular way, that care for all the Churches which is shared by all the bishops.

The renewed sense of the collegiality of the episcopate is especially important at a time when most schemes for unity are being developed at a national level, because the collegiality of the episcopate helps to stress the worldwide and universal character of the Church. This collegiality must be a guiding principle in the growth of the relationships between the provinces of the Anglican Communion and those Churches with which we are, or shall be, in full communion. Within this larger college of bishops, the primacy would take on a new character which would need to be worked out in consultation with the Churches involved.

As a result of the emphasis placed on collegiality at the Second Vatican Council, the status of bishops in the Roman Catholic Church was in great measure enhanced, though the teaching of the First Vatican Council on the infallibility and immediate and universal juris- diction of the Pope was unaffected. We are unable to accept this teaching as it is commonly understood today. The relationships between the Pope and the episcopal college, of which he is a member, are, however, still being clarified, and are subject to development. We recall the statement made in the Lambeth Conference of 1908, and repeated in 1920 and 1930, "that there can be no fulfillment of the Divine purpose in any scheme of reunion which does not ultimately include the great Latin Church of the West, with which our history has been so closely associated in the past, and to which we are still bound by many ties of common faith and tradition." We recognize the Papacy as a historic reality whose developing role requires deep reflection and joint study by all concerned for the unity of the whole Body of Christ.

Although the declaration and guardianship of the faith has tra- ditionally been regarded as belonging fundamentally to the episcopal office, the collegiality of the episcopate must always be seen in the context of the conciliar character of the Church, involving the *consensus fidelium*, in which the episcopate has its place.

Lambeth Conference 1968 Actions

The Roman Catholic Church

52. The Conference welcomes the proposals made in the report of Section III which concern Anglican relations with the Roman Catholic Church.

53. The Conference recommends the setting up of a Permanent Joint Commission, for which the Anglican delegation should be chosen by the Lambeth Consultative Body (or its successor) and be represen- tative of the Anglican Communion as a whole.

54. In view of the urgent pastoral questions raised by mixed mar- riages the Conference welcomes the work of the Joint Commission on the Theology of Marriage and its Application to Mixed Marriages, and urges its speedy continuance.

Collegiality

55. The Conference recommends that the principle of collegiality should be a guiding principle in the growth of the relationships between the provinces of the Anglican Communion and those Churches with which we are, or shall be, in full communion, and draws particular attention to that part of the Section III report which underlines this principle.

Pope Paul VI
Remarks on the Canonization of the Uganda Martyrs

From its earliest planning, it was Our earnest desire that in the course of this brief visit to Uganda We should come here, to Namugongo. We wished to meet the Anglican Church which flourishes in this country. We wished to pay homage to those sons of whom it is most proud: those who—together with our own Catholic Martyrs—gave the generous witness of their lives to the Gospel of the Lord we have in common, Jesus Christ. For all of them, there is the same inspired word of praise: "These all died in faith, not having received what was promised, but having seen and greeted it from afar, and having acknowledged that they were strangers and exiles on the earth" (Heb 11:13).

In the Martyrs' spirit of ecumenism, we cannot resolve our differences by mere re-consideration of the past, or judgement upon it. Instead, we must press on in confidence that new light will be given us, to lead us to our goal; we must trust that new strength will be granted us, so that, in obedience to our common Lord, we may all be able to receive the grace of unity.

The Uganda martyrs were brought together by suffering, and died in faithful witness and hope. They now see, as we must, much to thank God for, "since God had foreseen something better for us, that apart from us they should not be made perfect" (Heb 11:40).

Among ecumenical enterprises, the Christian Council in Uganda is particularly flourishing. Since there can be no growth towards unity without strong deep local roots, it is Our prayer and, We feel confident, your prayer also, that the spiritual quality of this association may increase as collaboration extends into new fields.

Thus, not only in Uganda, but in all the great African continent, spiritual hunger will intensify to bring healing to that division of which the Second Vatican Council said that it "openly contradicts the will of Christ, scandalizes the world, and damages that most holy cause, the preaching of the Gospel to every creature" (*Unitatis Redintegratio*, no. 1). May the Lord bless the work of the All-Africa Christian Conference, as it bends its efforts towards the unity of all Christians!

A notable achievement in Christian co-operation is the common effort among the various confessions to provide readily accessible translations of Sacred Scripture, that rich source from which the minds and hearts of men receive the life-giving nourishment of divine Revelation. As the Council declared, "in the ecumenical dialogue itself, the Sacred Word is a precious instrument in the mighty hand of God, attaining to that unity which the Saviour holds out to all men" (*ibid*, no. 21).

This and many other forms of common work in Christ are gathered up in a single resolve. For this is the search we all pursue together, for that true, visible and organic unity which Christ so clearly willed, in order that the world might believe—that consummation for which, on the eve of His saving death, He so solemnly prayed to the Father.

In Jesus We express to you, Our Christian brethren, heartfelt greetings and good wishes, in firm and lasting hope, in ardent and sincere charity, invoking rich divine favours and graces.

The Nature of Baptism and Its Place in the Life of the Church

A Common Statement by the Joint Study Group of Representatives of the Roman Catholic and Scottish Episcopal Churches

Foreword

The Joint Study Group was formed after consultation between the Most Reverend Gordon Joseph Gray (now His Eminence Cardinal Gray), Archbishop of St. Andrews and Edinburgh, the Most Reverend James Donald Scanlan, Archbishop of Glasgow, the Most Reverend Francis H. Moncrieff, Primus of the Scottish Episcopal Church, and the Right Reverend Kenneth M. Carey, Bishop of Edinburgh.

The Group was to report back in the first instance to the National Ecumenical Commission of the Roman Catholic Church and to the Inter-Church Relations Committee of the Scottish Episcopal Church.

The subject chosen for discussion was "The nature of Baptism in the life of the Church."

The Group first met in Plenary Session on October 10th, 1968. It then met in two regional groups, based on Edinburgh and Glasgow. Two meetings were held before Christmas, 1968, by each regional group. After these meetings the Steering Committee (composed of the four Conveners listed below) met to discuss future regional meetings, to be held in the New Year. Three meetings were held by the Eastern Group and two by the Western Group. These were followed by a final meeting of the Steering Committee, in preparation for the closing Plenary Session, held on May 28th, 1969.

The Joint Study Group now presents its Report, which is unanimous. It asks the sponsoring bodies to continue its general remit, and suggests that the next subject for discussion should be "The ecclesial nature of the Eucharist."

The Group is happy to place on record its satisfaction at the friendship and understanding that have grown out of its meetings. It hopes that its work will further in some degree the cause of Christian unity in Scotland.

Members

Scottish Episcopal Church

Western Group:

The Very Reverend Provost H. McIntosh (Convener)
The Reverend Canon A. O. Barkway
The Reverend A. S. Black
Miss Gillian Carver
Dr. Robert A. Shanks
The Reverend J. A. Trimble

Eastern Group:

The Very Reverend Provost A. I. M. Haggart (Convener)
Mrs. Mary Burn
The Very Reverend W. B. Currie
The Reverend E. J. C. Davis
The Reverend D. Guthrie
Neil Macvicar, Q.C.

Roman Catholic Church

Western Group:

The Reverend D. Strain (Convener)
James Breen, Esq.
The Reverend Henry Docherty
The Reverend John Fitzsimmons
F. MacMillan, Esq.
The Reverend J. McShane

Eastern Group:

The Reverend J. Quinn, S.J. (Convener)
The Reverend C. Barclay
The Very Reverend B. Cavanagh, O.F.M.
The Reverend M. Donoghue
Dr. P. G. Walsh
The Reverend H. G. White

Owing to his appointment as Sheriff-Substitute, Mr. Macvicar was unable to attend the meetings and felt obliged to tender his resignation. Father Strain's illness in February of this year prevented

him from attending subsequent meetings: his place on the Steering
Committee was taken provisionally by Father Fitzsimmons.

A. I. M. Haggart
(*Chairman*)

James Quinn, S.J.
(*Secretary*)

June 1969.

I.   The Meaning of Baptism

There is a wealth of teaching about Baptism which is common to both
Churches. We have selected the following points as likely to help
towards a renewed understanding of the place of Baptism in the life
of the Church.

Introduction

It is a fact of experience that we are all born into an alienated world,
in which we are separated from God and from each other.

God in his love sent his Son to restore the world to that unity
with himself which is his will.

This unity has been restored to us through the life, death and
resurrection of his Son, Our Lord Jesus Christ.

The restoration of the unity that God wills for us is brought about
in us initially through the Holy Spirit in the sacrament of Baptism.
Through Baptism we are united to Christ and made members of his
Body, the Church.

**(a) We are baptized "in the name of the Father and of the Son
and of the Holy Spirit."**

Through Baptism God calls us into a new relationship with himself.

We share the divine life.

We become children of the Father, brethren of the Son, and Tem-
ples of the Holy Spirit.

We are heirs of the Kingdom of heaven.

(b) In Baptism we die and rise again with Christ.

Baptism is our Easter, our sharing in the Paschal Mystery of Christ's
death and resurrection.

Members of a humanity alienated from God, we die with Christ to all that is sin.

We rise again with him to newness of life in the Holy Spirit.

We become one with Christ in his risen life: our Baptism will be fulfilled in our resurrection to glory.

(c) Baptism is our entry into the Church.

By Baptism we are "incorporated" into Christ, i.e., we are made members of his Body, which is the Church.

Baptism is therefore important not only to the person baptized, but also to the whole Church.

By Baptism we are given a permanent status, function and responsibility within the Church, and for the sake of the Church.

We may be unaware of this status, function and responsibility; we may choose to ignore them; but we cannot lose them. Baptism, though given once only, is for the whole of life; it is a permanent consecration.

The status, function and responsibility of the baptized are defined by the nature of the Church, i.e., the royal, priestly and prophetic community of the New Israel, proclaiming God's kingship, his reconciling love and the values of the world to come.

(d) Baptism is a sacrament of Christian unity.

Baptism is our entry into the one Church of Christ.

Those who are baptized are one in confessing their faith in the Blessed Trinity. They are one also in sharing the life of the Blessed Trinity.

They are one in Christ and with each other.

The "one Baptism" which Christians share looks to its fulfilment in the visible Church in which all share the same faith, the same ministry and the same sacraments.

(e) Baptism is fulfilled in the Eucharist.

Baptism is a sacrament of initiation into the life of the Church.

The life of the Church on earth reaches its fullest expression in the celebration of the Eucharist.

The Eucharist therefore throws light on the status, function and responsibility of the baptized.

It is in the celebration of the Eucharist that the royal, priestly and prophetic community of the New Israel finds its true identity: it is seen at the Eucharist as the reconciled and reconciling community of faith, hope and love.

(f) Baptism is for the world.

From the Eucharist the Church goes out to serve the world.

The world was created to be one in Christ. It is made one in Christ through the Church, the great sign of the unity of all mankind.

It is the privilege, and the responsibility, of the baptized to build one world for Christ.

The reconciled community of the baptized are sent out from the Eucharist to be the reconciling community in the world.

II.   The Social Implications of Baptism

Awareness of the meaning of Baptism should have important consequences in practice for our individual and social lives as well as for the life of the Church.

The first step in a spiritual renewal of our country should be a renewed understanding of the implications of Baptism.

Baptism is for daily Christian living.

The Christian life is lived not only within the life of the Church, but also within the Christian family and within the social community.

Baptism lays important obligations upon parents, upon the Church and upon Christians in their social life.

Parents, Church and Christian society are jointly responsible for enabling children to fulfil their Baptism.

All Christians have a responsibility to create the kind of society in which God's will, revealed in Baptism, can be fulfilled, not frustrated, and in which all men can find their fullness of maturity in Christ.

III.   The Ecumenical Implications of Baptism

A renewed understanding of Baptism is important also for growth in Christian unity.

Fundamental to Christian unity is spiritual renewal within each communion.

The basis of such renewal is to be found in a renewed understanding of the meaning of Baptism.

We must live as baptized. We must recognize what we are through Baptism: the supernatural family of God.

The unity of Christians in Baptism is unique. It is a unity incomparably more profound than that of members of the same family in their kinship of blood.

The kinship of Christians is based not on nature but on grace. It is kinship in the Blood of Christ.

To recognize this kinship is the first step in ecumenical understanding.

It is within this context of supernatural kinship that differences between Churches must be examined.

The differences are differences within one family.

Such differences may be important. They may be based on principle, and may humanly be irreconcilable in conscience. But they should not blur the fundamental fact of an already existing Christian unity.

If this unity is to grow, it must first be recognized, and its implications acknowledged.

The fact of Baptism is thus the primary growth-point in Christian unity.

Subsequent Actions

The Provincial Synod of the Scottish Episcopal Church meeting at Perth on Tuesday, 4th November, 1969, received, through its Inter-Church Relations Committee, the Report of the Joint Study Group of Representatives of the Roman Catholic and Scottish Episcopal Church, entitled,

"The Nature of Baptism and its place in the life of the Church."

The Synod warmly welcomed the Report and unanimously resolved:
1. To continue to recognise the validity of Baptism as administered by the Roman Catholic Church.
2. To produce, in co-operation with the Roman Catholic Church in Scotland, a common certificate of Baptism for use in each Church, as recommended in the Report.
3. To co-operate with the Roman Catholic Church in Scotland, through the appropriate Liturgical bodies, in the production of a Common Rite of Baptism for separate use in each Church.
4. To share, with the Roman Catholic Church in Scotland, the costs of publishing the Report as received.
5. To continue the conversations of the Joint Study Group on the subject of "The Ecclesial Nature of the Eucharist."

At their meeting on the 6th of November, 1969, the Scottish Hierarchy made the following statement on the paper, "The Nature of Baptism and its place in the life of the Church," presented by the Joint Study Group of Representatives of the Roman Catholic and Scottish Episcopal Churches:

"In general, we commend the Report drawn up by the Joint Study Group of Representatives of the Roman Catholic Church and the

Scottish Episcopal Church on 'The Nature of Baptism and its place in the life of the Church.'

"We are particularly pleased with the practical proposals in which the requisites for valid Baptism are clearly stated.

"We hope that discussions between the Liturgical Commissions of the Scottish Episcopal Church and the Roman Catholic Church will draw us together through a common ceremonial for the conferring of the sacrament.

"Regarding the sections in the Report concerned with the meaning of Baptism and its social and ecumenical implications, we wish to make this comment. Because of its brevity there is room for misunderstanding in the interpretation of, especially, paragraphs c. and d., should sentences be quoted out of context. Consequently, we note that our understanding of these paragraphs is in accordance with the teaching contained in the documents of Vatican II (cf. *Decree on Ecumenism*, nos. 3 and 22; and *Instruction on the implementation of the Decree*, no. 10), lest the impression be given that through valid Baptism unity among baptized Christians has already been achieved without that fullness of unity desired by Christ for his Church."

ARC VII Statement

The Malta Report had been distributed to all the
participants of the 1968 Lambeth Conference. At the suggestion of
Bishop John S. Higgins and Father Herbert J. Ryan, SJ, ARC spent
its seventh meeting drafting a statement that would summarize its
progress and provide a context for specific recommendations for
practical cooperation between the Episcopal Church and the Roman
Catholic Church in the United States. The *ARC VII Statement* was
brought by three ARC members (Fathers Arthur A. Vogel, George
Tavard, and Herbert J. Ryan, SJ) to the first meeting at Windsor in
January 1970.

Anglicans and Roman Catholics in the United States have been meeting officially since June of 1965. The group of representatives named
by the Roman Catholic Bishops' Committee for Ecumenical and Interreligious Affairs and the Joint Commission on Ecumenical Relations
of the Episcopal Church in the United States of America has subsequently been known as the Joint Commission on Anglican-Roman
Catholic Relations in the United States (usually informally abbreviated
to ARC).

Seven meetings have been held to date. These were ARC I, in
June of 1965, in Washington, D.C.; ARC II, in February of 1966, at
Kansas City, Missouri; ARC III, in October of 1966, at Providence,
Rhode Island; ARC IV, in May of 1967, at Milwaukee, Wisconsin;
ARC V, in January of 1968, at Jackson, Mississippi; ARC VI, in Decem-
ber of 1968, at Liberty, Missouri; ARC VII, in December of 1969, at
Boynton Beach, Florida.

From the beginning, members of ARC have sensed the creative
theological and ecumenical possibilities in the situation of their two
churches in the United States. At their first meeting, they came to a
speedy agreement on several questions relating to the sacraments of
Christian initiation. In particular, they were agreed that the instances
of conditional baptism of Episcopalians upon admission to the Roman
Catholic Church or of confirmation of Roman Catholics by Episcopalians were abuses. With their common sacramental emphasis, the
group chose at the same time the topic of the ensuing conversations
to be: "The Eucharist, Sign and Cause of Unity; the Church as a

Eucharistic Fellowship." ARC studied this theme continuously in meetings II through V.

At ARC II, the question was immediately raised, as the conclusion to one of the several papers presented it: "Could not we, in the controlled situation which is ours, celebrate together the Eucharist? If not, why not? What precisely are the barriers?"

It became clear that some of both Roman Catholic and Anglican members felt it possible, on the basis of principle, to propose that discriminate Eucharistic communion be celebrated, now or in the near future, by the group as a legitimate ecclesial action. In all of the ARC meetings, on successive days, Anglican and Roman Catholic liturgies have been celebrated with all of the members attending. In every instance, only Anglicans have received communion at the Anglican liturgy and only Roman Catholics have received at the Roman Catholic liturgy.

ARC II considered a number of barriers which have existed to the full communion and organic unity of our Churches. Many of these appeared no longer to be obstacles to the participation of Anglicans and Roman Catholics together in the Eucharist in one another's churches. Some important difficulties remained, barring such an action insofar as could be seen at that time. Still some expressed the sentiment that perhaps such communion was not so far away, especially when the urgency of the Churches' united presence to the world was sufficiently realized. In the press conference which followed, it was this optimism which overshadowed the report on the specifics of the conference and, consequently, several newspapers had headlines suggesting imminent intercommunion or a new joint rite. While such suggestions did not become actualities in succeeding meetings, nevertheless, a certain expectation, which cannot be ignored, was created among our people and, indeed, among certain members of the commission itself.

ARC III advanced agreements by clarifying language, the meaning of liturgical practices and the general theological nature of holy orders and of the priestly ministry. Both churches hold firmly for the necessity of an ordained ministry in which are included the three orders of bishops, priests (presbyters) and deacons. Problems and practices of intercommunion were again discussed and not entirely resolved.

ARC IV took up the study of Eucharistic sacrifice, studying the Documents of the Second Vatican Council, the Lambeth Conference Report of 1958, the 1948 Statement of Faith and Order of the Episcopal Church, and other statements of the contemporary position of both our Churches. It concluded that while, since the time of the Reformation, the doctrine of Eucharistic sacrifice had been considered a major obstacle to the reconciliation of the Anglican Communion and the Roman Catholic Church, this was no longer true. It based its conclusion on the findings of the modern biblical, liturgical and theological studies which, ARC members believed, had transcended the polemical formulations of an earlier period.

This same consultation considered it to be of the utmost importance for the clergy and laity of the two Churches to acknowledge their substantial agreement in this area of Eucharistic doctrine and to build upon it as they go forward in dialogue. In elucidation, ARC IV published a statement as a kind of brief summary of such consensus (see Appendix I).

The next consultation again studied official documentation and theological papers, this time on the necessity and role of the ordained priesthood and the relationship of this ministry to the common priesthood and to the role of the laity in the church. It concluded that there was no basic difference of understanding on these topics and that whatever minor differences of understanding did exist, they did not *in themselves* constitute the barrier to the two Churches celebrating and receiving communion together.

The sixth consultation heard papers exploring the problem of unity from the viewpoint of a layman's experience and of a bishop's experience as a guardian and representative of church unity. However, most of the dialogue was devoted to consideration of the future of such bilateral consultations as ARC and to the procedures for the issuance of releases, interim statements and the occasional publishing of the proceedings of such sessions.

Most of the meeting was spent clarifying such procedures. An Executive Committee was set up to expedite internal housekeeping matters in the future. A careful statement of the competence of ARC and of its relation to the news media was drawn up and is appended to this report (see Appendix II).

A. Pastoral Situation

ARC members, as they work toward Christian reconciliation, feel the demands of urgency pushing them ahead. The religious situation in the United States today is challenging and, we believe, pressing. Its salient characteristics are these:

1.   American cultural patterns have changed. During the past two generations the mobility of people—in residence, in social interaction, and in income level—has weakened the sense of dependence upon cultural and national traditions linking people to their background in the Old World. Present tensions of race and region are uniquely American problems existing within an emerging American culture. Attachments to religious affiliations embedded in other national traditions increasingly are no longer dominant influences. In this emerging socio-cultural context, a fragmented Christianity finds it difficult

to contribute the healing and cohering influences so clearly needed.

2.   The Second Vatican Council spoke to the hearts of all people. In the American setting it was heard as the promise of a renewed Christianity and raised hopes for a united Christendom.

A variety of influences have combined in the United States to bring about a pattern of consultations, involving both Roman Catholics and Episcopalians, in separate exploratory discussions with other Christian groups. Especially noteworthy is the Consultation on Church Union, an effort at shaping a united church in which nine Churches, including the Episcopal Church, are engaged. Renewal and the rediscovery of the Christian commitment influence the American religious scene. The Anglican-Roman Catholic Commission understands itself as part of this movement.

3.   Because the Roman Catholic and Anglican Communions in the U.S. share a greatly treasured Christian tradition, they are deeply aware of their common commitment to preserve these inheritances and to carry them forward into the emerging fabric of American religious life. At the same time, both are sensitive to the larger worldwide scope of their communions, and they are resolved through ARC both to contribute to the Permanent Joint Anglican-Roman Catholic Commission the fruits of their efforts in the American context and also to utilize the accomplishments realized by the International Consultation.

4.   The members of ARC feel strongly the urgency to move soundly and positively toward a position of organic unity of their communions. Concerned Christians are already finding ways for the expression of their shared commitment. Often these are beyond the bounds of the formal church structures.

B. Projections

We, the members of the Joint Commission on Anglican-Roman Catholic Relations, now declare that we see the goal as to realize full communion of the Roman Catholic Church with the Episcopal Church and the other Churches of the Anglican Communion. For the past four and one half years we have given our energies to the task of this consultation. Nothing in the course of this serious enterprise has emerged which would cause us to think for a moment that this goal, given the guidance and support of the Spirit of Christ, is unattainable. To the contrary, the progress which we hope we have achieved in the Holy Spirit has deeply encouraged us to press forward with a sense of earnest responsibility toward this achievement, insofar as this lies within our strength and capacity. This we want to do, not only with a sense of the seriousness of our undertaking, but with a profound sense of responsibility to the now separate churches to which we belong. We wish to submit all our findings, and the proposals which we offer, to the serious, searching scrutiny and judgment of our Churches. We shall be most attentive to their response.

At the same time, we hasten to add that we cannot conceive our efforts in this bilateral consultation as divorced from the other significant efforts which in our times we are privileged to witness being made to achieve the goal of further reconciliation and full ecclesial unity among all Christians. We would never wish our own specific efforts and our own specific goal to be regarded as prejudicial to the many different efforts that are being made by our Churches toward this end. Specifically, we wish to mention in this regard the Consultation on Church Union, in which the Episcopal Church is engaged, and the other bilateral consultations in which both our Churches are honored to participate. All of these endeavors have been a source of gratification to the members of the ARC and we, in turn, hope that our endeavor may be seen as a source of encouragement to them.

Moreover, we cannot see the task that is set before us as unrelated to the agonizing and critically important quest of the men of our times, amid the deeply painful experiences of our century, to achieve a fuller unity among all the members of the human family. Our faith impels us to look to the Church of Christ as a visible sign of the possible unity of mankind. We are, therefore, keenly distressed that the one Church, of which all baptized Christians are members, is seen to be divided more than it is perceived to be one Church. We understand all too well how this state of affairs has come to be and how it persists. But we wish to encourage all faithful Christians who, with us, regard this present condition of the Church as a source of suffering to her members and of scandal to others.

We offer our efforts to be joined with those of all others who seek to alleviate this suffering and remove this scandalous state both from the Church and from the whole human family as well. If the full significance of the Anglican and Roman Catholic ecumenical quest for unity cannot be perceived apart from the quest of all Christians for their fullest unity, neither will our furthest hopes be fulfilled apart from the need of all men for a much greater realization of the fitting unity of all mankind.

This we regard as an important imperative of the Church of Christ among men in human history, there both serving and rejoicing over the possibilities that God has bestowed upon us. We see our communities as intimately linked with mankind and its history. "The joys and hopes, the griefs and anxieties of the men of this age, these too are the joys and hopes, griefs and anxieties of the followers of Christ." (Vatican II, *Gaudium et Spes*, n. 1.)

In the recommendations of the Preparatory Commission for Anglican-Roman Catholic Relations, we are able to discern three possible stages in the restoration of full communion between our churches.

(I) Re-encounter through Personal Exchange and Dialogue

After four centuries of estrangement, we have witnessed the beginning of reconciliation between Anglicans and Roman Catholics. The visit of the Archbishop of Canterbury to Pope Paul VI marked in a visible way the success, not only of the program for ecumenical effort proposed by the II Vatican Council, but also of many earlier, courageous initiatives on the part of Anglicans and Roman Catholics. This meeting of our leaders and especially their participation in a Service of Prayer, gave proof of their personal commitment to the quest for full organic unity.

This meeting led happily to the establishment of an international Preparatory Commission and to its results, namely, *The Malta Report* and the creation of an international Permanent Commission for Anglican-Roman Catholic Relations.

It is now our purpose in ARC to pursue, as far as possible, in the United States of America, the recommendations of the international Preparatory Commission as they have been approved by the Holy See and Canterbury.

ARC already has a history and has laid a foundation upon which we can build. Our earlier statements stand as our testimony. Still we await expectantly further response and criticism of these efforts from our Churches.

Around the world and across our nation there are many signs of a developing rapport between Anglicans and Roman Catholics. There is need at this time, however, to signalize in new ways our commitment to the cause of unity. Among the recommendations of *The Malta Report* is one which calls for fraternal meetings between Roman Catholic and Anglican bishops. Given our common belief in the role of bishops as bearers of an apostolic office and as "the visible principle and foundation of unity" in their particular churches (Vd. Vatican II, *Lumen Gentium*, n. 23), we look forward to such exchanges in the U.S.A.

At some appropriate time in the not too distant future, we also hope for an event which, following the example set by Pope Paul and Archbishop Michael, will manifest anew the character of the close relations between our churches. At the national level, some public service, both a solemn celebration of our given unity and a humble prayer for full unity, should take place under the leadership of representative bishops of both Churches and with participation by representatives of the clergy and laity of both Churches. This event would be intended as a common pledge of our resolve to seek full communion and organic unity.

(II) Growing Together: Interim Steps

We in ARC feel the necessity for a common declaration of faith between Catholics and Anglicans, but we feel that this project would be more appropriately undertaken by the newly formed international Permanent Anglican-Roman Catholic Commission than by ARC. As we now see it, such a statement would affirm, in the description of the Preparatory Commission,

> our common faith in God our Father, in our Lord Jesus Christ and in the Holy Spirit; our common baptism in the one Church of God; our sharing of the Holy Scriptures, of the Apostles' and Nicene Creeds, the Chalcedonian definition, and the teaching of the Fathers; our common Christian inheritance for many centuries with its living traditions of liturgy, theology, spirituality, Church order, and mission (Paragraph 3 of *The Malta Report*).

Having achieved agreement in our past meetings of ARC on the Church as a Eucharistic fellowship, on the theology of the celebrant, and on the nature of Eucharistic sacrifice, we now feel our next step in ARC should be to move on toward mutual recognition of ministry in a statement that we can forward to our respective church authorities for action.

We endorse the following statement from the international Anglican-Roman Catholic Preparatory Commission:

> We are agreed that among the conditions required for intercommunion are both a true sharing in faith and the mutual recognition of ministry. The latter presents a particular difficulty in regard to Anglican Orders according to the traditional judgment of the Roman Church. We believe that the present growing together of our two communions and the needs of the future require of us a very serious consideration of this question in the light of modern theology. The theology of the ministry forms part of the theology of the Church and must be considered as such. It is only when sufficient agreement has been reached as to the nature of the priesthood and the meaning to be attached in this context to the word 'validity' that we could proceed, working always jointly, to the application of this doctrine to the Anglican ministry of today. We would wish to reexamine historical events and past documents only to the extent that they can throw light upon the facts of the present situation (Paragraph 19 of *The Malta Report*).

We feel that ARC should immediately study the question of orders together with the related topics of episcopal collegiality, the papacy, and the authority and teaching office in the whole church. Our next meeting will examine these subjects also in the context of developments in other bilateral conversations, such as the Roman Catholic-

Lutheran dialogue, and the findings of the Consultation on Church Union.

Further agreements on the topics already listed may give us more light on possible stages or steps of partial Eucharistic communion on the way to full communion between the Roman Catholic Church and the Churches of the Anglican Communion. Without attempting to predict the shape of such stages because of our limited perspective at this point and the new developments in polity and theology, we feel we should examine the following relationships as offering, not static nor fully satisfactory models, but some possible points of departure for new developments between our churches:

1.   The Concordat establishing communion between the Old Catholic and Anglican Churches.

2.   The nature of uniatism within the Roman Catholic Church.

3.   The proposals of the Second Vatican Council about relationships between the Roman Catholic and the Orthodox Churches.

4.   The Services of Reconciliation in the many proposed church unions involving Anglicans, such as the Consultation on Church Union, the North-India/Pakistan Plan (now officially approved by the constituting churches), and the Plans in England, Ceylon, Nigeria, Ghana, Canada and New Zealand.

If we can achieve a mutually acceptable statement concerning episcopacy and priesthood, we hope to recommend the reconciliation of the ordained ministries of the two churches without "reordination" or "conditional ordination."

(III) Toward Full Communion and Organic Unity

Following the completion of the above-mentioned tasks, we can hope for the restoration of full communion and organic unity. The terms "full communion" and "organic unity" need further definition, but both of them signify an intention to arrive at the oneness for which Christ prayed in his high priestly prayer: a unity which shows forth the relationship between the Father and Son in the Spirit, so that the world may see the glory of God revealed in the relationship of His disciples with one another.

Full communion must not be interpreted as an agreement to disagree while sharing in the Eucharistic gifts, nor may organic unity be understood as a juridical concept implying a particular form of Church government. Such a unity is hard to visualize, but would include a common profession of faith and would mean a sufficient compatability of polity to make possible a united mission to the human family. Whatever structural forms emerge, it is hoped that cultural and liturgical variety will remain so that the values of both the Roman and the Anglican ethos will survive and develop.

We hope also to further the reconciliation of our respective Churches in such a way as to promote the still wider reconciliation with other Christian Churches.

C. Diffusion

Since the goal of ARC is full communion and organic union between our two Churches, we recognize the need for making this goal, and our progress toward it, widely known among the bishops, priests, religious and laity of the two Churches. Accordingly, we would like to see the following programs set in motion.

1. In the press and the television news, with the assistance of our press officers, we should arrange for an announcement of our joint acceptance of this goal, accompanied by interviews with our two chairmen and two other members of the consultation.

2. Promotion of spiritual ecumenism is necessary to make us all realize that the varieties of spirituality within our two communions can be a source of mutual enrichment, and that loyalty to our relationships with God will be strengthened, not eroded, by participation in each other's spiritual activity and resources (*communicatio in spiritualibus*).

3. The projected meeting of bishops, combining a day of recollection with a day of discussion of pastoral concerns and problems, should serve several purposes besides the direct goals of the meeting itself: (a) making our efforts toward union visible to the world; (b) establishing continuing collaboration between bishops with overlapping jurisdictions; (c) providing a model for further conferences, perhaps on a regional basis, to strengthen relationships between our two hierarchies throughout the nation.

4. Joint clergy conferences should be encouraged, and our ecumenical officers and diocesan ecumenical contacts should become resources for subjects and speakers (perhaps as "traveling teams") to assure successful programs that would move our two Churches toward the common goal.

5. The movement toward sharing in theological training should be systematically encouraged with the aim of raising up a new generation of priests who know and understand their common spiritual heritage.

6. Cooperation should be fostered between our program resource persons, especially in the areas of adult education, professional leadership development, and missions. Steps should be taken toward unifying our basic approaches toward religious education of the young.

7. The religious orders should be made aware of the desirability of closer relationships between orders of similar inspiration as recommended in *The Malta Report* and approved by authority.

8.   Participation of the laity in joint retreats and conferences, in living room dialogues, and in the week of prayer for Christian unity, should be systematically encouraged.

9.   Our Christian brotherhood should issue in theologically based joint action for the whole family of man. Together we must bear witness to Christ's love for persons of all races and identify with them in their struggle for justice. Together we must work to build or preserve a natural environment fit for the dignity of each human person and help to create a community in which every man can live in peace, free from fear, hunger and poverty. In doing these things our mutual love will grow to include all men.

10.   The special relationship springing from our many areas of common life and tradition should not only be a source of mutual enrichment for our two Churches, but should also serve the purpose of moving toward the greater goal of unity of the whole Christian fellowship. There should be continuing consultation, in particular, on the subject of Anglican union discussions with other Churches to help assure that they will fulfill their declared purpose of being steps toward the unity of the whole body of Christ.

11.   The Ecumenical Commissions of our two Churches, through their staffs, should assume responsibility for these and other means of diffusing ecumenical knowledge and understanding through our Churches at all levels.

Conclusion

The participants in the ARC present this statement, prepared and reviewed by us at our seventh session, as one which records our substantial agreement. As a group we also recognize the fact that we must continuously seek more and more adequate ways to express the insights that come to us and the hopes that we share. It is in this spirit and with this clear understanding that we submit this statement to the judgment of the authorities of our Churches and offer it for the consideration of our fellow workers in the ecumenical undertaking.

Co-chairmen

The Most Reverend
   Charles H. Helmsing
Bishop of Kansas City
  —St. Joseph

The Right Reverend
   Donald H. V. Hallock
Bishop of Milwaukee

Participants

The Most Reverend
  William D. Borders
Bishop of Orlando

The Most Reverend
  Aloysius J. Wycislo
Bishop of Green Bay

Reverend Monsignor
  William W. Baum
Reverend Lawrence Guillot
Reverend John F. Hotchkin
Reverend Monsignor
  Bernard F. Law
Reverend Herbert Ryan, S.J.
Reverend George Tavard

The Right Reverend
  John M. Allin
Bishop of Mississippi

The Right Reverend
  John S. Higgins
Bishop of Rhode Island

The Right Reverend
  Edward R. Welles
Bishop of West Missouri

Reverend Arthur A. Vogel

Reverend William J. Wolfe
Mr. Peter Day
Mr. Clifford P. Morehouse
Mr. George A. Shipman

Boynton Beach, Florida—December 8-11, 1969

Appendix I

The Church is the Body of Christ and is built up by the Word through the Eucharist.

Baptism is the entrance into the Eucharistic community. In the Holy Eucharist Christians are united with Christ as the fulfillment and perfection of their baptismal union with Him.

In the Lord's Supper we participate at the same time in Christ's death, resurrection, and ascension; the Christian community is thus transformed in grace and the pledge of future glory is given to us.

Our communion with Christ in the Holy Eucharist is also communion with one another. Such union is achieved through the Holy Spirit.

Christian people participating in Christ's priesthood through baptism and confirmation are meant to be a living sacrifice to God. That sacrifice finds its fullest expression in the Eucharistic offering of the priesthood of the people of God. Such sacramental offering of the whole people is made possible through the special action of the ministerial priest, who is empowered by his ordination to make present Christ's sacrifice for His people.

The Sacrifice of the Holy Eucharist is not just the sacrifice of the cross but the sacrifice of Christ's whole life of obedience to the Father which culminated in His death on the cross and His glorious resurrection. We offer nothing we have not first received; because of our incorporation into Christ at baptism, He offers us in Himself to the Father.

Appendix II

The Joint Anglican-Roman Catholic Commission recognizes that it can make only recommendations, not decisions, concerning closer relations and doctrinal agreements between our two Churches. Such decisions must be arrived at by the appropriate authorities of each Church after consideration and recommendation by our parent bodies, the Bishops' Committee on Ecumenical and Interreligious Affairs and the Joint Commission on Ecumenical Relations.

However, the work in which we are engaged is not secret by nature and from time to time may be of interest and concern to the people of God in general. They too are part of the process whereby the Church makes its decisions and their reactions, whether favorable or unfavorable, are significant to the authoritative decision-making bodies.

The mass media are, with all their limitations, a major means of informing the people of God as to the ideas and opportunities being proposed to the two parent bodies. We believe that a policy of openness, in spite of occasional confusion or mistakes, will result in the long run in more positive achievements than a policy of close control of the dissemination of information. The group itself must, of course, be sensitive to its responsibilities not to misrepresent either its own status or the actual state of ecumenical agreement between our two Communions.

Cardinal Willebrands' Address in Cambridge, England

January 18, 1970

Following is the text of an address given by Jan Cardinal Willebrands, president of the Vatican Secretariat for Promoting Christian Unity, in Great St. Mary's Church, Cambridge, England.

Delivered within a week of the close of the first ARCIC meeting, Cardinal Willebrands' address underlined the importance of ARCIC's work and the important task also of national ecumenical dialogues, such as ARC, to provide "balance" to the International Commission. The cardinal's address was seen by many as explicating what Pope Paul VI meant in his October 25, 1970, reference to the Anglican Church as the Roman Catholic Church's "ever beloved sister in the one authentic communion of the family of Christ." The cardinal outlined a *typoi* ecclesiology and saw this type of vital unity as sufficient for organic unity. The cardinal appeared to endorse the work of Belgian theologian Emmanuel Lanne, OSB, who had first proposed this notion.

Let me first of all express my great joy and deep gratitude for the fact that at your gracious invitation I am able to join you before God in this prayer service to thank Him and to beg of Him full and complete unity in faith and love.

May I begin by quoting some words which you will not suspect of being taken from an ecumenical prayer or pamphlet:

> . . . come with me you fools, Into Unity of Holy Church—and hold we us there. . . . And call we to all the commons—that they come unto Unity and there abide and do battle—against Belial's children.

The blunt words are from the great prophetic poet of fourteenth century England, Piers Plowman. They remind us that the unity of the Church, that effective sign of Christ living in her, is always a matter of urgency to visionary minds. The New Testament is full of this urgency; the fourth Gospel makes it the mark of the heirs of eternal life, of those who look with the eyes of faith beyond this world. It is the glory of those whom God has given to Christ his Son.

45

"Holy Father, keep them in Thy name which Thou hast given me, that they may be one even as We are one" (Jn. 17, 11). He sent them into the world for the centuries to come and prayed "for those who believe in me through their word, that they may all be one" (Jn. 17, 20-21). If there is some glory in unity, in togetherness, in a bond of love, it is the glory of Christ, "the glory which Thou has given me. I have given to them, that they may be one even as We are one" (Jn. 17, 22). This glory, or, as the Greek expresses it—"doxa," marks the transcendence of God as it is appearing and manifesting itself to this world. This glory appears and manifests itself first of all in Christ, "As Thou Father art in me and I in Thee," but then also in us "I in them" (Jn. 17, 21) in so far as we remain united in Him. Therefore, it is through that glory in unity that the world may know that Christ has been sent by the Father and that the love of the Father is in us. John the evangelist, who is called also the divine, is really the troubadour of love and unity. His Gospel and his first Letter are filled with this idea.

This unity is not only the inspired ideal of a troubadour. In the first record of Church history, the Acts of the Apostles, the primitive community of Jerusalem is described as gathered in the upper room "with one accord devoted to prayer" (Acts 1, 14). St. Paul, in his Letter to the Romans, expresses his desire that they may "live in such harmony with one another in accord with Christ Jesus that together you may with one voice glorify the God and Father of Our Lord Jesus Christ" (Rom. 15, 6). St. Paul's wishes for the community in Rome are not merely a matter of local concern. In various ways he directs them to all the Christian Churches and communities. He tells the Corinthians, "Because there is one bread, we who are many, are one body for we all partake of the one bread" (1 Cor. 10, 17). To the Ephesians he speaks of the strength of unity, the integrity, candour and courage it brings to Christian witness. In his Letter to the Philippians, Paul has preserved for us the old Christian hymn on the divinity of Christ and the emptying of Our Lord in the humility of the cross. This hymn, in which the primitive Christian community professed its faith, is introduced by Paul with the plea to "complete my joy by being of the same mind, having the same love, being in full accord and of one mind" (Phil. 2, 2).

Now we all are conscious of the fact, and we confess it with repentance before God, that we have not preserved, in the obedience of faith, that unity through which we may all partake of the same bread, through which we should be in full accord and of one mind. However, we may thank God that humility and courage in the spirit of Christ have begun again to inspire the relations among Christians, among their Churches and Communities. This new spirit has also been manifest in a particular way in the relations between the Roman Catholic Church and the Anglican Communion during these recent years, years so charged with events of heavy import for Christianity.

For the Roman Catholic Church the Second Vatican Council has been a great event for what it is contributing to theological reflection, to the renewal of the mission of the Church to the world of today, to the orientation it has given for relations with our Christian brethren of other Churches and Communities. From the very beginning, when he first announced the calling of an Ecumenical Council, Pope John made it clear to the world that the restoration of Christian unity was one of his great hopes. Pope Paul, in his speech opening the second session, indicated the restoration of Christian unity as one of the main objectives of the Council.

In December 1960, after a pilgrimage to the Holy City of Jerusalem, Archbishop Fisher of Canterbury paid a visit to the Churches of Constantinople and Rome. For the first time since the Reformation the Archbishop of Canterbury met the Pope. This fraternal encounter in historical perspective so much more than a mere gesture of courtesy, was a stroke of vision pointing firmly towards the future. The Archbishops of Canterbury and York responded to the spirit and the words of Pope John and, already during the preparatory period of the Second Vatican Council, sent a personal representative to Rome. The Archbishop of Canterbury, as the head of the Anglican Communion, led the way in accepting Pope John's invitation to send observers to the Council. When the Vatican Council turned to formulate Catholic principles on ecumenism and its practice, both Roman Catholics and Anglicans rejoiced that the *Decree on Ecumenism* spoke of the "special place" held by the Anglican Communion "among those in which some Catholic traditions and institutions continue to exist" (*Decree on Ecumenism*, n. 13).

Insight and a clear understanding of the many factors involved led Archbishop Ramsey to await the end of the Council's work before visiting Rome and the Pope. The Archbishop wanted to avoid giving any impression of wishing to influence the development of the discussions in the Council. Furthermore, he wished to give a firm basis to his visit by setting it within the context of the decisions already taken by the Vatican Council. The human warmth, the spiritual elevation and the geniality of those days caught the imagination of a world still sensing the movement of the Spirit over the waters. Whatever difficulties or setbacks may arise from history or emotions, the spirit and the fruit of the common prayer of the Pope and the Archbishop, as well as the conviction and the faith expressed in their common declaration, will remain a source and guiding principle for the further development of our relations and will lead us to that unity which is the object of our prayers and desires and which is the promise and gift of the Lord to His Church. The spiritual elevation and the geniality of the visit, prolonged so to speak in the life of the Anglican Center founded at that time in Rome, firmly established the tone of the dialogue which Pope and Archbishop set in motion then. It continues to shine through the earnest purpose of the report which the Joint Preparatory Roman Catholic/Anglican Commission made— a document full of hope, on which a letter of the revered Cardinal Bea set the mark of Roman Catholic approval, while the resolutions of the Lambeth Conference showed how much it mirrored the aspirations of the Anglican episcopate.

This very week the first fruits of these proposals are being gathered: for six days a new commission has seriously discussed the great issues on which, in appearance or reality, we remain divided. But be sure that it has also discussed what unites us—our resolve, under God, to accept the great command of unity given by Christ and echoed in all the writings of the New Testament, to accept also the great challenge of Christian witness in this new age—a challenge as broad and as deep as life itself. Some speak of this Commission as a "permanent" commission. If the title were to represent a forecast of the Commission's span of life, its pessimistic outlook would frighten me, as I am sure it would frighten the commission members and yourselves. But this is not the case. The title reflects rather the happy irreversibility of the ways we have taken together.

What is the true meaning of these ways of dialogue? Theological discussion is a necessary help to discover and to manifest the unity in faith which we already enjoy and to restore that unity where it has been lost. However, the heart of the matter, I am sure, is what the *Roman Catholic Ecumenical Directory* calls *Communicatio in spiritualibus*, i.e., a sharing of spiritual activity and resources. The basis of this is our Christian brotherhood, securely grounded in the baptism by which we are reborn in Christ. Through this we turn confidently in prayer to the Source of all that we hold good and true, drawing new things and old out of a deep, rich treasure. This treasure holds many things deriving from our common inheritance, many reflecting our particular genius and witnessing to the vitality of our particular history. Within the framework of such a sharing we need have no fear of candour and straight speech in theological discussions. We can be sure of blessing and ripeness in Christian cooperation which will increase and find many fields of practical application in local circumstances. This will be due to the fact that a solid basis of agreement in faith underlies such spiritual sharing and such common labour, as it provides the spur for that intense effort of prayer, of thought and imagination, that humble and courageous stretching of minds, which will in God's time discover, manifest and reintegrate unity in faith and give it its expression in Church unity.

None can deny that this unity in faith is indispensable; it is no less sure that diversity of theological approach and explanation is legitimate and can be acknowledged within the unity of faith, and within the Church. This important fact was expressed by Pope John in his address at the beginning of the Council: "One thing is the deposit of faith, that is the truths preserved in our sacred doctrine, another thing is the way they are expressed while retaining the same meaning and substance." This distinction has been reaffirmed by the Council itself (*Decree on Ecumenism*, n. 6).

Another important idea introduced by the Vatican Council, when it speaks of dialogue, was to acknowledge a "hierarchy of truths": "When comparing doctrines, theologians should remember that in Catholic teaching there exists an order of "hierarchy" of truths, since they vary in their relationship to the foundation of the Christian faith." The importance of this idea has not escaped the theological world, but what is meant by the phrase is no less important. It does not mean that any part of Revelation is less true than another, nor does it deny that we have to accept with the same act of faith all revealed truths. However, besides the formal aspect of revealed truths we have to consider also their content. In this respect religious truth is more important in proportion to its relationship to the foundation, or we may also say, to the Center of Christian faith. In the explanation of this phrase given by the responsible conciliar commission, it was said: "Truths upon which all Christians agree as well as truths in which they differ, should rather be weighed than counted" (*Potius ponderentur quam numerentur*).

Without disparaging any truths, this principle gives a guideline for every ecumenical dialogue and is of great importance and help for those who participate in theological dialogue. They carry a serious responsibility in their search for the manifestation and the restoration of unity. However, dialogue is not an end in itself, by remaining such, it becomes sterile. Accompanying work such as that done this past week at Windsor, there must be an enlargement, a process, an awakening of interest and aspiration, a sharing of spiritual activity and resources which always looks out towards the concerns of Christian mission and the challenge of the present age. Theological dialogue remains an indispensable service to arrive at this end. Dialogue on world level, inevitably tempted to great abstractions, is balanced by national and regional dialogue—in U.S.A., in South Africa, Australia, in this country and elsewhere. For this balance to be realized we need full exchange of information between all these enterprises, and the authorities to whom their work is referred must face up to the task not only of passing on its benefits by various degrees of distribution and publication, but also of integrating its results and aiding in their further developments.

If they work with this common mentality and are strengthened by God's grace, are obedient to our Lord's commands, and are enlightened by the Holy Spirit, might not our theologians then expect to see in the none too distant future, a vision of that unity in truth given us in Christ? I would go so far as to hope that a limited period, say five years, might allow them to give, conscientiously and loyally, this service they are qualified to give to the Churches.

This would not mean that by that time we would have before us a full program and concrete outline for a schema of unity. Dialogue, however, would have entered upon a new stage, studying concrete ways and modalities of future unity. We would face then the challenge, most difficult yet most bracing of all—to explore what unity might mean in practice. We should not feel tempted to imagine ourselves at the gates of the promised land—there is plenty of recent experience even of far advanced unity negotiations to moderate our euphoria—but rather than tempt us to superiority it would lead us to consolidation and to courage. Would it be courage or rashness to offer some further perspective, some pattern for the future?

May I invite you to reflect on a notion which, it seems to me, has received much fruitful attention from theologians recently? It is that of the *typos* in its sense of general form or character, and of a plurality of *typoi* within the communion of the one and only Church of Christ.

When I speak here of a *typos* of the Church, I do not mean to describe the local or the particular Church in the sense the Vatican Council has given it. In the *Decree on the Bishops' Pastoral Office in the Church* the Council describes the local Church or the diocese as

> that portion of God's people which is entrusted to a bishop to be shepherded by him with the cooperation of the presbytery. Adhering thus to its pastor and gathered together by him in the Holy Spirit through the gospel and the Eucharist, this portion constitutes a particular church in which the one, holy, catholic and apostolic Church of Christ is truly present and operative.

From this description it becomes clear that the local Church is not merely a part of the whole but that the fullness of the whole universal Church is present in the local Church, or if that fullness is not present in it, the local Church is not perfect and complete. Here we are not making a distinction between the essence of the Church and its empirical manifestation. The New Testament never makes this distinction when it speaks of Churches. We are talking about the universal Church which is manifest in a particular place. It is this meaning of the local Church which the Vatican Council has discovered again.

As distinct from this notion of the local Church, with all of the theological meaning it contains, the notion which I submit to your attention, that of a *typos* of a Church does not primarily designate a diocese or a national Church (although in some cases it may more or less coincide with a national Church). It is a notion which has its own phenomenological aspects, with their particular theological meaning.

In the *Decree on Ecumenism* we read: "For many centuries the Churches of East and West went their own ways, though a brotherly communion of faith and sacramental life bound them together"

(n. 14). The theological element which must always be present and presupposed is the full "communion of faith and sacramental life." But the words "went their own ways" point in the direction of the notion which I would like to develop a little more. What are these "own ways" and when can we speak of a *typos*? A bit further on the *Decree on Ecumenism* explains "the heritage handed down by the apostles was received in different forms and ways, so that from the very beginnings of the Church it has had a varied development in various places, thanks to a similar variety of natural gifts and conditions of life" (n. 14).

Where there is a long coherent tradition, commanding men's love and loyalty, creating and sustaining a harmonious and organic whole of complementary elements, each of which supports and strengthens the other, you have the reality of a *typos*.

Such complementary elements are many. A characteristic theological method and approach (historical perhaps in emphasis, concrete and mistrustful of abstraction) is one of them. It is one approach among others to the understanding of the single mystery, the single faith, the single Christ.

A characteristic liturgical expression is another. It has its own psychology; here a people's distinctive experience of the one divine Mystery will be manifest—in sobriety or in splendor, inclining to tradition or eager for experiment, national or supranational in flavor. The liturgical expression is perhaps a more decisive element because "the liturgy is the summit toward which the activity of the Church is directed; at the same time it is the fountain from which her power flows" (*Constitution on the Sacred Liturgy*, n. 10).

A spiritual and devotional tradition draws from many springs— the bible, the fathers, the monastic heritage, its own more recent classics. It meets new needs in its own way; its balance of joy and contrition, of action and contemplation, will be determined by history and temperament.

A characteristic canonical discipline, the fruit also of experience and psychology, can be present. Through the combination of all of these, a *typos* can be specified.

In the *Constitution on the Church* of the Second Vatican Council we read: "By divine Providence it has come about that various Churches, established in various places by the apostles and their successors, have in the course of time coalesced into several groups, organically united, which, preserving the unity of faith and the unique divine constitution of the universal Church, enjoy their own discipline, their own liturgical usage, and their own theological and spiritual heritage" (n. 23). It is through such deeply seated realities as these, and not because of mere territorial or national boundaries, that we can find the expression of a typology of Churches. Different *typoi* exist in countries where eastern and western Churches live together.

If within one nation two *typoi* are so closely related, that in a situation of full communion between them, Providence draws them into coalescence, the authentic and strong elements of each will take their place in an enriched unity. Such a strengthening and enrichment will manifest itself primarily where it finds its highest motive—in a renewal of witness to Christ, a renewal of mission. A reunion which would not be a new Pentecost, a fresh manifestation of the eternal mystery to a time with its own spiritual needs, would be a nine days' wonder and little else.

It seems to me that Pope Gregory in his famous letter to Augustine, Archbishop of the English nation, opened the way for a new *typos* of the Church in western countries. He writes

> My brother, you are familiar with the usage of the Roman Church, in which you were brought up. But if you have found customs, whether in the Roman, Gallican, or any other Churches that may be more acceptable to God, I wish you to make a careful selection of them, and teach the Church of the English, which is still young in Faith, whatever you can profitably learn from the various Churches. For things should not be loved for the sake of places, but places for the sake of good things. Therefore select from each of the Churches whatever things are devout, religious, and right; and when you have arranged them into a unified rite, let the minds of the English grow accustomed to it (Bede, *A History of the English Church and People* 1, 27, 2).

Obviously the very existence of different *typoi* "added to external causes and to mutual failures of understanding and charity" can also "set the stage for separations" (*Decree on Ecumenism*, n. 14). Through the grace of God, the ecumenical movement is creating understanding and charity and restoring unity between those who have grown asunder. The life of the Church needs a variety of *typoi* which would manifest the full catholic and apostolic character of the one and holy Church. If we are only going to fossilize, common sense would seem to suggest that it is not very important whether we do so together or separately. Unity is vital only if it is a vital unity.

None of us, I fancy, underestimates what is needed of wisdom and discernment, of strength and patience, of loyalty and flexibility, of forbearance, of willingness to teach and to learn, if we are to make progress towards this goal. Nor, happily, is any of us in doubt as to the sources whence we shall derive what we need. The movement we aspire to make together is within one great dynamic, the *aedificatio Christi*. The tradition which is shared and enriched in a true typology is a *living* tradition—something which looks to the past only as it has vital meaning for the present and contributed dynamically to the future.

If a typology of Churches, a diversity in unity and unity in diversity, multiplies the possibilities of identifying and celebrating the presence of God in the world; if it brings nearer the hope of providing an imaginative framework within which Christian witness can transform human consciousness for today, then it has all the justification it needs.

For us, especially during this week of prayer for unity, there remains the call to perseverance, to a closer union of prayer in our common enterprise. St. Paul in his Letter to the Philippians has something to say to us here: "So if there is any encouragement in Christ, any incentive in love, any participation in the Spirit, any affection and sympathy, complete my joy by being of the same mind, having the same love, being in full accord and of one mind" (Phil. 2, 1-2).

Pope Paul VI
Remarks at Canonization of Forty Martyrs

Pope Paul VI called for the eventual reunion of the Anglican and Roman Catholic Churches in his address at the canonization of the forty Roman Catholics in England and Wales who were martyred in the sixteenth and seventeenth centuries. The quotations from him are as follows:

"While we are particularly pleased to note the presence of the official representative of the Archbishop of Canterbury, the Rev. Dr. Harry Smythe, we also extend our respectful and affectionate greeting to all members of the Anglican Church who have likewise come to take part in this ceremony. We indeed feel very close to them. We would like them to read in our heart the humility, gratitude and hope with which we welcome them. We wish also to greet the authorities and those personages who have come here to represent Great Britain, and together with them, all the other representatives of other countries and other religions. With all our heart we welcome them, as we celebrate the freedom and the fortitude of men who had, at the same time, spiritual faith and loyal respect for the sovereignty of civil society. . . .

"May the blood of these martyrs be able to heal the great wound inflicted upon God's Church by reason of the separation of the Anglican Church from the Catholic Church. . . .

"Is it not one—these martyrs say to us—the Church founded by Christ? Is not this their witness? Their devotion to their nation gives us the assurance that on the day when—God willing—the unity of the faith and of Christian life is restored, no offence will be inflicted on the honor or the sovereignty of a great country such as England. There will be no seeking to lessen the legitimate prestige and the worthy patrimony of piety and usage proper to the Anglican Church when the Roman Catholic Church—this humble 'Servant of the servants of God'—is able to embrace her ever beloved sister in the one authentic Communion of the family of Christ: a communion of origin and of faith, a communion of priesthood and of rule, a communion of the saints in the freedom of love of the spirit of Jesus.

"Perhaps we shall have to go on, waiting and watching in prayer, in order to deserve that blessed day. But already we are strengthened in this hope by the heavenly friendship of the forty martyrs of England and Wales who are canonized today."

Rome, October 25, 1970

Archbishop Ramsey's Response to the Forty Martyrs Address

From the text of a sermon given by the Archbishop of Canterbury, Dr. Michael Ramsey, in Canterbury Cathedral, during the week of Prayer for Christian Unity, 1971.

So, be of good cheer. Be thankful. There is much for which we shall thank God. . . .

As to the Church of Rome I have two things to say. First, I believe that the new Papal Motu Proprio on mixed marriages brings a good deal of help to a vexed problem, so long as it is acted upon to the full. Second, I welcome gratefully the words used by His Holiness the Pope on October 25. "There will be no seeking to lessen the legitimate prestige and the worthy patrimony of piety and usage proper to the Anglican Church when the Roman Catholic Church . . . is able to embrace her ever beloved sister in the one authentic communion of the family of Christ . . ." Responding to the warmth of these words I said in my Christmas letter to the Pope: "I read with happiness the words which Your Holiness spoke of warm and friendly feeling towards the Anglican Communion . . . and you can be sure that your warmth of feeling to us Anglicans is reciprocated in Anglican hearts and minds in the hope that one day there will be between us a consummated unity which conserves all that is true and good in our several traditions." The implications of the Pope's words can be rightly examined by Roman Catholics and Anglicans together, and this lies within the ongoing task of the Anglican/Roman Catholic International Commission.

Canterbury, January 24, 1971

Doctrinal Agreement
and Christian Unity:
Methodological Considerations

*This statement on methodology was intended
to aid persons in understanding Agreed Statements on doctrinal matters, such as the Windsor Agreed Statement on* Eucharistic Doctrine.
*Drafted by Bishops Arthur Vogel and Peter Day, and Fathers Avery
Dulles, SJ, and Herbert J. Ryan, SJ, and approved at the eleventh
meeting of ARC (January 23, 1972), at New York City, it was thought
of as providing a means to achieve the "balance" Cardinal Willebrands felt would come from the national dialogues. Moreover, The
Malta Report had suggested, "We should examine further and together
both the way in which we assent to and apprehend dogmatic truths
and the legitimate means of understanding and interpreting them
theologically" (no. 5).*

"We are all to come to unity in our faith and in our knowledge of
the Son of God, until we become the perfect Man, mature with the
fullness of Christ himself" (Eph 4:13 BJ).

With its call to unity in truth and to living the truth in love, the
Epistle to the Ephesians depicts the Christian life as the growth of a
body to maturity or, in another passage, as the erection of a building
whose cornerstone is Christ. The goal is completeness, a perfection,
a fullness that lies ahead and toward which each Christian and the
Christian fellowship as a whole must grow.

Ecumenical dialogue among separated Christians is a part of this
process of growth. Its aim is not to produce a statement of minimum
essentials by which one Church can measure the orthodoxy of another,
but to deepen, strengthen, and enrich the life of both. As Vatican II
declares in the *Constitution on Divine Revelation*:

> There is growth in the understanding of the realities and the words
> which have been handed down. . . . As the centuries succeed one
> another, the Church constantly moves toward the fullness of divine
> truth until the words of God reach their complete fulfillment in her
> (*Dei Verbum*, 8).

Churches coming out of the isolation imposed by the divisions
of the past find that they are able to contribute to each other's growth
in the fullness of divine truth. But unless the origins and purposes

of theological discourse are rightly understood differences in terminology and in modes of conceptualization, due in part to past isolation, can lead to failure of communication and even impasses in doctrinal discussion. Theological discourse must always be interpreted
within the horizon of man's experience of the divine mystery because
it grows out of that experience. From this it follows that no formal
or conceptual statement can ever be fully adequate to the religious
data. Because of man's nature, however, his religious experience must
come to expression by every means available to him.

Whenever man speaks about the engulfing mystery of God he
speaks from within a particular situation—geographical, temporal,
cultural, sociological, psychological, linguistic. . . . Because of the
transcendence of God's mystery, one must always speak about him
symbolically, but these symbols, taken from man's experience of the
world, always have the stamp of human particularity. Even statements made by groups of men in representative councils bear this
stamp of particularity. For example, when the early councils apply
to God and Christ terms such as substance, person, and nature, they
are using the terminology and conceptual tools available in a given
culture. When these terms in another time and culture take on different connotations their effectiveness for expressing the truths of
faith may be impaired. Human discourse even under the working of
grace is perspectival and hence also pluralistic.

To acknowledge the relativity of theological statements is not to
fall into relativism but to escape it. Because encounter with God always
calls man beyond himself it must be recognized that all religious
expression may itself be transcended. The abiding presence of the
Holy Spirit moves communities of believers to express their life in
Christ in ways that may not be abstractly deducible from their previous statements.

The result of the preceding analysis is to recognize that Christians
who are orthodox in their faith may express it in varying formulations,
as the Bible and the creeds of the early Church so well exemplify.
This does not mean that all formulations are equally appropriate.
Some may in fact express, and conduce to, a misapprehension of God
and his relationship to man, and thus be impediments to the Christian
life.

The participants in this dialogue, fortunately, rejoice in the possession of the same Sacred Scriptures, the same creedal formulations
of the ancient Church, and a substantial body of shared intellectual
and spiritual tradition. They also acknowledge the need for critical
scholarship if the meaning of the ancient texts is to be accessible to
modern man. There are, however, some other doctrinal formulations
which, in the course of a sadly separated history, have been adopted
by one communion or the other and are generally seen as obstacles

to full communion between the Anglican and Roman Catholic Churches.

In order to promote the cause of full mutual recognition and full ecclesiastical communion, the participants commend the following operative principles in the assessment of whether such divergent formulations do indeed constitute an essential obstacle to full communion:

1. *Paradoxical Tension*

As previously pointed out, theological language never adequately corresponds to the reality to which it refers. In revelation itself there is always an inherent tension between God's self-disclosure and man's capacity for understanding: human thought and language can never encompass the divine mystery. For this reason there is a peculiar ambiguity in theological statements. The grammatical opposite of a true statement of faith, therefore, may in some sense be also true. E.g., man is—or is not—saved by faith alone; the Bible is—or is not—the word of God.

2. *Contextual Transfer*

It should be recognized that past doctrinal utterances were made in definite cultural situations that are not our own, and hence that they reflect the presuppositions, terminology, and concerns of their times. This means that a Christian today, in order to be orthodox and to maintain continuity with the tradition expressed in the language of another day, may need to find new language and even new concepts to express the same truth; e.g., the descent into hell.

3. *Relative Emphasis*

It should be acknowledged that some statements made in the past as "definitions" and imposed under anathema, are no longer insisted upon because, at least today, they do not seem to be of crucial importance in relationship to salvation. E.g., the teaching of the Council of Vienne on the soul as the substantial form of the human body (*DS* 902).

4. *Doctrinal Pluralism*

(a) Within a single Church one and the same formula often receives different theological interpretations—e.g., the Banesian and Molinist interpretations of the Tridentine canons on grace; the use of the Thirty-Nine Articles in the Church of England. We see these as instances of the principle of comprehensiveness which, rightly understood, involves living in tension and does not admit of easy compromise or superficial syncretism.

(b) Because the same mystery can sometimes be conveyed more effectively by different formulas in different cultural contexts, one may support a variety of theological expressions among different groups of Christians. In Churches entering into full ecclesiastical communion, different creedal formulas are sometimes mutually acknowledged—e.g., the use or omission of the "Filioque" in the agreement between Churches of the East and West at the time of the Council of Florence.

Both these forms of doctrinal diversity should be taken into consideration in assessing the possibilities of overcoming obstacles to union among separated Churches.

5. *Empathetic Evaluation*

Any Church, in deciding whether it can enter into communion with another, should seek to appraise the role played by the formulations of the other community in the life of that community. One should not condemn all that one would not personally wish to say.

In this connection one may apply the principle of St. Ignatius Loyola, prefixed to the *Spiritual Exercises:* ". . . It is necessary to suppose that every good Christian is more ready to put a good interpretation on another's statement than to condemn it as false. If an orthodox construction cannot be put on a proposition, the one who made it should be asked how he understands it. . . ."

6. *Responsive Listening*

Since no Church exists by itself in this world, every Church should listen respectfully to what the others find unacceptable in its own formulations, and consider whether its own official doctrinal commitments can be re-expressed in contemporary statements that remove the occasion for offense. In this way the Churches will be of mutual help to one another in their ongoing expression of the faith.

Mindful of the fact that the revelation once for all given to man is the person of Christ present in the Spirit, Christians are called to be faithful to that presence at all times in their living tradition. The foregoing principles should be applied in conformity to that abiding presence, and thus in a way that leads to an ever richer appropriation of the gospel. "So the body grows until it has built itself up in love" (Eph 4:16).

Prospects for Anglican-
Roman Catholic Relations

A Lecture Delivered by Cardinal Willebrands
at the Great Hall, Lambeth Palace,
on 4 October, 1972

This is Cardinal Willebrands' careful summary
of the events of the twelve-year period, 1960-1972, a period that was
important in improving official contacts and relations between Rome
and Canterbury. The cardinal insists that the most important element
in organic unity is faith. "The root of our division lies there, where
organic unity, the unity of the body or of the family of Christ should
have its origin: in faith. We are still divided in matters of faith, there
is our greatest difficulty, and since faith rests 'in the power of God'
[1 Cor 2:5], there must be our most ardent prayer that we may be
restored to the unity of faith." The cardinal expresses his support for
ARCIC and the Windsor Agreed Statement on *Eucharistic Doctrine*,
and he reveals the process of how the statements of ARCIC will be
reviewed by the Church.

Your Grace, Beloved brothers and sisters in Christ,

The invitation of His Grace, the Archbishop, to speak on the
occasion of this visit about the prospects for Anglican-Roman Catholic
relations provides me with the opportunity to assess, in the light of
the Gospel of Jesus Christ, the present state of our relations, the
stages passed through since the renewal of our relations, the hope
which inspires our holy purpose and guides us towards the final goal.
This assessment should at the same time be an examination of conscience before God and before the Church.

I will of course avoid every attempt at or even appearance of
foretelling the future, since we speak here about a subject to which
I would like to apply the saying: "one sows and another reaps."

In speaking about recent and present sowing, we may easily repeat
platitudes. Nevertheless it seems to me necessary, if we will consider
the prospects for the harvest, to study first what has been sown.

When Pope John announced the first time, on the memorable
25 January 1959, that the Church was to have a new ecumenical
Council, he expressed the hope that this Council would serve the
holy cause of Christian Unity, the restoration of which, he said, all

Christians desire so ardently. His words stirred immediately the emotions and expectation of the whole Christian world, because they announced a new attitude of the Roman Catholic Church not in a platonic phrase, but in connection with such an important event as was to be the second Vatican Council. Moreover they revealed the personal feeling of the Pope, who was himself so deeply possessed by this desire. Some months later, on 5 June 1960, he created the Secretariat for Promoting Christian Unity, under the leadership of Cardinal Bea. The reactions of the Christian world to the initiatives of the Pope were generally positive and warm. The then Archbishop of Canterbury, Dr. Geoffrey Fisher, decided even to conclude his pilgrimage to Jerusalem with a courtesy visit to the Pope of Rome, thus ending his service as Archbishop of Canterbury under the sign of the cross and the resurrection of the Lord, by opening a new period in the relations between the two Churches. He was the first Archbishop of Canterbury to cross the threshold of the Vatican since the Reformation. This fact was in the event more important than the cautious restrictions expressed, qualifying the visit as a courtesy visit and recalling the serious doctrinal differences and prejudices separating the two Churches. The same year Bernard Pawley, Canon of Ely, was appointed as the liaison officer of the Archbishops of Canterbury and York in Rome, nearly two years before observers were invited to attend the Vatican Council. In this way a link, real and official, between Canterbury and Rome was created for the first time since the Reformation.

The relationships thus established were multiplied and intensified during the Council, when representatives of different provinces of the Anglican Communion guided by a bishop were present at all the sessions. If we compare this regular conversation at the Vatican Council with the Malines Conversations, we can measure the difference. In a certain way the conversation at the Council was a silent one, because the observers had no right to speak at the sessions, but their presence was highly eloquent and fruitful in the conversations with the Secretariat. It was also quite official and the observers were acknowledged and received as brothers in the faith. It seemed normal and appropriate that Bishop Moorman, one of the observers who attended all the sessions of the Council, spoke in the name of all the observers at the farewell audience with the Pope, and if we study the writings of several Anglican observers after the Council and on the Council, we can notice with gratitude the impact of the Council on our relations, and the increase of mutual knowledge and love, which was expressed, too modestly even, in the phrase about the "special place" which the Anglican Communion occupies in relation to the Roman See (*De Oecum.* 13). The commemoration of the fortieth anniversary of the Malines Conversations took place in an atmosphere very different from that of the period of those Conversations themselves.

Even during the Council the present Archbishop of Canterbury expressed his desire to pay an official visit to the Church of Rome, but he intended to make it only after the Council, in order to have a clear and solid base for a meeting between the two Churches and for an exchange of views on their common desire to find a way, with the grace of God, towards the restoration of full communion between them. This visit laid the foundation for the present state of relations between the Anglican Communion and the Roman Catholic Church and for their further development. Of course it is not my intention to tell again the story of the visit. But I would like to pay attention to some aspects of the visit which seem to me significant in themselves and in their consequences.

1. The visit had the consent of the metropolitans of the Anglican Communion, who therefore in some way were all involved in this event. So two Christian traditions, which have a common origin but had grown asunder in conflict, came together resolved to overcome the conflict and to restore communion. From the time of Gregory the Great a legitimate variety within the one Church had developed; in fact the letter of Pope Gregory to Augustine of Canterbury had laid the foundation for this. Can the break be healed and "the unity in truth" of which the Common Declaration of the Pope and the Archbishop speaks, be restored, "founded" as the same Declaration says, "on the Gospels and on the ancient common traditions"?

After the visit a preparatory joint Commission was established, which had to survey the whole field and make concrete proposals not only in theological matters but also in matters of practical difficulty. This Commission was deeply convinced of its responsibility and declared with decision in its first communication: "After four hundred years of separation between the Roman Catholic and Anglican Churches, official representatives from both sides have taken the first steps towards restoring full unity." Was it superficial, irresponsible or reckless to use this language? It expressed doubtless the firm conviction of the Commission which after three meetings in one year drew up a programme of theological matters and practical recommendations and proposed different stages through which, with the grace of God, the goal of full unity could be reached. Rome answered to this work in a personal letter of the Holy Father expressing his gratitude, and in a detailed answer from the Secretariat for Unity explaining how the continuation, on the basis already laid down, should be planned. This programme is so multiple and varied, that if it were to be executed in all its details, every concrete and decisive step would be postponed to an unforeseeable future. But the strength and the weakness of the programme do not lie in this. Its real significance is in the readiness to consider every possible problem, theoretical or practical, with the earnest desire to overcome it on the basis of the Gospel and the ancient common traditions. Moreover it is obvious that progress and a positive result in some central and essential points would carry with it progress in the whole texture. I would like, however, to remind you of the first point approved for further study, which was: "A common declaration of faith between Catholics and Anglicans." There are some who claim that common declarations have to be avoided as being necessarily ambiguous and creating confusion. However a result only becomes clear if it is expressed and ambiguity is only seen as necessary if the desire for real and honest agreement is absent. A common declaration of faith on points which have separated us or have been controversial during four centuries supposes a creative work concerning language and expression. There is no sense in repeating the old controversial and polemical formulas. Already the Council declared

> The manner and order in which Catholic belief is expressed should in no way become an obstacle to dialogue with our brethren. It is, of course, essential that doctrine be clearly presented in its entirety. Nothing is so foreign to the spirit of ecumenism as a false conciliatory approach which harms the purity of Catholic doctrine and obscures its assured genuine meaning. At the same time, Catholic belief needs to be explained more profoundly and precisely, in ways and in terminology which our separated brethren too can really understand (*De Oecum.* 11).

And in the document on dialogue issued by the Secretariat for Promoting Christian Unity it is said

> Approaching together the mystery of Christ, men discover the difficulty of speaking the same Christian language. By language is meant not just the vocabulary, but above all mentality, the genius of a culture, philosophical tools, traditions and style of life. (*Reflections and Suggestions concerning Ecumenical Dialogue IV, 4, c*).

This text may remind us of the profundity and complexity of the difficulties which surround a dialogue between Christians of different traditions at the initial stage. Once they have come to understand each other, and perhaps even to agree, the question arises: how to convey this shared enrichment to those who did not share the dialogue and its evolution or are even outsiders to the whole ecumenical movement but nevertheless belong to the people of God.

The document on dialogue goes on:

> With each one using the language of his own Communion, the same words may signify quite different realities in one Church and in another, while different words may express the same reality. Since it is a question of establishing real and complete communication, of

eliminating the risk of misunderstandings and of not travelling unaware along parallel ways, it is absolutely necessary that those taking
part in dialogue, even though they be formed by the spirit of the
Scriptures and express themselves in a language inspired by the
Scriptures should submit the language they use to a hermeneutic,
a critical study (*loc. cit.*).

The Joint Commission which succeeded the Preparatory Commission chose three main topics for further study: Eucharist—Ministry—Authority.

On 31 December 1971 the Commission published an Agreed
Statement on the Eucharist. I want to express sincere gratitude for
the work done by the Commission. This kind of work is exactly what
we hoped for. I appreciate the difficulty in taking up this central and
essential subject and I respect the efforts and decision shown by the
Commission in giving this arduous service to the Church. Those who
have mixed feelings and reserves about this Statement, I ask: Had
we the right to expect more from the Commission? Can we ask from
the Commission what can only be done by the Churches themselves?
At present the statement is submitted to further study and discussion
by the theologians. The Commission will examine their suggestions
and criticisms. The official authorities of the Church will not take over
the task proper to the theologians, but follow their further work with
confidence. Moreover the work will be completed by the study on
ministry, closely related to the theme of the Eucharist, and we hope
and pray that it will be possible to express also a common faith on
the ministry in the Church. A final judgment on the result, its implications and consequences can only be given at a later stage. But we
may say that the intention, expressed in the Common Declaration of
the Pope and the Archbishop has been seriously pursued, that the
work achieved so far has given new hope and inspires our prayers.

Though doctrinal matters are of great importance on the way
towards unity in truth, "matters of practical difficulty" (to use the
expression of the Common Declaration) are often felt more directly,
are part of the daily life of the Churches, touch from close by and
intimately the people of the Church. The Malta report listed a certain
number of them. With the development of the ecumenical movement
several of them have been solved and suggestions have been fulfilled
almost unnoticed, such as common prayer, development of relationships between religious orders of similar inspiration, consultation on
pastoral problems. But one of the most sensitive points was doubtless
the question of mixed marriages. As in many other cases, the practical
and pastoral problems are here intimately linked with a theological
question: the doctrine of marriage, its sacramental character, its indissolubility, its relation to Church and State, etc. On the doctrinal questions, a special joint Commission has been very helpful in clarifying

the positions on both sides; concerning the practical difficulties one can measure the difference between the provisional instruction published on the eve of the Archbishop's visit and the later, final norms, given in the *Motu Proprio* of 1970. The latter gives general instructions and norms, founded on Catholic principles, which in practice allow different applications according to the local situation and concrete circumstances, on which the local authority has to judge and to decide.

Practicalities

As practical difficulties I would consider also questions of psychological and historical heritage in relationships, lack of knowledge, of understanding, attitudes of mistrust, fear of the unknown future. It is often said that the desire of the people to go ahead, to overcome all obstacles on the way towards unity is greater than the readiness of the leaders to go. This may be true with regard to some aspects, but there are also examples where authorities or leading theologians are ahead of the situation among the people. Clarification and honest, responsible agreement on principles and doctrine are basic and necessary also in this field. Then follows communication in order to establish general and deep conviction. In this context also the work of competent, engaged men, in steady contact with the authorities of the Church, is very important.

What I have said about "a serious dialogue" between the R.C. Church and the Anglican Communion concerns one aspect of the Archbishop's visit and its consequences.

2. The other aspect which I would like to submit to your consideration is the spiritual nature of our relationships. The Second Vatican Council declared

> There can be no ecumenism worthy of the name without a change of heart. . . . We should therefore pray to the divine Spirit for the grace to be genuinely self denying, humble, gentle in the service of others, and to have an attitude of brotherly generosity towards them. . . . Let all Christ's faithful remember that the more purely they strive to live according to the gospel, the more they are fostering and even practising Christian Unity (*De Oecum. 7*).

When the Pope welcomed the Archbishop at the Vatican, he stressed the ecumenical importance of the visit without dissimulating "the serious and difficult problems" which "remain as difficult as ever." But he opened a perspective of hope, indicating the new spirit in which we approach them: "we can study and meditate upon them together, without any dissimulation or human pride, without any shadow of earthly interests, and in accordance with the word of Christ and with the help of the Holy Spirit." And concluding his address of welcome, the Holy Father developed a motive which underlines his whole talk:

> the truly spiritual and religious value of our meeting. . . . Its importance lies in our seeking together, seeking to profess our common fidelity to Christ together, to discover prayers, both new and old, which can bring our hearts and our voices together in celebrating the greatness of God and of his plan of salvation for the whole of mankind, which he brought about through Christ.

I hope you will forgive me the length of these quotations, but personally I attach a great importance to the spiritual nature of ecumenical relationships and of the search for unity. I think it is characteristic of the way in which the Archbishop of Canterbury speaks about Christian Unity, that he puts together the notions of unity and holiness, or the idea of unity in Christ and unity among ourselves, being all members of the one body of which Christ is the Head. So did he express himself in Rome, speaking to Cardinal Bea: "The work of Christian Unity is inseparable from the work of Christian holiness. As God calls us all to unity so he calls us to a closer union with Our Lord Jesus Christ in the way of holiness." In a sermon on "the recovery of unity," preached at Geneva on 24 March 1966, immediately after his visit to Pope Paul VI, he said

> Such is Christian Unity, the only Christian Unity. It is the binding together of men and women to one another in the common life of the body of Christ. It is the binding of lives to God himself through the forgiveness of sins. It is the binding up of each life so that its name can truly be not legion but one. These aspects of Christian Unity are properly inseparable. So in the high-priestly prayer at the supper Our Lord says, "Father, I pray that as thou art in me and I in thee, so they may be one in us." The unity of disciples with one another goes with their union with the Father and the Son, in truth and holiness (*One in Christ*, 1967, p. 3).

I find it highly significant that the Archbishop, who has emphasised on several occasions the necessity of having unity in truth, here amplified and completed this idea, putting together "truth and holiness." This reminds us of the word of our Lord in his high-priestly prayer: "Sanctify them in the truth" (Jn. 17, 17). Recently in a similar way the Archbishop spoke in the Episcopal Cathedral of New York on the text: "No one can say 'Jesus is Lord' except by the Holy Spirit."

These principles are beautifully expressed in the prayer for unity which we find in the accession service of the Book of Common Prayer and which was said by the Archbishop at the Service of Prayer in the Basilica of St. Paul Without-the-Walls.

A Spiritual Relation

A spiritual sense has so deeply permeated Catholic-Anglican relations that an occasion which in earlier days would have stirred up feelings of bitterness and opened old wounds now led to the warmest expression of respect and affection. I mean the canonisation of the forty martyrs in England and Wales of the sixteenth and seventeenth centuries. The words spoken on that occasion by the Holy Father calling for unity were full of implications, as we will see, and found fraternal response from the Archbishop of Canterbury in his Christmas letter to the Pope and in a sermon in Canterbury Cathedral, during the week of Prayer for Christian Unity, 1971.

If ever we deserve the blessed day of grace on which we will embrace each other "in the one authentic Communion of the family of Christ," we will need all the spiritual strength which is the gift of the Holy Spirit.

My reflections are doubtless based on a choice of facts and events, which is very incomplete and perhaps arbitrary. I make no apology for being incomplete, because I had no intention of giving a survey and moreover facts and events have been so numerous and significant in all parts of the world, where Catholics and Anglicans meet, that it would be impossible to take them all into consideration. It is a reason for hope and consolation that whenever we receive in the Secretariat for unity reports on the ecumenical movement from local Churches, the relations between Catholics and Anglicans are generally said to be marked by fraternal co-operation, mutual trust and love. This means that new and positive developments are not limited to a few persons and places.

Already in 1968 the Lambeth Conference, in its sectional report on relations with the Roman Catholic Church, was able to point to a number of fields in which progress was being made "to varying degrees in various places." That progress has since undoubtedly been furthered and its front broadened, in some places quite remarkably; this has sometimes been stimulated by such official guidance as that given in the second part of the *Directorium Ecumenicum* on "Ecumenism in Institutions of Advanced Learning." But local energy is in the end decisive. One can point in this country, for instance, to developments at Durham, at Oxford and in the relationships between Heythrop and London University—developments which are bound to broaden and strengthen the solid learned foundations on which official dialogue necessarily rests.

Speaking of the work of the Permanent Joint Commission then about to be set up, the 1968 report hoped that it would "be representative of the Anglican Communion as a whole" and that it would give early attention to "the theology of ministry which forms part of the theology of the Church." As we know, the Permanent Joint Commission has now begun the study of this problem. It is my personal hope that the members of the Commission will not look back to the past for its own sake, but try to ascertain whether *at present* Catholics and Anglicans are able to profess in conscience the same faith about the Sacrament of Orders.

What has been said by the Lambeth Conference of 1968 about episcopacy justifies the phrase of the *Decree on Ecumenism* of the Second Vatican Council: "Among those in which some Catholic traditions and institutions continue to exist, the Anglican Communion occupies a special place" (n. 13). This however does not affect the necessity of the joint theological research now undertaken by the Catholic-Anglican international Commission about the nature of the ministry, including episcopacy, and about apostolic succession. For both Churches, episcopacy is not only an historical form of organisation of the Church, but a structure which we have received from the Lord through the Apostles and which is accepted in faith for our salvation. The documents of the Second Vatican Council, especially the *Constitution on the Church* and the *Decree on the Bishops' Pastoral Office in the Church* will help us to discern whether we share really a common faith about episcopacy. The Lambeth Conference set great value on the notion of collegiality. In this context it may be interesting to notice that the Secretary of the Synod of Bishops of the R.C. Church is a member of this present delegation. The sense of collegiality at the same time enhances the sense of the primacy in the Church, since no college exists without a president or as the Lambeth Conference said, "Within the college of bishops it is evident that there must be a president." As we believe that episcopacy is a structure within the people of God, given by its divine Founder, so we Roman Catholics believe, that the primacy of Peter and his successors within the college of the bishops was given by the Lord. We therefore see in the Papacy something essentially more than "a historic reality" and we welcome the words of the Lambeth Conference when it speaks of a Papacy "whose developing role requires deep reflection and joint study by all concerned for the unity of the whole Body of Christ." As the theology of the ministry forms part of the theology of the Church, so also the theology of the primacy.

I have chosen some significant events in the past, such as the Second Vatican Council, the meeting of the Archbishop of Canterbury with the Pope, the Lambeth Conference, as a basis and starting point for my reflections. Other facts and events, other documents could have been chosen. But if my premises have been solid and true, then my choice has not been arbitrary.

The Future

Looking to the future I would like to develop a consideration which seems to me important. If ever unity or full communion is bestowed upon us as a divine grace, to use the words of the Pope: "one authentic communion of the family of Christ: a communion of origin and of faith, a communion of priesthood and of rule, a communion of the saints in the freedom of love of the spirit of Jesus," if ever this full communion is given to us, it has to be organic but it has not to be a unity of organisation.

There has always been a widespread fear, tacit or expressed, that union with Rome would mean unity of organisation, the loss of one's own characteristic traditions, the yoke of uniform, foreign rule. The consequence of this was quite naturally an aversion from reunion. I think that it has become abundantly clear that this kind of unity does not constitute a Church. We know the phrase of the Malines Conversations: "united not absorbed." In several places the Second Vatican Council has been much clearer and more explicit on this point, in the dogmatic *Constitution on the Church* in the pastoral *Constitution on the Church in the Modern World*, in the *Decree on Ecumenism*, in the *Decree on the Church's Missionary Activity*, in the *Declaration on Religious Freedom* and we can generally find in these documents the conviction that the unity of the Church is a reality which transcends all human power of organisation and is, with its sanctity, its Catholicity, its apostolicity, a divine gift which belongs to its mystery rather than being a product of human skill. The *Decree on Ecumenism* paraphrases the well known aphorism: "in essentialibus unitas, in dubiis libertas, in omnibus caritas," in this way:

> While preserving unity in essentials, let all members of the Church, according to the office entrusted to each, preserve a proper freedom in the various forms of spiritual life and discipline, in the variety of liturgical rites, and even in the theological elaborations of revealed truth. In all things let charity be exercised (n. 4).

In an address given during the Week of Prayer for Christian Unity in 1970 in Great St. Mary's Church, Cambridge, I developed the notion of a *typos* of a Church and the possibility of a plurality of *typoi* within the communion of the one and only Church of Christ. In this context I quoted the Second Vatican Council, which provides us authoritatively with a basis for this idea when it says

> By divine Providence it has come about that various Churches, established in various places by the apostles and their successors, have in the course of time coalesced into several groups, organically united, which, preserving the unity of faith and the unique divine consti-

tution of the universal Church, enjoy their own liturgical usage, and their own theological and spiritual heritage (*Lumen Gentium*, n. 23).

The idea expressed in this text, like its more general idea of a *typos* of a Church, goes surely beyond the mere notion of organisation, since the idea of a *typos* includes not only the external elements of organisation, but also elements touching the life of a particular Church. I went on to say

> The life of the Church needs a variety of *typoi* which would manifest the full Catholic and Apostolic character of the one and holy Church. . . . None of us, I fancy, underestimates what is needed of wisdom and discernment, of strength and patience, of loyalty and flexibility, of forbearance, of willingness to teach and to learn, if we are to make progress towards this goal.

The fear of uniformity stretches out beyond mere organisation and touches all the elements which make up the life and traditions of a particular Church. I hope that what I have said will go some way towards dispelling these fears, where they persist. To go further in the same direction, I can quote the words of Pope Paul VI, spoken at the canonisation of the forty martyrs:

> on the day when—God willing—the unity of faith and of Christian life is restored, no offense will be inflicted on the honour or the sovereignty of a great country such as England. There will be no seeking to lessen the legitimate prestige and the worthy patrimony of piety and usage proper to the Anglican Church.

But if uniformity is not sought and even not desirable, there must be true unity. Vatican II speaks of "various Churches . . . organically united" (*L. Gentium*, 23) and the Pope, as we have just seen, speaks of "the one authentic Communion of the family of Christ." We have our difficulties regarding organisation, uniformity, typology. I would not say that they are not real, but they are surely not the greatest or the most serious. Organic unity means the unity of the body of Christ. "For just as the body is one and has many members, and all the members of the body, though many, are one body, so it is with Christ. For by one Spirit we are all baptised into one body . . . and all were made to drink of one Spirit" (*1 Cor.* 12, 12-13) wrote St. Paul to the Corinthians, and to the Ephesians: "There is one body and one Spirit" (*Eph.* 4, 4). Organic unity is based upon faith, as the same Apostle explained to the Romans: "since we are justified by faith, we have peace with God through our Lord Jesus Christ" (*Rom.* 5:1). The root of our division lies there, where organic unity, the unity of the body or of the family of Christ should have its origin: in faith. We are still divided in matters of faith, there is our greatest difficulty and since faith rests "in the power of God" (*1 Cor.* 2, 5) there must be our most ardent prayer that we may be restored to the unity of faith. One baptism should lead into one faith. Since it is a task of theology to explain to us the content of our faith, so that we may "always be prepared to make a defence to anyone who calls you to account for the hope that is in you" (*1 Pet.* 3, 15), we are grateful for every effort made by theologians for the cause of unity. Since faith is before and above all a gracious and merciful gift of the Father in heaven, we will be "with one accord devoted to prayer" like "the women and Mary the mother of Jesus and his brethren" (*Acts* 1, 14) expecting the descent of the Holy Spirit, and our prayer will join the sacerdotal prayer of Christ. We are all called to one hope (*cf. Eph.* 4, 4) and "hope does not disappoint us, because God's love has been poured into our hearts through the Holy Spirit who has been given to us" (*Rom.* 5, 5).

The Ecclesial Nature of the Eucharist

A Report by the Joint Study Group of Representatives of the
Roman Catholic Church in Scotland and the
Scottish Episcopal Church

The present Report was examined by the National Ecumenical Commission for Scotland of the Roman Catholic Church at its meeting in Glasgow on September 22, 1973. The Report was approved in the following terms:

> The National Ecumenical Commission receive with pleasure the Report on the Ecclesial Nature of the Eucharist. They wish to thank the Joint Study Group for their excellent work, and warmly commend the Report as a most useful basis for study. The National Ecumenical Commission are particularly pleased to note the clear expression in the Report of so much agreement between the Scottish Episcopal Church and the Roman Catholic Church in Scotland on fundamental present-day belief about the Eucharist. The National Ecumenical Commission, while satisfied with the Report as a whole, would not wish to be committed however, to any particular historical judgment on Reformation doctrine on the Eucharist.

Subsequently, the Report was discussed at a meeting of the Roman Catholic Bishops' Conference of Scotland and it was accepted in the same terms as by the National Ecumenical Commission.

The Report was likewise presented to the Provincial Synod of the Scottish Episcopal Church at its meeting on October 9-10, 1973. The Synod expressed appreciation of the Report and suggested its widespread study.

Membership of the Joint Study Group
Roman Catholic Church

Western Group:

Rev. Desmond Strain (Convener)
Mr. James Breen
*Rev. Henry Docherty
Rev. John H. Fitzsimmons
Mr. Frank G. MacMillan

---

*Later Resigned

Eastern Group:

Rev. James Quinn, S.J. (Convener)
*Rev. Charles Barclay
*Rev. Brian Cavanagh, O.F.M.
Rev. Matthew J. Donoghue
Rev. Robert Hendrie
Professor P. G. Walsh
Rev. Hugh G. White

Scottish Episcopal Church

Western Group:

Rev. Hugh McIntosh (Convener)
*Mr. Walter H. A. Abbott
Rev. A. Oswald Barkway
Dr. Robert A. Shanks
Rev. Samuel S. Singer
Rev. John A. Trimble

Eastern Group:

Rev. Donald A. Guthrie (Convener)
Rev. Alexander S. Black
*Miss Gillian M. Carver
Rev. W. B. Currie
*Rev. E. J. C. Davis
*Mr. Thomas Glen
Dr. Robert Gould
*Principal Alistair I. M. Haggart
CONSULTANT-OBSERVER
Rev. Richard F. Baxter (Scottish Churches' House)

Foreword

The Joint Study Group of representatives of the Roman Catholic Church in Scotland and the Scottish Episcopal Church was formed in 1968. The details of its formation and composition are given in the Foreword to its common statement on "The Nature of Baptism and its Place in the Life of the Church," which was published in 1969 with the authority of the Scottish Hierarchy of the Roman Catholic Church and of the Provincial Synod of the Scottish Episcopal Church.

---

*Later Resigned

The procedure whereby groups of Roman Catholics and Scottish Episcopalians, both clerical and lay, met in Edinburgh and Glasgow for detailed and frank discussions, and then met in plenary session to draw together the results of their deliberations, seemed a happy and fruitful arrangement. The immediately sponsoring bodies of the Joint Study Group are the National Ecumenical Commission of the Roman Catholic Church and the Inter-Church Relations Committee of the Scottish Episcopal Church, and in presenting their common statement in 1969, the members of the Joint Study Group asked these authorities to continue their remit, suggesting as the next subject for discussion "The Ecclesial Nature of the Eucharist." This was agreed, and the present report represents the extent to which the Joint Study Group has been able to pursue its chosen but difficult goal.

The composition of the Group has understandably not remained unchanged, and several members for one reason or another were unable to continue. More grievous was the departure of the Chairman, Provost Haggart, whose appointment as Principal of the Scottish Episcopal Theological College in Edinburgh compelled him to relinquish a position he had filled admirably. On the credit side, we were glad to welcome newcomers to our Group, and in particular to welcome an observer from the Scottish Churches' Council at plenary sessions.

Necessary changes notwithstanding, the bond of friendship and understanding which was so notable a feature of our discussions on Baptism, grew in warmth and openness: it is true to say that we have not been able fully to complete our remit by including consideration of "The Ministry" or "Intercommunion," but none of us now has the same fear of grasping the nettle of our historic divisions on these two subjects as we should have felt had we not learnt to know each other so well.

Both Chairman and Secretary are only too conscious of the debt of gratitude they owe to several members for many a long stint at home preparing documents for discussion. We must also thank our colleagues for a forbearance in discussion without which our tasks would not have been possible.

Above all, we have been humbly aware that in spite of the limitations and imperfections of our report, our prayers for the guidance of the Holy Spirit were not entirely unanswered.

Robert A. Shanks
Chairman

James Quinn, S. J.
Secretary

Introduction

On first acquaintance, "The Ecclesial Nature of the Eucharist" as a topic for ecumenical discussion has a recondite air far from the problems of individual Christians who are disturbed by their divisions and yet unmoved by the spectacle of theologians at play. This report will try to make plain that the unique inter-relationship between Eucharist and Church is as *central* to our common faith as it is to our divisions. From earliest times, the Eucharist has been held to be the supreme gift of God, and has been celebrated in obedience to the express command of Our Lord. While there have been historical differences both within and between our two communions, the *centrality* of the Eucharist has never been in question. Not the least of our difficulties has been that of nomenclature, and we have chosen the term "Eucharist" in preference to "The Mass," "The Lord's Supper," or "Holy Communion" for reasons of euphony, brevity, and neutrality.

The heart of our problem could not be reached without some preliminary discussions: some subjects might seem peripheral, but had to be dealt with to clear the way for unambiguous consideration of our views on the Eucharist and the Church. From time to time, ecumenical groups have been accused of agreement by ambiguity— a polite glossing over differences of interpretation of phrase or concept. "For all colours will agree in the dark," wrote Francis Bacon in his essay, "Of Unity in Religion," and it was precisely in order to avoid this error that the Joint Study Group decided to spend some time on antecedent considerations, such as differing eucharistic practices, and the theology of Presence and Sacrifice, before going on to consider the nature of the Eucharist and the light it throws on the nature of the Church.

The plan of this report was to begin with Eucharistic Practice and Eucharistic Theology, and to follow this with the main section on the Ecclesial Nature of the Eucharist. We had intended to complete the report with two final sections on the Ministry and Intercommunion, in that order.

We have not departed from this plan, although it soon became clear that we should not be able to complete it in time for our first report—itself delayed beyond our expectations. To those who are familiar with the difficulties of such discussions this will come as no surprise. It is worth stressing that some of the delays occasioned by protracted discussions were because of an unexpected measure of agreement between us, allowing a deeper exploration of our beliefs.

A discussion of the nature of the Eucharist inevitably involves consideration of what is meant by "The Real Presence"; for many Protestants there is difficulty over the meaning of the word "sacrifice" as applied to the Eucharist; and there is the ever-present difficulty of the nature of the act of Communion and the basis for the authority of the presiding minister of the Eucharist. It is a tribute to the individual members of the Joint Study Group that our often protracted discussions seldom ranged beyond the use of words and always returned to the Narrative of Institution—the words of Our Lord himself—as the centre of our eucharistic theology.

Preliminaries were clearly needed for a meaningful consideration of our remit, and it should be emphasised that the work involved was considerable. Individual pairs from both groups produced papers on items for discussion, only to find them torn to pieces in argument, and so requiring that another draft be prepared and offered for similar treatment. It is our earnest hope that the mutual respect and understanding that we reached in our deliberations will be reflected in this report.

The succeeding chapters are largely self-explanatory, and it remains perhaps to explain the *title* of our report. It might be thought that to explain the choice of the word "ecclesial" as a title for a report over which so much time and consideration has been spent would be only too easy. In one sense, it may be so: "ecclesial" is an obsolete form of the current adjective "ecclesiastical," according to the Shorter Oxford Dictionary (although the New Chambers Dictionary allows "ecclesial" as the adjective from "ecclesia"). The word "ecclesiastical," however, has more overtones than are desirable if it is to be used to imply the essential nature of the Church; but in distinguishing between these two words and using "ecclesial" to refer to the essential nature of the Church while reserving "ecclesiastical" to include aspects of Church organisation, we are in danger of implying a dichotomy that is not intended. The matter is dealt with in some detail in chapter III.

Two sections of this report remain to be studied, namely "The Ministry" and "Intercommunion." These are subjects that we have not yet been able to discuss in depth, yet we are in no way reluctant to do so. We know very well that the nearer we move to the practical implications of our agreement on the centrality of our faith, the closer we come to the problems of entrenched positions and attitudes of mind rooted in history rather than reason. Yet we remain convinced that this report, which indicates how little of truly *ecclesial* importance separates the Scottish Episcopalian from the Roman Catholic in the three aspects of eucharistic theology so far considered, can only lead us to hope for a similar agreement on the other two, and so lead us nearer to that unity which is Our Lord's will for his Church.

I. Eucharistic Practice

The basic fact to emerge from our discussions was the *centrality* of the Eucharist in the worship of both Churches.

In Roman Catholic practice, this is reflected in the tradition of daily celebration, while the Scottish Episcopal Church has a tradition of celebrating "frequently, but always on a Sunday and on the greater festivals." The Eucharist takes the same essential form in both Churches: there is the same two-fold pattern of "Liturgy of the Word" and "Liturgy of the Eucharist," the latter being expressed by means of a four-fold action—Offertory, Consecration, Breaking of the Bread, and Communion.

In the Scottish Episcopal Church, Communion is received "under both kinds," while the Roman Catholic practice is for it to be received by the laity under one kind only, although the practice of receiving under both kinds is gradually being renewed. In both Churches, Communion is usually received kneeling; but whereas Episcopalians receive the consecrated Bread in their hands, Roman Catholics normally receive it in the mouth.

In all Roman Catholic churches and many Episcopalian ones, the Blessed Sacrament is reserved: in both traditions, where the consecrated elements remaining after Communion are not to be reserved, they are reverently consumed by the ministers. With regard to ceremonial, the use of lights (candles), vestments, and genuflections is "universal" in the Roman Catholic Church, and "widespread" among Episcopalians.

In the matter of admission to the Eucharist, the present discipline of the two Churches differs, in that the Scottish Episcopal Church recognises wider areas of admission for "Christians duly baptised in the name of the Holy Trinity and qualified to receive Holy Communion in their own Churches," who "may be welcomed at the Lord's Table in the Anglican Communion" in order to meet "a special pastoral need," and in certain authorised ecumenical situations.[1] The Roman Catholic Church does not admit to Communion anyone except those in full communion with Rome, though there are some excep-

---

1. Cf. "Intercommunion. A Scottish Episcopalian Approach," being a Report of the Commission on Intercommunion to the Provincial Synod of the Scottish Episcopal Church, together with a Postscript recording the decisions of the Provincial Synod at its meeting in Perth on 4th-5th November, 1969, published for the Provincial Synod by the Representative Church Council, 13 Drumsheugh Gardens, Edinburgh, nos. 21-22, pp. 9-10.

tions to this with regard to Eastern Christians and other Christians in special circumstances.[2]

There are thus many liturgical elements held in common by our two Churches, and in many respects our practice is identical. Since a common, "Lex Orandi" would be a factor making for a common "Lex Credendi," we feel it is important to recognise how much is already done in similar ways, as well as to press forward wherever possible with the development of other common elements. Although it is clearly necessary for each tradition to develop in harmony with its own past and heritage, nevertheless agreement to use a common Lectionary and to observe a revised Christian Year, together with the incorporation of internationally agreed texts for the Creed, the Lord's Prayer, and other elements of the Liturgy, and the creation of a common store of hymns and church music—all of these are factors which would promote further unity between our two Churches.

II. Aspects of Eucharistic Faith

Sacrifice

Down the centuries both our traditions have developed a theology about the sacrificial nature of the Eucharist; and in both cases the roots of this theology are to be found in the biblical tradition of the Old and New Testaments, together with the interpretation of its data embodied in the traditional teaching of the Church.

On examining together the New Testament narratives of the institution of the Eucharist, we have seen how the evangelists have taken over the themes and motifs of the Old Testament's own theology of sacrifice.[1] Their central idea is that of the Eucharist as the "Christian Passover": just as the Passover of Israel is anticipated and signified in the meal shared in Egypt (cf. *Ex.* 12, 1-36), so the Passover of Christ and Christians is anticipated and signified in the Last Supper. The

---

2. Cf. "Guidelines for Ecumenical Activity," issued by the National Ecumenical Commission for Scotland of the Roman Catholic Church, Glasgow, 1970, nos. 16-18, pp. 13-15; the discipline of the Roman Catholic Church on this point has been further elaborated by the Secretariat for Promoting Christian Unity in its Instruction of June 1st, 1972, and the interpretative "Note" issued on October 17th, 1973.

1. Above all else, the Old Testament's theology of sacrifice is concerned with a personal response of man to a God who is personal: Jahweh, the Lord, is Master, Creator, the Transcendent, but above all he is a person. Sacrifice is the external expression of an internal attitude of service and dedication. The different kinds of sacrifice which we find in the religion of the Old Testament each emphasise various aspects of the total reality—the highest expression of man's self-giving to God, and an act of communion between God and man.

context of the narratives of institution (at least in the tradition of the Synoptic Gospels) is the Passover meal shared by Jesus and his followers. While the image of Christ as the Paschal Lamb is none too clear, the words of the institution interpret his death as an atonement sacrifice—his Body and Blood are "for many" and "for you."

The sacrificial aspect of the Eucharist is further heightened by its definition as the sealing of the New Covenant between God and man.[2] Here again the immediate reference is to the covenant sacrifices of the Old Testament. As in the Old Testament sacrifices the ritual words and actions interpret the offering of the victim, so the words and actions of Jesus in the Upper Room interpret his offering of himself on the Cross as the Victim reconciling God and man.

The Last Supper provides us with a key to the understanding of Calvary, and the Last Supper and Calvary together provide us with a key to the understanding of the Eucharist. The author of the Letter to the Hebrews takes up these ideas and expresses them succinctly: the sacrifice of Christ was offered "once and for all," and this offering of Christ achieves perfect forgiveness for all men; through the sacrifice of Christ, the Christian can approach God with faith and hope that he is delivered from sin (cf. *Heb.* 9-10).[3]

In the light of this interpretation offered by the New Testament writers, the Eucharist was early understood in terms of Christ's offering of himself as a sacrifice for the reconciliation of God and man. As the perfect sacrificial offering, he fulfils in himself the aspirations and intentions of the Old Testament in its worship. There are, however, other aspects of the New Testament understanding of the Eucharist which are significant for us, in that they have been integrated into the theology of both our traditions.

The words of institution contain the injunction to celebrate the Eucharist as a "memorial" of Christ, and to this St. Paul adds the further notion of the Eucharist as a "proclamation" of the death of Jesus (*I Cor.* 11, 26), so allowing the Church to see in the Eucharist the source and fullest expression of its mission.

If the idea of communion with God through the offering of sacrifice is essential to the Old Testament theology of sacrifice, it is also

---

2. Cf. "My blood of the covenant" in Mt. 26, 28, and Mk. 14, 24, and "The new covenant in my blood" in Lk. 22, 20, and I Cor. 11, 25. We have understood this idea against the background of Ex. 24, 8.
3. It is significant that exegetical opinion recognises in these chapters the "central section" and "essential message" of the entire Letter. The author institutes a comparison between the Old Covenant and its religious expressions and the unique, effective, and definitive sacrifice of Christ which brings the New Covenant into being; the priesthood of Christ replaces the former priesthood, and so "we have confidence to enter the sanctuary by the blood of Jesus" (10, 19) and can "draw near with a true heart in full assurance of faith" (10, 22).

an essential aspect of the New Testament theology of the Eucharist. The eucharistic sharing of the Body and Blood of Christ makes all Christians one—the many are one body, for they all partake of the one bread (*I Cor.* 10, 17). Further, the Eucharist is celebrated until the Lord "comes" (*I Cor.* 11, 26), and so stands as a sign and guarantee of the final fulfilment of the salvation in which the Christian is already caught up through his sharing in the Lord's Body and Blood. Thus what God's people of the Old Testament hoped for and looked forward to in the celebration of the Passover meal, the Church now possesses in the celebration of the Eucharist. The Messianic Banquet, which expresses the full and final union of all men with God and with one another, is already anticipated in the eucharistic meal.[4]

Inspired by this interpretation of the Eucharist offered by the New Testament writers, both Churches have understood the Eucharist as the presence here and now in the Christan community of Christ's once-and-for-all offering of himself as a sacrifice for the reconciliation of God and man. The communion with God in a sacred meal or banquet which belongs to the New Testament appreciation of the Eucharist has been the source and context of our understanding of the real presence of Christ. Our idea of the Church as the "Body of Christ" is derived from the New Testament idea of the Eucharist as the sharing of one bread which makes us who are many, all one with God and with one another. Our hope and our expectation for the future are nourished by the Eucharist, which points to the fulfilment of our salvation. The eucharistic sacrifice indeed has been understood by both Churches as a pattern for the life of the Christian community: "Be imitators of God, as beloved children. And walk in love, as Christ loved us and gave himself up for us, a fragrant offering and sacrifice to God" (*Eph.* 5, 1-2).

In examining the interpretation of biblical data embodied in the traditional teaching of both our Churches, we have seen how the Eucharist has been understood as a "re-presentation" of the one sacrifice of Christ, through the re-enactment of the words and actions of the Upper Room, which make the reconciling work of Christ present and effective for us, and through us for all men. Through the eucharistic mystery celebrated by the Church in the Spirit, the sacrifice of the Cross, achieved "once and for all," is brought to mind in the "memorial" of Christ, and thus made sacramentally present,

---

4. Each of these notions has an important bearing on the total New Testament picture of the Eucharist, and consequently on the traditional theology of both Churches: the biblical idea of "memorial," the Pauline idea of "proclamation," the Eucharist as "effective" sign of unity, and the Eucharist as a share in the eschatological future.

so that its saving power may be communicated to us.[5]

From the very beginning, the Church has gathered to celebrate the Paschal Mystery of Christ's death and resurrection, reading all that the Scriptures have to say about the "things referring to himself" (*Lk.* 24, 27) and celebrating the Eucharist in which "the victory and triumph of his death are again made present."[6] It is clear that there can only be one sacrifice: the eucharistic sacrifice is the same sacrifice as that of Christ on the Cross, and this one sacrifice is now offered by the ascended and glorified Lord in his Church. The Eucharist is the celebration not only of the death, but also of the resurrection and ascension of Christ: it is the sacrament of the whole Paschal Mystery. The Eucharist is not simply the commemoration of Calvary as of a past event, nor is it simply an offering of praise and thanksgiving for Calvary and its reconciling and atoning effects. On the contrary, the Eucharist is the continuing presence in our time and situation of Christ's sacrifice. This presence, which signifies and brings about the reconciliation of men with God and with one another, is his gift to those who, through the Spirit, are incorporated with him in his Body the Church. It is this identification of the faithful in the Spirit with the risen humanity of Jesus Christ that guards the "once and for all"-ness of Christ's sacrifice and yet makes that sacrifice the sacrifice of the Church itself.

In this connexion we have looked at the Anglican Articles, esp. Art. XXXI. What is repudiated in this Article is something that never had been part of the authentic teaching of the Roman Church. The "sacrifices of Masses" referred to there is part of a conception which would understand the eucharistic sacrifice as *adding* something to the sacrifice of Christ on Calvary. This idea is rightly denied and the traditional faith of the Church remains what it always has been: there is but one sacrifice, the sacrifice of Christ on Calvary of which the Eucharist is the "memorial" or "representation."[7]

---

5. Cf. Council of Trent: "Doctrina de Sanctissimo Missae Sacrificio," esp. ch. 1. Vatican II has expressed the same idea concisely and in the form of a synthesis: "At the Last Supper, on the night when he was betrayed, our Saviour instituted the eucharistic sacrifice of his Body and Blood. He did this in order to perpetuate the sacrifice of the cross throughout the centuries until he should come again, and so to entrust to his beloved Spouse, the Church, a memorial of his death and resurrection: a sacrament of love, a sign of unity, a bond of charity, a paschal banquet in which Christ is consumed, the mind is filled with grace, and a pledge of future glory is given to us." (Const. on the Sacred Liturgy, ch. 2, no. 47.)
Cf. also Lambeth Conference Report, 1958, p. 2. 84; and Anglican-Roman Catholic International Commission (ARCIC), Agreed Statement on the Eucharist, para. 3.
6. Cf. Council of Trent, "Decretum de Sanctissima Eucharistia," ch. 5 Cf. also Encyclical Letter, "Mysterium Fidei," no. 34, and ARCIC Agreed Statement, para. 5.

The Real Presence

In speaking of the eucharistic sacrifice, we have referred to the idea of the sacred banquet, that communion with God which we share in the Eucharist, as the source and context for our understanding of the real presence of Christ. From St. Paul onwards, the Church has always maintained that a *change* takes place in the eucharistic elements after the consecration.[8]

---

7. Article XXXI states that "the sacrifices of Masses," *not* the sacrifice of the Mass, were "blasphemous fables and dangerous deceits." It asserts that "the Offering of Christ once made is the perfect Redemption, Propitiation, and Satisfaction," which again is not in question today. It is the idea that the Mass adds something to Calvary that is rightly denied, and the notion that the more Masses are offered, the greater is the redemption. The writings of Elizabethan and later Anglican divines to the effect that in the Eucharist the one sacrifice of Christ is offered to the Father make clear that the notion of "representation" here stated is not contrary to the teaching contained in this article. Indeed Ridley, at his trial, referred to the Eucharist as an "unbloody sacrifice." Thus the agreement in this statement is not a contravention of Anglican faith.
8. The doctrine of eucharistic change in contemporary Roman Catholic theology is not tied to any particular philosophy. "The word 'transubstantiation' is commonly used in the Roman Catholic Church to indicate that God acting in the Eucharist effects a change in the inner reality of the elements. The term should be seen as affirming the fact of Christ's presence, and of the mysterious and radical change which takes place." (ARCIC Agreed Statement, footnote to para. 6.)
    The Thirty-Nine Articles *appear* to deny transubstantiation as a doctrine. A letter from the author of the article in question, no. XXVIII, insists that it did not exclude the presence of Christ's Body from the sacrament, but only the grossness and sensibleness in the receiving thereof. He goes on: "Though he took Christ's Body in his hand, received it with his mouth, and that corporally, naturally, really, substantially, and carnally as the doctors do write, yet he did not for all that see it, smell it, nor taste it." What Bishop Guest, the writer, appears to be denying is the belief that gave rise to the legend of bleeding hosts and blood-stained corporals. It is clear that what is here controverted is an idea that no one would assert today. He affirms a presence that is not in a "corporal, carnal, or natural manner." He quotes Bishop Jewel, who claimed that the presence is "invisible, unspeakably, supernaturally, divinely, and by way to him only known." Thus no denial of what is currently held by Roman Catholics is contained here; indeed, it is asserted.
    It is also relevant to note that the so-called Black Rubric added at the last moment to the Communion service of the 1552 English Prayer Book, and rewritten in modified form in the 1662 Prayer Book, has never appeared in any Scottish Prayer Book. In its 1552 form the Rubric stated that kneeling to receive communion did not imply "any real or essential presence there being of Christ's natural flesh and blood." In the 1662 Book this was changed to "any Corporal Presence of Christ's natural flesh and Blood."
    The Scottish Prayer Book of 1929 includes the following among its rubrics for Holy Communion: "According to long-existing custom in

After the consecration, the Bread of the Eucharist is a different kind of bread: the bread of human life has been changed into the Bread of everlasting life. This change, though it does not affect the physical or chemical properties of bread, is nevertheless a real change—not one imposed by our purpose, minds, or faith. It is more than a change in the use to which we put bread; it is more than a change in its meaning for us. It is a change by which the bread of human life has become the Bread of everlasting life, has become the "Body of the Lord" (*I Cor.* 11, 29).

We do not think of eucharistic sacrifice and the real presence as separate, nor do we believe that they should be thought of in this way. Christ is present, i.e., the change takes place in order that we may offer him and his oblation on behalf of ourselves and the world, and receiving the full benefits of his death and resurrection in his gift of Holy Communion may be reintegrated in him so as to participate more effectively in his mission and service to the world.

It is important also to recall that Christ is the Giver as well as the gift bestowed, and that he is present and active in more than one way in the Eucharist—in his People gathered together, in the minister who presides, in his Word read and proclaimed, in the world's needs brought forward in the Intercessions (*Mt.* 25, 40).[9]

The priesthood which is exercised in the eucharistic offering is the priesthood of Christ himself. He is at once Priest and Victim. In the Church's offering of his sacrifice, the officiating priest and the whole community share in his Priesthood. Hence, those who say that the ministry of an episcopally ordained priest is necessary for the eucharistic offering do not deny that the whole People of God offers the sacrifice together.[10] The presence of Christ's sacrifice in the eucharistic offering is the work of the Holy Spirit acting in the community, as the liturgical traditions of both our Churches constantly attest. In the Christian community's exercise of his priesthood, which it shares, the Eucharist is offered by Christ in and through the Church.

III. The Ecclesial Nature of the Eucharist

Introduction

The understanding of the Eucharist expressed in Chapter II calls our attention once more to a fundamental but somewhat neglected feature

---

the Scottish Church, the Presbyter may reserve so much of the consecrated Gifts as may be required for the Communion of the Sick and others who could not be present at the celebration in Church."
9. Cf. ARCIC Agreed Statement, para. 7.
10. Cf. Vatican II: Const. on the Church, ch. 2, no. 10. Cf. also Lambeth Conference Report, 1968, "Renewal in Ministry," pp. 93 ff.

of our common Eucharistic heritage: viz. *the unique relationship of mutual dependence between the Eucharist and the Church*. It is not without significance that from the earliest times, as acknowledged in the New Testament and faithfully maintained in both traditions, the Eucharist has been cherished as the supreme gift of God to his Church and that the celebration of the Eucharist has always held a place of pre-eminence in the growing life and work of the Church. For it is in the celebration of the Eucharist that the faithful experience and express most fully that unity which must always be the first characteristic of the Church of Christ. The eucharistic sacrifice "is the fount and apex of the whole Christian life . . . Strengthened anew at the Holy Table of the Body of Christ, (the faithful) manifest in a practical way that unity of God's people which is suitably signified and wondrously brought about by this most awesome sacrament."[1]

The Eucharist—Sacrament of the Church: A Biblical Approach

It was his appreciation of this intimate connection between the Eucharist and the Church which allowed Paul to speak of both the Eucharist (*I Cor.* 10, 16) and the Church (*Eph.* 1, 23) as the "Body" of Christ, meaning by body "person."

> "Because there is one bread, we who are many are one body for we all partake of the one bread" (*I Cor.* 10, 17).
> ". . . and he has put all things under his feet and has made him the head over all things for the church, which is his body, the fullness of him who fills all in all" (*Eph.* 1, 22).

Already, Paul finds in the celebration of the Eucharist the sign and source not only of the union of the faithful with Christ, but of their unity with one another—"a single body." As such, Paul prompts us to an understanding of the Church as *first and foremost a Eucharistic Community*—what is achieved by and witnessed to in the fellowship of the Eucharist is the normative guide for the Church. The Eucharist reveals the nature of the Church, and in each celebration of particular communities the Church continues to discover afresh the dynamic source of its own membership, growth and renewal, the origin of its structure and the ultimate meaning and purpose of all its activity. Without the Church there can be no Eucharist, but without the Eucharist there would be no Church—each stands as a sign and source of the other.

---

1. Cf. Vatican II: Const. on the Church, ch. 2, no. 11.

When the New Testament authors came to set down in writing the tradition of the words and deeds of Jesus, they were acutely aware that they were not handling facts of the past which belonged exclusively to the past. It is for this reason that we can see an underlying conviction in all that they wrote: the conviction that the Jesus of whom they write is still alive, exalted at the right hand of the Father and present and active in his Church. This explains why Luke refers to the details of the Gospel story as events which "have been accomplished" and which have been fulfilled "among us," thereby identifying himself and his readers with the witness of the past (*Lk.* 1, 1). In the same way, John speaks of the Word's becoming flesh and dwelling "among us," in such a way that "we have beheld his glory" (*Jn.* 1, 14). The same conviction animated Matthew when he wrote of the birth of Jesus as the coming of Emmanuel, "which means God with us" (*Mt.* 1, 23), and when he concluded his version of the Gospel with the promise of Jesus: "I am with you always to the close of the age" (*Mt.* 28, 20).

When we use the language of contemporary theology and speak of Jesus Christ as "the sacrament of the Father," we are simply expressing something that responds to the New Testament portrayal of the person and mission of Jesus. (Here it is enough to remark that "sacrament" is taken in its most general sense—an effective sign: a sign, first of all, which can be seen and understood as such, and one which actually effects what it signifies, makes it real and present.) In this case, what is meant, therefore, is that in Christ the Father is present and active. The Gospel picture of the ministry (and more specifically of the miracles) of Jesus underlines this active presence of the Father in him. They all involve an encounter between men and Jesus: this encounter is effective, for the "blind receive their sight, and the lame walk, lepers are cleansed and the deaf hear, and the dead are raised up, and the poor have the good news preached to them" (*Mt.* 11, 5). The Gospels, then, show us how the presence of Christ is the presence of the redeeming love of God in the midst of men (cf. Mt.'s quotation of *Hos.* 6, 6 in 9, 13), in such a way that they can see it and respond to it. The whole technique of the handing on of the tradition which we find in the New Testament is based on the conviction that what Jesus once did, he does still. This is the heart of sacramental theology, and it is the key concept with regard to the existence and nature of the Church. Just as the leper, the blind, and the lame receive a fuller life through their encounter with Jesus, so the Christian shares a new kind of life through his encounter in faith with the Risen Christ. Christ is "the sacrament of the encounter with

God,"[2] the infinite love of God coming into contact with men in a tangible and personal form. "In Christ God was reconciling the world to himself . . . and entrusting to us the message of reconciliation" (*II Cor.* 5, 19). Here, we begin to touch upon the very essence of the Church—it is to be the meeting between Christ and men through the ages.

So, when we use the language of contemporary theology and say that "the Church is the sacrament of Christ,"[3] we are simply expressing the basic New Testament vision of the Church and its function. What Christ has done, that is the Church's task—"He who receives you receives me, and he who receives me receives him who sent me" (*Mt.* 10, 40). It is the abiding presence of Christ himself which enables the Church to carry out its mission—"where two or three are gathered together in my name, there am I in the midst of them" (*Mt.* 18, 20). The community of those who have gathered in his name is to be the bridge between Christ and the world in all places and in all times. Just as Christ, raised on the Cross, draws all men to himself (*Jn.* 12, 32), the Church must be an ensign for the nations (*Is.* 11, 12), carrying out and continuing the mission which Christ himself was sent to fulfil. It was Christ himself who commissioned the Church to go "and make disciples of all nations" (*Mt.* 28, 19); the witness of the Church to the abiding presence of Christ is the work of the Holy Spirit—"the Spirit of your Father speaking through you" (*Mt.* 10, 20). It is for the Holy Spirit to lead the Church to a deeper awareness of itself and its mission, to lead it "into all the truth" (*Jn.* 16, 13).

Against this background, it is easier to see how the New Testament writers regarded the Church as being most fully itself, as expressing most completely the abiding and active presence of Christ, when it came to the celebration of the Eucharist. In the Synoptic tradition, there is the highly symbolic presentation of the miracle of the feeding of the multitude (cf. *Mk.* 6, 32-44, par. *Mt.* 14, 13-21; *Lk.* 9, 11-17), where the disciples are involved in the miracle in such a way that they become partners of Jesus in feeding the people; further, the narratives of the institution of the Eucharist itself (cf. *Mk.* 14, 22-25, par. *Mt.* 26, 26-29; *Lk.* 22, 17-20), are short and to the point because they simply make explicit something which lies at the heart of the whole Gospel tradition—the abiding presence of Christ. There is a logic which imposes itself here: if Christ is the sacrament of the Father, and if the Church is the sacrament of Christ, then the sharing of the

---

2. Cf. Schillebeeckx, E.: "Christ the Sacrament of Encounter with God," London and Melbourne, 1963.
3. Cf. Ibid., ch. 2: "The Church, Sacrament of the Risen Christ." Cf. also Vatican II: "By her relationship with Christ, the Church is a kind of sacrament or sign of intimate union with God and of the unity of all mankind." (Const. on the Church, ch. 1, no. 1.)

eucharistic meal is the sacrament of the Church. The formula with the wine is all the more significant: "This is my blood of the covenant" (*Mt.* 26, 28); the covenant between God and man is what brings the people of God into existence, and it is the covenant in the blood of Christ which brings the Church into existence. In the sharing of the Eucharist is the full affirmation of the Church's identity. But not only is it an affirmation of identity, it is also an affirmation of what the Church *does*—to unite men to Christ and to unite them with one another: that is the mission of the Church. That is why the Fourth Gospel speaks of the Eucharist in terms of the giving of eternal life: "He who eats my flesh and drinks my blood abides in me, and I in him" (*Jn.* 6, 56). It also explains why the Fourth Gospel interprets the Last Supper in terms of a parting gift and instruction to the Church.— "by this all men will know that you are my disciples, if you have love for one another" (*Jn* 13, 35). It is for this reason that St. Paul was able to move from the real presence of the body of Christ in the Eucharist to the identification of the Church itself as "the Body of Christ." It is for this reason also that he sees in the Eucharist the remembrance of the death of the Lord and in the partaking of the Eucharist, the proclamation to the world of the Lord's death (cf. *I Cor.* 11, 23-26).

Just as John concentrates on the relationship between Christ and the individual Christian in his eucharistic doctrine, so the other New Testament writers emphasise this aspect, each in his own way. The identity between Christ and the Christian is basic to the meaning of Matthew's Mission Discourse (cf. *Mt.* 9, 35—11, 1). The mission of the Christian, however, which makes of him a "sacrament" of Christ, is consequent upon the call he has received to follow Christ. Men are "called" in the Gospels, and they are "baptised" in the letters of Saint Paul. It is those who have been "called"/"baptised" who are sent to preach under the guidance of the Spirit; so the New Testament perspective helps us to see the integral elements of Christian Initiation. The culmination of this initiation into Christ comes with the sharing in the Eucharist. It is Christ himself who called men to witness to his death and resurrection, to preach his Gospel, to forgive sins, to suffer with him, to share his authority, to be his companions, i.e., to live their lives in his company through to an eternal destiny. This is the ultimate sense of the Eucharist in the Church: it is the continuation (or "re-presentation") of the self-giving of Christ, and the guarantee of his lasting presence in the community of those who bear his name. The man who has been initiated into Christ becomes part of his work and his life becomes fused with the life and action of Christ. This is the new covenant between God and man, and it is sealed in the Eucharist.

The Eucharist—Model of the Church

In the Eucharist, the Church is always aware that here is the continuing action of God himself, Father, Son and Holy Spirit, by whose life the Church lives. The Church sees itself in the Eucharist as the mystery of the Trinity, revealed and actualised in our world and our history with the purpose of bringing all men into personal communion with the Father through the Son in the Holy Spirit. Incorporated into Christ so as to form his living Body, the faithful live in the fellowship of the Spirit as true sons of the Father.

Hence in the Eucharist the Church is built up by the Spirit into the fullness of Christ, and, through the saving work of Christ there made present, has access to the Father. *The Church knows itself as the object of the Father's loving initiative, mediated by the Son, in the power of the Spirit.*

In the Eucharist the presence of Christ is known through the signs of his self-giving love: his broken Body and outpoured Blood are shown forth in the consecrated elements. *The Church knows itself to be, like Christ, the suffering and redeeming Servant of God and of all men.*

In the Eucharist the Church is caught up into God's heavenly glory, and receives the promise and foretaste of the life of the age to come. *The Church knows itself to be a pilgrim people, travelling in hope towards that goal of which it already has the foretaste.*

In the Eucharist the Church blesses God for all creation by offering that creation to its Lord under the symbols of bread and wine, and the Church is herself nourished with the life of God through these same symbols, now made Christ's Body and Blood. *The Church knows itself to stand as the priestly people within creation* and through the whole universe of matter God works out his purposes of love.

In the Eucharist the Church is summoned to a sacred meal, which is a foretaste of the perfect fellowship with God which is to come. The Church knows itself to be a fellowship of men and women, having a vocation to build itself up as the universal family of mankind and thus committed to overcoming everything that breaks or hinders the fellowship of men with each other and with God.

The Eucharist and the Structure of the Church

Since the Church is the sign of Christ's saving action in the world and the means of that saving action, it lives at two levels. Its inner life and its structure are revealed in the Eucharist. It is here that we can see the need for holding two aspects of the Church in a dynamic tension. The Church is the visible society founded on the apostles, and at the same time the mystery of salvation always present. The Church is at once the community of the redeemed and the redeeming community. Acts 2, 42, holds the balance—"These remained faithful to the teaching of the apostles, to the brotherhood, to the breaking of bread and to the prayers." In the community gathered together to celebrate the Eucharist we see a visible society; this gathered community not only recalls and ratifies again the new covenant between God and man, but is also here and now caught up in the very acts of Christ by which it is gathered together and established as the People of God. *The Eucharist is the mystery of salvation constituting the Church in its inmost being—the People of God gathered together in the unity of the Father, Son and Holy Spirit.*

Wherever and whenever the tension between these two aspects of the reality of the Church is not maintained, the nature of the Church as a visible society is distorted and the presence of the saving activity of God in the Church is obscured. In other words, there is a constant danger that the "ecclesial" aspect of the Church can be taken for the "ecclesiastical" and vice versa. In distinguishing these two aspects, we are provided with a means of describing the mystery of the Church in its fullness. For, in the actual life of the Church, there is an unchanging element, a "givenness," forever to be found where the People of God are gathered together in the new and eternal covenant sealed with the Blood of Christ: this is its "ecclesial" nature, willed by God and given by Christ. It is God's will that men will be made holy and saved, "not merely as individuals without any mutual bonds, but by (his) making them into a single people, a people which acknowledges him in truth and serves him in holiness. . . . Established by Christ as a fellowship of Life, charity and truth, it is also used by him as an instrument for the redemption of all." Side by side with this, however, it must be recognised that the Church exists in history and subject to the changes, the stresses and the strains of history, in the same way that the men and women who make up the People of God are subject to them. Because of this, in the course of history, the Church takes on many different shapes, many different structures. This is what is meant by its "ecclesiastical" nature: it is the product of the guidance of the Holy Spirit coupled with the goodwill and activity of the members of the Church in any historical situation to make the Church a clearer expression of what God wills that it should be in every age, to make it a more effective "instrument for the redemption of all." The ecclesiastical may be Spirit-inspired for times and circumstances or it may be consequent on human genius or frailty, and it is in this area that the Church is "semper reformanda." Consequently, there is always a priority of the "ecclesial" over the "ecclesiastical": the shape and structure of the Church must be judged by its effectiveness in allowing the Church to be as fully as possible "the Sacrament of Christ," his visible embodiment in the power of the Spirit.

However, since the Eucharist is "the sacrament of the Church" and "the model of the Church," it likewise has implications for an estimate of the *structure* of the Church. The "ecclesial" shape of the Church is proclaimed in the Eucharist: at the Eucharist, the Church is most fully itself, and it is there that the characteristic roles and attitudes of the People of God find expression. The witness of the Church to the saving event of God in Christ cannot be separated from its unity in faith, hope and love. "I in them and you in me, that they may become perfectly one, so that the world may know that you have sent me and have loved them even as you have loved me" (*Jn.* 17, 23). The unity of the Church in the Body and Blood of Christ is both source and sign of its unity in faith, hope and love. When we pose the question of what is essential for the Eucharist, then we become conscious of what we are really asking—the question of what is essential for the Church itself. It is the Eucharist which lays bare the "ecclesial" nature of the Church, and helps us to distinguish it from the Church's "ecclesiastical" aspect. As ever, the Last Supper serves as guide and paradigm: The People of God are all equally served by Christ and called to serve one another: "If I then, your Lord and Teacher, have washed your feet, you also ought to wash one another's feet" (*Jn.* 13, 14). The "example" of Christ is a rule for his Church, and since "a servant is not greater than his master, nor he who is sent greater than he who sent him" (*Jn.* 13, 16), it follows that those who have authority in the Church are called to serve the community in the spirit of Christ.

It is in the light of these considerations that we can consider the existence and exercise of authority in the Church, the nature and function of the ministry in the Church. There we can discover the same kind of distinction between what is "ecclesial" and what is "ecclesiastical"; in making this vital distinction and in drawing out its implications, the Eucharist will be our guide because it enables us to see clearly what the structure of the Church is.

The Eucharist and Membership of the Church

All that is implied by Baptism and Confirmation is fulfilled in the Eucharist. There the Christian expresses the fullness of responsible membership of the Church. There he brings to completion what his Baptism and Confirmation looked forward to, rejoices in Christ's risen life within his Church on earth, and is drawn into his reconciling work in the world. Through his incorporation into Christ's Paschal Mystery, made present in the Eucharist, the Christian shares in the divine life (*Rom.* 6, 3-11).

Often, the New Testament places the close relationship between Christ, the Christian, and the Church in a eucharistic context. With the words, "Unless you eat the flesh of the Son of Man and drink his blood, you can have no life in you," St. John draws out the eucharistic implications of the community of faith (*Jn.* 6, 52-58).

Later, in the great discourses of Our Lord at the Last Supper with his disciples, we find this relationship described as so intimate that it is like a vine and its branches (*Jn.* 15, 1-7).

St. Paul goes even further, illustrating membership of the Church in terms of being so closely one with Christ that we may think of the Church as his Body. Once again the relationship is seen as expressing itself in the Eucharist. The cup of blessing which we bless, the bread which we break—these are a sharing in the Body of Christ (*I Cor.* 10, 16-17). By the action of the Holy Spirit in the Eucharist, our union with Christ is continually deepened and our fellowship with one another is strengthened.

But it is perhaps in the First Letter of St. Peter that we have the clearest picture of the eucharistic community in action—a priestly people called by God to holiness, a New Israel set for a light in the world (*I Pt.* 2, 4-10). The Christian goes out from the Eucharist to serve the world, able to share in this work through the power and grace of Christ's Paschal victory, which was first mediated to him in Baptism and is ever renewed for him in the Eucharist.

The Eucharist and Mission

The New Israel has been a missionary body from the first: "Go therefore and make disciples of all nations," was the command of Christ (*Mt.* 28, 19). The primary and chief agent of mission is the Father himself, who loves the world so much that he sent the Son. The Church's calling is to continue the mission of Christ in the power of his Spirit (*Jn.* 20, 21-23), and this is symbolised by the fact that the coming of the Spirit at Pentecost gives to the disciples the courage and capacity to spread the Gospel (cf. *Acts* 2).

God's Mission—the Father's sending of the Son to redeem the world—is focused, actualised and celebrated above all in the Eucharist. There the Church is called together, reintegrated in Christ, and sent out in his Spirit to share in his mission and service to the world. It is a world made new in Christ, and in which he comes to meet us in many forms. But the Lord who meets, beckons, challenges and judges us variously through his world, meets us by appointment, so to speak, and most plainly in the Eucharist. Christians recognise Christ's saving presence not only in the Eucharist but in the world, and are therefore committed to co-operate with him and to help others to realise his saving presence for themselves.

The relationship in Christ with God, with other Christians and with the world, which is explicit in the Eucharist, must increasingly be lived out in daily life. At the Eucharist we stand before the Father as those who have received forgiveness; we must then go out and forgive others. Because we are united with one another as well as with Christ, we must go out and draw men together. Because we have been loved, we must go out and love. Thus the world should see in the living community of the Church its own true face, and the possibility of bringing to birth its own potentialities in the power of Christ.

A great aspiration of present-day Christians is "One Church renewed for mission." This phrase emphasises our conviction, based upon the words of Jesus in John 17, 21, that the Eucharist is the sign and source of unity, and that unity at the Eucharist is part of the gospel of reconciliation, to be preached to the whole world.

Final Statement

Having come to the end of our study of the topic proposed to us, namely, "The Ecclesial Nature of the Eucharist," we can take great encouragement from the fact that our discussions have led to extensive and thorough agreement on the doctrine of our respective traditions with regard to the Eucharist, sacrament and sacrifice. The preliminary discussion of the eucharistic practice of the Scottish Episcopal Church and the Roman Catholic Church helped us to find a common ground, in that both traditions agree on the continuing application of the principle: "Lex orandi, lex credendi." Our study of two essential aspects of eucharistic faith—the eucharistic sacrifice and the real presence—have brought us to an agreement which is not only "substantial," but which can fairly be described as "complete." This is already something for us to rejoice over; further, it is a sign of hope for future discussions.

It is, however, in our conversations centring on the relationship between the Eucharist and the Church that we have felt ourselves breaking new ground and moving closer to the heart of all ecumenical endeavour. Not only have we been able to reach a similar degree of agreement in this context, but we have been able to see as a result the way in which our future discussions must go: the way is clear for us to open up the topic of the Ministry, and ultimately of Intercommunion.

We have felt it necessary to pause at this stage, so that we can estimate the gains we have made, and so that we can clarify as far as possible the precise questions which now face us. The fact that we have concurred in relating the Eucharist to the Church, and in this way clarifying our understanding of the Church itself, means that we have to go further in this direction; the recognition of elements which are "ecclesial" as distinct from "ecclesiastical" is crucial for our estimate of the Church and for our understanding of the ministry within the Church. It will be remembered that our study of the Eucharist in relation to the Church has meant that we had to discuss the Church's inner nature, its structure and its mission, as well as the connexion between the Eucharist and membership of the Church. From the fact that we recognise the connexion between the Eucharist and membership of the Church, it follows that we must consider this connexion in relation to the vexed question of intercommunion. What we have done, we believe, is to clear the ground for such further discussions. In the experience of the representatives of both communions, there has been a great deal of clarification of thought gained through our study to date, as well as a mutual growth in awareness and appreciation of the theological and liturgical traditions of both communions. Throughout our work we have been activated by a desire to hasten the time when "all Christians will be gathered, in a common celebration of the Eucharist, into that unity of the one and only Church which Christ bestowed on his Church from the beginning."[1]

We have gained encouragement from the "Windsor Statement" of the Anglican-Roman Catholic International Commission, and we would hope that what we have agreed together serves to clarify some of the questions alluded to in that document, and indeed carry the discussion further.

It is our conviction that what we have studied together is of supreme importance to the life of the Church of Christ; it is our earnest hope that what we have concluded will serve as a step on the way to the restoration of unity between our two communions. With this in mind, we submit our work to the authorities of our respective Churches.

---

1. Cf. Vatican II: Decree on Ecumenism, ch. 1, no. 4.

Covenants

Covenant Relationship

What Is It?

A "Covenant Relationship" is an agreement between two communities—e.g., a Roman Catholic parish and a parish or congregation of a non-Roman Catholic church—in which the members of these communities commit themselves to pray for each other, and together; to cooperate in whatever ways they determine are mutually desirable; and to come to know and support one another in the LORD.

Why?

Concern for Christian Unity has been a growing awareness in the lives of Christians and their churches during this century. For Roman Catholics, this awareness was confirmed in official Church policy at the Second Vatican Council, where Catholics—"faithful and clergy alike"—were charged with the responsibility of being concerned for restoring unity. The Council called for closer cooperation among all Christians.

Yet ecumenism—or, working for Christian Unity—has often remained on a theoretical, upper-echelon level. Its practical meaning is not clear to the people in the pew, nor often to their parish clergy, either.

Practical steps at the parish level are needed if we are to become aware of our call as a people to work for that unity for which Christ prayed. To enter a "Covenant Relationship" is one such practical step to build understanding and trust, cooperation and support, on the firm foundation of prayer and faith in Christ.

What Does a "Covenant" Contain?

The Covenant is primarily a willingness on the part of members of both parishes to enter into a relationship of prayer, cooperation and mutual support in Christ. Unless this attitude is firmly rooted in the hearts of people, a document will be meaningless.

The Covenant must also be reflected in the activities and programs of each parish, in their internal concerns and priorities. If it is a simple "good idea" which everyone approves but no one acts upon, the "Covenant" will be empty.

Finally, the Covenant should be written up in such a manner as to express the attitude and commitment of the people and parishes, and as a reminder for self-evaluation to determine periodically what the relationship truly means. Such a written document should contain at least the names of the parishes involved, the purposes for the Covenant, how they have mutually agreed to express this relationship in various programs or activities, and any other special provisions the two parishes may agree upon.

How Is It Developed?

The following is suggested approach for Roman Catholics:

1.   The parish staff should consider the idea carefully. Once they fully understand it, they should determine whether they would be willing to carry through on such a relationship.

2.   The Parish Council should consider the idea in the light of the Church's official position on Christian Unity. The question is whether this is an effective step to be taken locally to build greater understanding and love. If it is not, then alternatives to the "Covenant Relationship" should be decided upon: not to act for Christian Unity may be a betrayal of our Catholic convictions.

3.   If the parish staff and Parish Council are agreed that a Covenant Relationship is desirable, conversations should be initiated by the parish staff with a parish or congregation with which the Catholic parish already enjoys a certain level of understanding and mutual cooperation. At least, this would appear the most effective first choice.

4.   The staff and appropriate agencies of the other parish or congregation should be encouraged to consider the proposal as thoroughly as the Catholic parish has just done.

5.   If there is agreement that the idea is worth pursuing, joint study committees drawn from both communities should be established to investigate the various possibilities for what the Covenant Relationship might entail.

6.   The parish staffs and councils of the two communities should eventually determine the extent of the Covenant Relationship, approve the statement of it, and prepare the people of their respective communities for this relationship.

7.   For Roman Catholic parishes, approval of the Covenant by the Bishop is required before it may be signed by the local parish. Approval by the proper authorities of the other Church is encouraged.

A Suggested Time-Table

Careful preparation is needed to achieve a genuine Covenant Relationship.

Before June 30—steps 1 through 4

Before November 30—step 5 should be completed

Before December 30—steps 6 and 7

During the Week of Prayer for Christian Unity (January 18-25), formal signing of the Covenant document and initiation of the relationship.

> —The Ecumenical Commission of The
> Roman Catholic Diocese of Helena.

Toward a Theological Understanding of Clusters

The term "cluster" occurs in ordinary language when, e.g., we say, "That cluster of birches makes a brilliant scene," or, as a model in physics, such as a "cluster of molecules." Clusters of churches normally refers to two or more neighboring churches who associate in any way. The phenomenon of clustering reflects the local, regional, or grass roots turn in contemporary ecumenism.

We should more appropriately speak of "covenants," not clusters. In fact, covenant is the term used in Wales where churches have been involved in this process since 1964. It has a firm basis in Scripture and Tradition in the concept of the People of God as a covenantal community. While clusters implies pragmatic cooperation based upon geographical proximity, covenant means conscious intention to bring about a new relationship of community based upon a recognition of the faith which we share.

This means that the covenant is primarily a relationship. It is neither sacramental nor voluntary association. It is a relationship created by the love of God and sustained by the faith of its constituents. It is intentional, conscious, freely made, involves a community of persons, and carries specific responsibilities. The churches who comprise the covenant each recognize that the present state of affairs is not the final one. Purification and renewal are constantly needed. Death for an exclusive identity and resurrection to a more inclusive identity can then occur.

A covenant of churches may take a variety of shapes depending on the makeup of its constituents and their current state of development. They may be denominational—Orthodox, Protestant, Catholic or ecumenical.

Theologically speaking, any covenant model must include four basic features. Each one is indispensable and all four are equally important and must be held in balance: spiritual, intellectual, moral, and organizational. Indeed, it is the purpose of a covenant of churches to assure that all four dimensions of our ecumenical and religious life flourish together.

A covenant of churches is a worshipping community. In the process of mutually recognized and shared worship, it begins to create new ecumenical liturgies based on its own experience together.

A covenant of churches is a thinking community. It takes seriously the need to supply vision and to be informed as Christians and as people of the 20th Century. Accordingly, it provides occasions to engage in dialogue, reflection, and action with any person.

A covenant of churches is an acting community. It understands the basic meaning of the word "ecumenism" as "the inhabited world" and so acts courageously as an agent of reconciliation, change, and transformation among persons and institutions (including its own) in the world.

A covenant of churches is a conciliar community. That is, how it reaches decisions and organizes its life is as important as what it does. Honesty, openness, humility, fairness, e.g., equal male-female representation and toleration characterize its total organizational life.

A covenant of churches will grow to the degree that it allows all four dimensions to develop fully and in balance. It can help ecumenism move beyond the stalemate between the diplomatic ecumenism of polite conversation on the one hand and the utilitarian ecumenism of mere community service on the other.

The impetus for a covenant of churches should spring from our faith. It may arise though from the sudden realization that the existence of five or ten separate, unrelated, or competing churches in a community each with its own budgets, programs, staff, buildings, etc., raise serious moral not to say economic questions today. Instead of all the wasted energy and ineffective (shall we say faithless?) witness which that scene increasingly represents, think of what it might mean to begin seriously building a covenant of churches, a community of Christians worshipping, thinking, acting and planning together.

If we thoughtfully recognize the faith which we as churches share, then it will be our intention to really build covenants of churches. In the process, the twin luxuries of denominationalism and ecumenism as we now know them will vanish. Think of what that might mean in our neighborhoods, towns, and region!

Prepared by
Rev. Daniel L. Anderson

Commission on the Theology of Marriage and Its Application to Mixed Marriages

Final Report

From February 26 to March 4, 1967, the Vatican Secretariat for Promoting Christian Unity and the Faith and Order Department of the World Council of Churches sponsored a meeting at Nemi, Italy, to study the ecumenical difficulties inherent in marriages between Roman Catholics and other Christians. When *The Malta Report* of January 1968 recommended the setting up of a special commission to consider the theology of marriage, with special reference to mixed marriages, the Vatican, based on the experience of the Nemi meeting, accepted the need to pursue discussion of these topics on a bilateral basis. The Pope and the Archbishop of Canterbury appointed a commission that began its work at Windsor in April 1968. After six meetings, the commission issued its report at Venice in June 1975.

Contents

Members of the Commission

Roman Catholic Members

The Most Revd. Ernest L. Unterkoefler, Bishop of Charleston, S. Carolina, USA (*Co-Chairman*).

The Right Revd. Langton D. Fox, Bishop[1] of Menevia, Wrexham, N. Wales.

The Most Revd. Francis J. Spence, Bishop of Charlottetown, Prince Edward Island, Canada.[2]

The Right Revd. Mgr. Professor P. F. Cremin, DD, IUD, St. Patrick's College, Maynooth, Ireland.

Secretary: The Right Revd. Mgr. W. A. Purdy, Vatican Secretariat for Promoting Christian Unity.

Anglican Members

The Most Revd. George O. Simms, DD, Archbishop of Armagh, and Primate of All Ireland[3] (*Co-Chairman*).

The Right Revd. Donal H. V. Hallock, Bishop of Milwaukee, USA (*resigned on resigning his see, 1974*).

The Right Revd. Ralph S. Dean, Bishop of Cariboof Canada (*resigned, on resigning his see, 1974*).[4]

Professor the Revd. Canon G. R. Dunstan, DD, FSA, King's College, London.

The Revd. L. Mason Knox, JCD, Sacred Heart School of Theology, Hales Corners, Wisconsin, USA (*since 1974*).

The Revd. Barnabas Lindars, SSF, DD, Faculty of Divinity, University of Cambridge (*since 1974*).

Secretaries: The Revd. Canon J. R. Satterthwaite, Church of England Council of Foreign Relations (*until 1971*).[5]

The Revd. Prebendary Henry Cooper, Adviser to the Archbishop of Canterbury on Roman Catholic Pastoral Matters (*since 1971*).

---

1. Auxiliary Bishop at the time of his appointment.
2. Auxiliary Bishop to the Military Vicar, Canadian Forces, at the time of his appointment.
3. Archbishop of Dublin at the time of his appointment.
4. Replacing (as Anglican Executive Officer) the Most Revd. Edwin Morris, formerly Archbishop of Wales, who was overtaken by illness between appointment and the First Meeting of the Commission.
5. Subsequently consecrated Bishop of Fulham.

Consultants

At the Fourth Meeting: Dom Henry Wansbrough OSB, and the Revd. Fr. Michael Sharratt; Lady Oppenheimer[6] and the Revd. Dr. Barnabas Lindars, SSF.

At the Fifth Meeting: The Revd. Dr. Brian O'Higgins;[7] The Worshipful Chancellor the Revd. E. Garth Moore.

The following other persons, to whom the Commission is indebted, contributed papers at the request of members of the Commission:

The Revd. Fr. A. M. Ambrozic, "Indissolubility of Marriage in the New Testament: Law or Ideal?" (1973).[8]

The Right Revd. Mgr. H. G. J. Beck, "Proposed Pastoral Guidelines for Inter-Christian Marriages" (1968).

The Right Revd. Bishop B. C. Butler, OSB, "Vatican II's Ecclesiology" (1974).

The Revd. John Coventry, SJ, "Theological Trends: Inter-Church Marriage" (1974).[9]

The Revd. William J. La Due, "Marriage: Sacramentality, Validity, Indissolubility" (1974).

John Lucas, Esq., "The Doctrine of a Metaphysical *Vinculum*" (1973).[10]

Professor the Revd. Canon John Macquarrie, "The Nature of the Marriage Bond (*Vinculum Conjugale*)" (1973).[11]

The Report

Section A

Proceedings of the Commission

1. The Commission was established jointly in 1967, on the one part by the Roman Catholic Secretariat for Promoting Christian Unity with the approval of His Holiness Pope Paul VI and on the other part by the Most Revd. and Rt. Honble. A. M. Ramsey Lord Archbishop of Canterbury on behalf of the Anglican Communion.

---

6. Written submission published in *Theology* LXXVIII, May 1975.
7. Written submission published in *The Irish Theological Quarterly* XLI, July-Oct. 1974.
8. Published in *Studia Canonica* 6, 1972, pp. 269-288.
9. Published in *The Way*, April-July 1974.
10. Written submission published in *Theology* LXXVIII, May 1975.
11. *Idem.*

2.   The problems arising from mixed marriages[1] had been recognized as one of the chief of those "practical questions" referred to in the Joint Declaration made by the Pope and the Archbishop in Rome in March 1966; and when the Anglican/Roman Catholic Joint Preparatory Commission met at Gazzada in January 1967, one of its first acts was to recommend the setting up of a special commission to consider the Theology of Marriage with special reference to Mixed Marriages. The recommendation was immediately accepted on both sides.

3.   These events fitted in with other ecumenical developments. Early in 1967, from 26 February to 4 March, a group designated by the same Secretariat for Promoting Christian Unity had met at Nemi with a group convened by the Faith and Order Department of the World Council of Churches to discuss prepared papers on the pastoral and ecumenical difficulties inherent in marriages between Roman Catholics and other Christians. The Secretariat accepted the need to pursue "bilateral" discussions of the problem with major groups or communions of Churches, with the possibility of continuing relevant exchanges with the WCC as occasion arose.

4.   The members of the Commission are named on p. 2. Membership on the Roman Catholic side remained unchanged, though illness regrettably prevented the Bishop of Menevia from attending the Fifth Meeting. On the Anglican side, an early illness and two episcopal retirements occasioned the changes which we have recorded. At all our meetings Archbishop Simms and Bishop Unterkoefler presided over alternate sessions.

5.   The Commission has met six times; at St. George's House, Windsor Castle, from 16 to 18 April, 1968; at Pineta Sacchetti, Rome, from 27 to 30 November, 1968; in London, from 22 to 25 November, 1971; at Haywards Heath, at the Priory of Our Lady of Good Counsel, from 9 to 12 April, 1973; at the Divinity Hostel, Dublin, from 1 to 5 April, 1974; and at Casa Cardinale Piazza, Venice, from 23 to 27 June, 1975, when this final report was given unanimous approval.

6.   At the first meeting (1968), among the documents used to initiate discussion was a working paper on "Mixed Marriages," prepared by the Secretariat for the colloquy at Nemi, in which one member of the Commission had participated. This occasioned a preliminary survey of our problem in its entirety: the nature of marriage, its sacramentality and indissolubility, and the procedures of our Churches in relation thereto; the mixed marriage, requiring, in both its difficulties and its opportunities, pastoral action from the Church, in some respects juridical in form; hence the law and practice of Roman Catholic Church

---

1. "Ecumenical marriages" and "inter-Church marriages" are terms in experimental use in some places; we have retained the formal term "mixed marriages" for convenience, without prejudice to others.

relating to "canonical form," to the *cautiones* (as they were then called) concerning the upbringing of children, and to dispensation from the impediment of "mixed religion"; and the necessity of pastoral care, exercised within both Churches and, where possible, jointly between them, in preparation for the mixed marriage and in its continued support in the life of the Church. At the end of this meeting agreement was recorded on "The Fundamental Theological Principles," which, because they have governed our deliberations, in some sense, ever since, are here quoted in full:

Three Fundamental Theological Principles

i. That Holy Baptism itself confers Christian status and is the indestructible bond of union between all Christians and Christ, and so of Christians with one another. This baptismal unity remains firm despite all ecclesiastical division.

ii. That in Christian marriage the man and the woman themselves make the covenant whereby they enter into marriage as instituted and ordained by God; this new unity, the unity of marriage, is sacramental in virtue of their Christian baptism and is the work of God in Christ.

iii. That this marriage once made possesses a unity given by God to respect which is a primary duty; this duty creates secondary obligations for the Church in both its pastoral and its legislative capacity. One is the obligation to discourage marriages in which the unity would be so strained or so lacking in vitality as to be both a source of danger to the parties themselves and to be a disfigured sign of or defective witness to the unity of Christ with his Church. Another is the obligation to concert its pastoral care and legislative provisions to support the unity of the marriage once it is made and to ensure as best it can that these provisions be not even unwittingly divisive.

7.   Our Second Meeting (1968) was held at a time when it was known that new legislation was in prospect to replace the Instruction, *Matrimonii Sacramentum*, of 1966, and some hope was entertained that our unanimous Report might influence its content. In fact, upon advice, our Second Report was drafted and presented with this in view, and in accordance with the advice which we had sought the Report was brought to the notice of the relevant Vatican authorities. In particular, while aware on the one side of the theological principles underlying the guarantees for the Roman Catholic upbringing of the children of mixed marriages, and on the other aware that the pastoral and ecumenical consequences of these requirements are disturbing to many people, we could recommend that "no more be asked of the Anglican party than was proposed by the Synod of Bishops in Rome on 24 October 1967, namely that he knows of the obligation in conscience of the Roman Catholic party and at least does not rule out the Roman Catholic baptism and education of the children." This modification

was, co-incidentally, we believe, allowed in the new legislation, the Apostolic Letter *Matrimonia Mixta* issued *motu proprio* by Pope Paul VI on 31 March 1970 (*AAS* 62, 1970, p. 261). The other legislative proposal in our Second Report concerned canonical form. Adhering closely to the intention of the Decree of the Sacred Congregation for the Oriental Churches, *Crescens Matrimoniorum*, dated 22 February 1967 (*AAS* 59, 1967, p. 166), we suggested a similar provision for marriages between Roman Catholics and Anglicans in the following terms (expressly leaving the details to be worked out if the principle were accepted):

> The contracting parties are the ministers of Holy Matrimony. When one party is Anglican it seems to us entirely reasonable that the parties should decide between themselves whether they shall contract marriage before a Roman Catholic minister or before an Anglican minister, and whether in a Roman Catholic or an Anglican church. Therefore we would recommend that, on condition that joint pastoral preparation has been given, and freedom to marry established to the satisfaction of the bishop of the Roman Catholic party and of the competent Anglican authority, the marriage may validly and lawfully take place before the duly authorized minister of the Church of either party. Should a minister of the Church of the other party assist in the solemnization, as he might, on the invitation of the parties and with the concurrence of the local minister, we would hope that he would be assigned an appropriate part of the rite used in that Church and not any addition to it.

Again we urged the importance of good pastoral care to enable the spouses (in the words of the Pastoral Constitution of Vatican II) to "experience the meaning of their oneness and attain to it with growing perfection day by day" (*Gaudium et Spes*, 48).

8.   Before our Third Meeting (1971) there was a long interval, occasioned, first, by our waiting for the new legislation, and secondly (its contents having been perceived) for some general picture to be obtained of the diverse interpretations given to it by Episcopal Conferences in the liberty and discretion which it extended to them. We had to recognize that no new legislation could be expected for a considerable time; it was important, therefore, to take the measure of what we had. During this time also the Anglican/Roman Catholic International Commission (ARCIC) was developing its theological study which would, in time, strengthen the ecumenical foundation of our own work—as it did when it published its agreements on the Eucharist (1971) and the Sacred Ministry (1973). The Archbishop of Canterbury, meanwhile, had appointed a small commission to examine the doctrine of marriage and its application to some questions of discipline in the Church of England, and the Report of this commission, *Mar-*

riage, Divorce and the Church (1971) was also before us. Here, therefore, with *Matrimonia Mixta* and the reports of local episcopal direction and local pastoral activity, were ingredients for the agenda of our Third Meeting. From it emerged the pattern of our future work, and, indeed, of this Final Report.

9.   We were soon made aware that behind the differences of practice, both pastoral and juridical, lay deeper problems of theology. Behind the requirement of a promise concerning the baptism and upbringing of children, not simply as Christians and therefore members of a Christian Church (an obligation which none of us would dispute) but particularly as Roman Catholics, lay a doctrine of the Church which Roman Catholics cannot abandon and which Anglicans cannot accept. Behind the various means developed in our respective traditions for dealing, juridically and pastorally, with marriages which have broken down or other defective marital situations—of which more will be written explicitly later—there lay the possibility of deep dogmatic differences concerning the strict indissolubility of marriage, whether "natural" or "sacramental"; and this possibility called to be explored. Behind the Roman Catholic requirement of "canonical form" for the valid celebration of a mixed marriage, as for any marriage of a Roman Catholic, although historically the legislation was disciplinary and regulative in intent, there lay in some minds the possibility that its retention in the new *motu proprio* implied some ecclesiological defensiveness also, some notion that the Anglican priest could not, for reasons concerning Holy Orders, be empowered to perform for a Roman Catholic partner that office in marriage which a priest in communion with the see of Rome could perform. In short, by the time of our Third Meeting our Commission had, on the one hand, achieved a sufficient degree of mutual trust, and, on the other, experienced a sufficient degree of mutual provocation, to seek out and face the material which occasions suspicion and mistrust between our Churches concerning marriage and mixed marriages. Our task henceforth was to examine this, piece by piece, and in this way to work towards a resolution of our difficulties. We hoped, and we formally requested, that the ecclesiological questions would be undertaken for us by ARCIC, which had within itself greater theological competence than we could command. This request could not be met: ARCIC had already an agenda too heavy and a timetable too strict for any such diversion to be entertained. Accordingly, we had to attend to these questions ourselves; and, having attempted them, we were the more convinced that there remained much in them requiring more thorough theological analysis (v. *infra*, §6).

10. For our Fourth Meeting (1973), therefore, we made more extensive provision. We published our Third Report, with the permission

of our respective authorities,[2] in order that others in our Churches might know and, if willing, comment upon the questions which we had raised. We invited scholars from both Churches to contribute papers on the philosophical and theological aspects of indissolubility, particularly as these had found expression in the terminology of the *vinculum matrimonii*. We invited four consultants to assist us at our meeting, two exegetes and two philosophical theologians, in a concerted effort to encompass at least the major theoretical dimensions of the indissolubility of marriage. We benefited greatly from this assistance, and we record our thanks to the authors of it. As a result we were able to state agreements and disagreements on the methods and results of exegesis of the relevant texts of Holy Scripture (see below, § 32). We were able to re-affirm our earlier agreement in our understanding of marriage as being of its nature a lifelong and exclusive union, and in our requirement of an intention to enter into such a union in everyone contracting a true marriage. At the same time we were able to distinguish more sharply the lines of disagreement among canonists and theologians—lines *not* co-terminous with those demarcating our Churches—over the propriety of the various responses made to marriages which have broken down or otherwise been found defective. Both the theology of marriage and responses to defective marital situations receive fuller treatment in later sections of this Report. The Fourth Meeting left for the Fifth a further discussion of the question, posed by each Church to the other in relation to its theory and practice, "If this is what you do to enable your Church to recognize (if not actually to solemnize) a new marital union after the termination, otherwise than by death, of a first, how can you still maintain that you hold marriage, of its nature, to be exclusive and indissoluble?"

11. For our Fifth Meeting (1974) we were prepared by the replies received to a Questionary sent to all Roman Catholic Episcopal Conferences, and to all Anglican Primates and Metropolitans, in areas where our two Churches co-exist, and by more papers prepared by consultants as well as by some from among our number.[3] Two consultants gave valued help at the meeting. The yield of the Questionary was not weighty, grateful as we were to our respondents; a wide diversity in the manner and quality of answers given to questions, not always (in hindsight) framed precisely enough, yielded little information from which valid generalizations or conclusions could be drawn;

---

2. *Theology* LXXVI, April 1973, p. 195; *The Tablet*, 227/6926 March 1973, p. 316; *One in Christ* IX, 2, 1973, pp. 198-203.
3. Cf. G. R. Dunstan, *Natural and Sacramental Marriage*, printed in *Beyond Tolerance: The Challenge of Mixed Marriage*, ed. Michael Hurley, Geoffrey Chapman 1975, pp. 67-72; and see below, § 20, note.

though encouraging pictures of determined pastoral development emerged here and there.

12. Our discussion at this stage centred mainly on the relation between marriage as grounded in the "natural order," the order of creation, and marriage in the sacramental order, the order of redemption and of sanctifying grace. It had seemed from our very first meeting that we agreed in finding no dichotomy here. Thus the Anglican doctrine, given formal expression in its liturgy, conceives marriage as God's ordinance in the order of creation, taken by Christ and the Church into the sacramental order as representing the covenanted unity of Christ and the Church, and signifying effectively the sanctification of the marriage and its partners within the communion of Christ and the Church.

13. For the Catholic members the impression gained at the first discussion was confirmed that, despite traditional differences of linguistic usage,[4] this account is one with which they can fully agree; though they would not immediately understand how it was consistent with a discipline which recognizes subsequent marriage during the lifetime of the previous partners. Similarly discussions about the Catholic discipline of the Pauline privilege and the wider *privilegium fidei* made it necessary for the Anglican members to try to understand how this doctrinal position was consistent with a distinction between the natural and sacramental orders sharp enough to allow the Roman Catholic Church to dissolve a marriage when for lack of valid baptism the marriage does not enjoy the absolute security of a "sacramental" marriage. At the end of the Fifth Meeting provision was made for the drafting of this Final Report, the Commission itself having indicated its content and tendency.

14. At our Sixth Meeting (1975) the Report, which had been sent to members late in 1974, criticized by them and revised, was further scrutinized, amended, accepted by us all and signed. Thus we present this our unanimous Report.

---

4. We may quote here, in relation to Anglican use of the word "sacrament" with reference to marriage what ARCIC wrote of it with reference to ordination, namely that is "limited by the distinction drawn in the Thirty-nine Articles (article 25) between the two 'sacraments of the Gospel' and the 'five commony called sacraments.' Article 25 does not deny these latter the name 'sacrament,' but differentiates between them and the 'two sacraments' ordained by 'Christ' described in the Catechism as 'necessary to salvation' for all men" (*Ministry and Ordination*, p. 11 n. 4, SPCK 1973).

Section B

The Relevant Theology

Of Baptism and the Church
15. Though it was accepted from the beginning as a fundamental principle of our discussions "that Holy Baptism itself confers Christian status and is the indestructible bond of union between all Christians and Christ and so of Christians with one another," and that "this baptismal unity remains firm despite all ecclesiastical division," none the less it was quickly evident that the central theological difficulty that underlay Anglican/Roman Catholic tensions about the discipline governing mixed marriages was ecclesiological, it stemmed from divergent conceptions of the Church.

16. The discipline embodied in the 1917 *Codex Iuris Canonici,* and the language in which it was expressed, reflected a conception of the Church which was hardly questioned among Roman Catholics down to the Second Vatican Council. This conception received its latest classical expression in such encyclicals as *Mystici Corporis* and *Humani Generis;* it tended to identify the Church, the mystical body of Christ, with that juridical *societas perfecta,* the Roman Catholic communion. It survived to dominate the preparatory *schema* of Vatican II's treatment of the Church, but the Council's constitution *Lumen Gentium* and the decree on Ecumenism, *Unitatis Redintegratio,* both showed significant development, both in their fresh presentation of the Church as sacrament of salvation, as Communion and as pilgrim on earth, and in their assessment of the status and salvific efficacy of non-Roman Catholic Churches and communities.

17. It is predictably a slow and difficult business for a renewed ecclesiology to be brought to bear on canonical legislation with its long-established juridical categories and language. In the matter of marriage, many pastoral considerations have to be weighed before changes can prudently be made. None the less many saw the relaxations of the 1966 Instruction *Matrimonii Sacramentum* and of the 1970 *motu proprio Matrimonio Mixta* not simply as theologically unrelated ecumenical gestures but as canonical changes logically linked with developments in ecclesiology. The many included Anglicans, some of whom however were disappointed at the halting way in which it seemed discipline followed theological advance.

18. A significant and much-discussed change in the ecclesiological language of Vatican II was the account of the Church as "subsisting in" the Roman Catholic communion (*Lumen Gentium* 8; *Unitatis Redintegratio* 4). The *relator* at the Council made it clear that the scholastic phrase was deliberately chosen to replace mere identification, in order to harmonize with the very much more positive language used of non-Roman Catholic communions.[5]

19. It would be wrong to minimize the significance of these changes. In historical perspective they loom large. They could hardly have co-existed with the former, static, juridical, "societary" emphasis in the presentation of the Church, and because they reflect a new, dynamic way of thinking of the Church, they are capable of further development. While they do not provide ground for supposing that a Roman Catholic may no longer have an obligation in conscience concerning the Catholic upbringing of his children, they do mean that insistence on this obligation is not to be seen merely as institutional defensiveness, nor as dismissive of other traditions, nor as over-riding all other possible obligations, such as those which arise from the nature of marriage itself: the obligation simply reflects the Church's understanding of itself.

20. So far we have spoken only of Roman Catholic ecclesiology and its implications; but though Anglican ecclesiology is less precisely formulated, makes less exclusive claims and consequently of its nature leaves more room for choice to the conscience of the believer, we were reminded at our Fifth Meeting that there are marriages between Anglicans and other Christians in which the community concerned will be ecclesiologically so "seriously deficient that the Anglican will be compelled to insist that the children be baptized and reared as Anglicans."[6] Some Anglicans indeed would be sufficiently unhappy about certain Roman Catholic doctrines and practices to feel bound to insist on an Anglican upbringing for the children of an Anglican/Roman Catholic marriage, even though they would not impugn baptism administered in the Roman Catholic Church. Members of the Commission, in reporting these views, are not to be understood as identifying themselves with them.

Of Marriage

21. On marriage itself the Commission finds no fundamental difference of doctrine between the two Churches, as regards what marriage of its nature is or the ends which it is ordained to serve. The language of Vatican II in *Gaudium et Spes* (47-52), grounding marriage in the natural order, in the mutual pact or covenant (*pactum, foedus*) of the spouses, is entirely at one with the covenantal interpretation of marriage written into the Anglican liturgies. The sacramental nature of marriage is also affirmed, partly in the moral sense of enduring obli-

---

5. Cf. *Acta Synodalia Sacrosanti Concilii Ocumenici Vaticani II*, Vatican City, 1973, vol. III, Pars I, p. 177.
6. L. Mason Knox, *How important is it to Anglicans that the children of mixed marriages be brought up as members of their own Communion, and why?* A paper submitted to the Commission at its Fifth Meeting, 1974.

gation (*sacramentum*) expressed in the marriage vow, partly in the sense of sign (*signum*): a sign to the world of what marriage in the natural order by God's ordinance is and ought to be; a sign to the world and to the Church of Christ's irrevocable covenant with the Church and of the mutual love which finds expression between Him and the Church, and which ought to exist between the Church's members; and a sign to married people, to the world and the Church, that continuance within the covenant is dependent upon the continued forgiving and renewing grace of God; and finally in its being made by Christ into an effective sign of grace when it is celebrated between the baptized. It is from all this, with continuance in the sacramental life of the Church, that Christian marriage takes its specific character and achieves its fulness. Natural marriage had, in the beginning, the full potentiality of being made sacramental in the order of redemption: the sacramental significance was declared as part of the "mystery" (*sacramentum*) dispensed and revealed in the fulness of time by God through his Son and recognized as such by the Apostle; so the language of Ephesians 5, interpreting conjugal love in terms of Christ's love for the Church and *vice versa*, aptly expresses our common theology of marriage, and is as aptly entrenched in our respective marriage liturgies. This substantial convergence in doctrine, despite differences in the language used to express it, is a welcome fact of our time, too precious to permit us to rest on the polarities suggested by the time-conditioned formulations of the Reformation and Counter-Reformation. On our respective responses to marriages in which the moral unity and the integrity of the sign are together marred more will be written below. The differences in these responses are not such as to deny or impair our full agreement on what marriage in its created and sacramental nature is.

Of Reliance on Law

22. In a mixed marriage there is a meeting, not only of the two Churches represented by the parties, and not only of the doctrines and traditions of those Churches, but also of two jurisdictions, two societies whose lives are regulated, to different extents, by law. The Roman Catholic Church legislated for marriage comprehensively in the *Codex Iuris Canonici* and subsequent regulations, devising laws for every aspect of marriage, irrespective of what civil laws may provide (cf. § 26). This comprehensiveness derived logically from the Catholic Church's awareness of itself as a *societas perfecta*, having a jurisdiction of its own to regulate the internal life of a community which transcends all national and regional jurisdictions throughout the world. For Roman Catholic Christians, in so far as their life in the Church is concerned, the canon law operates, as we have said above in § 19, as a juridical expression of the Church's doctrine about itself, and of its pastoral responsibility for bringing the faithful to the complete awareness of and response to the redemption once wrought for them by God in Christ: in short, for their renewal in the image of God, for the enjoyment of his presence and his glory eternally. The canonical regulation of marriage, like the dispensation of the sacraments generally, is seen to be part of this whole.

23. In the Churches of the Anglican Communion law, particularly in respect of marriage, has a much more limited function. The fundamental regulation of marriage—competence to marry, impediments to marriage, prohibited degrees of kindred and affinity, the public acceptance of forms for the contracting or solemnizing of marriage etc.—is seen to be the function of the law of the State, not of the Church. For this there is a simple historical reason. At the Reformation in England jurisdiction in matrimonial causes continued to be exercised by the Church, now the Church of England, and was not taken over by the State, and the substantive law on marriage was carried over from the common canon law of Western Christendom, modified only in some important particulars, chiefly concerning impediments. When, over two centuries later, the State began to legislate for marriage in its own capacity, at first to guard against clandestinity and its attendant abuse, and then to provide for the dissolution of marriage by civil process, it left the solemnization of marriage as the responsibility of the Church virtually unimpaired (providing only alternatives for marriage before the civil registrar or according to the rites and ceremonies of other religious bodies), although it made the canonical grounds for separation *a mensa et thoro* the basis of its own substantive law for total dissolution. Consequently the Church of England feels no need for comprehensive ecclesiastical or canonical legislation to govern the fundamentals of marriage: it accepts its "own" law back again as enjoying the authority of and administered by the State. And since a similar pattern of relationship spread throughout the common law countries in which the Anglican Communion took its early roots, the emergence of comprehensive codes of canon law for marriage is a rare and late phenomenon.

24. Behind these differences lie others, less tangible but real. Even before the Reformation co-existence between the canon law of the Church and the common law of England was never easy. Not only did they differ in substance; not only had they different sources of ultimate authority and courts of final appeal, the Papacy in the one, the Crown in the other; they differed radically in procedure and even more in that sensitive area of the relation of authority to consent. The common law tradition was quicker to respond to public opinion, through the interplay of parliamentary legislation, judicial interpretation and the jury system, than was the canonical tradition with its closer involvement with a curial, and predominantly clerical, structure. These facts of history have influenced the unspoken attitude of

Anglicans to the proportionate place of law in the government of their Church.

25. The Anglican canon law does indeed state obligations incumbent on the laity as well as the clergy. Yet these obligations are legally enforceable on laymen only in respect of their holding ecclesiastical office, e.g., as churchwarden, or as judge in an ecclesiastical court. In his ordinary Christian living the Anglican accepts the authority of the Church as a moral obligation; the sense of there being a law to keep seldom occurs to him.

26. The Roman Catholic conception of the Church's legislative authority and function was and is considerably different from this; hence also the Roman Catholic's traditional attitude to the Church's law and to his corresponding obligation (though few of these things are exempt from the contemporary discussion of authority in general). He sees the Church as a supra-national institution endowed with power both to teach and to legislate comprehensively for marriage because it is a sacramental act and status. Marriage may be and is the subject of circumscribed agreements with the law of the land, the State's competence in some parts of the matter being recognized; yet marriage for the Roman Catholic could hardly be the subject of such relations between Church law and State law as those described above in § 23. Though he might feel particular Church regulations to be irksome and even in extreme instances to be an abuse of the Church's authority, he would hardly recognize a general separation of moral obligation from ecclesiastical law such as that described in § 25.

27. It follows, therefore, that in a mixed marriage an acceptance of ecclesiastical requirements which seems natural to one party might well occasion surprise and even resentment in the other. The Anglican partner would see a wider range of matters which he would think it right that the partners should "work out for themselves" than the Roman Catholic partner, whose disposition is to recognize the authority of his Church in these matters. This difference would inevitably occur whenever questions of Christian conscience arise. We shall point below to the two matters where the difference particularly affects a mixed marriage, namely in the requirement of a promise about the baptism and education of children and the requirement of marriage according to the "canonical form."

Section C

Defective Marital Situations

The Problems

28. We use the phrase "defective marital situations" to cover many types of broken or otherwise defective marriage which together make up a major problem of contemporary society. These situations may arise from known defects in the initial covenant, from defects subsequently discovered, or from various degrees of breakdown in personal relation. At the very outset the problem is personal to those directly involved in such situations—the married partners; this remains true whatever the contributory factors may be—social or psychological tensions, economic stress, spiritual defect or decline, and whatever their ratio to each other. An awareness of the primary personal nature of the problem and of the variety of possible factors at play is necessary for a valid approach to defective marital situations as they are encountered by the pastor. He must be aware of the requirements of Church discipline, but not as something isolated from its theological foundation or from the spiritual needs and anxieties of the persons involved.

29. From this point of view, what our two traditions have in common needs to be stressed at least as much as the divergences in discipline which attract more immediate attention. We have stressed earlier (in § 21) the fertility of the common ground we have on the sacramental nature of marriage. We would see value in developing this further, seeing Christian marriage as contributing to the world's self-understanding, as a sign revealing to the world the real meaning of marriage, and presenting living criteria by which the world is judged for its acquiescence in attitudes to marriage which are not consistent with the dignity, freedom and moral seriousness of full and mature personality.

30. If laws which the Church makes about marriage are to fulfil the time-honoured requirements for law so succinctly stated by Thomas Aquinas (I^a II^{ae}, qq. 90-97) they must mirror this theological conception and also serve the pastoral purpose which is linked with it, to make not marriage in the abstract, but marriages, a sacramental sign to the world. Discipline must be appropriate to real marital situations and their defects, without obscuring or damaging this witness to the world, or jeopardizing the common good.

31. We believe that our traditions are fundamentally at one in recognizing these principles and acknowledging these demands, however difficult they are to reconcile. But divergence appears when we compare practical solutions. For whereas we may properly derive from Christ's teaching the unchangeable theological principles of marriage which must be upheld, the fashioning of marital discipline, and its just adaptation to changing circumstances, remain always the responsibility of the Church, though always under the control of these principles.

The Relation of Discipline to Theological Principle

32. We have spoken of principles derived from Christ's teaching. The extent of agreement in this field was outlined at our fourth meeting (above § 10) and is set down here exactly as our consultants gave it.

Exegesis of New Testament texts on divorce and remarriage—areas of agreement and disagreement

i. *In general* we agreed that our differences on exegetical questions raised were not confessional, but reflected the varieties of critical opinion which are to be found within both communions.

ii. *Details* We agree:

on a text-critical approach;

on the priority of Mark's version in this pericope (*Mk* 10, 1-12; *Mt* 19, 1-12, cf. *Mt* 5, 32).

that the exceptive clauses in Matthew are additions to the words of Jesus;

that the most probable interpretation of *porneia* is as marriage within the forbidden Jewish degrees, and that this clause is inserted not as a mitigation but to preserve the full rigour of Jesus' words;

that *Mk* 10, 10-12 was not originally joined to *Mk* 10, 1-9, but that its authenticity as a word of Jesus is not thereby impugned;

that Jesus' statements on marriage are uncompromising;

that *Mk* 10, 1-9 intends to throw into relief the hardness of heart involved in making use of the legislation of *Deut* 24 allowing a bill of divorce, and that its direct concern is with the failure of the married couple to stay together, rather than with remarriage. *We disagree*, however, in that Henry Wansbrough thinks that Jesus intends to abrogate this permission, Barnabas Lindars that he does not;

that in *Mk* 10, 10-12 Jesus stigmatizes remarriage after divorce as adultery and therefore against the ten commandments.

Thus far we both agree that the views expressed would be endorsed by the great majority of critical scholars of all Christian confessions.

iii. *Status of the words of Jesus* We agree that the words of Jesus are treated by the evangelists as having force of law, for which reason Mark adds the corollary of verse 12 for the sake of his Roman readers, and Matthew adds his exceptive clauses.

We disagree, however, as to whether Jesus intended his words to be taken as having force of law. Henry Wansbrough regards them as a directive to the disciples which would be normative for the future Christian community, Barnabas Lindars as concerned with bringing people face to face with themselves in the reality of the marriage bond when they contemplate divorce and remarriage. Barnabas Lindars holds that Jesus sets out neither to correct the existing law nor to establish a new law; it is a mistaken undertaking to attempt to construct a law on the basis of Jesus' sayings: rather the sayings of Jesus will continue to stand in judgement on any law.

We consider that Henry Wansbrough's view is consonant with the view of the majority of informed opinion in both communions, while Barnabas Lindars's view represents current tendencies in biblical scholarship which have hardly yet made their full impact on discussion of the questions.

Barnabas Lindars, SSF
Henry Wansbrough, OSB

Procedures for the Regulation of Defect

33. We must now consider how the Church's discipline is to be related to unchangeable theological principles, particularly in establishing procedures for the regulation of marital defect. We are agreed that the "juridical" and the "pastoral" should never be at odds in the discipline of a Church. "Defective marital situations" may take many different forms and call for many varieties of pastoral solicitude, whether exercised by the parish priest, the theologian or the jurist (cf. *infra*, § 53). But, from the Roman Catholic point of view, what are here called "procedures for the regulation of defect" (that is, juridical procedures) are *not* examples of pastoral solicitude in the sense that they are devices for easing difficult situations. Whatever may be the motives of the parties for advancing a plea of nullity or petition for dissolution (and obviously these motives will normally be a "defect" in the marital relationship as it is lived, issuing in a desire, unilateral or shared, to be rid of it), not only will the judges of the case begin from the principle "marriage enjoys the favour of the law" (*C.I.C.*, can. 1014) but also their enquiry will be directed towards a canonical "defect" issuing in annulment or a reason for dissolution, deriving from the Church's teaching and practice concerning marriage and its properties.

34. Catholic teaching is that all marriages are *intrinsically* indissoluble. This means that the marrying parties effect something that they themselves cannot undo and which cannot of itself perish except by the death of a partner. In this sense the Church makes no distinction between natural and sacramental marriage. Similarly all marriages are held to be *extrinsically* indissoluble by any *human* power (*C.I.C.*, can. 1118).

35. Distinctions come in when we turn to the Church's power (mediating God's power) to dissolve *extrinsically*. But first the ground must be cleared by emphasizing the distinction between the dissolution of a valid marriage and a simple declaration of nullity. This latter is a declaration of fact, namely that no marriage has existed, and to speak of it as a dissolution (still more to use such a tendentious phrase as "divorce under another name") is improper.

36. The Church's claim to a vicarious power to dissolve certain marriages undoubtedly involves a distinction at least in degree of firmness between the natural and the sacramental bond. A marriage duly solemnized and physically consummated between two baptized persons, *matrimonium validum ratum et consummatum*, is absolutely indissoluble intrinsically and extrinsically. All such marriages are sacraments (because Christ elevated them to that dignity, canon 1012, § 1) and from this their essential properties of unity and indissolubility "acquire a particular firmness" (canon 1013, § 2).

37. The papal practice (documented since the early fifteenth century) of dissolving for an adequate cause, practical and pastoral, a non-consummated marriage is governed by strict procedural rules and seems not to cause great difficulty for most Anglicans.

38. Our discussions suggested that for some Anglicans the same is true of the "Pauline Privilege," by which a marriage between two unbaptized persons may, even after it is consummated, be dissolved if, following the conversion and baptism of one party, the other is unable or unwilling to continue co-habitation peacefully and "without offence to the Creator" (the facts of the case having been confirmed by interrogation). It appears however that other Anglicans regard this as a theologically doubtful pastoral application of St Paul's teaching *1 Cor 7, 12-17*. The exercise of the papal prerogative *in favorem fidei*, by which a marriage involving at least one unbaptized person, even if celebrated with a dispensation *disparitatis cultus*, can be dissolved, is seen by many Anglicans as a progressive extension of a claim which is theologically no less doubtful. They point to the fact that the moratorium on such favours declared in recent years—though in fact removed in December 1973—was in part motivated by doubts about whether the extensions of the privilege had been the result of adequate theological reflection.[7] Above all, the existence of the privilege, however prudently used, seems to them to imply a depreciation of natural marriage which at best is hard to square with the general principles of Catholic marriage doctrine (cf. *supra*, § 11).

39. The Commission has more than once directed its attention to literary evidence[8] of new Roman Catholic thinking, both by theologians and by canon lawyers, about the fundamental notions of consent, of consummation and of sacramentality. The practical tendency of much of this thinking, were it to influence legislation and the practice of the courts, would be to enlarge the grounds on which nullity might be declared, and to restrict the range of the category *matrimonium ratum et consummatum* within which alone absolute indissolubility applies, thus—obversely—extending the scope both of

---

7. Cf. an interview granted by Cardinal Seper, President of the Sacred Congregation for the Doctrine of the Faith, to the Executive Coordinator of the Canon Law Society of America, 30 April 1971, *CLSA Newsletter*, Sept. 1971, pp. 3f.

8. E.g., J. Bernhard, *A propos de l'indissolubilité du mariage chrétien*, in *Mémorial du Cinquantenaire* 1919-1969, Université de Strasbourg, 1969 J. G. Gerhartz *L'indissolubilité de mariage et la dissolution du mariage dans la problématique actuelle*, in *Le Lien Matrimonial*, ed. R. Metz and J. Schlick, Université de Strasbourg, CERDIC, 1970; Denis O'Callaghan, *How far is Christian Marriage Indissoluble?* in *The Irish Theological Quarterly*, XL 2, April 1973; and recent numbers of *Theological Studies* (Baltimore Md, for the Theological Faculties of the Society of Jesus in the United States) and of *The Jurist* (Washington, D.C. for the Department of Canon Law in The Catholic University of America), *passim; Theological-Praktische Quartalschrift*, 1973, pp. 335-346, quoted in *The Tablet* 29, March 5, April 1975, p. 325f.; Maurice Dooley, *Marriage Annulments*, in *The Furrow*, April 1975, pp. 211-219.

annulment processes and of dissolution by papal prerogative. Some members of the Commission strongly deprecate much of this thinking and consider it unlikely to have any influence on legislation in the foreseeable future; but all recognize the mounting influence of new thinking about consent upon the practice of the courts.

40. The Anglican understanding of the duty of the Church in the regulation of defective marital situations at some points coincides with the Roman Catholic understanding and at some points differs from it. It begins by distinguishing defective situations of three sorts. The first is where the defect is one for which the only appropriate action is a declaration of nullity, whether the parties seek or want it or not, because the "marriage" is no marriage, but a relationship not permitted by the law. The second is in a marriage, e.g., a non-consummated marriage, voidable at the instance of one or both of the parties, but not void in itself. In both of these situations there is no difference in principle between the Roman Catholic and Anglican disciplines, because they both derive from the same canon law.

41. The third situation is where there is a breakdown of relationship within a valid marriage, which is brought into cognizance, whether of the law or of the pastoral discipline of the Church, because relief is sought by one or both of the parties from a situation judged no longer tolerable. For these the only relief known to the canon law of the Church of England and, until recently, of the other Churches of the Anglican Communion, is a separation *a mensa et thoro*, without liberty to re-marry during the lifetime of the other spouse. In the Anglican *theological* tradition, however, there have always been those who, accepting as legislative the words of Jesus including the so-called "Matthaean exception," would have allowed re-marriage after a divorce occasioned by adultery, had the canon law permitted, which it did not. This tradition is still alive today, maintaining the possibility of a discipline, faithful to the words of Jesus, based on the principle of what might be called a modified exceptive indissolubility; that is, on the principle that while marriage is properly indissoluble, the authority of Jesus would allow of exceptions where sin of some sort had invaded or destroyed the marriage bond. This position is maintained in disregard of the exegesis of the critical passages of Scripture generally maintained among New Testament scholars.

42. The introduction of the possibility of divorce and re-marriage by civil process, in the mid-nineteenth century, enabled these "exceptive indissolubilists" to authorize action in accordance with their conviction.[9] The general tendency in modern Anglicanism, however, until the last two decades, has been towards a full indissolubilist position,

---

9. They had already done so, of course, since the late seventeenth century in the rare cases of divorce by private Act of Parliament.

and resolutions of Lambeth Conferences have declared this unequi-
vocally. At the same time, however, Anglicans found themselves
increasingly unable to live with the logical consequences of their own
affirmed position; they began to develop expedients to mitigate its
rigour.

43. The most general of these is, while refusing the re-marriage of
divorced persons by the rites of the Church, to accept their re-
marriage before the civil registrar and to receive them as man and
wife into the full communicant life of the Church (sometimes after a
period of voluntary abstention from sacramental communion) exactly
as though they had been married in Church; a service of prayer in
church, in varying degrees of elaboration, frequently follows the civil
ceremony of marriage. There is considerable unease at the logical and
theological oddity of such a compromise. It drives some, resolved to
remain "indissolubilist" at all costs, to follow with eager sympathy
developments in the practice of the Roman Catholic courts and in
serious discussion outside them which test the bearing of the principle of indissolubility in cases where its strict application might seem
to result in injustice or frustrate the pastoral function of the Church
(cf. *supra*, § 39; *infra*, § 49).

44. The same unease has driven some Churches in the Anglican Communion to abandon the strict principle of indissolubility, and to legislate, by canon in Provincial Synod, for the controlled admission of
divorced persons to re-marriage in church during the lifetime of former spouses: Canada, the USA, Australia and New Zealand have
already canons of this sort in operation or in process of enactment.
There are Anglicans in all these provinces and in others who deeply
regret this development, as there are Anglicans who welcome it. The
signatories of the Church of England Report, *Marriage, Divorce and
the Church* (1971) sought, while adopting an exegetical position which
ruled out reliance upon "the Matthaean exception," to secure relief
by means designed to safeguard more closely the theological control
which ought to be exerted over discipline, and to minimize the hurt
done to the Church's essential task of maintaining its witness to the
first principles of marriage as stated by our Lord; but their proposals,
though welcomed in numerous diocesan synods, and by many in the
General Synod, narrowly failed to secure a bare majority of votes in
the General Synod and cannot therefore be held to command general
consent in the Church itself. The attempt to hold together a first-
order principle that a marriage is of its nature indissoluble and a
second-order discipline which recognizes or permits re-marriage after
divorce rests on two suppositions: the first is a theology of the grace
of God which can release, forgive and re-create, even though inevitably the second marriage must be in some sense defective as a "sign"
as posited in § 21 above; the second is that the discipline itself, in its
private and public processes, must not obscure but rather must re-

emphasize what marriage, in its nature, characteristically is. The pursuit of these means still occupies concerned minds in the Churches of the Anglican Communion.

45. Roman Catholics take the point that Anglican discipline regarding the indissolubility of marriage was for long among the strictest of all. They are proportionately disconcerted by developments in theory and discipline within the Anglican Communion (of which an extreme case is the recent canon 18, Tit. I, of the General Convention of the Episcopal Church in the USA) which appear to them to compromise the doctrine of indissolubility. Though the Roman Catholic members of the Commission found much of the treatment of marriage in the Report *Marriage, Divorce and the Church* profoundly sensitive, scholarly and edifying, the carefully-considered recommendations of the Report concerning the re-marriage of divorced persons led the Commission at its Fourth Meeting to consider the question whether the notion of "irretrievable breakdown" was compatible with any concept of an indissoluble *vinculum*. This discussion cleared up several misconceptions and pointed to several imprecisions of linguistic usage, yet it left the Catholics and some of the Anglicans in the Commission unconvinced that the proposition "marriage is characteristically indissoluble but some marriages turn out to be dissoluble" allowed any meaning to the notion of life-long commitment.[10]

46. It may be questioned however whether the contrast between the "unitary" Catholic position and the threefold Anglican approach on this grave contemporary problem (§§ 43, 44) is as clear-cut as it seemed to us at an earlier stage.

47. While the Catholic position remains "unitary" and "solidly indissolubilist" in the sense of maintaining the proposition that *matrimonium validum ratum et consummatum* can be dissolved by no earthly power, there is, as suggested earlier (§ 39), considerable new thinking about the terms of this description and hence what marriages truly come within it. Even those Catholics who do not subscribe to this

---

10. Incidentally the tripartite conversations between the Roman Catholic Church and the Lutherans and Reformed have led some Catholic theologians to see the analysis of indissolubility and life-long commitment as most fruitfully made in terms of a durable and lasting promise of grace, given by Christ, experienced and continually renewed by the spouses in the reality of marriage, yet an objective gift for the upbuilding of the Church and the world. When a marriage breaks down "the couple's specific experience no longer corresponds to Christ's gift, but that does not imply that the sign received from Christ has been destroyed; indeed the nature of Christ's involvement with the couple cannot be annulled by the manner in which he is received" (From an unpublished *Report of the Third Meeting of the Roman Catholic/Lutheran/Reformed Study Commission on Marriage*, Basel, 22-27 October, 1973, pp. 61-3).

thinking would, however, agree that it does not make the line between nullity and divorce blurred and arbitrary.

48. Is there then a point of reconciliation between these two understandings, the Anglican and the Roman Catholic, of the Church's duty in respect of defective marital situations? First, it is clear that there is no essential difference between their attitudes to what are objectively non-marriages, in which the only proper course (saving the Roman Catholic possibility of rendering the marriage valid, for example, by dispensation from a diriment impediment) is a declaration of nullity by a competent court, leaving the parties as free to marry as though the previous situation had never existed. Anglicans, no less than Roman Catholics, may follow with close attention the academic discussions and complicated tribunal and rotal actions trying to determine what sort of cases properly lie or may be brought within this category for which a declaration of nullity is appropriate; indeed, the same course has been publicly favoured and pursued in some provinces of the Anglican Communion. It is not, however, useful or indeed proper to advance unsubstantiated allegations that this process is simply a granting of divorce under another name; within the given logic, the process is morally justifiable in its own right. The argument of this present report is conducted on the assumption that the process is undertaken in entire good faith in both Churches.

49. There is a further common element in the two traditions. It lies in the fact that the initiative in most cases is taken at the instance of parties seeking relief from a marital situation in which they find severe difficulty, or which they may find intolerable, often though not always with a new marriage in view. (Where no new marriage is contemplated an easier solution is available in a formal separation—though it is to be noted that this in itself marks some departure from the stated will of God that they should "cleave" together, and as such mars the "sign" of their marriage). Here the Roman Catholic would examine the case objectively to find whether it presents features appropriate to a declaration of nullity, or features which excluded it from the category of *matrimonium validum ratum et consummatum* between baptized persons which alone is intrinsically and extrinsically indissoluble (cf. §§ 34, 35, 36). The Anglican courses have been described: some Anglicans would adhere as closely as possible to the strict indissolubilist position; others would disclaim the possibility of divorce in itself and of re-marriage after it, but nevertheless accept a *fait accompli* by civil process for all subsequent ecclesiastical purposes; others would frankly accept and even solemnize re-marriage in particular cases after divorce. Now from the Anglican side it is submitted that these processes, Roman Catholic and Anglican alike, are *all* means of pursuing a common end, namely the continuance of the Church's pastoral responsibility for its members in a situation in which, because of sin, inadequacy or weakness, or for whatever reason, the sign of marriage is *already* marred and in which *no* course *absolutely* consonant with the first order principle of marriage as a life-long union may be available. The Church has a duty to work out such procedures and has done so from the beginning. From this activity we have evidence in the New Testament in the so-called Matthaean exception (*Mt* 5, 32 and 19.9) and the so-called Pauline privilege (*1 Cor* 7, 15) whatever their precise interpretation may be. This recognition of the integrity of the other Church's attempts need not carry with it unqualified approval of the means in themselves—Roman Catholics may think Anglican admission of re-marriage after divorce too weak, Anglicans may think the logic of Roman Catholic processes too strained. But in the view of the Commission neither attitude of disapproval is of such a degree as seriously to hinder ecumenical convergence in the two fields which are our immediate concern, the growing together of the Roman Catholic and Anglican Churches, and a more positive pastoral approach to the contracting and support of mixed marriages (cf. *infra*, § 55). Each Church can accept the assurance of the other that it maintains, and has a settled will to maintain, the full Christian doctrine of marriage, as outlined in § 21 above, and that in each Church an intention to accept marriage as a permanent and exclusive union is and will be required of all who seek marriage according to the Church's rites (cf. § 34, 43, 44).

50. The common ground we have established on the nature, properties and purposes of Christian marriage clearly implies common pastoral aims though not necessarily common methods of achieving those aims.

51. The pastor is aware at once of a responsibility to Christ and the Gospel—a responsibility for integrity of witness—and of a responsibility to the people of God, to enable them to bear their burdens and to live the Christian life in the conditions in which they find themselves. If tension is evident between these two responsibilities, he cannot resolve it by ignoring it, or by paying attention to only one of the responsibilities.

52. Applying these principles to Christian marriage, not as a theological abstraction but as a lived reality, the pastor is aware at once of the tension between the ideal, the sign to the world which is marriage as presented and illuminated by the word of God and the hard realities of a contemporary situation in which social, economic and other factors, opinion and custom, the trends of legislation, all militate perhaps as never before against the embodiment of the ideal and the witness in institutional forms.

53. Saying this we see at once that in this context we cannot simply equate the term pastor with bishop or priest working in a parish: the theologian, the canon lawyer, the official of the marriage court, is pastoral in his concern and in his operation. To scrutinize the notions of sacramentality, of consent, of consummation is not simply to juggle with or stretch the law; it is to face up to both aspects of pastoral responsibility and the tension between them. To seek a resolution of this tension in the theology of forgiving and re-creating grace is a complementary pursuit of the same end.

54. In view of what has been said earlier about the difference between Roman Catholic and Anglican attitudes, it is inevitable that the same awareness of having two pastoral responsibilities (§ 51), with the same need to face up to the inescapable tension between them, should issue in different solutions. It is indispensable to further understanding and convergence that each side should recognize and respect in the other the integrity of responsibility which produces these divergent solutions, even though recognition and respect may not make possible in all cases an acceptance of the solutions.

55. This leads us to say that, in setting this problem of defective marital situations and their pastoral care in the total perspective of the Roman Catholic/Anglican search for unity, one established principle is to be re-called which has underlain all adumbrations of the form that unity might take: it is that any such form of unity must preserve what is integral and acceptable in both our traditions in a variety-in-unity. What is or is not mutually acceptable will emerge in the course of this search. A fact perhaps significant in this context— and in any case one which raises profound questions in itself—is that in the Orthodox Church, whose communion with Rome has been described by Pope Paul VI as "almost perfect,"[11] long established marriage discipline includes the practice of re-marriage in church after divorce.

Section D

Mixed Marriages

The Roman Catholic Legislation

56. It has been said above that the *motu proprio Matrimonia Mixta* represents the latest stage in Roman Catholic modification both of discipline and of its expression. Though mixed marriages are still discouraged and seen only "in some cases" as an ecumenical opportunity and means of unity, yet it is recognized that the rapidly changing conditions of today and the development of thought reflected in

---

11. Speech at a Public Audience during the Week of Prayer for Unity, 20 January 1971: *L'Osservatore Romano*, 21 Jan. 1971, p. 1, col. 1; letter to Patriarch Athenagoras, 8 February 1971, quoted in *Tomos Agapis*, 283 (Rome-Istanbul); address to Delegates of the Commissions for Ecumenism of the Episcopal Conferences and of Synods of Catholic Oriental Patriarchates, 22 November 1972. Printed in *Information Service* of the Secretariat for Promoting Christian Unity, 20, April 1973, p. 23.

such Vatican II documents as *Dignitatis Humanae* and *Unitatis Redintegratio* involve substantial changes in the classical attitudes reflected in the Code of Canon Law. Mixed marriages are seen as a fact of life and an object of pastoral solicitude—solicitude which, where both parties are baptized, is proper to both Churches involved and a proper object of "sincere openness and enlightened confidence" between the respective ministers. The Catholic conviction that marriage between the baptized is necessarily sacramental, now combined with the more positive ecclesiological assessment of other Churches, seems to open up new prospects, especially for marriage with Anglicans, whose special relationship with the Roman Catholic Church was mentioned during the Second Vatican Council and emphasized on important occasions since,[12] besides being supported by important advances towards doctrinal agreement as is evidenced by the Windsor and Canterbury Joint Statements of the Anglican/Roman Catholic International Commission as well as in the theology of marriage outlined above.

57. These new prospects are however affected by the retention, for reasons we have described, of the requirement of promises by the Catholic party as a condition of dispensation to marry an Anglican (*Matrimonia Mixta*, 4-5) and by the insistence, also for reasons stated, that the "canonical form" (marriage before an authorized Roman Catholic minister and two witnesses) is necessary for the validity of the marriage. Moreover it may be observed that, in spite of the "special relationship" referred to in the previous paragraph, English-speaking areas of the world are, with certain exceptions, and doubtless for sufficient reasons, among the less ready to avail themselves of the considerable latitude granted to episcopal conferences by the *motu proprio* (nn. 7, 9, 10). Experience shows that on all these points certain confusions need to be forestalled.

58. First, the use of the phrase "divine law" is attached by the *motu proprio* to the obligations of the Roman Catholic party, which the Church believes herself not empowered to remove; it is not attached to the ecclesiastical discipline of promise concerning the obligation, which has been modified considerably during recent years. The divine authority attached to the obligation simply reflects the Catholic doctrine about the Church referred to above (§§ 16 ff.).

59. Secondly, interpretation seems to make it increasingly clear that this obligation is not to be thought of as absolute, i.e., unrelated to

---

12. E.g., "Inter eas in quibus traditiones et structurae catholicae ex parte locum specialem tenet Communio anglicana" (*Unitatis Redintegratio*, 13); cf. words of Pope Paul VI on 25 October 1970, to which the Archbishop of Canterbury responded on 24 January, 1971, quoted in *Theology*, London, SPCK, LXXIV, May 1971, p. 222.

any other obligations and rights. We would wish to reaffirm here what was said in our Third Report:

> **7.** In our (First) Report we agreed that "the duty to educate children in the Roman Catholic faith is circumscribed by other duties such as that of preserving the unity of the family." In the Apostolic Letter the promise required of the Roman Catholic partner is to provide *pro viribus* for the Roman Catholic education of the children of the marriage. This Latin adverbial phrase is usually translated into English "do all in his power." This English phrase might be and often is adduced to justify the Roman Catholic party acting in a way which disregards the equal rights in conscience of the non-Roman Catholic party, and even to justify the Roman Catholic adopting an attitude or pursuing his purpose in ways which might endanger the marriage. It is recognized that responsible Roman Catholic commentators on the Letter (including many episcopal conferences) do not put this interpretation on the Latin phrase, but rather confirm our first statement quoted above. The Roman Catholic undertaking *pro viribus* is given envisaging the marriage situation with all the *mutual* rights and obligations which the theology of marriage sees as belonging to the married state.
>
> **8.** The use of the Latin phrase in the official text also marks recognition that, as our Second Report from Rome in 1968 put it: ". . . no dispositions which the Churches can make can wholly determine the future of a marriage." "We acknowledge that as the spouses after their marriage 'experience the meaning of their oneness and attain to it with growing perfection day by day' (*Gaudium et Spes*, 48) they must be encouraged to come to a common mind in deciding questions relative to their conjugal and family life."

It is because these facts have not been sufficiently recognized that the application of this obligation has aroused fear of subjection to pressure whether social, psychological or ecclesiastical, not to mention the impression of mere obstinancy. On neither side have these fears proved wholly unfounded, and all of us, on both sides, have reason to examine our consciences.

60. The *motu proprio* warns that "no one will be really surprised to find that even the canonical discipline on mixed marriages cannot be uniform," and indeed there are considerable contrasts between the application of the *motu proprio* made by the various episcopal conferences, all of which are accepted by the Holy See. At one extreme there is strong insistence on the Catholic teaching that the sanction for the Roman Catholic obligation is divine, even introducing the expression into written formulae for the promises. This is evidently aimed at making the sense of the obligation as comprehensively felt as possible. At the other extreme there is an equally clear insistence on the limiting force of the phrases *quantum fieri potest* and *pro viribus*, and on the importance of setting decisions within the context of the

marriage and of a mutual respect for conscience. Anglicans are somewhat dismayed to find that, among English-speaking conferences
whose dispositions are familiar, the only one that seems to come well
into the second category is the Canadian.

61. As well as the contrasts just referred to very various understanding is to be observed of the importance, within the wide category of
mixed marriages, of those between committed members of the two
different Churches. It is generally agreed that these latter form a small
minority of all mixed marriages but sometimes this seems to lead,
illogically, to a tacit assumption that they are of little importance or
even that regulations or pastoral practice need take no specific account
of them. Difficult as it may be to provide for unidentifiable minorities,
it is necessary to do so nevertheless, if respect is to be paid to the
realities of personal commitment inherent in the marriage of Christians and to that ecumenical growth to which both Churches are
committed.

On Canonical Form

62. The requirement of "canonical form" for the validity of a marriage
has a long history rooted in the medieval problem of clandestine
marriages. It is not therefore a discipline which arose out of the divisions within Christianity or out of the ecclesiological teaching of the
Roman Catholic Church described earlier, nor does it prejudice the
fact that the parties themselves are the ministers of holy matrimony.
It may, however, unfortunately, appear to do so. To persons not well
versed in ecclesiastical matters (and at weddings the Church encounters these more than perhaps at any other time), the requirement—
whatever its justification—suggests, however unfairly, "Roman Catholic
intransigence and exclusiveness": it can excite memories, irrelevant
in this context, of the declaring invalid of the orders and ministries
of other Churches; it can even provoke or aggravate tensions between
the families of persons marrying; and in general it may tend to increase
irritation at the involvement of the Church with marriage at all. An
unreasonable mood may thus be created in which, instead of being
seen, as properly it should be, as hallowing marriage and bringing
grace to the partners in their responsibilities, the Church too easily
appears to be a nuisance, a source of discord. In the interest of ecumenical convergence, the clergy, Anglican as well as Roman Catholic,
should consider it a duty through their pastoral presentation to promote true understanding of the nature and intent of the Catholic
legislation about the canonical form.

63. Accepting the fact that the Roman Catholic Church judges it better to retain the discipline, yet recognizing, as reluctantly we must,
that in its present form it can arouse this kind of resentment, we
repeat here a proposal which we have twice, as a commission, submitted unanimously before:

Upon Canonical Form, we made concrete recommendation in our Second Report, namely that "on condition that joint pastoral preparation has been given, and freedom to marry established to the satisfaction of the bishop of the Roman Catholic party and of the competent Anglican authority, the marriage may validly and lawfully take place before the duly authorised minister of the Church of either party." Though the Apostolic Letter makes different provisions (*Matrimonia Mixta*, 9), further reflection would lead us to reiterate our original suggestion, for the following reasons. First, it is preferable for any practice to be brought within the general law rather than be made the object of frequent dispensation. Secondly, to extend the scope of Canonical Form to include Anglican ministers celebrating the Anglican rite would be an ecumenical act of profound significance, giving notable substance to those official utterances which, in various ways, have declared a "special relationship" to exist between our two Churches.

We do this in the hope that, with the development of theological dialogue, the movement towards unity between our Churches may make such progress that this recommendation may be implemented.

The Promise

64. Anglican objections to the requirement of the promise are simply stated. The first is that it rests on a doctrine of the Church which the Anglican cannot accept. That he is under divine obligation first to make on behalf of his children the response of faith to God's love revealed in Christ—that is, to bring them to Christian baptism—and then to enable them to respond themselves to that love—that is, to build them into the life of the Church of Christ—he readily admits. But he cannot recognize such a distinction between the words "Christian" and "Roman Catholic" in this context of such a force as to justify the requirements of an explicitly *Roman Catholic* baptism and upbringing, and not of an explicitly Christian one. [There is here a difference of doctrine which, in an earlier Report, the Commission asked that ARCIC (Anglican/Roman Catholic International Commission) should explore on our behalf. When the problem was returned to us, as being too far down on ARCIC's list of commitments for attention in the foreseeable future, we made a serious attempt to work at it ourselves, with the help of papers from one of our members and from a consultant.[13] These papers were found most valuable by all members of the Commission and they promoted enlightening discussion which we should have been glad to have had time to develop further. We strongly recommend them to readers of this report but it would be beyond the scope of the report to summarize them here; yet it should

---

13. L. Mason Knox, *supra*, § 20, note; and Brian O'Higgins, *supra*, p. 13.

not be thought that either Church's ecclesiological position was either inadequately stated or unsympathetically examined. The problem is a fundamental one which, moreover, ranges far beyond the field of marriage, and we must hope that ARCIC will eventually be able to speak adequately on it.]

65. The other objections that Anglicans feel carry us beyond ecclesiology although they are not unrelated to it. The second objection is that the requirements are insensitive to the conviction and conscience of the committed Anglican partner. They consider that it is no answer to this objection to say that in the majority of mixed marriages the non-Roman Catholic partner is religiously indifferent and unattached; such an answer puts a premium on absence of commitment in the sense that a dispensation for marriage to an uncommitted partner would be more easily obtained. It is the committed Anglican whose convictions are ignored who constitutes the problem—and the whole Anglican Communion stands with him.

66. The Roman Catholic would reply to this that there might indeed be concrete examples of insensitiveness and ignoring of conviction in the administration of the regulations. But far from admitting that the regulations were framed in this spirit, he would argue that the more intense the conviction recognized in the Anglican, the more acutely the problem is posed and the greater is the pastoral responsibility to recall the Catholic to a similar sense of commitment. The problem is not indeed thus solved, but a dialogue such as that here reported could have had no meaning except on a basis of mutual respect for conviction.

67. The third objection is that the requirements ask of one partner a unilateral decision in a matter so fundamental to the nature and essential properties of marriage as to require the achievement of a *joint* decision. Marital unity grows on the discipline and exercise of achieving a common mind on all that most intimately concerns the common life. The requirement of the promise lifts one essential matter out and forecloses it. It requires the Roman Catholic partner either to treat the matter as decided, because of the promise already made, or to be submitted to the extra strain of deciding when concession to the non-Catholic spouse is in breach of the promise, and so of personal integrity. Similarly it puts the other partner to the strain of deciding whether to adhere to his own religious conviction, and so discomfort his spouse, or whether mercifully to abandon it and so disquiet his own conscience. It were better, in the Anglican view, for the obligation concerning children to be stated in terms which treat the partners as equally bound and equally free. Such terms should not be impossible to devise.

68. Roman Catholics would see the imputation that they are removing the Catholic partner's obligation from the context of the marriage as exaggerated, because although the Catholic is reminded of and remains aware of his obligation, the whole tendency of recent modifications of the requirements is to set them in the context of the marriage. This is particularly true of the qualification *quantum fieri potest/pro viribus*. In this sense they would contend that indeed the partners remain "equally bound and equally free," with the exception that lesser demands are made by his Church on the Anglican partner.

69. A welcome reconciling factor may be seen in a recognition of the limiting force of the qualifiers *quantum fieri potest* and *pro viribus*. This of course supposes the persistence of the discipline of the promise, which is, as we have just seen, unwelcome to Anglicans. Before offering any further solution (which not all Roman Catholics on the Commission think is likely to prove possible) we feel that §§ 65 and 67 should be clarified still further.

70. Let us suppose a judgment of conscience by the Catholic party which assesses the actual marital situation and decides that, through no fault of his own, perhaps through nobody's fault, perhaps even because of his conscientiousness in pursuing his duty in the matter, he is brought to a point where it is clear that a conflict between the claims of the marriage and the requirements of the Roman Catholic Church is inevitable. Then the Roman Catholic partner can justifiably say "I have in conscience done *quantum fieri potest*, because if I do more I shall certainly be seriously prejudicing the prior claims of the marriage." This remains a judgment of fact about the marital situation, and not a judgment on or repudiation of the Church's right to insist on the obligation. The Church's pastoral practice, sacramental and other, should consistently support this interpretation, and support the faithful in continuing the Christian life on this footing.

An Alternative to the Promise

71. This having been said, the question remains, is there an alternative to the promise, a course by which the Roman Catholic Church can do what its doctrine requires of it in a way which encounters less objection? In the opinion of a majority of the Commission there is. It would be for the Church to require of the Roman Catholic parish priest responsible for the marriage a written assurance to his bishop that he had duly put the Roman Catholic partner in mind of his obligations concerning the baptism and upbringing of the children and, according to opportunity, satisfied himself that the other partner knew what these obligations were. He would not be empowered to exact a promise in the matter from either partner, though he might well ask formally if the obligations were understood. The bishop, if satisfied in other respects, might then issue a dispensation for the marriage on the strength of this assurance. Such a procedure would be more consistent than the present one with the spirit of Vatican II documents on ecumenical relations and religious liberty, and would, it is believed, earn more respect, and so command more attention,

from the non-Roman Catholic partner as well as from the Catholic.
72. This procedure is offered in an earnest attempt to make possible a real step forward in charitable relations between the two Churches. It is offered as a deliberate and more desirable alternative to the expedient now all too often adopted, and likely still to be encouraged, namely, in crude terms, to match force with force, that is, to grudge co-operation, to "make difficulties" from the non-Roman side matching in intensity what they feel they have encountered from the Roman. One example is an instruction from an Anglican bishop to his clergy not to assist at a mixed marriage in a Roman Catholic church if the promise has been given. Such a spirit of antagonism is inconsistent with the good which ought to be sought in the solemnizing of a marriage, and with the spirit in which Christians and Churches ought to act together.

Pastoral Care

73. The proposals made above for alterations in the law concerning canonical form and the requirement of a promise presuppose a high degree of mutual understanding and trust between our respective Churches, and particularly between the clergy. The clergy have a duty to lead in this matter; and if they are unconvinced themselves they will be unable to convey conviction to others. There is no room for complacency about the degree of understanding and trust prevailing at present, encouraging as the growth is here and there. We are bound, therefore, to return to the imperatives which we wrote into our Third Report designed to promote better joint pastoral preparation and support for mixed marriages. We began by recalling the words of Pope Paul VI in *Matrimonia Mixta* (words which, unhappily, have in many places received very much less attention than the more controversial provisions of the *motu proprio*):

> 14. Local Ordinaries and parish priests shall see to it that the Catholic husband or wife and the children born of a mixed marriage do not lack spiritual assistance in fulfilling their duties of conscience. They shall encourage the Catholic husband or wife to keep ever in mind the divine gift of the Catholic faith and to bear witness to it with gentleness and reverence and with a clear conscience (cf. 1 Pt 3, 16). They are to aid the married couple to foster the unity of their conjugal and family life, a unity which, in the case of Christians, is based on their baptism too. To these ends it is to be desired that those pastors should establish relationships of sincere openness and enlightened confidence with ministers of other religious communities.

74. This passage, without diluting the pastoral responsibility of the Roman Catholic priest to those of his own flock or the charge which he bears to support them in the obligations arising from their Church

allegiance, puts a clear and welcome emphasis on the specific duties imposed by the mixed marriage in which there is well-founded unity as well as possibility of division. Above all it implies that those duties cannot be fully discharged without generous cooperation with the other minister concerned.

75. Pastoral care in these times has its special difficulties, particularly as it involves visiting homes, whether mixed marriage homes or not. It may well be fortunate that the scope for clerical paternalism has much narrowed; it is thus easier to realize that the solution of delicate personal problems involved in mixed marriages (not one of which is exactly like another) is to be found only in the maturing and sensitive growing-together of the family itself, and that any outside assistance, clerical or other, must be no less delicate and sensitive if it is not to be rejected as insufferable interference. Where joint pastoral care is assumed, as it should be, any hint of competitiveness, suspicion or possessiveness will inhibit the necessary sensitiveness from the start.

76. It is not for the Commission to offer a guide to joint pastoral care, which must remain in the fullest sense an experimental and inexact science, or better, an art. But it is not for that reason an activity which can be put aside. The various experiments that have been made in different parts of the world should be sympathetically studied bearing in mind that what serves one national temperament or social pattern may be of little value to another. What will count in the end will be the dedication, wisdom and sensitivity of the individual pastor, whether working with individual families or with groups of families; this will help to determine whether mixed marriages are to be an occasion of spiritual growth or decay, an ecumenical opportunity or an ecumenical menace.

Acknowledgements

Members of the Commission would put on record their deep appreciation of the help which they have been given in the discharge of their task. They would thank their hosts in the various houses in which the Commission has met. They would thank their Secretaries, Mgr. Purdy whose contribution has been distinctive throughout, and Canon Satterthwaite (as he then was) and Prebendary Cooper who shared the task on the Anglican side. They would thank also Miss Anne Tyler of the Archbishop of Canterbury's Counsellors on Foreign Relations, Miss Margaret Orrell, and members of the secretarial staff of the Vatican Secretariat. Last they would thank the Revd. Prebendary J.H.B. Andrews, Sub-Dean of Exeter Cathedral, whose hospitality in his North Devon vicarage enabled the writing of this Report to be literally a joint undertaking.

June 1975

Ernest L. Underkoefler	George O. Simms
(Co-Chairman)	*(Co-Chairman)*
Langton D. Fox	G. R. Dunstan
Francis J. Spence	Barnabas Lindars, SSF
Patrick Francis Cremin	L. Mason Knox
W. A. Purdy	Henry Cooper

Correspondence between the Archbishop of Canterbury and the Pope on the Ordination of Women

In 1975 the Archbishop of Canterbury wrote to Pope Paul VI as well as to Orthodox and Old Catholic leaders concerning discussion within the Anglican Communion about the ordination of women. This is his initial letter to the Pope.

"After our predecessor's visit to Rome in 1966, together with him you inaugurated a 'serious dialogue' between the Roman Catholic Church and the Anglican Communion. The agreed statements of the consequent Anglican-Roman Catholic International Commission on the eucharist and the ministry are not authoritative statements of faith of either the Roman Catholic Church or the Anglican Communion; nevertheless they do bear witness to the steady growth of mutual understanding and trust developing between our two traditions.

"It is with this in mind that we write now to inform Your Holiness of the slow but steady growth of a consensus of opinion within the Anglican Communion that there are no fundamental objections in principle to the ordination of women to the priesthood.

"At the same time we are aware that action on this matter could be an obstacle to further progress along the path of unity Christ wills for his church. The central authorities of the Anglican Communion have therefore called for common counsel on this matter, as has the General Synod of the Church of England. Thus in view of our concern, both for the truth as it is understood within the Anglican tradition, and for ecumenical counsel, we are already in correspondence with His Eminence Cardinal Jan Willebrands, president of the Secretariat for Promoting Christian Unity and the Right Rev. Bishop John Howe, secretary-general of the Anglican Consultative Council, and we anticipate mutual discussion on this question in the future.

"It is our hope that such common counsel may achieve a fulfillment of the apostle's precept that 'Speaking the truth in love,' we 'may grow up into him in all things, which is the head, even Christ.'"

Your affectionate
brother in Christ,
Archbishop Donald Coggan

July 9, 1975

Some time later Pope Paul VI sent this letter in reply.

"We write in answer to your letter of July 9 last. We have many times had occasion to express to your revered predecessor, and more lately to yourself, our gratitude to God and our consolation at the growth of understanding between the Catholic Church and the Anglican Communion and to acknowledge the devoted work both in theological dialogue and reflection and in Christian collaboration which promotes and witnesses to this growth.

"It is indeed within this setting of confidence and candor that we see your presentation of the problem raised by the developments within the Anglican Communion concerning the ordination of women to the priesthood.

"Your Grace is of course well aware of the Catholic Church's position on this question. She holds that it is not admissible to ordain women to the priesthood, for very fundamental reasons. These reasons include: the example recorded in the sacred scriptures of Christ choosing his apostles only from among men; the constant practice of the church, which has imitated Christ in choosing only men; and her living teaching authority which has consistently held that the exclusion of women from the priesthood is in accordance with God's plan for his church.

"The Joint Commission between the Anglican Communion and the Catholic Church, which has been at work since 1966, is charged with presenting in due time a final report. We must regretfully recognize that a new course taken by the Anglican Communion in admitting women to the ordained priesthood cannot fail to introduce into this dialogue an element of grave difficulty which those involved will have to take seriously into account.

"Obstacles do not destroy mutual commitment to a search for reconciliation. We learn with satisfaction of a first informal discussion of the question between Anglican representatives and those of our Secretariat for Promoting Christian Unity, at which the fundamental theological importance of the question was agreed on. It is our hope that this beginning may lead to further common counsel and growth of understanding.

"Once again we extend every fraternal good wish in Christ our Lord."

Pope Paul VI

November 30, 1975

Early in the following year the Archbishop wrote to the Pope a second time.

"It is now almost ten years since our beloved predecessor visited the city of Rome. On the 23rd of March 1966, in the Sistine Chapel, Your Holiness and His Grace the Archbishop of Canterbury met to exchange fraternal greetings; this encounter was of profound significance for the future relationship between the churches of the Anglican Communion and the Roman Catholic Church. For this we thank God.

"We also recall with deep gratitude that on the 24th of March, in the Basilica of St. Paul-Without-the-Walls, Your Holiness and His Grace made your common declaration announcing your intention to inaugurate the serious dialogue between our respective traditions which has already borne notable fruit in the work of the Anglican-Roman Catholic International Commission and the Anglican-Roman Catholic Commission on Mixed Marriages.

"As Your Holiness recalled in your letter of November 30, 1975, which we were most grateful to receive, the goal which we jointly seek is that visible unity of the church for which Christ prayed. We believe this unity will be manifested within a diversity of legitimate traditions because the Holy Spirit has never ceased to be active within the local churches throughout the world.

"Sometimes what seems to one tradition to be a genuine expression of such a diversity in unity will appear to another tradition to go beyond the bounds of legitimacy. Discussion within the Anglican Communion concerning the possibility of the ordination of women is at present just such an issue. We are glad that informal discussion between Anglicans and Roman Catholics has already taken place about this matter at the Vatican Secretariat for Promoting Christian Unity. We hope such dialogue will continue in order that our respective traditions may grow in mutual understanding.

"While we recognize that there are still many obstacles to be overcome upon that road to the 'restoration of complete communion of faith and sacramental life,' called for by our predecessor and Your Holiness, we nevertheless believe that in the power of the Spirit Christ's high priestly prayer for unity will be fulfilled.

"We humbly make this prayer our own as we offer Your Holiness our warm greetings and recall that historic meeting in Rome ten years ago. Moreover we look forward to the day when we too shall be able to meet Your Holiness so that together we may take further steps upon the path to unity."

Yours most sincerely in Christ,
Archbishop Donald Coggan

February 10, 1976

Shortly thereafter Pope Paul again replied.

"As the tenth anniversary comes round of your revered predecessor's visit to Rome, we write to reciprocate with all sincerity the gratitude and the hope which, in recalling that historic occasion, you express in a letter recently handed to us by Bishop John Howe.

"It is good to know that the resolves taken, the dialogue entered upon ten years ago, have continued and spread to many places, and that a new spirit of mutual consideration and trust increasingly pervades our relations.

"In such a spirit of candor and trust you allude in your letter of greeting to a problem which has recently loomed large: the likelihood, already very strong it seems in some places, that the Anglican Churches will proceed to admit women to the ordained priesthood. We had already exchanged letters with you on this subject, and we were able to express the Catholic conviction more fully to Bishop John Howe when he brought your greetings.

"Our affection for the Anglican Communion has for many years been strong, and we have always nourished and often expressed ardent hopes that the Holy Spirit would lead us, in love and in obedience to God's will, along the path of reconciliation. This must be the measure of the sadness with which we encounter so grave a new obstacle and threat on that path.

"But it is no part of corresponding to the promptings of the Holy Spirit to fail in the virtue of hope. With all the force of the love which moves us we pray that at this critical time the Spirit of God may shed his light abundantly on all of us, and that his guiding hand may keep us in the way of reconciliation according to his will.

"Moreover, we sincerely appreciate the fact that you have expressed a desire to meet us, and we assure you that on our part we would look upon such a meeting as a great blessing and another means of furthering that complete unity willed by Christ for his Church."

Pope Paul VI

March 23, 1976

Anglican/Roman Catholic Commission in the U.S.A. Agreed Statement on the Purpose of the Church

For many Roman Catholics and Episcopalians,
loyalty to their respective Churches seemed to preclude acceptance of the "organic unity" proposed by the ARC VII Statement. Could ARC show that this very loyalty demanded ecumenical commitment? ARC proposed to produce a pastoral instrument, which would be of immediate value to the laity of both Churches, to show that Roman Catholics and Episcopalians were one in their faith, concerning the nature and purpose of the Church. From 1972 to 1975, ARC worked on this statement. Developing an outline provided by Bishop Arthur Vogel and Father George Tavard, Fathers J. Robert Wright and Herbert J. Ryan, SJ, drafted the statement, drawn from the liturgies of the Episcopal and Roman Catholic Churches.

I. Introduction

1. As Roman Catholics and Episcopalians living in the United States today, we have been charged by our churches to explore the possibility that there is a fundamental unity between us on the deepest levels of Christian faith and life. Roman Catholics and Episcopalians believe that there is but one Church of Christ,[1] yet we find ourselves living in separate churches.
2. Those who went before us in the faith lived in one communion for many centuries. This fellowship was broken in the sixteenth century, yet our two churches continue to share "many elements of sanctification and truth" which "possess an inner dynamism toward Catholic unity."[2] We follow one Lord; we profess the ancient Creeds and confess one Baptism; we hear God's Word in the Scriptures; we revere the Fathers and the ancient Councils; we cherish similar struc-

---

1. Constitution of the Episcopal Church, preamble; Vatican Council II, Dogmatic Constitution on the Church *Lumen Gentium*, 5 and 8, ed. Walter M. Abbott, S.J., pp. 17-18, 22-23.
2. Vatican II, *Lumen Gentium*, 8; Decree on Ecumenism: *Unitatis Redintegratio*, 3 and 13; ed. Abbott, pp. 23, 345-46, 356.

tures of worship and episcopal succession. Thus, our estrangement of four centuries has been far from complete. In fact, recent authoritative statements and liturgical texts of both our churches which we have examined[3] show a remarkable convergence in their answers to fundamental questions such as these:

> Where does the Church come from and why does it exist?
> Where is the Church going and what should it be doing here and now? In short, what is the *purpose* of the Church?

3. Since the prayer of the Church is the most intense expression of our faith in God and commitment to his purpose for the world, and since the Eucharist is seen in both our churches as bringing us into a new relationship of union with Christ and with one another in his sacramental Body and Blood,[4] we have decided together to write our common belief about the Church's purpose or mission, in answer to the above questions, in a context interwoven with prayers from our contemporary Eucharistic liturgies. We invite the reader to reflect upon this relationship between prayer and belief in the statement that follows. In the parallel passages that we quote, liturgical texts used in the Episcopal and Roman Catholic Churches are placed, respectively, in the left and right hand columns.[5]

---

3. At these meetings: ARC XIII, Cincinnati, Ohio, March 19-22, 1973; ARC XIV, Vicksburg, Miss., January 6-10, 1974; and ARC XV, Cincinnati, November 10-13, 1974. The following papers, among others, were considered: Charles H. Helmsing, "Some Reflections on the Mission of the Church"; George H. Tavard, "The Church as Eucharistic Communion"; and J. Robert Wright, "The Purpose or Mission of the Church as seen by the Episcopal Church." The documentation for this present statement has been largely drawn from these papers, which were themselves documented from authoritative statements and liturgical texts of both our churches.
4. Anglican/Roman Catholic International Commission, Windsor Statement on Eucharistic Doctrine, paras. 2-4 (see pp. 234-235).
5. Episcopalian texts are taken from *Services for Trial Use* (1971) and *Authorized Services* (1973). Roman Catholic texts are taken from *The Roman Missal: The Sacramentary* (Liturgical Press 1974). The aim of ARC in this statement has been to describe the Church's purpose or mission as it is seen in the present faith of our two churches, and in our selection of texts we have not intended to urge the superiority of any one particular form of liturgical expression over another. It is acknowledged that liturgical revision is still in process in both our churches.

II. Where Does the Church Come from and Why Does It Exist?

4.   Both our churches witness to the fact that the Church comes from God who sent Jesus Christ his Son in the power of the Spirit to accomplish the mystery of salvation and redemption. Christ announced the Kingdom and proclaimed the Good News. The Church is that community of persons called by the Holy Spirit to continue Christ's saving work of reconciliation.[6] As Christ proclaimed the Kingdom, so the Church serves the Kingdom, so that "the entire world may become the people of God, the Body of the Lord, and the Temple of the Holy Spirit, that in, by, and through Christ there may be rendered to God the Creator and Father of the universe all honor and glory."[7]

God of all power, Ruler of the Universe,
you are worthy of glory and praise.
Glory to you for ever and ever.

At your command all things came to be,
the vast expanse of interstellar space,
galaxies, suns, the planets in their courses,
and this fragile earth, our island home:
By your will they were created and have their being.

From the primal elements you have brought forth the race of man,
and blessed us with memory, reason, and skill;
you made us the rulers of creation.

Therefore, we praise you,
joining with the heavenly chorus,
with prophets, apostles, and martyrs,
and with men of every generation who have looked to you in hope:
to proclaim with them your glory,
in their unending hymn:

Father in heaven, it is right that we should give you thanks and glory:
you alone are God, living and true.
Through all eternity you live in unapproachable light.
Source of life and goodness, you have created all things, to fill your creatures with every blessing and lead all men to the joyful vision of your light.

Countless hosts of angels stand before you to do your will;
they look upon your splendor
and praise you night and day.
United with them, and in the name of every creature under heaven,
we too praise your glory as we sing:

Holy, holy, holy Lord,
God of power and might.
Heaven and earth are full of your glory.
Hosanna in the highest.
Blessed is he who comes in the name of the Lord.
Hosanna in the highest.

---

6. ARCIC, Canterbury Statement on Ministry and Ordination, paras. 3-5, 12, 17 (see pp. 244, 247, 249).
7. Vatican II, *Lumen Gentium*, 17; cf. Decree on the Ministry and Life of Priests: *Presbyterorum Ordinis*, 1; ed. Abbott, pp. 36-37, 532-33.

Holy, holy, holy Lord,
God of power and might.
Heaven and earth are full of your
    glory.
Hosanna in the highest.
Blessed is he who comes in the name
    of the Lord.
Hosanna in the highest.

III. Where Is the Church Going and What Should It Be Doing Here and Now?

5. Many in our churches ask the questions, "Where is the Church going?" and "What should it be doing here and now?" Some feel the Church is engaged in a fruitless, self-serving enterprise which fails to come to grips with the challenges posed by the world today. Others ask in bewilderment whether the Church has abandoned its spiritual calling. We find this restlessness and bewilderment among clergy and laity in both our churches. On the one hand, this situation is partially rooted in the churches' awareness of "the cry of those who suffer violence and are oppressed by unjust systems and structures (in a world whose) perversity contradicts the plan of its Creator."[8] On the other hand, it is partially produced by movements of renewal and new responses to the Spirit within our churches, such as the charismatic movement, the liturgical movement, new forms of piety, and developments in biblical study and catechesis.

6. In the midst of the long history of human selfishness and sin, we hear the story of God's redeeming action for us and all mankind calling us to re-examine our faithfulness to our mission.

Holy and gracious Father,
in your infinite love you made us for
    yourself;
and when we fell into sin
and became subject to evil and death,
you, in your mercy, sent Jesus Christ,
your only and eternal Son,
to share our human nature,
to live and die as one of us
to reconcile us to you,
the God and Father of all.

Father, we acknowledge your
    greatness:
all your actions show your wisdom
    and love.
You formed man in your own likeness
and set him over the whole world
to serve you, his creator,
and to rule over all creatures.
Even when he disobeyed you and lost
    your friendship

---

8. Roman Catholic Church, Second General Assembly of the Synod of Bishops, *Justice in the World* (1971), introduction; cf. Lambeth Conference 1948, pp. 26-28.

*you did not abandon him to the power
    of death,
but helped all men to seek and find
    you.
Again and again you offered a
    covenant to man,
and through the prophets taught him
    to hope for salvation.*

7.   In our re-examination, we need to be constantly reminded that "the Church is not a man-made society of like-minded people who are trying to live Christian lives and to exert some kind of Christian influence upon the world."[9] Rather, it is a community created and called by God. Its task is evangelization and salvation: to be an instrument of God's work in the world focused in the saving and liberating mission of Jesus Christ. It must, therefore, look to him for the example and style of its mission and to the Holy Spirit for the power to accomplish it.[10]

8.   Our churches have understood that this mission of witness to Jesus Christ is to be carried out by the proclamation of the Good News, the praise of God's Name, and service to all people. This mission is carried out in the context of the fellowship of believers, and it is the responsibility of all—not just some—of the Church's members.[11] The corporate character of this witness springs from the nature of the Church as the Body of Christ.

9.   The witness which the Church is called upon to give must first find expression in the lives of its individual members and in the Church's regulation of its own structures and agencies. Only then can it become a light to the world[12] and find expression in the structures of society.

---

9. Lambeth Conference 1948, p. 26.
10. Vatican II, Pastoral Constitution on the Church in the Modern World: *Gaudium et Spes*, 3 and 21; ed. Abbott, pp. 201, 219. *The Book of Common Prayer* (Episcopal Church), p. 38 (Prayer for Missions). Cf. General Convention of the Episcopal Church, 1973, definition of evangelism: "The presentation of Jesus Christ, in the power of the Holy Spirit, in such ways that persons may be led to believe in him as Savior and follow him as Lord, within the fellowship of his Church."
11. Episcopal Church, canon I.3, article 1: membership of the Domestic and Foreign Missionary Society comprises "all persons who are members of the Church." Cf. Vatican II, Decree on the Church's Missionary Activity: *Ad gentes*, 1, 11, 15, 20, 21, 35, ed. Abbott, pp. 585, 597, 602, 609-11, 623.
12. Vatican II, *Lumen Gentium*, 1; ed. Abbott, pp. 14-15.

Almighty and everliving God, you
  have fed us with the spiritual food
  of the most precious Body and
  Blood of your Son, our Saviour
  Jesus Christ;

You have assured us, in these Holy
  Mysteries, that we are living
  members of the Body of your Son,
and heirs of your eternal kingdom.

And now, Father, send us out to do
  the work you have given us to do,
to love and serve you as faithful
  witnesses of Christ our Lord.

To him, to you, and to the Holy
  Spirit, be honor and glory now and
  for ever. Amen.

Lord Jesus Christ,
we worship you living among us in
  the sacrament of your Body and
  Blood.
May we offer to our Father in heaven
  a solemn pledge of undivided love.
May we offer to our brothers and
  sisters a life poured out in loving
  service of that kingdom
where you live with the Father and
  the Holy Spirit,
one God for ever and ever.

A. *Proclamation of the Gospel*

10. The first thing the Church should be doing here and now is proclaiming the Gospel. The original Gospel was not only a message preached but also a life lived, and for this reason our proclamation today must involve not only preaching in words but also witness in deeds.[13] The Church proclaims Jesus as Lord and Savior, both in its preaching and in its witness, and the response it asks is a following in both word and deed. The task of proclamation and likewise the necessity of response, moreover, are an obligation not only for individuals but also for the Church as a whole.

Therefore, O Lord and Holy Father,
  we your people
celebrate here before your Divine
  Majesty,
with these holy Gifts which we offer to
  you,
the memorial of the blessed Passion
and precious Death of your dear Son,
his mighty Resurrection and glorious
  Ascension,
looking for his Coming again in power
  and great glory.

Father, calling to mind the death your
  Son endured for our Salvation, his
  glorious resurrection and ascension
  into heaven, and ready to greet
  him when he comes again,
we offer you in thanksgiving this holy
  and living sacrifice.

---

13. *Book of Common Prayer,* p. 83; Lambeth Conference 1968, p. 24; Anglican Congress 1954, p. 199; Episcopal Church, House of Bishops, Pastoral Letters, November 12, 1953, and November 12–17, 1960; cf. Vatican II, *Lumen Gentium,* 25; ed. Abbott, p. 47.

And with these Gifts, O Lord, we
*   offer to you ourselves,*
for this is our duty and service.
And we pray you, in your goodness
*   and mercy, to accept,*
through the eternal mediation of our
*   Savior Jesus Christ, this our*
*   sacrifice of praise and*
*   thanksgiving.*
Gracious Father, in your almighty
*   power,*
bless and sanctify us and these holy
*   Mysteries*
with your Life-giving Word and Holy
*   Spirit;*
fill with your grace all who partake
of the Body and Blood of our Lord
*   Jesus Christ;*
make us one Body that he may dwell
*   in us and we in him.*
And grant that with boldness
we may confess your Name in
*   constancy of faith,*
and at the last Day enter with all
*   your Saints*
into the joy of your eternal kingdom.

Look with favor on your Church's
*   offering, and see the Victim whose*
*   death has reconciled us to yourself.*
Grant that we, who are nourished by
*   his body and blood, may be filled*
*   with his Holy Spirit, and become*
*   one body,*
one spirit in Christ.

May he make us an everlasting gift to
*   you and enable us to share in the*
*   inheritance of your saints,*
with Mary, the virgin mother of God;
*   with the apostles, the martyrs, and*
*   all your saints, on whose constant*
intercession we rely for help.

Lord, may this sacrifice, which has
*   made our peace with you, advance*
*   the peace and salvation of all the*
*   world.*

11. Both in proclaiming the Gospel and in responding to it, the Church remembers with its Lord the words of the prophet as recorded in the Good News according to St. Luke (4:18-19): "The Spirit of the Lord is upon me, because he has anointed me to preach good news to the poor. He has sent me to proclaim release to the captives and recovering of sight to the blind, to set at liberty those who are oppressed, to proclaim the acceptable year of the Lord." These words of Scripture, we believe, as well as the words of our Eucharistic liturgies, lead us to affirm that "action on behalf of justice and participation in the transformation of the world" are fully a "constitutive dimension of the preaching of the Gospel."[14] This is to say, the Gospel as a word of reconciliation must be embodied in efforts to bring about social justice,[15] and in particular the Church must address itself to the questions posed by technological change. Such change, which is inevitable in the modern world, adds urgency and brings new opportunities for

---

14. *Justice in the World*, introduction; cf. Episcopal Church, Position Statement of the Executive Council on Empowerment, February 22, 1972.
15. Cf. *Justice in the World*, part III.

Christian mission. To the negative effects of technology, the Church must proclaim a word of challenge and even, at times, confrontation, whereas the positive effects of technology should receive the Church's active promotion; in both cases, however, the Church must seek to evaluate these effects and then make its voice heard. The imperative of evangelism, therefore, has many dimensions.[16]

B. *Worship*

12. The Church which proclaims God's Word expresses its own life most fully when it gathers as a community for worship, especially the celebration of the Eucharist, which is the summit and source of its mission.[17] Worship, indeed, is part of the mission of the Church, for it testifies to the dependence of all people upon God and it affirms God's action for humanity in the death and resurrection of Jesus Christ, in the promise of the gift of the Spirit, and in our ultimate destiny of union with the Father.

He stretched out his arms upon the Cross,
and offered himself, in obedience to your will,
a perfect sacrifice for all mankind.

On the night he was handed over to suffering and death,
our Lord Jesus Christ took bread;
and when he had given thanks to you,
he broke it, and gave it to his disciples,
and said, "Take this and eat it:
This is my Body, which is given for you.
Do this for the remembrance of me."

After supper he took the cup of wine;
and when he had given thanks, he gave it to them,
and said, "Drink this, all of you:

Father, you are holy indeed,
and all creation rightly gives you praise.
All life, all holiness comes from you
through your Son, Jesus Christ our Lord,
by the working of the Holy Spirit.

From age to age you gather a people to yourself,
so that from east to west
a perfect offering may be made
to the glory of your name.

And so, Father, we bring you these gifts.
We ask you to make them holy by the power of your Spirit,
that they may become the body and blood
of your Son, our Lord Jesus Christ,
at whose command we celebrate this eucharist.

---

16. *Book of Common Prayer*, pp. 47-48 (Bidding Prayer), 74-75 (Prayer for Whole State); Lambeth Conference 1968, p. 77; Anglican Congress 1954, p. 44. Vatican II, *Lumen Gentium*, 8; ed. Abbott, pp. 22-24.
17. Vatican II, Constitution on the Sacred Liturgy: *Sacrosanctum Concilium*, 2 and 10; ed. Abbott, pp. 137, 142; Anglican Congress 1954, pp. 197-98. Cf. *Book of Common Prayer*, p. 291 (Second Office of Instruction, Bounden Duty).

This is my Blood of the new Covenant,
which is shed for you and for many
for the forgiveness of sins.

Whenever you drink it, do this for the remembrance of me."

Therefore, Father, we recall the mystery of faith:

Christ has died,
Christ is risen,
Christ will come again.

On the night he was betrayed,
he took bread and gave you thanks and praise.
He broke the bread, gave it to his disciples, and said:
Take this, all of you, and eat it;
This is my body which will be given up for you.
When supper was ended, he took the cup.
Again he gave you thanks and praise,
gave the cup to his disciples, and said:
Take this, all of you, and drink from it;
This is the cup of my blood,
The blood of the new and everlasting covenant.
It will be shed for you and for all men
So that sins may be forgiven.

Do this in memory of me.
Let us proclaim the mystery of faith:

Christ has died,
Christ is risen,
Christ will come again.

13. To many contemporary Christians; moreover, the witness of worship is only fully complete when it results in a commitment to service.

C. *Service*

14. The imperative of viewing the Church's purpose in the context of "Service" (*diakonia*) has deep roots both in Holy Scripture and in the documents of our respective traditions.[18] While this call to serve others and to place our resources at the service of others is recognized and widely discussed in each of our churches, we must confess that it does not appear that either of us has yet found the means to carry out this aspect of mission as successfully as we might. This presents a particular problem as well as a special opportunity to those Church

---

18. *Interpreter's Dictionary of the Bible* (1962), vol. 3. pp. 386 ff. ("Ministry," *diakonia*, by M. H. Shepherd, Jr.); Robert C. Dentan, *The Holy Scriptures* ("The Church's Teaching Series," Protestant Episcopal Church, 1949), pp. 167-69; Augustin Cardinal Bea, *We Who Serve* (1969), esp. pp. 171-184; Lambeth Conference 1968, p. 24; Anglican Congress 1963, p. 264; Vatican II, *Lumen Gentium*, 18; *Gaudium et Spes*, 3 and 45; ed. Abbott, pp. 37, 201, 247.

members who find themselves among the affluent, for they possess, under God, particular means whereby the Church may become more fully a servant people, a sign of hope on mankind's way.[19] One of the major challenges facing our churches is the cultivation of an awareness of "unjust systems and structures" that oppress human freedom, maintain situations of gross inequality, and facilitate individual selfishness.[20] Forms of Christian service which do not take these structures into account are not adequate for the complexities of our day.

Lord God of our Fathers,
God of Abraham, Isaac, and Jacob,
God and Father of our Lord Jesus
*   Christ:*
open our eyes to see your hand at
*   work in the world about us.*
Deliver us from the presumption of
*   coming to this Table*
for solace only, and not for strength;
for pardon only, and not for renewal.
Let the grace of this Holy Communion
make us one body, one spirit in
*   Christ,*
that we may worthily serve the world
*   in his name.*
Risen Lord, be known to us in the
*   breaking of the Bread.*

Father, you so loved the world
that in the fullness of time you sent
*   your only Son to be our Savior.*
He was conceived through the power
*   of the Holy Spirit, and born of the*
*   Virgin Mary,*
a man like us in all things but sin.
To the poor he proclaimed the good
*   news of salvation,*
to prisoners, freedom,
and to those in sorrow, joy.
In fulfillment of your will
he gave himself up to death;
but by rising from the dead,
he destroyed death and restored life.

15. Our contemporary re-examination of mission has emphasized the call of the Church to serve as an agent and forerunner, in this world, of God's Kingdom of justice and peace. "Mindful of the Lord's saying, 'By this will all men know you are my disciples, if you have love for one another' (Jn 13:35) Christians cannot yearn for anything more ardently than to serve the men of the modern world ever more generously and effectively. Therefore, holding faithfully to the Gospel and benefitting from its resources, and united with every man who loves and practices justice, Christians have shouldered a gigantic task demanding fulfillment in this world. Concerning this task they must give a reckoning to Him who will judge every man on the last day. Not everyone who cries, 'Lord, Lord,' will enter into the kingdom of heaven, but those who do the Father's will and take a strong grip on

---

19. Vatican II, *Gaudium et Spes*, 8, 9, and 10; ed. Abbott, pp. 205-9; Lambeth Conference 1968, p. 74. *Book of Common Prayer*, pp. 18, 32 (Prayer for All Conditions), p. 44 (Prayer for Social Justice).
20. Cf. *Justice in the World*, introduction; *Book of Common Prayer*, pp. 298-9, 579-80 (Duty Towards Neighbor).

the work at hand. Now, the Father wills that in all men we recognize Christ our brother and love Him effectively in word and in deed."[21]
16. Human liberation, we agree, is that aspect of the Church's mission of service which is most challenging for our time. We agree, also, with the context in which Pope Paul VI has recently placed it: [Human liberation] "forms part of that love which Christians owe to their brethren. But the totality of salvation is not to be confused with one or other aspect of liberation, and the Good News must preserve all of its own originality: that of a God who saves us from sin and death and brings us to divine life."[22]

IV. What Is the Purpose of the Church?

Conclusion

17. The Church, the Body of Christ in the world, is led by the Spirit into all nations to fulfill the purpose of the Father. Insofar as it faithfully preaches the Gospel of salvation, celebrates the sacraments, and manifests the love of God in service, the Church becomes more perfectly one with the risen Christ. Impelled by its Lord, it strives to carry out the mission it has received from him: to prepare already the structures of the Kingdom, to share with all persons the hope for union with God.
18. In humility and repentance, the Church shares the guilt of mankind in its disunity. Presenting men and women with hope in the fulfillment of their destiny beyond this life, it also assumes, under the cross of its Lord, the burdens and the struggles of the oppressed, the poor, and the suffering. Striving for justice and peace, the Church seeks to better the conditions of this world. To the divided, it offers oneness; to the oppressed, liberation; to the sick, healing; to the dying, life; to all persons, eternal salvation.

*But chiefly are we bound to praise you
    for the glorious Resurrection of
    your Son Jesus Christ our Lord,
    for he is the Paschal Lamb who by
    his death has overcome death, and
    by his rising to life again has
    opened to us the way of everlasting
    life.*

*Father, in your mercy grant to us,
    your children,
to enter into our heavenly inheritance
in the company of the Virgin Mary,
    the Mother of God,
and your apostles and saints.*

21. Vatican II, *Gaudium et Spes*, 93; ed. Abbott, p. 307; cf. Episcopal Church, *Actions of General Convention 1967*, pp. 303-7; *Summary of General Convention Actions 1970*, pp. 3-6; Position Statement of the Executive Council on Empowerment, February 22, 1972.
22. *L'Osservatore Romano*, English edition, November 7, 1974, p. 9.

Accept these prayers and praises,
Father, through Jesus Christ, our
great High Priest, to whom with
you and the Holy Spirit, your
Church gives honor, glory, and
worship, from generation to
generation. Amen.

Then, in your kingdom, freed from the
corruption of sin and death, we
shall sing your glory with every
creature through Christ our Lord,
through whom you give us
everything that is good.

Through him,
with him,
in him,
in the unity of the Holy Spirit,
all glory and honor is yours,
almighty Father,
for ever and ever.
Amen.

19. We, as Roman Catholics and Episcopalians charged by our churches to explore the possibility that there is a fundamental unity between us, find that we are in substantial agreement about the purpose or mission of the Church as we have set it forth above. We have uncovered no essential points on which we differ. And we know, also, that insofar as the Church appears visibly divided, its purpose is obscured, its mission impeded, and its witness weakened. We yearn, therefore, for a restoration of the unity that will serve our common purpose.[23] Listening to the signs of the times, we seek guidance from the Spirit, so that through our common witness all may acknowledge that Jesus is the Lord, to the glory of God the Father, and that, in this faith, all may have life and have it abundantly. We conclude with a prayer common to both our traditions:[24]

O God of unchangeable power and eternal light: Look favorably on your whole Church, that wonderful and sacred mystery. By the tranquil operation of your providence, carry out the work of man's salvation. Let the whole world see and know that things which were cast down are being raised up, and things which had grown old are being made new, and that all things are being renewed to the perfection of him through whom all things were made, your Son our Lord Jesus Christ, who lives and reigns with you, in the unity of the Holy Spirit, one God, for ever and ever. Amen.

---

23. Cf. John 17.
24. In the Episcopal Church: *Services for Trial Use,* in Eucharistic Intercessions form VI, and in the Solemn Collects for Good Friday. In the Roman Catholic Church: prayer following Reading VII in the Easter Vigil.

Anglican/Roman Catholic Commission in the U.S.A. Statement on the Ordination of Women

The scholarly papers from the special ARC consultation that formed the background to this Agreed Statement have been published as *Pro and Con on the Ordination of Women* (New York: Seabury Professional Services, 1976). Perhaps one of the key points to this statement is the acknowledgement that "any decision, whether for or against the ordination of women, will in fact require the Church to explain or develop its essential Tradition in an unprecedented way." A second key point is the agreement that if one of the two Churches should proceed to ordain women, "this difference would not lead to ARC's termination or to the abandonment of its declared goal . . . of full communion and organic unity"—a goal which, the statement implies, does not require uniformity in either doctrine or discipline. The statement attempts to strike a balance in presenting the opinions of both sides of the question found in both Churches, and perhaps, for this reason, did not get the publicity it might otherwise have attracted.

1. State of the Question

Since 1969 the Anglican-Roman Catholic Consultation has consistently affirmed that its goal is to help the two churches to arrive at full communion and organic unity.[1] Recently the question of ordination of women to the priesthood and episcopate has become an increasingly pressing issue in our churches, but the state of the question is not the same in both.

The General Convention of the Episcopal Church is expected to consider the question at its meeting in September, 1976; meanwhile the leadership of the Roman Catholic Church has recently reaffirmed its position that only men are to be ordained to the priesthood.

If a divergence on this subject eventuates in official action, it will introduce an important new element into officially appointed dialogues, as well as into conversations and covenants at many other

---

1. "ARC VII Statement," adopted at the seventh meeting, December 8-11, 1969, Boynton Beach, Florida. See pp. 33-44.

levels. However, the members of ARC are convinced that this difference would not lead to ARC's termination or to the abandonment of its declared goal. The reasons for this conviction will be dealt with more fully in later paragraphs.

2. Development of Tradition

A special consultation of scholars on this question, convoked in June 1975 by appropriate authorities of our two churches, reported as follows:

"In considering the relation of the question of the ordination of women to the authority of the church's Tradition, the following considerations must be kept in mind.

"1. There is what may be called an 'essential Tradition' which, as witnessed in the Scriptures, the ecumenical creeds, the church's liturgical tradition, and its proclamation and teaching, constitutes the basic identity of the Christian community. This Tradition has as its fundamental content the relation of human beings to the God and Father of Jesus Christ in the Holy Spirit.

"2. This Tradition is variously elaborated and interpreted in dogma and doctrinal tradition, according as inquiry and change within the church, or confrontation with intellectual, social, or political movements in the world require the church to move towards a deeper self-understanding through explication of the Tradition which constitutes its identity. It thus faces, from time to time, novel issues, which demand that on the basis of its given self-understanding, it explain itself in new ways for the sake of fidelity to the Gospel.

"3. In the current situation, the question of the ordination of women has raised issues which cannot be answered adequately by the mere citing of traditional practices or belief. Current discussion of the issue has shown that traditional reasons for refusing the ordination of women are not universally acceptable. It has further shown that problems relating to the doctrine of God, of the Incarnation, and Redemption are at least indirectly involved in its solution, so that any decision, whether for or against the ordination of women, will in fact require the church to explain or develop its essential Tradition in an unprecedented way. The church, therefore, faces an issue which demands of it a new effort at self-understanding in regard to certain elements of its Gospel.

"4. Such an effort involves a two-fold process: first, the theological exploration of the Tradition and of the new question in its bearing on the data of Christian revelation; second, an official decision by constituted authority in the church which encompasses the doctrinal and practical aspects of the issue. In the divided state of the Christian churches, separate processes will be gone through by the different bodies.

"5. The theological exploration mentioned above has been undertaken by both Roman Catholic and Anglican theologians. Offi-

cial pronouncements give no indication of any expectation of change
in the present position of the Roman Catholic Church on this issue
in the immediate future. At this meeting, a number of the Roman
Catholic participants felt that the implications of this matter had not
been explored sufficiently to offer a final decision. On the other
hand, the question of the ordination of women is expected to be
proposed for action at the General Convention of the Episcopal Church
in 1976. Anglican participants felt that the discussion in the Episcopal Church in the United States had reached a stage where decision was becoming possible.[2]

3. Understandings Already Shared

The process outlined in the fourth paragraph of the above statement
is now going on in both churches and consequently is of concern to
ARC. We have given careful consideration to several papers subsequently written by the scholars who were called to the special consultation. ARC's contribution is not to propose what either church
should do, but to place the question within the context of agreed
statements already issued by ARC and ARCIC—the national and
international commissions of the Anglican and Roman Catholic
Churches—notably the Windsor *Agreed Statement on Eucharistic Doctrine*[3]
and the Canterbury Statement on *Ministry and Ordination.*[4]

These statements are a strong indication that, though disagreement exists on the answer, the question is based on a common understanding of the issues involved and the meaning of terms common
to both churches. We are talking about the same Eucharist and the
same three-fold ministry; we share the same fundamental sources of
doctrine in Scripture and Tradition. Both churches make use of the
insights of theological research, incorporating the contributions of
anthropology, psychology, history and other aspects of culture to
arrive at authoritative decisions.[5]

4. Women in Ministry

A concept of the inferiority and subject status of women is reflected
in both the Old Testament and the New. However, the fundamental
equality of men and women is indicated in a number of key biblical

---

2. ARC Special Consultation on Ordination of Women, Mercy Center,
   Cincinnati, Ohio, June 22-25, 1975.
3. See pp. 233-242.
4. See pp. 243-253.
5. Cf. "Doctrinal Agreement and Christian Unity: Methodological
   Considerations," ARC eleventh meeting. See pp. 57-60.

passages[6] and has been developed in the teaching of the church. The expression of this equality in the roles assumed by men and women in society is a matter of cultural development and change. The church must measure this development in relation to grace—our new creation in Christ—and to the ultimate fulfillment of his victory over sin and death.

In addition to Christian witness within the family, women have long been engaged in teaching, nursing, social work, missionary service, and care for the young, the aged and the infirm. Although the diaconate has been opened to women in the Episcopal Church, the role of presiding at the Eucharist has not been opened to women in the practice of either church. Yet women are now serving as Christ's ministers in many new ways: for example, ministries of peace, social justice, theological education, and formal pastoral care of special groups, including leadership in hospital, campus and prison chaplaincies. Women now play an increasing part in the Liturgy as lectors and auxiliary ministers of Holy Communion. Today they stand on a level of equality with men in exercising the ministry of all baptized persons in the public forum.

5. Issues to Be Faced

The New Testament records that Jesus chose only males to be apostles, and this has been cited as a model. Moreover, the fact that the church has continued to ordain only males to the priesthood is a weighty precedent. However, one must explore the reasons for this practice to determine whether it holds for all time or is capable of change when cultural evolution presents new possibilities for witness to the Gospel.

Both our churches agree that no individual has an inherent right to be ordained priest. Nevertheless, the exclusion *a priori* of a large class of persons from this ministry must be justified by cogent arguments, since women are now widely recognized as capable of exer-

6. Genesis 1:27-28 (cf. 5:1,2, placed by an ancient editor after the fall). Judges 4:4; 2 Kings 22:14; Nehemiah 6:14 (judges and prophetesses). Joel 2:28-29 (cf. Acts 2:17-18).
   Mark 12:18-25 (sexes in the resurrection); Luke 8:1-3 (companions of Jesus); 10:40-42 (woman as disciple); Acts 1:12-14 (awaiting Pentecost with the eleven); 9:36, 16:14, 40; 17:4, 12, 32 (leaders in local churches); 18:1-26 (Priscilla as theologian); 21:8 (daughters of Philip).
   Romans 16:1-16 (Phoebe the deacon, various women workers in the Gospel); 1 Corinthians 7:1-16 (marital mutuality); 11:2-12 (though men are accounted superior, women pray and prophesy in Church); Galatians 3:26-29 (In Christ "neither male nor female"); Philippians 4:2 (women who "have labored with me in the Gospel along with Clement. . .").

cising leadership in many roles once regarded as appropriate only to men. If the churches are to change their agelong practice, however, the claim that there is no strong reason against the ordination of women must be reinforced by strong arguments for it, since the desirability of change does not automatically follow from acceptance of its possibility. In any case, whether a change is advocated or a tradition affirmed, adequate theological reflection is necessary on the part of all concerned, because a decision of either sort would involve a response to a question never before raised in this way. The depth of the issue is indicated in the third paragraph of the above report of the June, 1975 consultation.

The question of ordination of women presents problems within both the Roman Catholic and the Anglican communions; so also do the Marian dogmas. Both of these issues are relevant to a deep concern for womanhood in the life of the world and the economy of salvation. In both our churches there is a growing realization that women should have a more effective voice in all areas of church life, befitting their dignity as human persons made in the image and likeness of God.

6. Diversity in Unity?

A difference in practice between our churches on ordination of women would inevitably raise the question of its effect upon the goal of full communion and organic unity. If this goal is thought of as requiring uniformity in doctrine and discipline concerning candidates for ordination, the problem would indeed be a serious one. However, there is a development in theological thought about Church unity toward accepting diversity as a gift of the Holy Spirit who endows churches as well as individuals with varied gifts.[7] Theologians of both churches are writing on Church "typology" in terms which suggest that we might accept and even cherish "varieties of service" (I Cor. 12:5) among churches—differences appropriate to the characteristic theological method, liturgical expression, spiritual and devotional tradition, and canonical discipline of each. These differences have relationship to the cultural situation, psychological outlook, intellectual method, and forms of social organization of different communities.

The ecumenical task is to inquire whether one church can fully recognize another in the midst of differences; whether both can discern a substantial unity in faithfulness to the Gospel amid varied expressions and understandings of the single Mystery, the single Faith, the single Christ. Particular controverted issues of church life

---

7. "Doctrinal Agreement." See p. 60.

may represent different ways of manifesting God's grace, as the Spirit has guided us. Even the things we do not agree with in each other's traditions may have something to teach us about God's will for his people. We proceed in the faith and hope that the Spirit is leading us into unity.

7. Discerning, Deciding, Doing

There is a particular urgency for mutual consultation before important decisions are taken by either of the two churches which already share so much in common and which intend to persevere in seeking together that unity for which Christ prayed. This process of mutual consultation, however, must not interfere with the interacting roles of prophecy and authority within either church. The entire body of the faithful is in Baptism anointed with the Spirit, and this one same Spirit, distributing diverse gifts at will, at times manifests itself to the entire body through the prophetic witness of a few, for the sake of the whole. It is the proper role of authority in the Church to encourage and promote discernment of such witness, thus fostering an authentic development while at the same time maintaining the integrity of a normative Christian life and tradition.

"Speaking the truth in love" is the way in which the Church will best prepare and strengthen itself to carry out the mission God has given it. We have tried to express that mission in the concluding paragraphs of our statement on *The Purpose of the Church*:[8]

> The church, the Body of Christ in the world, is led by the Spirit into all nations to fulfill the purpose of the Father. In so far as it faithfully preaches the Gospel of salvation, celebrates the sacraments, and manifests the love of God in service, the church becomes more perfectly one with the risen Christ. Impelled by its Lord, it strives to carry out the mission it has received from him: to prepare already the structures of the Kingdom, to share with all persons the hope for union with God.
>
> In humility and repentance, the church shares the guilt of mankind in its disunity. Presenting men and women with hope in the fulfillment of their destiny beyond this life, it also assumes, under the cross of its Lord, the burdens and the struggles of the oppressed, the poor, and the suffering. Striving for justice and peace, the church seeks to better the conditions of this world. To the divided, it offers oneness; to the oppressed, liberation; to the sick, healing; to the dying, life; to all persons, eternal salvation.
>
> —October 1975

---

8. ARC XV Statement, October 31, 1975. See pp. 136-147.

Common Declaration by Pope Paul VI and the Archbishop of Canterbury

The Ceremony in the Sistine Chapel

Friday, April 29th, Pope Paul and the Archbishop of Canterbury came together in the Sistine Chapel in the presence of a symbolic group of clergy and faithful, Catholic and Anglican, united in prayer and in the hope of reconciliation. There were 29 Cardinals present, ten archbishops and bishops, the diplomatic corps accredited to the Holy See, the Substitute Secretary of State, Archbishop Benelli, and the Secretary of the Council for Public Affairs of the Church, Archbishop Casaroli. At places near the altar were the members of the group that had come with the Archbishop of Canterbury and Cardinal Willebrands, Archbishop of Utrecht and President of the Secretariat for Promoting Christian Unity, together with members of his Secretariat. Seminarians of the English College assisted in the service which took place.

After the choir of the English College had chanted a hymn, the Holy Father made the sign of the cross and recited a prayer introducing the Liturgy of the Word. The first reading by the Reverend Christopher Hill, counsellor of the Archbishop of Canterbury, was from the Book of Job, and the second reading was from the Letter of St. Paul to the Ephesians. The Sistine Chapel choir then began the « Veni Sancte Spiritus » and led the assembly in the chanting of it. Finally, the deacon, Peter Fleetwood, read the passage from the St. John's Gospel containing the sublime invocation "that they may be one."

The Creed was then sung by all and Pope Paul introduced the prayer of the faithful. The intentions were read alternately by Msgr. William Purdy, of the Secretariat for Promoting Christian Unity, and the Reverend Christopher Hill. The "Our Father" was then sung in Gregorian chant.

Pope Paul then introduced the final part of the celebration which had as its high point the exchange of a kiss of peace between the Pope and the President of the Anglican Communion. This moving and significant gesture was preceded by the chanting of the "Sanctus," a common prayer, and discourses given by the Pope and Archbishop Coggan.

154

Discourse of Pope Paul VI

Already we have welcomed you, Venerable Brother, and those who have journeyed with you to this ancient and holy place. Today we welcome you all the more cordially, as we meet in prayer, humbled under the mighty hand of God (cf. 1 Pt 5, 6), yet full of thanks for all the blessings that this liturgical season reminds us we owe to the divine goodness. As we meet in praise and thanksgiving, with petitions as wide and various as our troubled world, we are able to discern the profound reason for your visit and for our joy in receiving you. For with the Second Vatican Council we are convinced that "there can be no ecumenism worthy of the name without interior conversion" (*Unitatis Redintegratio*, 7).

If we examine the list of pioneers in the search for unity, we cannot but be reminded of the majestic survey in the eleventh chapter of the Letter to the Hebrews. It is a survey which puts the Holy Scriptures before us as a record of faith. And we are still "surrounded by so great a cloud of witnesses" (Heb 12, 1), for those who in recent years have laboured in the cause of unity have witnessed no less to faith and hope, and to the perseverance which is their outward manifestation.

Venerable Brother, your presence here is a living expression of this faith and hope, continually being renewed in the Spirit who will guide us "into all the truth" (Jn 16, 13). We wish to join with you in proclaiming this faith and hope, borrowing the words of the Vatican Council's *Decree on Ecumenism:* "Before the whole world let Christians confess their faith in God, one and three, in the incarnate Son of God, our Redeemer and Lord. United in their efforts and with mutual respect, let them bear witness to our common hope, which does not play us false" (*Unitatis Redintegratio*, 13).

We know well how near to your own heart lies this desire for common witness to Christian faith and hope, how much of your pastoral labour in many parts of your Communion has been untiringly devoted to it.

It is the experience of all of us today that the world desperately needs Christ. The young, in whose aspirations good is often seen most vividly, feel this need most strongly. Secular optimism does not satisfy them. They are waiting for a proclamation of hope. Now is our chance to bear witness together that Christ is indeed the way, and the truth and the life, and that he is communicated through the Holy Spirit.

Here is a task to which the Lord calls everyone who invokes his name. Those who are charged with the care of Christians, and who minister to them, feel especially the responsibility of fidelity to the apostolic faith, its embodiment in the life of the Church today, and its transmission to the Church of tomorrow. To discern "the signs of the times" calls for constant refreshment of mind and spirit at the Christian sources, and especially in the Holy Scriptures. In sending all ministers and teachers to the Scriptures, the Vatican Council borrows strong words from Saint Augustine: those ministers and teachers should remain in close contact with the Scriptures by means of reading and accurate study of the text, so as not to become like "one who vainly preaches the word of God externally, while he does not listen to it inwardly." And from Saint Jerome it takes words even more pointed: "Ignorance of the Scriptures is indeed ignorance of Christ" (cf. *Dei Verbum*, 25).

The supplications we make together this morning to our common Lord are steeped in the Christian love of God's word, and they renew the reality of that pledge made together with us by your revered Predecessor—the pledge to a serious dialogue which, founded on the Gospels and on the ancient common traditions, may lead to that perfect unity in truth for which Christ prayed. What a challenge, what an uplifting ambition is here! It is good that, while our experts continue their work, we should meet humbly to encounter our Lord in prayer. Indeed we might think of the example of Moses, supported by Aaron and Hur, holding up his arms in supplication for Israel (cf. Ex 17, 10-13). Today we raise our prayers in support of those who strive for reconciliation and unity in Christ.

To falter in prayer is to falter in hope and to put the cause at risk. We know that a long road remains to be travelled. But does not one of the most moving accounts of the Risen Christ in Saint Luke's Gospel tell us how, as two of the disciples travelled a road together, Christ joined them and "interpreted to them in all the Scriptures the things concerning himself"? (Lk 24, 27).

Let us listen as we walk, strong in faith and hope, along the road marked out for us.

Discourse of the Archbishop of Canterbury

In this place, hallowed by the prayers of the faithful over so many centuries, meetings have taken place over the last 17 years which have brought together brethren in Christ hitherto separated by the differences and misunderstandings of the centuries. I rejoice in the meetings between Pope John and Archbishop Geoffrey Fisher, between Your Holiness and our predecessor, Archbishop Michael Ramsey, and yesterday and today between Your Holiness and myself, the successor of these two good men. We are grateful for the warmth of the reception accorded to us during these days and for the frankness and love in which we have been able to take counsel together in the Name of our common Lord. I pray that the good work begun by the

Anglican-Roman Catholic International Commission may be continued and extended to cover a wider expanse of dialogue and to lead to further understanding and co-operation.

From this place we look out to a world enlightened in large part by the Gospel of Christ, but still dark in larger part where the Gospel has not penetrated.

Even where the Church of Christ is strong, in places such as Uganda, where the members of our Communions work in considerable strength, our brethren suffer greatly. We send to our brethren in Africa and in many other places where the rule of freedom and justice is impeded, the assurance of our united concern and prayers.

As our Lord prayed not only for his immediate disciples but also for those who in the future would believe in him, so together we ·pray for them, that they may be kept by the power of his Name, in truth, in peace, and in love.

Let us pray also for ourselves, that, as we are united by baptism and by a living faith, so, strengthened by the word of God's grace and by the Body and Blood of Christ, we may reach out in joint evangelistic action to those for whom our Saviour Christ was contented to be betrayed and given up into the hands of sinful men.

May God's kingdom come. May his will be done. And may we, in the intimacy of an increasingly deep communion, together be the agents of God's love and peace in the power of the Holy Spirit.

We greet Your Holiness with affection and gratitude.

At the end of the service in the Sistine Chapel Pope Paul and Archbishop Coggan together gave a blessing to those who were present. The Pope and the Archbishop then went to the Pauline Chapel where Msgr. Purdy read the text of a *Common Declaration*. The Pope and the Archbishop then affixed their signatures to the document, which is reproduced here in the original English text.

Common Declaration

1. After four hundred years of estrangement, it is now the third time in seventeen years that an archbishop of Canterbury and the Pope embrace in Christian friendship in the city of Rome. Since the visit of Archbishop Ramsey eleven years have passed, and much has happened in that time to fulfil the hopes then expressed and to cause us to thank God.

2. As the Roman Catholic Church and the constituent Churches of the Anglican Communion have sought to grow in mutual understanding and Christian love, they have come to recognise, to value and to give thanks for a common faith in God our Father, in our Lord Jesus Christ, and in the Holy Spirit; our common baptism into Christ;

our sharing of the Holy Scriptures, of the Apostles' and Nicene Creeds, the Chalcedonian definition, and the teaching of the Fathers; our common Christian inheritance for many centuries with its living traditions of liturgy, theology, spirituality and mission.

3.   At the same time in fulfilment of the pledge of eleven years ago to "a serious dialogue which, founded on the Gospels and on the ancient common traditions, may lead to that unity in truth, for which Christ prayed" (*Common Declaration* PPVI/ABC 1966) Anglican and Roman Catholic theologians have faced calmly and objectively the historical and doctrinal differences which have divided us. Without compromising their respective allegiances, they have addressed these problems together, and in the process they have discovered theological convergences often as unexpected as they were happy.

4.   The Anglican/Roman Catholic International Commission has produced three documents: on the Eucharist, on Ministry and Ordination and on Church and Authority. We now recommend that the work it has begun be pursued, through procedures appropriate to our respective Communions, so that both of them may be led along the path towards unity.

The moment will shortly come when the respective Authorities must evaluate the conclusions.

5.   The response of both communions to the work and fruits of theological dialogue will be measured by the practical response of the faithful to the task of restoring unity, which as the Second Vatican Council says "involves the whole Church, faithful and clergy alike" and "extends to everyone according to the talents of each" (*Unitatis Redintegratio*, 5). We rejoice that this practical response has manifested itself in so many forms of pastoral cooperation in many parts of the world; in meetings of bishops, clergy and faithful.

6.   In mixed marriages between Anglicans and Roman Catholics, where the tragedy of our separation at the sacrament of union is seen most starkly, cooperation in pastoral care (*Matrimonia Mixta*, para 14) in many places has borne fruit in increased understanding. Serious dialogue has cleared away many misconceptions and shown that we still share much that is deep-rooted in the Christian tradition and ideal of marriage, though important differences persist, particularly regarding remarriage after divorce. We are following attentively the work thus far accomplished in this dialogue by the Joint Commission on the Theology of Marriage and its Application to Mixed Marriages. It has stressed the need for fidelity and witness to the ideal of marriage, set forth in the New Testament and constantly taught in Christian tradition. We have a common duty to defend this tradition and ideal and the moral values which derive from it.

7.   All such cooperation, which must continue to grow and spread, is the true setting for continued dialogue and for the general extension and appreciation of its fruits, and so for progress towards that goal

which is Christ's will—the restoration of complete communion in faith and sacramental life.

8.   Our call to this is one with the sublime Christian vocation itself which is a call to communion; as St. John says "that which we have seen and heard we proclaim also to you, so that you may have fellowship with us; and our fellowship is with the Father and His Son Jesus Christ" (I Jn 1, 3). If we are to maintain progress in doctrinal convergence and move forward resolutely to the communion of mind and heart for which Christ prayed we must ponder still further his intentions in founding the Church and face courageously their requirements.

9.   It is their communion with God in Christ through faith and through baptism and self-giving to Him that stands at the centre of our witness to the world, even while between us communion remains imperfect. Our divisions hinder this witness, hinder the work of Christ (*Evangelii Nuntiandi*, 77) but they do not close all roads we may travel together. In a spirit of prayer and of submission to God's will we must collaborate more earnestly in a "greater common witness to Christ before the world in the very work of evangelisation" (*Evangelii Nuntiandi*, ibid.). It is our desire that the means of this collaboration be sought: the increasing spiritual hunger in all parts of God's world invites us to such a common pilgrimage.

This collaboration pursued to the limit allowed by truth and loyalty, will create the climate in which dialogue and doctrinal convergence can bear fruit. While this fruit is ripening, serious obstacles remain both of the past and of recent origin. Many in both communions are asking themselves whether they have a common faith sufficient to be translated into communion of life, worship and mission. Only the communions themselves through their pastoral authorities can give that answer. When the moment comes to do so, may the answer shine through in spirit and truth, not obscured by the enmities, the prejudices and the suspicions of the past.

10.   To this we are bound to look forward and to spare no effort to bring it closer: to be baptised into Christ is to be baptised into hope—"and hope does not disappoint us because God's love has been poured into our hearts through the Holy Spirit which has been given us" (Rom V, 5).

11.   Christian hope manifests itself in prayer and action—in prudence but also in courage. We pledge ourselves and exhort the faithful of the Roman Catholic Church and of the Anglican Communion to live and work courageously in this hope of reconciliation and unity in our common Lord.

From the Vatican, 29 April 1977

Anglican/Roman Catholic Commission in the U.S.A. Where We Are: A Challenge for the Future A Twelve-Year Report

The Malta Report of 1968 and Cardinal Willebrands' Cambridge Address of 1970 and his Lambeth Address of 1972 had stressed that unity in the faith, essential to organic unity, should be articulated in mutually agreed statements. For three years, ARC attempted this articulation. Using the ARC discussions as a base, Fathers J. Robert Wright and Herbert J. Ryan, SJ, drafted a summary report in June 1977, at Los Angeles. The report summarized ARC's doctrinal agreements and possible areas of disagreement between the Episcopal Church and the Roman Catholic Church. It also set proposals for ARC's future agenda and suggested the formation of five task forces for possible joint action by Episcopalians and Roman Catholics. ARC accepted the *Twelve-Year Report* on Friday, August 12, 1977, at Cincinnati.

Preface

Having met nineteen times over a twelve-year period, the national consultation of the Episcopal and Roman Catholic Churches in the U.S.A. now issues a report to its sponsoring communities. The report is both a summary of past work and a challenge for future cooperation. The Consultation believes it has discovered a significant and substantial unity of faith between the two Churches, a unity which demands visible expression and testimony now. At the same time, the Consultation honestly recognizes differences which continue to separate the two Churches. In the following pages we present, at this point in our work, conclusions and suggestions to our sponsoring bodies for evaluation, response, and action. We offer direction to the Churches which commission us, but we also seek direction and a continuing mandate from those Churches for the pursuit of the unity God wills for His church.

The Most Rev. Raymond W. Lessard, Bishop of Savannah
The Rt. Rev. Arthur A. Vogel, Bishop of West Missouri
Co-Chairmen
December 1977

Introduction

Since 1965 the Episcopal Church and the Roman Catholic Church have been in officially sponsored dialogue. At the request of these Churches, these meetings have been conducted in this country by the Anglican-Roman Catholic Consultation in the USA (ARC), whose members have been jointly appointed by the authorities in both Churches. The purpose of these official consultations has been to aid both Churches in realizing together that unity for which Christ prayed.

After 12 years of study ARC contends that the Episcopal Church and the Roman Catholic Church agree at the level of faith on such topics as the Holy Eucharist, Priesthood and Ordination, and the nature and mission of the Church. There is also a common understanding between us of the theological methodology necessary for ecumenical dialogue. Yet agreement even at the level of faith is not always evident in visible expression. The Episcopal and the Roman Catholic Churches differ in their forms of worship, their traditions of spirituality, their styles of theological reflection and in some of their organizational structures of church life. Despite these historically conditioned differences, however, ARC finds after 19 joint consultations that the Episcopal and Roman Catholic Churches share so profound an agreement on the level of faith that these Churches are in fact "sister Churches" in the one *Communio* which is the Church of Christ.[1]

How may this unity in faith be shown? We propose that such unity be given expression in an immediate responding together in the Spirit through Christ to the Father. In this report we suggest specific joint activities which can be undertaken by our two Churches, and we indicate some areas which we think require further investigation.

A. *Responding Together in the Spirit through Christ to the Father*

1. *Worship.* The ritual patterns in the liturgies of Baptism and Eucharist in both our Churches show that we both understand the Christian life as a response not only to historical events but also to a transcen-

---

1. Cf. Pope Paul VI, 25 October 1970: "There will be no seeking to lessen the legitimate prestige and the worthy patrimony of piety and usage proper to the Anglican Church when the Roman Catholic Church—this humble 'Servant of the servants of God'—is able to embrace her ever beloved sister in the one authentic Communion of the family of Christ: a communion of origin and of faith, a communion of priesthood and of rule, a communion of the saints in the freedom of love of the spirit of Jesus." Cf. pp. 54-55.

dent reality. In the historical person of Jesus Christ, crucified and risen, the all-holy God is both revealed and glorified by his people on earth. Initiated in Baptism, constantly renewed by repentance, service, and daily prayer, the Christian life finds its core in the worship of the eucharistic community as the apex and source of the Church's mission. Already in 1967 ARC-USA found our two Churches to be in substantial agreement on the meaning of the Eucharistic sacrifice,[2] and in 1972 ARC was happy to record its own endorsement of the ARCIC (Anglican-Roman Catholic International Commission) Windsor agreed statement on the meaning of the Eucharist as the spiritual but real presence of Christ and His sacrifice for us in the consecrated bread and wine.[3] Although there may be occasional differences in secondary matters of theology and practice, we are convinced that the centrality of the Eucharist in the Church's life and work is a major affirmation made by both Anglicans and Roman Catholics in their common faith. A convergence about ritual and worship, as we indicated in our joint statement on the Church's purpose or mission, is evidence in turn of a deeper convergence in faith and doctrine that can readily be discerned from a comparison of our contemporary liturgical texts.[4] It is in the sacrament of the Eucharist above all, and in the eucharistic way of life which flows from it, that we respond together in the Spirit through Christ to the Father.

2.   *Scripture.* Episcopalians and Roman Catholics believe that in the Bible the inspired word of God is expressed: through the Holy Scriptures the living God speaks to us still today. The Bible records Yahweh's self-disclosure throughout Israel's religious history and his definitive revelation in Christ Jesus, the Word made flesh, attested by the living faith of the early Christian communities. Both the Episcopal and Roman Catholic Churches hold that the collection of New Testament canonical writings, properly understood in their literary forms, is historically trustworthy concerning the life, death, and the resurrection of Jesus and is permanently normative[5] for the life and faith of the Christian Church. To help comprehend the meaning of Scripture the Episcopal and Roman Catholic Churches endorse and utilize historical, critical methods of exegesis.[6]

However, it is the conviction of both our Churches that the task of understanding the Bible and the biblical faith does not cease with

---

2. Cf. pp. 5-6.
3. ARC/DOC II, pp. 54-56.
4. Cf. pp. 136-147.
5. Cf. ARCIC 1976 Venice statement on Authority in the Church, para. 2. See pp. 254-255.
6. Vatican Council II, Dogmatic Constitution on Divine Revelation (*Dei Verbum*) 12, ed. Abbott p. 120; Decree on Priestly Formation (*Optatam totius*) 16, ed. Abbott p. 451. Cf. *Proposed Book of Common Prayer* (Episcopal Church), pp. 853, 888 ff., 934 ff.

the establishment of the historical context of a given text, section, or verse of the Bible. Biblical faith is a living response to the living God revealed in the Bible. Thus, appreciating how Scripture has been utilized to articulate the Church's living faith in its worship, preaching, spirituality, and outreach is also part of the task of understanding the biblical message.

3. *Articulation of the Faith.* Both Anglicans and Roman Catholics, we are convinced, share all the basic doctrines of classical Catholic Christianity and view them as normative for the Church's continuous living tradition. Neither of our Churches conceives of doctrine as developing in isolation from scriptural foundation or from historical and cultural forms of thought and speech. We both believe that one reason why the Church cherishes, studies, and teaches the whole canon of Sacred Scripture is so that articulation of the faith may be formed from it and reformed by it. Yet we also both maintain that doctrines do not remain verbally static—in a vacuum, so to speak—apart from the various thought patterns, historical factors, and modes of interpretation that produced them at a given time and that guide the Church, under the Holy Spirit, along its course.[7] The Church fathers, liturgy and devotion, catholic creeds, ecumenical councils, papal statements, theological reflections, scriptural exegesis, "sense of the faithful," and concrete decisions of the Church in every age, among other factors, all contribute to that dynamic process which in both our Churches is collectively called tradition.

Over these past 12 years the agenda of ARC has tended to concentrate on those points of doctrine that have divided us in the past— the Eucharist, the ordained ministry, and the question of authority. But in the process of investigating our respective beliefs on these points, as well as in preparing our agreed statement on the Church's purpose and mission, we have become increasingly conscious of the very great body of fundamental doctrine that our churches have inherited in common and still share with little or no divergence between us. We both affirm the Trinity of God as Father, Son, and Spirit. We both confess Jesus Christ as true God and true man in accord with the formula of Chalcedonian Christology.[8] Much ecclesiology in both our churches is the same: the Church is the mystical body of Christ,

---

7. ARCIC Venice statement, para 15. (see p. 259); 1972 ARC statement on Doctrinal Agreement and Christian Unity: Methodological Considerations, esp. paras. 2, 3, and 4 (see pp. 57-58).

8. Common Declaration of the Pope and the Archbishop of Canterbury signed in Rome, 29 April 1977, para. 2 See pp. 157-158. For the Chalcedonian text, cf. *Proposed Book of Common Prayer*, p. 864. It is acknowledged that some theologians of both our Churches, as well as others, are calling for restatement, reformulation, reinterpretation, or, in some cases, even rejection of the Chalcedonian terminology. For some Roman Catholic views, see W. Kasper, *Jesus the Christ*; Hans Küng, *On*

its structure of authority is truly episcopal, and its purpose is proclamation, worship, and service.[9] We both recognize Baptism and the Eucharist as the basic sacraments of Christian life, often called necessary to salvation. In both our traditions confirmation, penance, matrimony, orders, and the unction of the sick are also considered to be authentic sacramental means of grace, appropriate to specific situations in life.[10]

Further, the whole Christian view of the world may properly be called sacramental inasmuch as outward and material appearances conceal and at the same time reveal inward and spiritual realities visible to the eyes of faith. We also hold that faith is inseparable from hope, because for the Christian death itself is in the hands of a loving God and the final destiny by all human kind has already been anticipated in the resurrection of Christ. It is in this perspective that many of the faithful in our two Churches have found inspiration in countless holy men and women, among whom are the Virgin Mary, the apostles and the martyrs, and all the saints already sharing the divine glory in the Risen Christ.

We are painfully aware, of course, that no summary of the doctrine which our Churches hold in common can be thoroughly adequate. The foregoing has been only a brief attempt to survey some of the highlights, and our Consultation stands prepared to investigate any other areas which may be of concern to our respective communities. We do both share the conviction that not all doctrinal truths are of the same order of importance,[11] however, and although neither

---

Being a Christian; Gerald O'Collins, S.J., *What Are They Saying About Jesus*; K. Rahner, various articles on Christology in *Theological Investigations* vols. 1, 3, 4, 5, 7, 8, 9, and 10; P. Schoonenberg, *The Christ*; B. Vawter, *This Man Jesus*. For some Anglican views, see William Temple, *Christus Veritas*; Richard A. Norris, "Towards a Contemporary Interpretation of the Chalcedonian Definition," in *Lux in Lumine: Essays to Honor W. Norman Pittenger*; E. R. Hardy, "Chalcedon in the Anglican Tradition," and David Jenkins, "The Bearing of Chalcedon upon the Modern Discussions about the 'Humanum' and the Secular," both in *The Ecumenical Review* xxii:4 (Oct. 1970); Maurice Wiles, *The Remaking of Christian Doctrine*; J. A. T. Robinson, *The Human Face of God*.

9. ARC 1975 statement on the Purpose of the Church, paras. 10-16. See pp. 141-146.
10. *Proposed Book of Common Prayer*, pp. 860-861; Vatican II, Constitution on the Sacred Liturgy (*Sacrosanctum Concilium*) 59-82, ed. Abbott pp. 158-163. See also the study entitled *Subscription and Assent to the Thirty-nine Articles* (London, 1968), prepared for the Tenth Lambeth Conference by the Commission on Doctrine appointed by the Archbishops of Canterbury and York.
11. Cf. Vatican II, Decree on Ecumenism (*Unitatis Redintegratio*) 11, ed. Abbott p. 354; "When comparing doctrines, *Catholic theologians engaged in ecumenical dialogue* should remember that in Catholic teaching there exists an order or 'hierarchy' of truths, since they vary in their relationship to the foundation of the Christian faith."

of us has yet spelled out this order with exact precision it is the firm belief of ARC that the doctrines of Trinity, Christology, sacraments, ecclesiology, and eschatology are of the highest order in the faith of each of our Churches. To be sure, our verbal formulations of these doctrines may have differed from time to time over the centuries, but we in ARC judge that the methodological considerations already set forth in our agreed statement on "Doctrinal Agreement and Christian Unity" show that these differences are less important than what our Churches hold in common.[12] The object of our faith is not the earthen vessels but the treasure which they contain, and we have become convinced from our papers, investigations, and conversations over the past 12 years that substantial agreement does exist between us at the level of faith and doctrine.

4. *Relations of Bishops to Worldwide Church.* The structure of authority as it is understood in each of our Churches is obviously undergoing considerable scrutiny, analysis, and clarification at present. In view of the diversity of Church structures that were operative within the New Testament churches and in view of an imminent expectation of our Lord's second coming at that time, it seems impossible for scholars in both our Churches to prove on historical grounds alone that Jesus himself intended any one particular structure of authority to be determinative and normative for all earthly time. Yet neither of our Churches has been or is willing to conclude from this observation that questions of authority and structure are unimportant. Even the substantial agreement on the Eucharist in the Windsor statement has ecclesial implications for the problem of authority since the Church is there considered as eucharistic community.[13]

In fact, we both share a common tradition of theological reflection, extending over many centuries and rooted both in Holy Scripture and in the ancient fathers, concerning the basic structures of authority necessary for the Church to pursue its mission. We both agree, moreover, that the structure of authority cannot be static, that its renewal involves and always has involved a forward development and not merely a backward return to some pristine *status quo*, and that in every age the Church must conceive its structure of authority not as a self-giving end but rather as a means of proclaiming the Gospel and serving the Church's mission. This measure of agreement, our Consultation believes, led ARCIC to affirm, in its Canterbury statement on Ministry and Ordination in December of 1973, that an essential element in the earliest ministry of the Church is that of the ancient term *episcopé*, meaning "oversight," which involves "fidelity to the apostolic faith, its embodiment in the life of the Church

---

12. Cf. pp. 57-60.
13. Cf. pp. 234-237.

today, and its transmission to the Church of tomorrow."[14] ARC has previously recorded substantial agreement with the Canterbury statement,[15] and we do not propose to reiterate its contents here.

We do note, however, that beginning with the time of the Reformation in the Sixteenth Century, our two Churches placed differing emphases upon the expression and interpretation of this ministry of *episcopé*. For Roman Catholics, this episcopal ministry was increasingly centered in the Bishop of Rome and its nature has appeared to be too authoritarian in the eyes of many Anglicans. For Anglicans, on the other hand, the ministry of bishops has been less centralized and the nature of their authority has appeared too vague and indefinite in the eyes of many Roman Catholics. At the same time, over the past few centuries each of our Churches has continued to grow and develop in its own separate way without the benefit of close contact or conversation with the other.

Yet in the last decade or so, thanks to a movement of change which we are entirely unable to explain apart from the providence of God, deeper understandings and fresh perspectives about the nature of *episcopé* among both Anglicans and Roman Catholics have led many of us to suspect that perhaps we are not so far apart as we seemed and indeed that perhaps we are in fact growing closer together even on this very basic question. We do both affirm, after all, that the fundamental structure of the Church should be "episcopal." In the past many Roman Catholics have seen an Anglican tendency to impose excessive constitutional limitations on the episcopal office. Many Anglicans in the past have seen a Roman Catholic tendency to impose excessive papal controls on the episcopal office. Yet both structures are in their very nature *vere episcopalis*, that is, "truly episcopal." Some Anglicans now seem increasingly convinced of the need for a greater degree of worldwide organization and focus, not only for the sake of doctrinal and liturgical cohesion but also in order to facilitate the Church's work of evangelization and service. Some Roman Catholics seem increasingly concerned to recognize and indeed protect a greater degree of local self-government, individual expression, and plurality of theological affirmation within their various regions, episcopal conferences, and even dioceses and parishes.

Neither of our Churches is entirely certain how present structures will be affected in the future, but ARC-USA is convinced that an empathetic evaluation of our past histories and present situations, an effort to enter into the experience of the other Church and to under-

---

14. Cf. I Timothy 3:1; ARCIC Canterbury statement, para. 9; Arndt and Gingrich, *Greek-English Lexicon of the New Testament*, p. 229; G.W.H. Lampe, *Patristic Greek Lexicon*, p. 532.
15. ARC/DOC III, pp. 82-84.

stand what lies behind its formulations and customs, will enable us both to work together and learn from each other. Our joint statement on "Doctrinal Agreement and Christian Unity: Methodological Considerations" proposes some principles for such a serious effort towards mutual understanding.[16]

In particular, on the question of the way in which bishops in their individual dioceses serve and relate to the worldwide mission of the universal Church, ARC believes that a certain degree of convergence may be developing between Episcopalians and Roman Catholics about the ministry of the Bishop of Rome. It is a ministry of service to his fellow bishops as well as to other Christian churches.[17] The "Synod of Bishops," for example, is a structure of recent evolution in the Roman Catholic Church that encourages us to look at the papal ministry to and with other bishops in new perspectives as a "truly episcopal" office. Among the proposals for pastoral action concluding this report we suggest a study by ARC and also the naming of a joint task force of bishops to facilitate our greater cooperation and mutual understanding of the question: What are the structures of episcopal ministry that will best enable our bishops to care for all the churches by teaching, leading, and serving the Church and peoples in the Christian life for our day?

The relation of bishops to one another and of the Bishop of Rome to other bishops, we may add, should in no way detract from the ministry bishops also share with priests, deacons, and lay people. The co-responsibility of all the people of God, both in deliberations and in the decision-making process of the Church, which received renewed emphasis for Roman Catholics in the Second Vatican Council, has long been a concept of vital importance to Anglicans and is now another aspect of convergence that both our Churches share.

While the Roman Communion has given increased importance to national and regional councils of bishops, with other forms of decentralization, history has required Anglicanism to develop means of closer communication and cohesion as a world communion. In this further example of convergence, the two churches have moved toward each other from different starting points.

The Archbishop of Canterbury, during the worldwide expansion of the Anglican Communion in the nineteenth century, instituted, as *primus inter pares,* the custom of inviting his brother bishops to Lambeth Palace every ten years to take counsel together on matters of common concern in faith, morals, and the mission of the Church. The first such conference met in 1867.

---

16. Cf. pp. 57-60.
17. See the ecumenical study *Peter in the New Testament,* ed. Raymond E. Brown, Karl P. Donfried, and John Reumann (1973).

Though the Lambeth Conferences do not claim synodical authority, they have had great influence on the life of the Communion. As the Anglican Communion grew and separate national churches were formed, more organized ways of maintaining relationships of mutual support and communication were needed. In 1968, 101 years after the first meeting, the Lambeth Conference created the Anglican Consultative Council (ACC) to meet this need.

The ACC includes bishops from all the Anglican provinces and, recognizing that priests and lay people share the ministry of Christ along with bishops, also includes representatives of these orders in its membership. Each province or national church is encouraged to identify the current goals of mission among its dioceses and to take counsel with representatives of other Anglican provinces for ways of mutual support, providing money and personnel from the stronger provinces for those that need help. These "Partners in Mission" conferences, as they are called, began in the younger churches and then expanded into similar conferences in the older churches concerning help they needed from the younger ones. Carrying out its assigned task of enabling Anglicans "to fulfill their common inter-Anglican and ecumenical responsibilities in promoting the unity, renewal, and mission of Christ's Church,"[18] the ACC assisted inter-Anglican communication among the churches on the question of ordination of women opened by the 1968 Lambeth Conference.

·At its most recent meeting, in 1976, the ACC devoted much of its report to current trends in ecumenism. Such new terms as "visible unity" and "conciliarity" seem to be opening a way to a different idea of Christian unity from the older concept of one monolithic church in each city, province, and nation. This line of thought, the report noted,[19] appeared to show convergence with Roman Catholic thinking on the *communio* model of church-to-church relationships.

5. *Ethics of the Christian Community.* The people of the Old Testament were made a unique community by the covenant God established with them. As that community, they led a visible, corporate life of witness to Yahweh. The New Covenant established in Christ, through his life, death, and resurrection, forms of a new community. By Baptism the believer enters this community of visible, corporate witness to Christ. "But you are a chosen race, a royal priesthood, a consecrated nation, a people set apart to sing the praises of God who called you out of the darkness into his wonderful light. Once you were not a people at all and now you are the People of God; once you were

---

18. Lambeth Conference 1968, *Reports and Resolutions*, p. 145 and cf. pp. 46-49.
19. Anglican Consultative Council, *Report of the Third Meeting: Trinidad 1976*, p. 16.

outside the mercy and now you have been given mercy." (1 Pt 2: 9-10)

The Christian witness of worship in the Spirit through Christ to the Father involves the entire Church in a corporate response of love and service both to God and to the whole of humankind. Such response is sometimes simply called the "Christian life-style."

The Christian life-style is based on the belief that the Triune God has redeemed all creation in Christ. Because God has first loved us, as a people as well as individually, so must we as Christians corporately and individually express our love for God and for each human being. Upon the corporate or social character of the Trinity's redemptive action for the whole human family the morality of the Christian community is built. Christian life or the Christian life-style begins as a covenant response of a people witnessing to God's love in Christ. Therefore in Christian ethics there is a primacy given to the social or corporate character of life in Christ.[20]

Episcopalians and Roman Catholics agree on the primacy given to the corporate witness of the Christian life-style. Both agree that the Church as Church has a responsibility of compassionate service to the whole of humankind, to manifest in the Spirit the Father's love shown us in Christ Jesus. How the individual Christian appropriates to himself or herself what the Church proposes as the Christian life-style has been and is a source of apparent discrepancies between the Episcopal and Roman Catholic Churches.

Christians living in the world of today are confronted with a confusing array of philosophies and values. These touch upon what it means to be a human person. Consequently new questions have risen in related areas such as human sexuality, marriage, and the family. In this kind of situation diversity in the manner of forming Christian conscience—a traditional difficulty between Roman Catholics and Episcopalians—is exacerbated as both Churches grapple separately to find what is the proper Christian response to the new questions. Though both Episcopalians and Roman Catholics hold that the ultimate subjective norm of morality is the properly informed individual conscience and therefore share the same solution to many moral problems, there is insufficient agreement as yet between them in facing the new and serious questions now before the Christian community. The initial studies made of these questions by Episcopal and Roman Catholic theologians indicate answers that are not in agreement with one another. In this situation for both our Churches

---

20. Vatican II, Pastoral Constitution on the Church in the Modern World (*Gaudium et spes*) 47-93, ed. Abbott pp. 249-308, and Dogmatic Constitution on the Church (*Lumen gentium*) 11, ed. Abbott p. 29; cf. Lambeth Conference 1968, *Reports and Resolutions*, pp. 78-81.

pastoral responsibility is all the more arduous as Christians find it increasingly difficult to reach certitude among the conflicting answers suggested to these troubling questions. Thus dialogue between the Episcopal and Roman Catholic Churches is urgently required in this new area of growing disagreement.

6.   *Personal Life in Christ.* Episcopalians and Roman Catholics believe that the relationship of Jesus with his heavenly Father is both the summit and model of the spiritual life. To be a Christian today is to believe that through the Spirit an individual now can also somehow share Jesus' self-giving love leading through the Cross to the glory of the Resurrection.

Because the human nature of Jesus is uniquely related to the Second Person of the Blessed Trinity, Jesus is both true God and true man, "consubstantial" with the Father and "consubstantial" with us. The hypostatic union of the human nature of Christ and the Word or *Logos* in no way prevents Jesus' experience of God from being truly human. It is Jesus' relationship with God that the Christian religion seeks to convey to all human beings. "He became what we are in order that He might bring us to be even what He is."[21]

Jesus' relation with God the Father is communicated to Christians in many ways. Among these are the reading and study of Scripture, meditation on the mysteries of salvation, and the devotional exercises of the Christian life. The eucharistic liturgy, with its renewed emphasis on the proclamation of the word of God, and its celebration of the presence of Christ, is regarded in both our traditions as "the summit toward which the activity of the Church is directed; at the same time it is the fountain from which all her power flows."[22] It is in liturgical worship, and especially in the eucharistic celebration, that the Christian as a member of the community worshipping the transcendent and indwelling God can realize the deepest implications of what it is to be a person, find the impetus for ethical action in the Christian style, and learn the destiny to which one is called by God in Christ through the Spirit.

Human beings live in a world that is ever changing. Christian doctrine and the visible social structure of the Christian Church are therefore necessary in order for Christians living in a world of change to discern, communicate, adapt, and transmit through different times and cultures their historical identity in Jesus as Lord and Saviour. Christians believe that this process of adaptive continuity springs

---

21. Irenaeus, *Against Heresies*, book V, preface; cf. Athanasius, *On the Incarnation*, 54.
22. Vatican II, Constitution on the Sacred Liturgy (*Sacrosanctum concilium*) 10, ed. Abbott p. 142.

from the Spirit's abiding in the Church and from the charisms that the Spirit brings.

B. *Conclusion: Pastoral Recommendations*

Part I. Areas for Further Investigation
ARC's Proposals for Future Agenda

ARC asks of its sponsoring bodies whether it should study the following problem areas:

1. In view of the ARCIC statement "Authority in the Church" and recent papers prepared for ARC on authority, the episcopacy, and papacy, we now see the possibility, after some further investigation, of drawing up a set of mutual affirmations about the ministry of the Bishop of Rome. There are points on which we believe there may well be substantial agreement between the Episcopal and Roman Catholic Churches and which should therefore be drafted on paper for further consideration by our respective bodies and authorities. Should such a statement on authority, however, be limited to more theoretical questions touching the pope and other bishops, or should it extend to more practical realities—such as the way in which Episcopalians are treating the issue of women's ordination and the way in which the recommendations of the Detroit "Call to Action" conference are being handled by Roman Catholics?

2. In view of the growing claims of Christian women for full participation and partnership with men in the life of the church and the world—a fact of contemporary life—we now recommend a study of the new and perplexing questions which arise for both our Churches. Behind the issues of changing sex roles in family and work and the still deeply divisive questions raised around the ordination of women to the presbyteral and episcopal ministries, lie fundamental theological issues. The imaging language of Fatherhood and Sonship in Christian theology and devotion has shaped our experience of God and ordained ministry as well as our experience of ourselves as women and men in relationship to each other and to God. Other images for the Holy are to be found, such as Bride, Queen, Mother, Nurturer. A careful study of the role of Mary, of other female saints, of sexual imagery for God, the Church and its ministries, and the soul, may provide important theological and spiritual guidance for our Churches today as we wrestle with the common perplexities raised by these issues of human wholeness (holiness), what it means to be a woman and a man, and how men and women image God in their being and their callings in the Church and the world.[23]

3. In view of apparent discrepancies concerning the formation of conscience in the Christian community as well as the resolution of certain moral questions in both our Churches, we recommend an investigation of the relation between normative tradition and individual conscience in our respective Churches. The relative weight that is given to the tradition of the earliest Christian centuries, as well as that given to the faith of the Church at present, in the way that consciences are formed and educated for life in Christ in each of our Churches, should be compared and then related to such current questions as abortion and the right to life, the pastoral approach to ecumenical marriages, and homosexuality.

4. In view of the particularly close relationship that both our Churches share with each other,[24] we recommend a study of the degree of unity that each of us feels necessary as prerequisite to sacramental sharing, and how each Church intends to relate this convergence between us to the ongoing ecumenical relations each of us has in many other ecumenical dialogues.[25] Must a closer relationship and even sacramental sharing between us be delayed until all Anglicans and all Roman Catholics throughout the world agree on every point that the other thinks is important, or is it possible that our growing together and sacramental sharing may be allowed to develop differently in different places? In view of the present situation, what can be said about Pope Leo XIII's *Apostolicae Curae* (1896) and the validity of Anglican Orders that will satisfy both Anglicans and Roman Catholics?

23. Cf. E. McLaughlin, "Christ My Mother: Feminine Naming and Metaphor in Medieval Spirituality," *Nashotah Review* xv (1975), and F. Jelly, O.P., "Marian Dogmas within Vatican II's Hierarchy of Truths," *Marian Studies* xxvii (1976).
24. Common Declaration of the Pope and the Archbishop of Canterbury signed in Rome, 29 April 1977; Vatican II, Decree on Ecumenism (*Unitatis Redintegratio*) 13, ed. Abbott p. 356; Pope Paul VI, statement quoted in note 1 above; *Annual Report*, Episcopal Diocesan Ecumenical Officers, 1976 survey of diocesan ecumenical priorities, showed Anglican/Roman Catholic relations "an overwhelming priority in interest and effectiveness" (p. 1).
25. For a survey of these up through 1974 see N. Ehrenstrom and G. Gassmann, *Confessions in Dialogue*, third ed., Geneva 1975. The survey of "Bilateral Conversations between the Roman Catholic Church in the U.S.A. and other Christian Communities" published in the 1972 *Proceedings of the Catholic Theological Society of America* (vol. 27) is now being updated, and a similar survey is under way for the Episcopal Church under the sponsorship of its Standing Ecumenical Commission.

Part II. Joint Task Forces
ARC's Proposals for Possible Action

ARC asks its sponsoring bodies whether ARC should now proceed to establish, with their authorization, any of the following:

1. *Joint Task Force on World Hunger.* This problem received the highest priority rating from Episcopalian diocesan ecumenical officers in their survey of February 1976 and was emphatically underlined by Pope Paul VI in his message to the International Eucharistic Congress at Philadelphia in August of the same year. What can our two Churches do together now to face this problem? There could be a joint task force of experts in social witness to be convened by our respective authorities. Possibilities: Joint letter from our bishops to our peoples, posters, conference of experts, raising of consciousness, meatless days every week, periods of fasting and abstinence, congressional legislation, etc.

2. *Joint Task Force on the Apostolate of the Church or Evangelism.* This task force would embody a common thrust in mission to which Archbishop Coggan and Pope Paul VI have jointly called us.[26] The task force could: 1) look carefully at the mission of the Christian Church to so present "Jesus Christ, in the power of the Holy Spirit, in such ways that persons may be led to believe in Him as Saviour and follow Him as Lord, within the fellowship of His Church"[27]; 2) compare the ways in which this is understood, implemented, and described in both Churches; and 3) recommend ways in which there could be a greater partnership in this common missionary imperative.

3. *Joint Task Force on Prayer and Spirituality.* The existing calendars of prayer in our two Churches, now based upon very similar liturgical years, might be enriched through the choice of special days for appropriate intercessions that would draw us more deeply into our common mission. Also, opportunities for a shared ministry of the word, through preaching, might profitably be explored. Persons gifted in spirituality, prayer, and liturgy, and other persons placed in positions

---

26. Common Declaration, 29 April 1977, para. 9: "Our divisions hinder this witness, hinder the work of Christ, but they do not close all roads we may travel together. In a spirit of prayer and of submission to God's will we must collaborate more earnestly in a 'greater common witness to Christ before the world in the very work of evangelisation. It is our desire that the means of this collaboration be sought: the increasing spiritual hunger in all parts of God's world invites us to such a common pilgrimage. This collaboration pursued to the limit allowed by truth and loyalty will create the climate in which dialogue and doctrinal convergence can bear fruit."
27. General Convention of the Episcopal Church 1973, definition of evangelism.

of leadership might be convened. Perhaps a booklet might be published jointly for widespread distribution and use.

4.   *Joint Task Force to Survey ARC Covenants.* Many of these already exist, between parishes, dioceses, seminaries, etc. Their positive accomplishments, their shortcomings and misgivings, their goals and needs, should be studied. This task force should include clergy and laity from groups already in covenant relationships.

5.   *Joint Task Force on the Pastoral Role of Bishops.* We propose a study and report on the similarities and differences in episcopal ministry between our two Churches. This task force, consisting of six or eight bishops, would be named by the Presiding Bishop of the Episcopal Church and the President of the National Conference of Catholic Bishops. How do our bishops see their roles in worship, evangelization, proclamation of the gospel, and service to the clergy and laity, as well as their relation and responsibility to the universal Church? This report should be published for the benefit of the general membership of both our Churches.

Archbishop of Canterbury's Westminster Cathedral Address

At the invitation of the Archbishop of Westminster the Archbishop of Canterbury attended an ecumenical worship service in the Catholic cathedral in London during the 1978 Week of Prayer for Christian Unity. He spoke on that occasion.

The background to the Archbishop of Canterbury's impassioned plea for eucharistic sharing now, delivered at Westminster (Roman Catholic) Cathedral in London, on January 25, 1978, at the end of the Week of Prayer for Christian Unity, is a similar address he had given on April 28, 1977, at the American Episcopal Church of St. Paul Within-the-Walls, in Rome. There, Archbishop Coggan asked, "Has not the time now arrived when we have reached such a measure of agreement on so many of the fundamentals of the gospel that a relationship of shared communion can be encouraged by the leadership of both our Churches? I would go further and ask whether our work of joint evangelization will not be seriously weakened until we are able to go to that work strengthened by our joint participation in the sacrament of Christ's body and blood." In the same address, he added that he was not, however, "asking for a blurring of the issues—and they are not inconsiderable—on which, at present, we cannot agree. Truth is not advanced by pretending not to see the divisions and disagreements which still exist."

. . . For many years it has been my great privilege to enjoy the friendship of my dear brother in Christ, Basil Hume. I have shared with him, as my friend and host, what I am saying to you in this address, and he has expressed himself happy that I should say it, even though he is unable to agree with me because of theological differences. Next week he will, I hope, speak to us with equal frankness when he is our guest at our general synod.

I think it is a measure of the maturity which dialogue between us has reached and, I would hope, a measure of the maturity of the dialogue between our two communions, that we can speak openly on matters on which as yet we are not fully agreed, one of which is the matter of our joint participation in the sacrament of the eucharist. Such frank dialogue, undertaken in deep love, is, I believe, the most fruitful way forward to the goal we both long for.

We are united in our common baptism into the triune name. We are united in our love for the Lord who loved us and gave himself up for us. We are united in our membership of his church, though there are still areas of theological interpretation in which we do not find agreement and which no doubt will continue to perplex us. We are united in our desire to be obedient to the Lord's commission to "go . . . make disciples . . . baptize . . . teach." We are united, as I have just said, in the ministry of spreading the printed word. This is a wonderful measure of unity. This is the result of the operation of the Holy Spirit. Thanks be to God.

But, let us confess it, the impact that we make on a world which, like the Greeks in St. John's Gospel, "would see Jesus," is pathetically feeble, the witness we bear is muted, the vision which we share is blurred. I ask: Why is this so? Can the reason be that we are divided at the deepest point of unity, the sacrament of the body and blood of Christ? Is this God's judgment on us for failing to grasp this nettle? We recognize our unity in baptism; we persist in disunity at the eucharist. So we go to our mission weak, where we should be strong and invigorated by joint participation in the supper of the Lord.

We shelter behind differences of doctrine, of expression, of explanation. But is there, underlying it all, almost in our subconscious, a failure to repent of the way we have injured one another in the past? My attention has recently been drawn to a passage in Dean Church's essay on Lancelot Andrews, where he says of the conflict in the reigns of Elizabeth and James I:

> Controversy, never silent, and always truculent and unsparing, was but a light matter compared with the terrible hostilities carried on, not by word, but by deed. . . . We may well be aghast at the horrors of the struggle. The deep hatreds and injuries of the political conflict gave to the theological controversy—the necessary theological controversy—an unfairness and virulence from which it has never recovered, and which have been a disgrace to Christendom, and fatal, not merely to unity, but in many ways to truth.

We are the heirs of those who shared in these terrible deeds. Our eyes, to a lesser or greater degree, have been blinded to the saving, healing truths of the Gospel. We rejoice at the three agreed statements produced by the members of the Anglican-Roman Catholic International Commission. We rejoice at the recent dedication of the memorial in Westminster Abbey to the martyrs who "divided at the Reformation by different convictions laid down their lives for Christ and conscience sake."

But should I not be asking—as indeed I now do—for the forgiveness of my Roman Catholic friends for the lingering attitudes of suspicion and coldness—even sometimes of contempt—which characterized us up to 15 or 20 years ago, and sometimes do so still? And should not that confession of sin be sealed in joint participation in the sacrament of holy communion? Is not that the way forward to that unity without absorption of which Pope Paul, echoing a phrase first used in 1925, spoke when we met in Rome last year?

Throughout the world, men and women, ordained and lay, in both our communions, are refusing to continue in disunity at what Christ intended to be the sacrament of unity, Roman Catholics receiving at Anglican hands the tokens of Christ's passion, and vice versa. I have seen this happen, and taken part in it, and been deeply moved by it, in Australasia and in other places beyond these islands. Order within the church matters, and encouragement must not be given to the breaking of the rules. But I ask: Is the Holy Spirit speaking to the leadership of our churches through the voice of the people who see, with a clarity sometimes hidden from our eyes, the scandal of disunity?

In the two famous passages in St. Matthew's Gospel (16, 19 and 18, 18) about "binding" and "loosing," it is generally recognized that in Aramaic the terms to "bind" and to "loose" are academic language for the decision of the rabbis as to what was "forbidden" or "permitted." Among us in the past, more attention has been given to binding than to loosing, to forbidding than to permitting. I ask again: Is the Spirit saying to the church: "Ye that do truly and earnestly repent you of your sins, and are in love and charity with your neighbors, draw near with faith—draw near *together* with faith—and take this holy sacrament to your comfort?"

As I pondered on this matter last week, I listened again to those words of St. Paul in which he spoke of the age-long barrier which separated Jews from Gentiles, Gentiles from Jews. He had been brought up under the old rules and regulations. Now they were annulled. The wall was down. The enmity was broken. Christ had done—was doing—his reconciling work. This is what he wrote:

> For he is himself our peace. Gentiles and Jews, he has made the two one, and in his own body of flesh and blood has broken down the enmity which stood like a dividing wall between them; for he annulled the law with its rules and regulations, so as to create out of the two a single new humanity in himself, thereby making peace. This was his purpose, to reconcile the two in a single body to God through the cross, on which he killed the enmity (Eph. 2, 14-16).

Let that be our text tonight, and let that be our guide tomorrow.

There is a Lord to be obeyed. There is a light to be passed on. There is a world to be won. We have talked about the pain of disunity long enough. Now let us act. And in the strength of the body broken and the blood outpoured, we will walk in love, and we will go in peace.

Archbishop Donald Coggan
Archbishop of Canterbury

January 25, 1978

ARC Joint Consultation: Versailles Report

Report of a meeting co-sponsored by the Anglican Consultative Council and the Secretariat for Promoting Christian Unity.

The findings of this consultation, which met at Versailles from February 27 to March 3, 1978, bear the authority only of the ten members (five from each Church) who were officially appointed by the Vatican's Unity Secretariat and by the Archbishop of Canterbury, with the Secretary General of the Anglican Consultative Council. The report notes that the Vatican decree against women's ordination (*Inter Insigniores*) does not affirm explicitly that the matter is *de jure divino*, and also—echoing similar observations made by ARC/USA in its statement on women's ordination and in its official response to the ARCIC Canterbury Statement—the report records that "those Anglican Churches which have proceeded to ordain women to the presbyterate have done so in the conviction that they have not departed from the traditional understanding of apostolic ministry (expressed, for example, in the Canterbury Statement of the Anglican-Roman Catholic International Commission)." For the list of signatories, see *One in Christ* (Turvey Abbey, England, 1978), pp. 389-392.

1. Given that certain churches of the Anglican Communion have ordained women to the presbyterate, the question posed to the consultation was not to discuss whether or not it is right to ordain women, but to consider "to what extent and in what ways churches with women priests and churches without women priests can be reconciled in sacramental fellowship."
2. A substantial majority in each Anglican church accepts the possibility of ordaining women to the presbyterate. Some churches have already proceeded to such ordinations. At this time no Anglican church has officially stated that such ordinations are impossible, though some churches have not yet considered the question officially and others have for various reasons decided not to ordain women at least for the present. The Roman Catholic Church believes that she has not the right to change the tradition "unbroken throughout the history of the church, universal in the East and the West, and considered to conform to God's plan for his church."

3. Given these two positions the question must be: Is it still possible for our two churches to establish full communion between them and if so how, since full communion presupposes the mutual recognition of ministry? On the one hand could the Roman Catholic Church, which judges it impossible, for theological reasons, to ordain women, recognize such ordinations in the Anglican Communion? How could she hold such ordinations impossible for her yet possible for the Anglican Communion?

4. On the other hand, many Anglicans find it difficult to accept the official Roman Catholic position (as expressed for example in the declaration *Inter Insigniores*) that the ministry of the church is not open to this development. Within the tension and divergence which they are experiencing over this question, the autonomous provinces of the Anglican Communion believe they are expressing their real sense of unity in diversity.

5. With the statements of the Anglican-Roman Catholic International Commission and with the sharing and collaboration which are growing everywhere between Anglicans and Roman Catholics, we continue to discover new hope of unity; hence it has seemed to us necessary to pose the problem in its clearest form. Because of their mutual esteem neither communion can take lightly the fact that the other seems either to do something not warranted by the will of Christ for Ւ church or to be lacking in sensitivity to the promptings of the Holy Spirit.

6. Two things may be seen as ground for hope. First there is the fact that those Anglican churches which have proceeded to ordain women to the presbyterate have done so in the conviction that they have not departed from the traditional understanding of apostolic ministry (expressed for example in the Canterbury Statement of the Anglican-Roman Catholic International Commission). In the second place there is the fact that the recent Roman Catholic declaration does not affirm explicitly that this matter is *de jure divino*. These facts would seem not to exclude the possibility of future developments.

7. These developments might well be stimulated by deeper dialogue on those noticeable differences which have been emphasized by this new obstacle—matters such as human sexuality, culture and tradition, freedom and authority, among others. Simultaneously, despite the difficulty in this issue, both Anglicans and Roman Catholics feel themselves committed to continue exploring the new shapes of ministry to which the Holy Spirit may be calling them, as well as to a new sense of unity with one another. The rapidity of change in our times, the great diversities of culture and circumstance in which the churches must minister, and the growing characteristic contribution of the Third World to theology, demand openness, flexibility and a readiness to accept and affirm differences in form and style. How this is to be achieved in fidelity to the tradition which we share is one of the challenges which face the church in our time.

8. While we do not underrate the reality of this obstacle, we are convinced that our communions ought to maintain that deep trust in each other which has been built up over recent years. We have a grave responsibility to continue and intensify cooperation and dialogue in everything that promotes our growing together toward full unity in Christ. In this the churches will be sustained by their confidence and hope in the Holy Spirit, who alone can bring the effort to fulfillment.

March 1978

The Roman Catholic members, appointed by the Vatican Secretariat, were as follows:

Father Yves Congar, OP, Couvent des Dominicains, Paris, France

Father Eric Doyle, OFM, Franciscan Study Centre, Canterbury, England

Father Pierre Duprey, WF, Under Secretary, Vatican Secretariat for Promoting Christian Unity

Father John Hotchkin, Secretary, United States' Bishops Ecumenical Commission—Co-Chairman

Msgr. William Purdy, Vatican Secretariat for Promoting Christian Unity, who also acted as Co-Secretary

The Anglican members, appointed by the Archbishop of Canterbury and the Secretary General of the Anglican Consultative Council, were as follows:

Rt. Rev. Donald Cameron, Assistant Bishop of Sydney, Australia

Rev. Professor Edward Fashole-Luke, Fourah Bay College, Sierra Leone

Rev. Professor James Griffiss, Nashotah House, U.S.A.

Miss Christian Howard, York, England

Rt. Rev. Barry Valentine, Bishop of Rupert's Land, Canada—Co-Chairman

(Rev. Christopher Hill, Assistant Chaplain, Archbishop of Canterbury's Counsellors on Foreign Relations, acted as Co-Secretary)

Lambeth Conference: Selected Resolutions

The Lambeth Conference, attended by the bishops of the Anglican Communion meets every ten years to take counsel and offer recommendations to the provinces of the communion on matters of importance before the Church. Among the resolutions of the Lambeth Conference of 1978 are the following.

The 1978 Lambeth statement, which was set in the context of generally positive ecumenical resolutions, was and is the most authoritative international Anglican statement on the question of unity within a worldwide Church divided over the fact of women's ordination. It attempts to maintain a delicate but classical Anglican balance in this situation, and its comments at the end are addressed particularly to the Roman Catholic Church. For further information on this topic, see chapter 7 of *Discerning God's Will: The Complete Eyewitness Report of the Eleventh Lambeth Conference*, by James B. Simpson and Edward M. Story (New York: Nelson, 1979).

Women in the Priesthood

1. The Conference notes that since the last Lambeth Conference in 1968, the diocese of Hong Kong, the Anglican Church of Canada, the Episcopal Church in the United States of America and the Church of the Province of New Zealand have admitted women to the presbyterate, and that eight other member Churches of the Anglican Communion have now either agreed or approved in principle or stated that there are either no fundamental or no theological objections to the ordination of women to the historic threefold ministry of the Church.

   We also note that other of its member Churches have not yet made a decision on the matter. Others again have clearly stated that they do hold fundamental objections to the ordination of women to the historic threefold ministry of the Church.

2. The Conference acknowledges that both the debate about the ordination of women as well as the ordinations themselves have, in some Churches, caused distress and pain to many on both sides. To heal these and to maintain and strengthen fellowship

is a primary pastoral responsibility of all, and especially of the bishops.

3. The Conference also recognizes
    1. the autonomy of each of its member Churches, acknowledging the legal right of each Church to make its own decision about the appropriateness of admitting women to Holy Orders;
    2. That such provincial action in this matter has consequences of the utmost significance for the Anglican Communion as a whole.

4. The Conference affirms its commitment to the preservation of unity within and between all member Churches of the Anglican Communion.

5. The Conference therefore:
    1. encourages all member Churches of the Anglican Communion to continue in communion with one another, notwithstanding the admission of women (whether at present or in the future) to the ordained ministry of some member Churches;
    2. in circumstances in which the issue of the ordination of women has caused, or may cause, problems of conscience, urges that every action possible be taken to ensure that all baptized members of the Church continue to be in communion with their bishop and that every opportunity be given for all members to work together in the mission of the Church irrespective of their convictions regarding this issue;
    3. requests the Anglican Consultative Council
        a. to use its good offices to promote dialogue between those member Churches which ordain women and those which do not, with a view to exploring ways in which the fullest use can be made of women's gifts within the total ministry of the Church in our Communion; and
        b. to maintain, and wherever possible extend, the present dialogue with Churches outside the Anglican family.

6. Consistent with the foregoing, this Conference
    1. declares its acceptance of those member Churches which now ordain women, and urges that they respect the convictions of those provinces and dioceses which do not;
    2. declares its acceptance of those member Churches which do not ordain women, and urges that they respect the convictions of those provinces and dioceses which do;
    3. with regard to women who have been ordained in the Anglican Communion being authorized to exercise their ministry in provinces which have not ordained women, we recommend that, should synodical authority be given to enable them to exercise it, it be exercised only
        a. where pastoral need warrants and

      b.   where such a ministry is agreeable to the bishop, clergy and people where the ministry is to be exercised and where it is approved by the legally responsible body of the parish, area, or institution where such a ministry is to be exercised.

7.   We recognize that our accepting this variety of doctrine and practice in the Anglican Communion may disappoint the Roman Catholic, Orthodox and Old Catholic Churches, but we wish to make it clear:

      1.   that the holding together of diversity within a unity of faith and worship is part of the Anglican heritage;

      2.   that those who have taken part in ordinations of women to the priesthood believe that these ordinations have been into the historic ministry of the Church as the Anglican Communion has received it; and

      3.   that we hope the dialogue between these other Churches and the member Churches of our Communion will continue because we believe that we still have understanding of the truth of God and his will to learn from them as together we all move towards a fuller catholicity and a deeper fellowship in the Holy Spirit.

8.   This Conference urges that further discussions about the ordinations of women be held within a wider consideration of theological issues of ministry and priesthood.

For the Motion	316
Against	37
Abstentions	17

Women in the Episcopate

While recognizing that a member Church of the Anglican Communion may wish to consecrate a woman to the episcopate, and accepting that such member Church must act in accordance with its own constitution, the Conference recommends that no decision to consecrate be taken without consultation with the episcopate through the primates and overwhelming support in any member Church and in the diocese concerned, lest the bishop's office should become a cause of disunity instead of a focus of unity.

Women in the Diaconate

The Conference recommends, in accordance with resolution 32(c) of the Lambeth Conference of 1968, those member Churches which do not at present ordain women as deacons now to consider making the necessary legal and liturgical changes to enable them to do so, instead of admitting them to a separate order of deaconesses.

The Anglican-Roman Catholic International Commission

The conference:
1. welcomes the work of the Anglican-Roman Catholic International Commission which was set up jointly by the Lambeth Conference of 1968 and by the Vatican Secretariat for Promoting Christian Unity.
2. recognizes in the three Agreed Statements of this Commission* a solid achievement, one in which we can recognize the faith of our Church, and hopes that they will provide a basis for sacramental sharing between our two Communions if and when the finished Statements are approved by the respective authorities of our Communions;
3. invites the ARCIC to provide further explication of the Agreed Statements in consideration of responses received by them;
4. commends to the appropriate authorities in each Communion further consideration of the implications of the Agreed Statements in the light of the report of the Joint Preparatory Commission (the Malta Report received by the Lambeth Conference 1968—see p. 134 of its report), with a view to bringing about a closer sharing between our two communions in life, worship and mission;
5. asks the Secretary General of the Anglican Consultative Council to bring this resolution to the attention of the various synods of the Anglican Communion for discussion and action;
6. asks that in any continuing Commission, the Church of the South and the East be adequately represented.

Anglican/Roman Catholic Marriages

The Conference welcomes the report of the Anglican-Roman Catholic Commission on "The Theology of Marriage and its Application to Mixed Marriages" (1975).

In particular we record our gratitude for the general agreement on the theology of Christian marriage there outlined and especially

---

*Eucharistic Doctrine (the Windsor statement, 1971), Ministry and Ordination (Canterbury, 1973), and Authority in the Church (Venice, 1976).

for the affirmation of the "first order principle"[1] of life-long union (i.e., in the case of a break-down of a marriage). We also welcome the recognition that the differing pastoral practices of our two traditions do in fact recognize and seek to share a common responsibility for those for whom "*no* course *absolutely* consonant with the first order principle of marriage as a life-long union may be available." We also endorse the recommendations of the Commission in respect of inter-Church marriages:

1. That, after joint preparation and pastoral care given by both the Anglican and Roman Catholic counsellors concerned, a marriage may validly and lawfully take place before the duly authorized minister of either party, without the necessity of Roman Catholic dispensation:

2. that, as an alternative to an affirmation or promise by the Roman Catholic party in respect of the baptism and upbringing of any children, the Roman Catholic parish priest may give a written assurance to his bishop that he has put the Roman Catholic partner in mind of his or her obligations and that the other spouse knows what these are.

We note that there are some variations in different regions in the provisions of Roman Catholic Directories on inter-Church marriages. We nevertheless warmly welcome the real attempts of many Roman Catholic Episcopal Conferences to be pastorally sensitive to those problems arising out of their regulations, which remain an obstacle to the continued growth of fraternal relations between us. In particular, we note a growing Roman Catholic understanding that a decision as to the baptism and upbringing of any children should be made within the unity of the marriage, in which the Christian conscience of both partners must be respected. We urge that this last development be encouraged.

The problems associated with marriage between members of our two Communions continue to hinder inter-Church relations and progress towards unity. While we recognize that there has been an improved situation in some places as a result of the Motu Proprio the general principles underlying the Roman Catholic position are unacceptable to Anglicans. Equality of conscience as between partners in respect of all aspects of their marriage (and in particular with regard to the baptism and religious upbringing of children) is something to be affirmed both for its own sake and for the sake of an improved relationship between the Churches.

---

1. See Anglican-Roman Catholic Marriages (London, CIO 1975) p. 21, para. 49.

Priesthood and the Eucharist

A Common Statement by the Joint Study Group of Representatives
of the Roman Catholic Church in Scotland and the
Scottish Episcopal Church

The present statement was accepted by the Commission for Christian
Unity (Scotland) of the Roman Catholic Church at its meeting in
Glasgow on 1 September 1979, and forwarded to the Bishops' Conference for discussion and comment. They replied:

> The statement was discussed at a meeting of the Roman Catholic
> Bishops' Conference of Scotland on 18 September 1979. The Conference wishes to thank the Joint Study Group for their excellent
> work and warmly commends the statement as a most useful basis
> for study.

At a meeting held on 17 October 1979, of the Provincial Synod
of the Scottish Episcopal Church, the following resolution was passed:

> That this Synod:
> i. thanks the members of the Episcopalian/Roman Catholic Joint
> Study Group for their work over the past eleven years and for the
> three common statements they have produced in that time;
> ii. welcomes the common statement 'Priesthood and the Eucharist,'
> hopes that it will be published as soon as possible, and commends
> it for serious study at all levels in the Church, wherever possible
> jointly with members of both Churches, and asks that reports be
> returned to the Inter-Church Relations Committee.

Membership of the Joint Study Group

Roman Catholic Church

Western Group:
Rev. Desmond Strain (convener)
Mr. James Breen
Rev. John H. Fitzsimmons
Rev. James Foley
Mrs. M. Josephine McMenamin
Mr. Frank McMillan (died December, 1974)
Rev. Columba Ryan, O.P.

Eastern Group:
Rev. James Quinn, S.J. (convener)
Rev. Matthew J. Donoghue
Rev. Robert Hendrie
Rev. Hugh White

Scottish Episcopal Church

Western Group:	Rev. Canon Hugh McIntosh (convener)
	Rev. Canon A. Oswald Barkway
	Rev. Canon John F. A. Farrant
	Mrs. E. Margaret Pocklington
	Dr. Robert A. Shanks
	*Very Rev. Samuel S. Singer
	Rev. John A. Trimble
Eastern Group:	Rev. Michael C. Paternoster (convener)
	Rev. Alexander S. Black
	*Rev. Canon Wilfred B. Currie
	Rev. James W. Duffy
	*Dr. Robert Gould
	*Rev. Donald A. Guthrie
Consultant-Observer:	*Rev. Richard F. Baxter (Scottish Churches' House)
	Rev. John S. Summers (Scottish Churches' House; died August, 1977)

Chairman:
James Breen

Secretary:
Rev. M. C. Paternoster,
The Rectory,
35 Gurney Street,
Stonehaven,
Kincardineshire, AB3 2EB

Foreword

The Joint Study Group was formed in 1968 after consultations between the Most Rev. Gordon Joseph Gray, Archbishop of St. Andrews and Edinburgh, the Most Rev. James Donald Scanlan, Archbishop of Glasgow, the Most Rev. Francis H. Moncreiff, Bishop of Glasgow and Galloway, Primus of the Scottish Episcopal Church and the Right Rev. Kenneth M. Carey, Bishop of Edinburgh.

At its first meeting in plenary session on 10 October 1968, the Group decided to form two regional groups based on Edinburgh and Glasgow. Each group, composed of clerical and lay members of both our Churches, discusses sometimes the same topic, sometimes a dif-

---

*later resigned

ferent part of our remit, exchanges papers which embody its thinking
and then we meet in plenary session to harmonise our views and
agree on their expression. Our final reports are submitted to our
sponsoring bodies: on the one hand, to the Commission for Christian
Unity and through it to the Bishops' Conference of the Roman Catholic Church in Scotland, and, on the other hand, to the Inter-Church
Relations Committee and through it to the Provincial Synod of the
Scottish Episcopal Church.

In 1969, we submitted the first-fruits of our discussion, a common
statement on "The Nature of Baptism and its Place in the Life of the
Church." Encouraged by the warm reception of this document, we
suggested that we might be permitted to continue our discussions
and proposed as a suitable subject "The Ecclesial Nature of the Eucharist." The appropriate Church authorities readily agreed. After four
years' discussion we published our report in 1973 and were highly
gratified not only by the agreement reached among ourselves, but
also by the public welcome accorded to the report both at home and
abroad. The increasing understanding that flowed from our meetings
and our desire to continue our search for unity led us to ask for a
continuation of our discussions. The document we now present,
"Priesthood and the Eucharist" is, we hope, worthy of the lengthy
and lively discussions which went into its composition. We are especially grateful to those members of our groups who, with infinite
patience, produced innumerable drafts before agreement was finally
reached.

During the past six years, we have had many changes in the
composition of our groups and, sadly, two deaths. Frank McMillan,
a founder member, died in December 1974, and Rev. John S. Sum-
mers, an observer from Scottish Churches Council, died in August
1977. Rev. James Quinn, S.J., our initial secretary who, with his metic-
ulous scholarship and wide ecumenical experience, had been so helpful in resolving many of our difficulties, left in October 1976, to become
spiritual director in the Beda College, Rome. Although he continued
to attend our meetings when his leave permitted and sent us his
written comments, he was not present at our final deliberations. We
should like to place on record our special thanks to Father Quinn and
to those other former representatives who contributed so much to
the content and warmth of our meetings. The new representatives
have brought their own special insights and have contributed signif-
icantly to the final form of our document.

Our scripture references are taken from the *Common Bible*, an
ecumenical edition of the *Revised Standard Version*, published by Collins (Glasgow) 1973.

Preamble

On completing our report on "The Ecclesial Nature of the Eucharist,"
the Joint Study Group decided it was opportune to turn to a related
theme: the nature of the ministry of bishop and priest in relation to
the celebration of the eucharist. In the course of our discussions, we
began to focus our attention on the meaning of "priesthood" in relation to the eucharist, thus leaving for future study the important topic
of the role of the bishop and priest as preacher, teacher and pastor.
Our present study came to be organised around three main headings:
1.   the unique priesthood of Christ;
2.   the priesthood of the faithful of the Church as a whole and of
the Christian as an individual;
3.   the "ministerial" priesthood of the bishop and priest.
    While the notion of priesthood is rightly used in speaking of the
Church and its ministers, it does not exhaust what can be said about
them.
    The nature and functions of bishop and priest are not dependent
on some pre-conceived notion of priesthood, but become apparent
only as we inspect what the Church intends its officials to do. For
this reason, we have looked carefully at the ceremonies of ordination
to determine what this understanding is.

Choice of Approach

From the variety of New Testament thinking on the priesthood, we
have chosen to approach our subject through the concepts of consecration and mission. This is the approach suggested by the Second
Vatican Council: "The Lord Jesus, 'whom the Father has made holy
and sent into the world' (Jn. 10, 36), has made his whole Mystical
Body share in the anointing by the Holy Spirit with which he himself
has been anointed. For in him all the faithful are made a holy and
royal priesthood" (*Decree on the Ministry and Life of Priests*, ch. 1 para.
2). It is also given pride of place in the Roman Pontifical (official
English translation, 1978) when the bishop addresses the candidate
for ordination with the words:

> It is true that God has made his entire people a royal priesthood in
> Christ. But our High Priest, Jesus Christ, also chose some of his
> followers to carry out publicly in the Church a priestly ministry in
> his name on behalf of mankind. He was sent by the Father, and he
> in turn sent the apostles into the world; through them and their
> successors, the bishops, he continues his work as teacher, priest and
> shepherd.

A divine consecration and mission are implied in the Code of Canons of the Episcopal Church in Scotland when reference is made to the divine institution of the threefold ministry (Canon 1, 1).

Definitions

The sense in which these key terms, consecration and mission, are to be understood is explored in the first part of this document. For the moment, it might be helpful to have before us a brief definition of their meaning. By "consecration," we understand initially the communication of God's holiness to the Incarnate Son, and through him to man. As a result of this consecration, man is reconciled to God. Sharing in the divine life, man becomes holy in the Spirit, and so able in his turn to consecrate and offer redeemed humanity to God. Similarly by "mission" we understand the Christian's vocation to communicate this holiness of God to the world. In other words, they are dynamic terms which express the inner life of God himself, Father, Son and Holy Spirit, and the communication of this life to man.

Christian Priesthood

In seeking to express our understanding of the priesthood of God's people, we have tried to concentrate our attention on what is specific and original in the Christian idea of priesthood as such. The marked reticence of the New Testament as a whole with regard to the actual expressions "priest," "priesthood" and "sacrifice" in relation to Christ himself is a fact that we have taken into account; we have recognised an attempt on the part of the New Testament writers to avoid confusion between what they are intent on communicating and the ritual aspects of the Old Testament's ways of thought in relation to the Levitical Priesthood. It is precisely because there is a specific and original element in Christ's priesthood that this reticence manifests itself. Even the great exception, the Letter to the Hebrews, develops its argument on the priesthood of Christ precisely by insisting on the differences between his priesthood and that of the Old Testament. As we follow the argument of the Letter to the Hebrews, it becomes reasonably clear that what is specific and original in the priesthood of Christ is this—his offering is the offering of himself, his personal obedience unto death—not merely through conventions and ritual, but in reality. His priesthood is rooted in the mystery of his being, and it is in recognising this that we can discern a value "once and for all" in his offering. As Son of God, Christ manifests in himself and in his offering a true union with God the Father—there is, in this unique case, no separation between the victim and God, between the priest who offers and God. Then as Son of Man and Servant of the Lord, he identifies himself with sinful humanity, and so we can see an identity between this priest and the people for whom he offers himself.

It is only with a theology of fulfilment as it subsequently developed that the earlier reticence was superseded by a later reflection which began to see in the priesthood of Christ the reality of which the Old Testament priesthood had been the shadow and figure. There is a pattern of continuity and at the same time of discontinuity running through the New Testament vision of the fulfilment of the Old Testament and its institutions, in Christ and the New Covenant. In relation to Christ's priesthood, this means that on the one hand there is the recognition of him as a priest in the line of Melchizedek, and on the other hand an awareness that his priesthood is not like Aaron's. The basic point is that Christ sums up in himself all the different types of mediation that the Old Testament had envisaged; so that he is not just a priest, he is the perfect priest. The access to God which the priesthood of the Old Testament looked to has become a reality for the people of God through the priesthood of Christ. "Since we are justified by faith, we have peace with God through Our Lord Jesus Christ. Through him, we have obtained access to this grace in which we stand, and we rejoice in our hope of sharing the glory of God" (Rom. 5, 1-2).

An important element in our study was concerned with a problem of language. The word "priest" in contemporary English is used in two senses:

1. to describe a rank;
2. to describe a function.

The first sense differentiates the priest from the bishop, the second, in an important sense, equates the priest with the bishop. Priest and bishop have different ranks and functions in the ordained ministry, but they share the same function as celebrants of the eucharistic sacrifice. The development of these two usages of the one word "priest" is treated in the third appendix to throw light on a latent source of ambiguity.

Chapter I
The Priesthood of Christ
"Consecrated and Sent"

The Starting Point: Christ the Good Shepherd

1. Our Lord presented himself to the world in the role of the Good Shepherd who would call his own sheep by name, who would go ahead of them and lead them to pasture, and who would finally lay

down his life for them. For this purpose, he had been "consecrated and sent" into the world (Jn. 10, 36). Both our traditions are united in embracing the constant teaching of the Catholic Church that there is one shepherd of the flock and one priesthood, the priesthood of Christ, and that this priesthood derives ultimately from the consecration and mission of the Incarnate Son of God by his Father.

2.   We begin with a brief reflection on the priesthood of Christ understood in terms of consecration and mission, and we do so in the conviction that the priesthood of the faithful and the ministerial priesthood, together with the other ministries in the Church, can be understood only in their relationship to the consecration and mission of Christ himself.

3.   In the rich variety of New Testament thought, we have explored the ways in which the consecration and mission of the Son are revealed, and we find there both the continuity of the divine plan of salvation and the stages in its revelation and unfolding in history. Each stage reveals a new dimension to the consecration and mission of the Son and as such contributes to our understanding of his priesthood.

The Salient Moments in the Priesthood of Christ

4.   (i) In the Eternity of God.

In considering the salient moments of this revelation, we see that the ultimate source of the consecration and mission of the Son is the unfathomable love of the Father.

> For God so loved the world that he gave his only Son, that whoever believes in him should not perish but have eternal life. For God sent the Son into the world, not to condemn the world, but that the world might be saved through him (Jn. 3, 16 f).
>
> Father, I desire that they also, whom thou hast given me, may be with me where I am, to behold my glory which thou has given me in thy love for me before the foundation of the world (Jn. 17, 24).

This divine decree, inspired by love for the world, is an act of election and consecration in that it designates the Son from all eternity for a specific mission, the salvation of mankind. In this sense, therefore, the consecration of the Son and his priesthood are eternal. They belong to the mystery hidden from all ages in the mind of the Father:

> The mystery hidden for ages and generations but now made manifest to his saints. To them God chose to make known how great among the Gentiles are the riches of the glory of this mystery, which is Christ in you, the hope of glory (Col. 1, 26 f).

5. (iia) The Incarnation—Unique Point of Man's Reconciliation with God.

This primordial act of consecration, hidden in the life of the Godhead, comes to light with the Incarnation. The Incarnation is presented in the New Testament as the same act of consecration and mission now unfolding in history. With the Incarnation, the divine plan, previously hidden in the mind of the Father, is revealed and begins to come into effect in the lives of men. Understood in this way, the Incarnation is a moment of consecration and mission when, in the fulness of time, the divine plan of salvation enters its definitive stage:

> For he has made known to us in all wisdom and insight the mystery of his will, according to his purpose which he set forth in Christ as a plan for the fullness of time, to unite all things in him, things in heaven and things on earth (Eph. 1, 9 f).

When we speak of the priesthood of Christ, therefore, we speak of the Incarnation which renders him the perfect mediator between God and man because in him God and man are perfectly reconciled. Here lies not only the essence of his priesthood, but also its uniqueness. In no one else do God and man come together so as to enjoy such personal union of the divine and the human.

6. (iib) The Incarnation within the History of Salvation.

Although the Incarnation is a privileged moment in history when God and man come together in a personal union, it should be understood against the background of the history of the Chosen People. The Incarnation is the high-point of the whole process of reconciliation which began with the promise of salvation at the beginning of human history and will continue till all things are restored in Christ. This sense of historical perspective, coupled with a vision of the final outcome of the Incarnation, finds clear expression in the prologue to the Letter to the Hebrews:

> In many and various ways God spoke of old to our fathers by the prophets; but in these last days he has spoken to us by a Son, whom he appointed the heir of all things, through whom also he created the world. He reflects the glory of God and bears the very stamp of his nature, upholding the universe by his word of power. When he had made purification for sins, he sat down at the right hand of the Majesty on high, having become as much superior to angels as the name he has obtained is more excellent than theirs (Heb. 1, 1 ff).

Such an understanding of the Incarnation in its entirety allows us to appreciate the continuation of the priesthood of Christ in the life of the Church, which is his body, as well as the preparation for that priesthood in the experience of the Chosen People.

7. (iic) The Incarnation and the Levitical Priesthood.

To relate the priesthood of Christ to the Incarnation is not to dissociate it entirely from the Old Testament priesthood. That priesthood was a significant part in the whole process of salvation and was an integral part in the Covenant between God and his people. The ritual and imagery of the Old Covenant priesthood were superseded by their fulfilment in the New. In the light of the New Covenant, the Letter to the Hebrews is able to interpret the final triumph of the Risen Christ in terms of the entry of the High Priest into the heavenly sanctuary at the head of his redeemed community:

> But when Christ appeared as a high priest of the good things that have come, then through the greater and more perfect tent (not made with hands, that is, not of this creation) he entered once for all into the Holy Place, taking not the blood of goats and calves but his own blood, thus securing an eternal redemption (Heb. 9, 11 f).

Yet it is with a sense of the uniqueness of the priesthood of Christ born of his identity as the Son of God that Hebrews takes inspiration from the figure of Melchizedek:

> This becomes even more evident when another priest arises in the likeness of Melchizedek, who has become a priest, not according to a legal requirement concerning bodily descent but by the power of an indestructible life. For it is witnessed of him, "Thou art a priest for ever, after the order of Melchizedek." On the one hand, a former commandment is set aside because of its weakness and uselessness (for the law made nothing perfect); on the other hand, a better hope is introduced, through which we draw near to God (Heb. 7, 15 ff).

The Levitical Priesthood and the Old Covenant give way to the priesthood of Christ and the New Covenant to which they bore witness and of which they were the imperfect image.

Christ's Priesthood: Unique Yet Shared

13. The Priestly Prayer of Christ, recorded in the fourth Gospel, speaks in similar terms of the hour of death and resurrection as an hour in which the consecration and mission of Jesus are seen in all their glory and in which the disciples are privileged to share:

> As thou didst send me into the world, so I have sent them into the world. And for their sake I consecrate myself, that they also may be consecrated in truth (Jn. 17, 18 f).

14. We began our consideration of the priesthood of Christ with an affirmation of its uniqueness, born of the uniqueness of his identity as the Son of God (cf. Para. 1). Yet our understanding of his priesthood would be far from complete if it did not take into account our own share in that consecration and mission.

15. Through baptism and confirmation, we are sealed by the Spirit of holiness (Eph. 1, 13) and as members of a priestly people we are made acceptable as an offering (Rom. 15, 16). We are exhorted to offer our "bodies as a living sacrifice, holy and acceptable to God" (Rom. 12, 1). This raises the question of how this sacrifice of our daily lives is related to the sacrifice of Calvary and of the eucharist. In what sense do we, as the people of the New Covenant, offer sacrifice to God in union with the sacrificial self-offering of Christ? This is the question to which we must now address ourselves.

Chapter II
The Priesthood of the Faithful

16. Over the years, both our traditions have grown in their understanding of the mystery of the Church. Side by side with this growth, there has been a concentration of interest on the idea of the "Priesthood of the Faithful." No doubt, there is a greater degree of "newness" in this idea for some than for others; but it remains a fact that in the understanding of both our Churches it has meant a conscious attempt to hold together in a fruitful tension two things: the "common priesthood" of all the faithful and the "ministerial" or "hierarchical" priesthood, along with an estimation of the similarities and differences between them.[1] There is always the danger that this tension will be resolved by the adoption of one or other of two extreme positions: complete separation of the two kinds of priesthood or a complete fusion of the two. The result of this extreme resolution of the tension is that, on the one hand, the "common priesthood" is reduced to the level of the purely metaphorical (in which case it is not "priesthood" in any proper sense) or, on the other hand, the laity are presented as already in possession of all the attributes of the "ministerial priesthood" (in which case there is no need for a distinct "ministerial priesthood" in the Church). In its last joint report, this Study Group has already touched on this matter in connection with

---

1. The terminology adopted here is that used by Vatican II in the Dogmatic Constitution on the Church—"Lumen Gentium" (21/11/64)—sect. 10. Cf. "The Documents of Vatican II" (ed. Wm. Abbott and J. Gallagher, 1966), pp. 26-27 and "Vatican Council II: The Conciliar and Post-Conciliar Documents" (ed. A. Flannery, 1975) pp. 360-361.

the eucharist.[2] What the Group intends at this point is a reflection on the nature of the "common priesthood" of all the members of the Church, in an effort to situate it in relation to the unique priesthood of Christ and to the "ministerial priesthood" as it is understood in the Roman Catholic and Episcopalian traditions.

17. In our preamble, we have already indicated what we believe to be specific and original in the Christian idea of priesthood, relating it to the priesthood of Christ, from whom all Christian priesthood derives.

18. *A New Religious Experience.*

What the faith of the Church is trying to express, then, when it speaks of the "priesthood of the faithful" is a totally new religious experience for humanity. The barriers are broken down; all separation between God and men is done away with; God and men are reconciled; through his offering of himself, Christ has become "our peace" (Eph. 2, 14). What the idea of the "priesthood of the faithful" seeks to express is this aspect of the mystery of Christ as it becomes a reality in the lives of his people. Through their baptism, Christians are introduced into this new religious experience which Christ's priesthood has made possible for them. In baptism, the faithful are made one with Christ who is their life, they are united with his priestly work and their lives take on the character of his priesthood. Their lives are "hid with Christ in God" (Col. 3, 3), and their whole existence takes on a priestly dimension, because the Christ with whom they are thus united is Christ the High Priest. In the light of this totally new religious situation in which all those who are baptised in Christ are caught up (and in which all men are destined to share) we can speak of the "common priesthood" of the faithful. We can follow the lead given by the New Testament and define the Christian people as "a chosen race, a royal priesthood, a holy nation, God's own people" (1 Pet. 2, 9). The focal point of Christ's priesthood we discern in his giving of himself: he is, above all, "Jesus Our Lord who was put to death for our trespasses and raised for our justification" (Rom. 4, 25). At the same time, his offering of himself brings with it a new dimension to our lives: since God "did not spare his own Son but gave him up for us all, will he not also give us all things with him?" (Rom. 8, 32). The gift of God is our own identification with Christ the priest: to share in his saving work is the task which is set before us, and the achievement of this work in us and through us is the work of the Holy Spirit.

---

2. Cf. "The Ecclesial Nature of the Eucharist. A report by the Joint Study Group of Representatives of the Roman Catholic Church in Scotland and the Scottish Episcopal Church," pp. 84-85.

It is for this reason that the priesthood of Christ becomes the criterion by which we judge the life and ministry of the Church and of the individual Christian. If there is any priesthood in our midst, then it must be his; if there is to be any priestly dignity, then it must be a share in his priestly dignity. Our lives are to be modelled on his, involving, therefore, the offering of ourselves in the likeness of his self-offering. Of ourselves, we have nothing to offer, and yet, through our incorporation into Christ, our lives in all their variety and in the different situations which they encounter, take on a priestly quality that enables us to consecrate all our work and activity in the worship and service of God, the Father of all. It is in this sense that we ought to understand the nature of the people of God as a priestly people. Here, we would recall what was said before about the Church as sacrament of Christ and the reasons why we have tried to locate the full affirmation of the Church's identity in the eucharistic presence, here and now, of Christ's own offering of himself as a sacrifice for the reconciliation of God and men.[3]

19. *Priesthood of the Faithful and Sacrifice.*

As members of a priestly people, all Christians are called upon to offer sacrifice. Such spiritual sacrifice, springing from the depths of an existence that is animated and transformed by the power of the Holy Spirit, is real, because it includes the whole of human life in all its different dimensions. What Christ has achieved in his once-and-for-all offering of himself has to take root in the lives of all those who belong to Christ through baptism and the Spirit, and so become the basis of a true offering of self to the Father on the part of every Christian. When we look at the involvement of the people of God in the world and its affairs in this perspective, the ideal of a priestly people consecrating and offering the whole of human life to God becomes clearer. As the Church grows in its understanding of itself in the light of the priesthood of Christ as shared by all who belong to him, then it is natural that it will spell out the implications of priesthood for the whole range of human experience. So, we come to understand that the transformation of all our activities and our responsibilities—personal, familial, professional, social, national and international—into an offering of our whole existence to the Father is our priestly action in the world. An awareness of the priestly nature of the Christian life enables the members of the Church to look upon their involvement in the world and its affairs in a new and positive light. Our social concern, our political action, our work itself—all of these are not pursued for their own sake, but as a real and tangible

---

3. Cf. "The Ecclesial Nature of the Eucharist," p. 89.

expression of the radically new religious situation in which we find ourselves because we have a share in Christ's priesthood. And just as there can be no true sacrifice without cost, the sacrifice of the people of God is costly. It is nothing short of the offering of ourselves, an offering made possible through our identification with Christ the High Priest.

20. *Priesthood of the Faithful and Mission.*

The last report of this Joint Study Group spoke of the relationship between the eucharist and the mission of the Church.[4] Further reflection enables us to place this mission more closely in its connection with the priestly nature of God's people. Just as Christ himself is "consecrated and sent," so those who belong to him are "consecrated" and "sent" in the power of the Holy Spirit in their baptism and confirmation to bring about that "recapitulation" which will unite all things in Christ (cf. Eph. 1, 10). This is of the essence of the Christian life. When St. Paul spoke in these terms of bringing all things in heaven and earth under Christ as head, he was in fact outlining the task which is committed to the priestly people of God. His vision, based as it was on the clear appreciation of the significance of Christ's self-offering and the reconciliation achieved by it, embraced a world given power and hope to overcome its divisions of race, culture, or politics, a human race formed into one family of God. The effort to bring about this unity, the striving towards the formation of this family, is the priestly activity of God's people by definition. Just as the real and decisive purpose of the life of Christ is to be discerned in his offering of himself, the aim and purpose of the priestly people, who have come into being as a consequence of his action and bear his name, are to be found in a similar giving of self, through which the priestly people transform this world and build it into the Kingdom of God.[5]

The final purpose of the sacrifices of the people of God, spiritual and real, is the building up of the body of Christ. It is in the light of this that we can say that the essence of the Christian life is priesthood, a share in the priesthood of Christ himself.

21. *Priesthood of the Faithful and the Kingdom of God.*

In Christ we are able to see a humanity which is introduced to a new kind of existence where the meaning of life and death is fully expressed

4. Cf. Ibid., pp. 91-92.
5. Cf. MacQuarrie, J.: "The Faith of the People of God" (London, 1972), pp. 101-109.

in total union with God. Here we discover the life of humanity as it is meant to be. The priestly people share in this new kind of existence already in virtue of their identification with Christ, and they serve the world to bring about the union of the whole human family with its creator and father. Men and nature together are bound up with the growth and completion of the "fullness" of Christ; the whole of creation which had once groaned, and still groans, for its redemption is now caught up in the experience of the people of God, starting out on its pilgrim way towards the final destiny which the divine wisdom has decreed for it. In this pilgrimage, the life and activity of the priestly people are decisive, for it is the priestly people of God, acting in the name of Christ and through the Spirit, who bring the whole of the divine plan of "recapitulation" to its fulfilment, a fulfilment which is set forth by God and not just arrived at by a natural process.[6] "According to his promise, we wait for new heavens and a new earth in which righteousness dwells. Therefore, beloved, since you wait for these, be zealous to be found by him without spot or blemish, and at peace" (II Pet. 3, 13 f). Once more, we can point to the fact that such an insight into the nature and activity of the priestly people of God has an intimate connection with the eucharist.[7]

22. The discovery and affirmation of the priesthood of Christ have been our starting point; of equal importance, however, is the recognition of this priesthood of Christ shared by those who belong to him. Precisely because they belong to him, they are brought into a new situation, a new relationship with God and with the world in which they live. "The status, function and responsibility of the baptised are defined by the nature of the Church, i.e., the royal, priestly and prophetic community of the new Israel, proclaiming God's kingship, his reconciling love and the values of the world to come."[8] In our baptism and the gift of the Spirit in confirmation, sealed and strengthened in the sharing of the eucharist, we recognise the foundation of the share in Christ's priesthood which is ours as members of his body, the Church. This is how we understand the "priesthood of the faithful." At this point we feel that we can move a stage further towards examining the nature of the ministerial priesthood, its relationship to Christ's priesthood and the priesthood of all the members of Christ's Church.[9] It proved impossible, as well as undesirable, to

---

6. Cf. Rahner, K.: art, "Parousia" in "Encyclopedia of Theology" (London, 1975), pp. 1158-1160.
7. Cf. "The Ecclesial Nature of the Eucharist," pp. 79-82.
8. Cf. "The Nature of Baptism and its Place in the Life of the Church. A Common Statement by the Joint Study Group of Representatives of the Roman Catholic and Scottish Episcopal Churches," pp. 30-31.
9. Cf. "Ministry and Ordination. A statement on the Doctrine of the Ministry agreed by the Anglican/Roman Catholic International Commission," para. 3, p. 244.

separate the eucharistic role of the priest from his roles as preacher, teacher, pastor and living testimony.

Chapter III
The Ministerial Priesthood
Ordination and Baptism

23. "Though they differ from one another in essence and not only in degree, the common priesthood of the faithful and the ministerial or hierarchical priesthood are none-the-less interrelated. Each of them in its own special way is a participation in the one priesthood of Christ," states Vatican II.[1] And speaking of Christian ministers, the Anglican/Roman Catholic International Commission said: "their ministry is not an extension of the common Christian priesthood but belongs to another realm of the gifts of the Spirit."[2] We understand this to imply that ministerial priesthood is a gift of God conferred through the Church, distinct from, though related to the gift of priesthood of the faithful.

24. The responsibilities and privileges of the priesthood of all Christians are spelled out in the initiatory sacraments of baptism and confirmation: the nature of the difference "in essence and not only in degree" is clearly expressed in the words and ceremonies by which the "ministerial priests" are charged and commissioned in both our Churches. Accordingly, we examined the Ordinal of the Scottish Episcopal Church and the Roman Pontifical. Our task was complicated by the fact that the Roman Pontifical has been thoroughly modernised (1978), whereas the Ordinal of the Scottish Episcopal Church remains as in the Scottish Prayer Book (1929), which is substantially that of 1662; we found, however, an underlying unity of structure and intention.

25. *A Threefold Ministry.*

Both our Churches recognise a threefold ministry: episcopate, presbyterate and diaconate. The Scottish Episcopal Church's Commission on Ministry reported that "Ministerial priesthood applies primarily to the bishop and secondarily to the presbyter."[3] This is in line with the teaching of Vatican II:

---

1. Dogmatic Constitution on the Church—"Lumen Gentium"—sect. 10 in "The Documents of Vatican II" (ed. Wm. Abbott and J. Gallagher, 1966).
2. "Ministry and Ordination," para. 13, p. 247.
3. "Varieties of Ministry," para. 40—a document received for study by the Provincial Synod of the Scottish Episcopal Church.

> Although priests do not possess the highest degree of the priest-hood, and although they are dependent on the bishops in the exer-cise of their power, they are, nevertheless, united with the bishops in sacerdotal dignity . . . (priests) constitute one priesthood with their bishop, although that priesthood is comprised of different func-tions. Associated with their bishop in a spirit of trust and generosity, priests make him present in a certain sense in the individual local congregations of the faithful, and take upon themselves, as far as they are able, his duties and concerns, discharging them with daily care. As they sanctify and govern under the bishop's authority that part of the Lord's flock entrusted to them, they make the universal Church visible in their own locality and lend powerful assistance to the upbuilding of the whole body of Christ.[4]

While "At a lower level of the hierarchy are deacons, upon whom hands are imposed 'not unto the priesthood, but unto a ministry of service'. For strengthened by sacramental grace, in communion with the bishop and his group of priests, they serve the people of God in the ministry of the liturgy, of the word, and of charity."[5] The nature of the priesthood of bishop and priest is seen most clearly in their roles in the Church's most specific activity, the celebration of the eucharist, but the Pontifical and Ordinal make it clear that their min-istry is not confined to that.[6]

(a) In the new Roman Pontifical, the bishop's full function is clarified as follows:

> In the person of the bishop, with his priests around him, Jesus Christ, the Lord, who became High Priest for ever, is present among you. Through the ministry of the bishop, Christ himself continues to proclaim the gospel and to confer the mysteries of faith on those who believe. Through the fatherly action of the bishop, Christ adds new members to his body. Through the bishop's wisdom and pru-dence, Christ guides you in your earthly pilgrimage towards eternal happiness.[7]

In various ways—questions, charges and prayers—the varied duties of the bishop are spelled out:

"Never forget that in the Catholic Church, made one by the bond of Christian love, you are incorporated into the college of bishops. You should therefore have a constant concern for all the Churches and gladly come to the aid of Churches in need."

---

4. Dogmatic Constitution on the Church (cf. note 1), ch. 3, sect. 28.
5. Ibid., sect. 29.
6. Cf. Roman Pontifical (official English translation, 1978) and Scottish Prayer Book Ordinal (1929).
7. Roman Pontifical (1978).

"Pray and offer sacrifice for the people committed to your care and so draw every kind of grace for them from the overflowing holiness of Christ."

The bishop-elect is asked: "Are you resolved to maintain the deposit of faith, entire and incorrupt, as handed down by the apostles and professed by the Church everywhere and at all times?"[8]

What emerges is the traditional role of the bishop to confirm the faith of his brethren, to be the leader and centre of unity of the local Church and its link to the Church Universal.

The duties of the bishop are similarly understood within the Anglican communion. The Ordinal of the Scottish Episcopal Church however does not define the duties of a bishop as clearly as it does those of priests and deacons. The Lambeth Conference of 1968 defines the characteristic functions of the bishop as follows:

> The service of the bishop has its centre in the liturgical and sacramental life of the Church, in his celebration of the eucharist and in ordination and confirmation. It is developed in his work of teaching and safeguarding the faith and in his general care for the upbuilding and equipping of the Church. It is concerned with deepening and broadening ecumenical relationships and reaches out in service, witness and prophetic word to the life of the human community as a whole.[9]

(b) Presbyterate in the Roman Pontifical is called "priesthood in the presbyteral order" because it is defined by its relationship to the episcopate. In the address of the ordaining bishop to the people, he speaks of the candidates for the presbyterate in these terms:

> They are to serve Christ the teacher, priest and shepherd in his ministry which is to make his own body, the Church, grow into the people of God, a holy temple. They are called to share in the priesthood of the bishops and to be moulded into the likeness of Christ, the supreme and eternal priest. By consecration, they will be made true priests of the New Testament, to preach the gospel, sustain God's people, and celebrate the liturgy, above all, the Lord's sacrifice.

Later they are urged to "seek to bring the faithful together into a unified family and to lead them effectively, through Christ and in the Holy Spirit, to God the Father."[10]

---

8. Ibid.
9. The Lambeth Conference, 1968: Resolutions and Reports, p. 108.
10. Roman Pontifical (1978).

In the Ordinal of the Scottish Episcopal Church, presbyters are reminded that they are

> to be messengers, watchmen and stewards of the Lord; to teach and premonish, to feed and provide for the Lord's family; to seek for Christ's sheep that are dispersed abroad, and for his children who are in the midst of this naughty world, that they may be saved through Christ for ever.[11]

(c) The diaconate is essentially subsidiary to the other two and is defined in relation to them. Deacons are to help in the duties of "ministers of the word, of the altar and of charity."[12]

26. *The Elements of Ordination.*

What emerges from the practice of both our Churches is the idea of ministry as an office or function in the Church conditioned by and dependent on visible deputation. This emerges from the four elements we find in the practice of the Churches, in their rites of ordination and in Canon Law. These essential elements concern:

(a) *The one who ordains.* The one who ordains is a bishop, representing the college of bishops and ultimately the whole Church and Christ.[13] While Christ, the eternal priest, exercises a unique role in ordination, he uses as his voice a bishop, representing the Church and himself. The act of ordaining is thus collegial and ecclesial, a sign for the sanctification of Holy Church, of continuity with the Apostolic Church, of communion with the Catholic Church and for building the unity of the One Church as well as the conferring of the Spirit on the ordinand.

---

11. Scottish Prayer Book Ordinal (1929).
12. Roman Pontifical (1978).
13. Cf. The Code of Canons of the Scottish Episcopal Church, which begins with this canon: "The Scottish Episcopal Church, being a branch of the One, Holy Catholic and Apostolic Church of Christ, retains inviolate in the sacred ministry the three orders of bishops, priests and deacons, as of Divine Institution. The right to consecrate and order bishops, priests and deacons belongs to the order of bishops only."
Cf. too, Codex Iuris Canonici, canon 951:
"Sacrae ordinationis minister ordinarius est episcopus consecratus; extraordinarius qui, licet charactere episcopali careat, a iure vel a Sede Apostolica per peculiare indultum potestatem acceperit aliquos ordines conferendi."
"The ordinary minister of sacred ordination is a consecrated bishop; the extraordinary minister is a priest who, though lacking episcopal consecration, has received the power of conferring certain orders either by law or by special indult from the Apostolic See."

(b) *The one who is ordained.* The one who is ordained does not choose himself nor is he chosen by acclamation of the congregation. The ordination rites allow for a measure of election, or at least of approval, on the part of the whole Church, of clergy and laity alike. But they make it clear that the role of the bishop in ordination is more than that of ratifying the approval of the people. The approval of the candidate is a sign of his fitness to represent Christ, the king, priest and prophet, and of his possession of charisms for the good of the whole Church, but something more than approval is required if he is to take his place in the ordained ministry as bishop, priest or deacon.

(c) *The act of ordaining.* The act of ordaining is the act of commissioning, a prayer for fidelity and the conferring of a special gift of the Holy Spirit. It is not merely a human arrangement for good order, but a solemn, ecclesial act. The Church, through the bishop, commits itself in full confidence to the consecration and mission of the candidate through a special gift of the Holy Spirit. The Church, traditionally and correctly, sees ordination as a sacrament and the ordained ministry is an ecclesial necessity, without which the Church would not be fully constituted as the Church. The special gift of the Holy Spirit is signified by the words of ordination accompanied by the traditional gesture for the giving of the Holy Spirit, the laying on of hands. In the Ordinal used at present not only in the Scottish Episcopal Church but throughout the Anglican Communion this is made explicit by the formula: "Receive the Holy Ghost for the office and work of a priest (bishop) in the Church of God." The Roman Pontifical likewise has in the prayer of consecration:

> *Almighty Father, grant to these servants of yours the dignity of the priesthood. Renew within them the Spirit of holiness. As co-workers with the order of bishops may they be faithful to the ministry that they receive from you, Lord God, and be to others a model of right conduct.*

(d) *The effect of ordination.* The gift of the Holy Spirit conferred in ordination is a new gift of the Spirit for a new function in the Church, a gift conferred on the individual for the sake of the Church. This new gift of the Spirit constitutes a new and special relationship with Christ and is manifested by the special role which the ordained minister has in representing Christ to his brethren within the Church. It is this gift which marks the essential difference between the ministerial priesthood and the priesthood of the faithful. Henceforth, the person and life of the bishop, priest and deacon in the service of the Church are part of the Church's sacramental witness to Christ. In this sacramental ministry, the love of God is made, not more real, but here and now more visible, tangible, and therefore more effective for the life of the Church and of the world.

The candidate for the priesthood in its two degrees is necessarily ordained to priesthood in the whole Church. Since the one who ordains is a bishop, representing the college of bishops, ordination is not simply ordination to the ministry of a local congregation or even of a particular diocese. It is ordination to priesthood within the whole body of Christ.

Ordination effects a permanent consecration of the individual with the promise of special help for fulfilling his ministry. Though it is a particular act at a particular moment, it creates a new and continuing responsibility. Like baptism and confirmation, it is a consecration for the whole of life and is unrepeatable.

In the light of this examination it becomes clear that it is the conviction of both our Churches that the doctrine of the priesthood of the Church, far from excluding a special priesthood of ministry, requires it for its own realisation. This appears more clearly when we look at the ministerial priesthood and the eucharist.

Ordination and Eucharist

.27. In our previous joint statement on "The Ecclesial Nature of the Eucharist" we expressed our common understanding of the eucharist as sacrament and model of the Church.[14] In the light of that understanding we stated

> In the eucharist the Church blesses God for all creation by offering that creation to its Lord under the symbols of bread and wine, and the Church is herself nourished with the life of God through these same symbols, now made Christ's body and blood. The Church knows itself to stand as the priestly people within creation and through the whole universe of matter God works out his purposes of love.[15]

28. *The Eucharist as the Sacrifice of the Church.*

Both Churches have understood the eucharist as the presence here and now in the Christian community of Christ's once-and-for-all

---

14. "The Ecclesial Nature of the Eucharist", chap. III (cf. note 2 on chap. II), pp. 85-89.
15. Ibid., p. 89.

offering of himself as a sacrifice for the reconciliation of God and man.[16]

The whole of life is the material of our sacrifice as Christians, a total self-giving to the Father in union with the one sacrifice of Christ. Our offering of ourselves finds its sacramental expression in the eucharist as Christ's self-offering found its expression on the cross. Our eucharist is not merely our grateful response to Christ's offering or our self-oblation inspired by it, but is, in very truth, the whole Christ (head and members) offering the whole Christ to the Father.[17] Hence the Church will make its offering in its structured reality. The people of God will be led by its ministers.

29. *The Eucharist and the Mission of the Church.*

God's Mission—the Father's sending of the Son to redeem the world—is focused, actualised and celebrated above all in the eucharist. There the Church is called together, reintegrated in Christ, and sent out in his Spirit to share in his mission and service to the world.[18]

As members of, and participants in, the body of Christ, all Christians have a part in the priestly mission of the Church and Christ. With Christ, they are consecrated and sent into the world. As Christ is seen in them individually and collectively, they mediate the Father to their brethren and to all mankind. This too "is focused, actualised and celebrated above all in the eucharist" as the Word of God is spoken in and to the Church in the reading of scripture, in preaching and in the broken body of Christ.

In this movement from God to man, this structured reality of the Church will again be apparent. By hearing its ministers, the people of God will be renewed for their mission.

30. *The Eucharist and the Ordained Ministry.*

It is our conviction that in the eucharist the Church should be most clearly seen in its structured reality. As the Anglican/Roman Catholic International Commission expresses it:

It is because the eucharist is central in the Church's life that the essential nature of the Christian ministry, however this may be expressed, is most clearly seen in its celebration.[19]

---

16. Ibid., p. 81.
17. Cf. "The City of God", St. Augustine Bk. 10, chs. 6 and 20.
18. "The Ecclesial Nature of the Eucharist," p. 92.
19. "Ministry and Ordination," para. 13, p. 247.

In our previous statement, we said

> The 'ecclesial' shape of the Church is proclaimed in the eucharist: at the eucharist, the Church is most fully itself, and it is there that the characteristic roles and attitudes of the people of God find expression.[20]

We repeat that the doctrine of the priesthood of the Church, far from excluding a special priesthood of ministry, requires it for its own realisation. As Vatican II put it:

> A bishop, marked with the fullness of the sacrament of orders, is the 'steward of the grace of the supreme priesthood' especially in the eucharist which he offers, or causes to be offered, and by which the Church constantly lives and grows.[21]

To sum up, the eucharistic roles of bishop and priest are not by delegation or appointment by the body of the faithful in order to make the common priesthood more visible. The bishop or priest presides at the eucharist, but not simply in the sense of acting as chairman at a meeting of the faithful for worship.

He acts on behalf of, and provides a focus for, the priestly ministry of the faithful, but the priesthood he exercises is different in kind from theirs and without the ministerial priesthood there is no eucharist. He leads them in their offering and speaks to them for Christ, building up the body in word and sacrament.

As the rites of ordination to the episcopate and the priesthood recognise, in ordination a special gift of the Holy Spirit is conferred for the fulfilment of an essential ecclesial ministry, distinct from that of the priesthood of the faithful. So far from overshadowing the priesthood of the faithful, the ministerial priesthood of bishop and priest is a service to the priesthood of the faithful in its mission as the people of God and its building up the body of the Church through the celebration of the eucharist. Thus the ministerial priesthood helps renew, develop and bring to fulfilment the life of the whole Church.

Final Statement

The appendices are not part of our common statement but we have included them in our document as part of the background to our

---

20. "The Ecclesial Nature of the Eucharist," p. 91.
21. Dogmatic Constitution on the Church, sect. 26.
    Cf. J. Zizioulas, "The Orthodox Understanding of the Ministry", cited in "Varieties of Ministry", para. 43.

thinking and discussion in the belief that they may be of interest to some of our readers.

Those familiar with our previous statements on "The Nature of Baptism and its Place in the Life of the Church" and "The Ecclesial Nature of the Eucharist" will readily recognise that we have followed the policy, adopted at the beginning of our discussions, of examining the present beliefs and practices of our respective Churches. Although very conscious of the influence of past events in shaping present attitudes we decided very early in our meetings that an examination of past controversies was likely to prove an endless and sterile exercise. We did not dismiss such controversies as unimportant, especially those concerning the validity of orders, but we considered that, in the Scottish context, we should meet as committed fellow Christians anxious to talk to one another, to find out to what extent, despite our different language usage, we concurred in belief and practice.

That our discussions over the past ten years have led to a remarkable growth in understanding and friendship is beyond question. As friends we have always been frank with one another and we have tried not to avoid or gloss over difficulties or to clothe them in ambiguous language. We are, consequently, much encouraged by the agreement that we have reached on the topics that we have discussed. We are, nevertheless, aware that there are other topics such as Authority and Inter-communion which invite us to further discussion and agreement if present friendship is to be consummated in that unity for which Christ Our Lord prayed. That is our purpose and our hope.

In the belief that our present document is a significant step towards the fulfilment of that hope, we submit our work to the authorities of our respective Churches.

First Appendix: The Ministry in the New Testament

1. It is a significant feature of the life and ministry of Jesus as presented in the New Testament that out of the wider group of his followers, known collectively as "disciples," he chose twelve men to be his "apostles." He chose them to be particularly associated with him and we are agreed that to them he gave his power and authority, including the power of binding and loosing and of forgiving sins. After the ascension and the return of Jesus to the Father, it was this group which took charge of the embryo Church. One of the distinguishing marks of the infant community, indeed, was that it formed the "fellowship of the apostles" (Acts 2, 42); this association with the apostles was an indication of a more fundamental relationship with Christ in his new body. The first task of the apostles was to restore their number to its original twelve, and so Matthias was elected. From that point onwards, however, we note that the title "apostle" covers a wider group than the "twelve."

2.   Within the original group, the "twelve," we note the importance and pre-eminence of Peter; in fact, we find him acting as spokesman for the group in many of the important decisions that have to be made, both during the earthly life of Jesus and afterwards. In speaking of the priesthood of Christ, we have underlined how it expresses the identity of the Son "consecrated and sent" by the Father in terms of the Servant of the Lord, and reaches its fulfilment in the sacrificial self-offering of Christ. It is of the essence of the apostolic ministry in the Church that it should continue this mission of Christ; it therefore expresses itself in *diakonia*, service of God and of the Church, and ultimately of the world. The *diakonia* of the apostles is related to the preaching of the Good News, to the community at large, and to the Father through Christ whose "service" it reproduces. The New Testament understands it also as a "service in the Spirit" and a "ministry of reconciliation." In all of these ways, the ministry of the apostles, with Peter at their head, is related to the "priesthood of Christ" as we have described it above.

3.   When we consider the actual functioning of this *diakonia* and discover how the apostles themselves are chosen and sent, how they are associated personally with Christ in his offering of himself, how their witness to the resurrection is fundamental to the preaching of the Church, and how they act as leaders of the community, then we can discern in their life and ministry the reproduction of that "priesthood of Christ" which we have already outlined. It seems that even though the New Testament evidence is not compelling, we can at least say that the essence of the apostolic ministry is to be to the Church what Christ was to them, to continue his work and his ministry. As we have to be guarded in using sacrificial and priestly language about Christ, so we have to be similarly guarded in using such terms of the apostles; as we can rest assured that the reality that lies behind the ministry of Christ as it is expressed by the New Testament is priestly, so we can say the same about the apostolic mission in the Church.

4.   The growth of the Church brought with it the need for a corresponding growth in ministry; hence, there are many forms of ministry attested in the New Testament. All of them, however, take their origin from the apostolic ministry, and there is evidence to support the view that what the varieties of ministry represent is simply the diversifying of that basic apostolic ministry within each community. Therefore, while we would not pretend that the threefold ministry which now exists in our two Churches is clearly identifiable with what we can discern in the New Testament, on the other hand, we should have to say that we recognise in such a threefold ministry the continuation in the Church of the basic and fundamental ministry of the apostles.

"Just as the formation of the canon of the New Testament was a process incomplete until the second half of the second century, so the full emergence of the threefold ministry of bishop, presbyter and deacon required a longer period than the apostolic age. Thereafter, this threefold structure became universal in the Church."[1]

Second Appendix: The Growth of the Threefold Ministry in the Sub-apostolic Church

1. In the preamble to this document, we have referred to the contemporary understanding in both our Churches of the origins and function of the threefold ministry of bishop, priest and deacon in the Church. The first canon in the Code of Canons of the Scottish Episcopal Church expresses this understanding where it reads:

> The Scottish Church, being a branch of the One Holy Catholic and Apostolic Church of Christ, retains inviolate in the sacred ministry the three orders of bishops, priests and deacons, as of divine institution.

Following the approach we have adopted in this document, and in the list of what has been said about the ministry in the New Testament, we are united in emphasising that the fundamental ministry in the Church is the ministry of Christ himself. There is no Christian priesthood or ministry that does not derive from him. His priestly and ministerial function is to reconcile the world to God in and through himself, by his incarnation and by his one sacrifice offered once and for all, delivering men from the power of sin and death.

2. The Church, as the body of Christ, derives its ministerial function from Christ. The official ministry is regarded by both our Churches as an original and essential element in the Church, but there has to be due attention paid to the period between the New Testament and the time when a fully developed and organised ministry appears; during this period, it is clear that evidence is scant for the ongoing process by which the varied ministry of the later New Testament became the threefold ministry in all clarity. Nevertheless, at the end of this period the episcopate emerged as the norm and an authentic expression of the Church's ministry and authority. Early second century evidence that the regular and official ministry was centred on the bishop comes from St. Ignatius of Antioch (c. AD 110) who sees in the bishop and his office a type of authority like that discerned in Christ himself.

---

1. "Ministry and Ordination," para. 6, p. 245.

3. During the New Testament period, the original apostles were dispersed but as they died a more established form of Church life evolved. Proclamation *(kerygma)* was accompanied by teaching *(didache)*; the missionary type of ministry gave way to the pastoral. There runs through the writings of the Fathers a strong emphasis on the office and work of the bishop which underlines, above all, that he "teaches with authority."

4. This emphasis can be noted in the document known as the "Didache" or "Doctrine of the Twelve Apostles." It shares with the New Testament and other early writers a tendency to be imprecise in its description of ministers, of whom there are certainly more than three terms used. Further, it envisages a situation where the peripatetic form of ministry still survived. On the other hand, we can find in this document a description of a settled local ministry, with bishops and deacons prominent as in the later New Testament. We can also find in the Didache a stress on the need for an ordered ministry in the Church.

5. The sub-apostolic period does present difficulties if we are looking for absolute and certain evidence of how the variety of New Testament ministry emerged as the threefold ministry of bishop, priest and deacon. However the threefold ministry emerged, we believe in both our traditions that it was in continuity with the ministry of the Apostolic Church. We believe that Jesus Christ himself is "the same yesterday, today and forever" (Heb. 13, 8) and, consequently, we believe that there is in his Church a continuity that enables the ministry as we know it to embody the commission and authority which he originally gave. In conclusion we may say that both our traditions believe that:

(i) priesthood is an expression of the mystery of Christ;

(ii) the apostolic ministry is priestly because it continues the ministry of Christ the High Priest;

(iii) the apostolic ministry is embodied in the Church in the threefold ministry of bishop, priest and deacon;

(iv) this threefold ministry represents an integral *diakonia* to the whole priestly people of God.

Third Appendix: A Summary Note on Language

The English word *priest* has an interesting but confusing history. It is now used to refer to a priest as distinct from a bishop. It is also used to underline the role of the priest as celebrant of the eucharistic sacrifice, a role he shares with the bishop. Both usages are the result of a process of development. The first is due to a development in ecclesiastical practice, while the second is due to a development in theological understanding.

1.   Etymologically, *priest* comes from the Latin *presbyter* (Greek *presbuteros*), which means "an elder" or "senior," a "member of a senate of *presbuteroi*" in association with an *episkopos* or "overseer" or "bishop." With the development of the system of monarchical bishops, the "priests" came to assume a subordinate position, forming the second rank of the ministry under the bishop.

2.   Thus, "priest" did not originally imply a "priest who offered sacrifice." It came to assume overtones of sacrifice when it replaced another word for the same rank of the ministry. *Sacerdos* in Latin was used of a sacrificing priest. In Christian times, it was used of pagan and Jewish priests, but came to be used also of the Christian priests.

3.   Thus, by the fourth century, there were two words in Latin for *priest: presbyter* and *sacerdos*, the first etymologically expressing rank and the second expressing function. It is worth noting that *sacerdos* was used also of the bishop.

4.   The use of *sacerdos* (Greek: *hiereus*) for the Christian priest is a development beyond the New Testament practice of reserving the singular *hiereus* for Christ, and the plural *hiereis* for the whole priestly people of God.

5.   The result of a development of language is that "priest" is now used for both *presbyter* and *sacerdos*, for the priest as distinct from the bishop and for the priest as celebrant of the eucharistic sacrifice, a role he shares with the bishop.

6.   The purpose of our report has been to explore the role of both priest and bishop as *sacerdos*, a sacrificing priest, and to see how it is related to the priesthood of Christ and of the whole Church.

Rome and Canterbury

Lenten address by the
Lord Archbishop of Canterbury, Dr. Robert Runcie,
given in Westminster Abbey, 11 March 1981.

United Not Absorbed

Just over fifty years ago the bishops of the Anglican Communion saw little hope of unity with Rome. They regretted that Pius XI appeared to contemplate 'complete absorption' (in his encyclical *Mortalium Animos* of 1928) as the only method of achieving unity. The bishops of that 1930 Lambeth Conference were particularly disappointed because the approach of the Malines Conversations had been set aside: that approach had encouraged the Anglican Church to think about being united, not absorbed. At the penultimate Malines Conversation in 1925 Cardinal Mercier had read the paper *'L'Église anglicane unie non absorbée'*. It had been prepared by an "anonymous canonist." It attracted immediate attention. Some of the details of the paper, now known to have been written by Dom Lambert Beauduin, seem rather fanciful today; his stress on the pallium, a woollen stole blessed by the pope for archbishops, which caused no end of prelatical rivalry in the Middle Ages; his contention that progress towards unity would be wrecked over the question of the precedence of archbishops of Canterbury over cardinals or vice versa—Cardinal Basil Hume and I will not lose much sleep over this. Nor did he really take seriously enough the indigenous English Roman Catholic tradition: on his view the new sees created at and after the restoration of the Roman Catholic hierarchy in 1850 would simply be suppressed.

Yet in spite of serious flaws—which were seen by the Lambeth Fathers in 1930—the paper remains significant, because it is the first clear recognition that the Churches of the Anglican Communion are bound to seek a unity which respects their autonomous tradition. It is a first systematic essay on the *kind* of unity Rome and Canterbury seek. The nineteenth-century debate had focused on "Anglican Orders." In the eighteenth century an archbishop of Canterbury thought of a union with an *Independent* Gallican Church. In the sixteenth and seventeenth centuries both sides saw unity in terms of the Crown imposing a statutory uniformity. So, in spite of its oversimplifications, Beauduin's essay makes its point: we cannot tolerate an Anglican Church *separated* from Rome and we cannot tolerate an Anglican Church *absorbed* by Rome: the Anglican Church, united not absorbed.

Unity and Diversity

However, once this is admitted as a fruitful approach (and such an approach was publicly endorsed by the late Pope Paul VI more than once) an immediate question arises: what range of diversity is compatible with unity or, to put the matter another way, what are the limits of acceptable diversity? The question has to be asked in *any* ecumenical discussion. It is a particularly pressing question for any Church in dialogue with Rome because of the Roman tendency towards an authoritarian centralization and uniformity. Forgive me for making this point somewhat crudely.

The character and model of the Church in the dominant Roman tradition owes a great deal to its origins and location in the centre of a great empire. Many of the detailed administrative practices, legal systems and even archives survived to mould the minds of the architects of the original papal monarchy. The tendency of such an order is to favour a stable ideology, both communicated and enforced by a bureaucracy functioning according to juridical models.

The precondition of the system was the Latin language which became even more useful to the Roman curia after it had died as a living language. An ideological stability is easier to maintain through the medium of a fixed language. The changes in living languages are always subversive to unchanging theological definitions—words do not only change their meaning in a living language, they also change their resonances and their place in a cultural economy.

The collapse of the Latin culture over the past two decades, the liturgical changes within the Roman Catholic Church, the new confidence of the non-European cultures into whose languages Christian truth needs to be baptized—all mean that the problem of perceiving unity in inescapable diversity is now a pressing one for the Roman Church which for so long had been able to fend off the difficulty by reducing diversity to matters of ornament and detail. The Anglican Church had to face the problems of serious diversity, but the Roman Church had to face problems of unity.

Not surprisingly, we have both been having a hard look together at the New Testament and the early Church.

The New Testament

But once we examine the New Testament—or listen to the siren voices of New Testament scholarship—we are confronted by an immediate and serious problem. There is no *one* New Testament picture of anything. To put it bluntly, we are presented with such a bewildering diversity that we begin to doubt whether the concept of unity may not be a reading back of later Orthodoxy. Indeed, the German New Testament specialist Ernst Käsemann writes as follows: "The New Testament Canon does not, as such, constitute the foundation of the unity of the Church. On the contrary, as such, it provides the basis for the multiplicity of the Confessions." What, then, can the New Testament teach us about unity in diversity?

Let me take the most important example of New Testament diversity—the clash between Jewish and Hellenistic Christianity, the first serious threat to the unity of the Church. Some of the New Testament documents, notably St. Matthew's gospel and the Epistle of St. James, strongly affirm the *continuing* validity of the Law of Moses and reject the teaching of St. Paul. You will remember that it is in St. Matthew that not one "jot or tittle" of the law will disappear (Matt. 5.17-19) and that Luther found James' treatment of the Pauline doctrine of justification by faith so unacceptable that he branded his letter an "Epistle of straw." Indeed, Jewish Christianity in the New Testament looks very much like what later became the heretical Jewish Christian sects, for example the Ebionites.

At the other end of the New Testament spectrum, specially in St. Paul and St. John, we find a certain speculative interaction with the philosophical theology of Hellenistic society. In St. John's Gospel in particular we see a recurring contrast between light and darkness, above and below, spirit and flesh, which is typical of Hellenistic dualism and characteristic of the later Gnostic syncretism.

Yet in spite of this very sharp diversity, a profound unity can also be discerned between Jewish and Hellenistic Christianity: that unity is the developing understanding of Christ himself. Jewish Christianity in the New Testament was already moving away from a *purely* Jewish understanding of Christ. Jesus in St. Matthew's Gospel is the Messiah, "the Son of the Living God" (16.15-17) and the birth narrative excludes an understanding of Jesus merely in terms of being a "prophet." In Hellenistic Christianity Paul preaches an uncongenial "*crucified* Christ" (cf. 1 Cor. 2.1-5) and John insists that the World has become "*flesh*" (1.14). However contrasting their expressions, Jewish and Hellenistic Christianity were fundamentally united in their identification of the *crucified* Jesus with the *exalted* Lord and this identification lies behind the earliest christological titles, in whichever Christian milieu they have their origin: Messiah; Son of Man; Son of God; Lord.

Donald MacKinnon, using different examples of diversity, once summed up the basic unity of the New Testament like this: "We cannot conjure the Jesus of Luke out of the Jesus of Mark, but we can see standing behind them both, shaping, controlling and even twisting their narratives, the sure hand of the one they strive to bear witness to in the fellowship of the Spirit."

The Early Church

When we turn to the early Church we have the impression that instead of looking for unity in diversity we are now looking for diversity in unity. From the point of view of the emergent Great Church, Fathers and heretics could be neatly separated—dad and cads, as G. L. Prestige used to say. Schism was not *in* the Church but *out* of it.

The question is now not how much diversity can be found in a general study of early Christian history but how much diversity can be found within the undivided communion of the Great Church of the first centuries. This appeal must not be uncritical, as if there were no divisions, no schisms, and all was sweetness and light. But no church historian could think that. Yet there is still a certain cogency in speaking of the undivided Church, whether one draws a line at the separation of the Oriental Churches from Byzantine Orthodoxy (a schism between Greek-speaking and Semitic-speaking Churches), or the later division between Rome and Constantinople (where language and culture again played their part in the cleavage between the Greek and Latin Churches). The point of an appeal to an "undivided tradition," however defined, is that once any Christian tradition develops an isolation from the wider Church its doctrine and life begin to be less than fully catholic—according to the whole.

What can we learn about diversity in unity from the early and undivided tradition of the Catholic Church? I do not want to offer purely liturgical or even disciplinary examples, even though disputes about new liturgies in both Churches raise a lot of steam and marriage discipline or clerical celibacy touches even more sensitive areas. The real issue, however, is the problem of theological and doctrinal pluralism. Was, and is, it possible to have unity in faith and difference in its expression?

This question was posed in its sharpest way for the early Church in the christological dispute between Antioch and Alexandria in the fifth century. At the risk of oversimplification: Alexandrine Christology stressed the unity of the incarnate Christ; Antiochene Christology stressed the reality of Jesus' humanity and so saw a distinction in the incarnate Lord. The Council of Chalcedon was a proper compromise which sought to do justice to the insights of both schools: *one* person in *two* natures. But the disputes before and after the Council were more than usually influenced by personalities and ecclesiastical empire-building.

Even so, just before the Council we have a very significant recognition of theological and even doctrinal pluralism in one communion. In 433 two of the major protagonists, Cyril of Alexandria and John of Antioch, exchanged remarkable letters. John wrote to Cyril and sent him his confession of faith. Though the letter was irenic, it contained the normal Antiochene theology of the "two natures" of Christ—directed explicitly against Cyril's "one nature"; but at the same time John clearly stated the unity of the "person" of Christ and the consequent legitimacy of describing Mary as "Mother of God." Cyril, a real hard-liner and no woolly-minded ecumenist, replied with great generosity and rejoiced that they shared a common faith and his reply was canonized by the Council fourteen years later. As Fr. Emmanuel Lanne puts it, Cyril "accepted a profession of faith in which the theological perspective was not his own."

Another example, of a different kind, which is actually found in the Creed, shows the early Church quite prepared to be reticent in defining the faith for the sake of unity. One of the reasons for convening the Council of Constantinople in 281 (we celebrate its sixteenth hundredth anniversary this year) was to settle the disputed status of the Holy Spirit. Was the Holy Spirit a creature, or, on the contrary, like the Son, of the same "substance" as the Father and so properly to be called God? The majority of the Council were clear enough that the Holy Spirit was indeed "of one being" with the Father and many were happy to go on and say he was God. Yet the form accepted and which we still use in the Creed was much more reticent: "We believe in the Holy Spirit, the Lord, the Giver of life, who proceeds from the Father. With the Father and the Son he is worshipped and glorified. He has spoken through the Prophets." This cautious phraseology accords very much with the teaching and 'ecumenical' sensitivity of St. Basil the Great. Basil was concerned to defend the legitimacy of the Church's worship of the Spirit, but—in John Kelly's phrase—he "practised diplomatic caution" in his actual language about the Spirit.

Once again different ways of expressing the faith, even in so central a matter as the divinity of the Holy Spirit, are compatible with unity.

Anglican Comprehensiveness

The point of our exploration of these aspects of the unity and diversity of the New Testament and the early Church has been to show that, far from being incompatible with unity, a very wide diversity is found among the earliest Christian communities and that, even when the Church developed its structures in a more unified way in the centuries which followed, this did not necessarily entail the acceptance of identical expressions of faith. In now going on to speak of Anglican comprehensiveness I do not wish to insinuate that the Anglican tradition is the direct or only heir to the primitive Church. Nor do I want to suggest that Anglican comprehensiveness is the only possible way of achieving unity in diversity presented to us by the Church of the New Testament, and the Fathers may put Anglican comprehensiveness, when rightly understood, in a more favourable light, as well as indicating the range of diversity feasible in any Anglican/Roman Catholic union.

At the English Reformation a number of forces were at work. There was a new nationalism and a "godly prince" to embody it. There was the desire for vernacular Scriptures and Liturgy. There was the influence of the continental Reformation, at first Lutheran but later Calvinistic. And there was a wish by many to preserve a continuity with the Church of the previous centuries. The Elizabethan Settlement was a more or less conscious attempt to comprehend within the Church of England all those who would accept the Scriptures, the Creeds, the Sacraments of Baptism and the Eucharist, a liturgy and the threefold ministry of bishops, priests and deacons. To achieve this comprehension it was absolutely necessary to make a clear distinction between fundamentals and non-fundamentals—a distinction probably taken from the "ecumenical" Lutheran reformer Melancthon. The clearest expression of this distinction is found as recently as the 1968 Lambeth Conference: "Comprehensiveness demands agreement on fundamentals, while tolerating disagreement on matters in which the Church may differ without feeling the necessity of breaking communion."

Yet immediately the distinction is made, an urgent question arises: where is the line to be drawn? At the close of the sixteenth century and during the seventeenth century, in the polemic with both Puritans and Recusants, the classical Anglican answer to this question emerged. The answer gave Anglicanism its distinctive ethos. It had three characteristics.

First, that the common Reformed appeal to Scripture was tempered by the role of tradition, not, of course, as an additional source of revelation, but as a sure guide to the uncertainties of scriptural interpretation. As a result of this, the study of the Fathers had great importance—with the interesting result that eventually the doctrine of the incarnation became more central to mainstream Anglicanism than justification by faith.

Next, that there was an appeal to reason which reflected the assurance of Renaissance humanism—an appeal powerfully developed by Richard Hooker and others. The Enlightenment, too, eventually became a characteristic of Anglican thought.

Finally, that doctrine was presented in the liturgical worship of the Church. The *lex orandi* was the guide to the *lex credendi*. Unlike other Reformed Churches, the Prayer Book was a formula of faith.

Now these three characteristics were, and are, by no means exclusively Anglican, but their particular combination gave Anglican theology, spirituality and pastoral practice its distinctive stamp. They gave Anglicanism not so much a distinctive theological content as a distinctive theological method. Hence, Richard Hooker wrote about methodology and precisely entitled it *Of the Laws of Ecclesiastical Polity*. He did not write a systematic *Summa* or an Anglican version of John Calvin's *Institutes*.

"In the mind of an Anglican, comprehensiveness is not compromise"—so said the 1968 Lambeth Conference. Rightly understood, it is the achievement of unity in diversity through the distinction of the essential from the non-essential by means of the holy Scriptures interpreted by tradition, in the light of reason, all expressed in and through the corporate worship of the Church.

Criticisms

In suggesting that Anglican comprehensiveness (and the distinction between fundamentals and non-fundamentals it entails) is a legitimate way of expressing the unity in diversity we find in the New Testament and the early Church, I am aware of a vulnerability to sharp criticism. Yes, a Roman Catholic or Orthodox critic will say, it sounds all right but it is a *paper* system—what kind of unity can we have with Anglicans, some of whom, and they include some professional teachers of theology, seem to believe nothing at all? Or it will be said that the party strife in the Church of England between "catholic," "evangelical" and "liberal" is so sharp as to negate internal Anglican unity, let alone unity with Rome.

The first thing to point out is that Anglicans themselves make similar self-criticisms. Professor Stephen Sykes's important book *The Integrity of Anglicanism* is on target here.

Second, "abuse does not take away the use of a thing"—a remark which seventeenth-century Anglicans were always addressing to the Puritans. There are some Anglicans who seem to be saying that there are no fundamentals at all, or rather, that one can never be certain what they are. Anglicanism depends, on the contrary, on the possibility of a public distinction between essentials of faith and non-essentials being made and embodied in the worship of the Church. To refuse to draw the line anywhere or to draw it in a highly personal and idiosyncratic way is in fact to abandon the classical Anglican method I have described. Now I have no wish to be oversimplistic: it is obvious to all Christians that there is a general crisis of doctrinal authority. The crisis has arisen for many reasons, but not least because of the acceptance of biblical criticism—and we can do no other. There is also a growing realization that some degree of "doctrinal" or credal criticism also has to be accepted. Add to these the contemporary lack of trust in human reason and the seventeenth-century Anglican appeal to Scripture, tradition and reason looks less secure. I am not a classical Anglican fundamentalist and want no witch hunts. To quote the 1968 Lambeth Conference again: "Comprehensiveness implies a willingness to allow liberty of interpretation, with a certain slowness in arresting or restraining exploratory thinking."

Third, in spite of some impressions to the contrary, comprehensiveness does not imply that plain contradiction can be a normal expression of Anglican diversity. Stephen Sykes has suggested that from the latter part of the nineteenth century, aided and abetted by F. D. Maurice, comprehensiveness has come to be thought of in almost Hegelian terms: Catholic thesis, Protestant antithesis and Anglican synthesis. No doubt there is a real truth in the idea of "a continuing search for the whole truth" in which Protestant and Catholic emphases "will find complete reconciliation" (Lambeth Conference 1968). But this idea has to be recognized as a modern one. It is quite alien to original Anglican thought that there could be logically opposite expressions of faith in fundamentals. To be an Anglican is not to be content with self-contradiction.

Lastly, comprehensiveness, properly understood as the distinction between fundamentals and non-fundamentals, will be seen to be not unrelated to the doctrine of the "hierarchy of truths," canonized by the Second Vatican Council, the implications of which have not yet been fully worked out.

Questions for the Future

I began with the idea of the Anglican Church united not absorbed. In the light of my very Anglican appeal to Scripture and the early Church, and of my attempt to relate Anglican comprehensiveness to the unity and diversity I believe we find there, I want to conclude by suggesting some questions Anglicans should now be asking Roman Catholics in order to elucidate what unity not absorption would mean.

Some hard questions must be asked about Vatican centralization. As early as the close of the second century, Pope Victor was threatening the excommunication of the whole of the Asian episcopate because they kept Easter on a different date from the West. Fortunately Irenaeus put him right. But the tendency to uniformity still seems to be a Roman attitude of mind (for the reasons I mentioned earlier). The Uniat Churches in the USA are forbidden the married clergy they have had from time out of mind in the Middle East because this clashes with "Latin" canon law. Or, to bring the matter nearer home, how much freedom does the Roman Catholic Episcopal Conference of England and Wales have to pursue moral and pastoral initiatives culturally relevant to the mission of Christ in this country? To put it more directly, would Anglicans be expected to accept the "Latin" attitudes and rulings of the various Vatican Congregations? The question is acute when we consider moral issues relating to particular interpretations of natural law and the Anglo-Saxon tradition of the informed Christian conscience.

Ultimately, the theological questions can be put like this: what is involved (and what is *not* involved) in acceptance of the universal ministry of the Bishop of Rome? Is this ministry not solely concerned with the basic unity of the faith in the worldwide communion of the Churches and their God-given diversity? Would this mean, at the most, a form of universal presidency in charity when essential matters of faith are at stake? What relation, then, would the Vatican have to the various Synods of the Anglican Communion? There are, therefore, some questions about the Anglican acceptance of a universal primacy which cannot be answered until Anglicans and Roman Catholics have come to some consensus on what acceptance actually involves.

Beauduin saw something of this even in the 1920s and expressed it in the concluding words of his paper:

> What will Rome think of this plan? It is clear that it suggests a principle of decentralization which is not in accordance with the actual tendencies of the Roman Curia, a principle that could have other applications. Would it not be a good and a great good? Yet would Rome be of this opinion? Nothing can allow us to foresee what would be the answer.

Beauduin did not know how Rome would react to his question. In the 1920s it was, in any case, certainly premature. But we are now at the stage of dialogue where the hard questions need to be put—and Rome will have some tough questions to put to Anglicans as well. In this exchange both traditions will be purified and renewed. Both will have something to give to the other.

In putting a few Anglican questions in the light of the New Testament and the early Church and arguing that Anglican comprehensiveness does not mean Anglicans have no faith, I do not think it will be assumed that I am not absolutely committed to Anglican/Roman Catholic unity. I ask questions precisely because I am, and deeply so, for both personal and theological reasons. It is therefore my profound hope that when the present successor of Pope Gregory comes to this country next year St. Augustine's present successor and he will be able to take a step together towards that unity—towards the mutual exchange which will show both traditions more clearly what visible structures that unity in diversity requires.

Practical Implications of the Anglican View of Authority

From the Statement of the Meeting of Primates of the
Anglican Communion held in Washington, D.C., May 1, 1981.

The background to this statement was a series
of three papers on this topic, specifically prepared for the April 1981
international meeting of primates of the Anglican Communion at
Washington, D.C. They were subsequently published by the Anglican Consultative Council in a booklet entitled *Authority in the Anglican
Communion.* Although not itself endorsed in any specific resolution
of the 1948 Lambeth Conference, the "theology of dispersed authority," here referred to in clause 1, was described in the report to that
1948 conference as follows: "It is thus a dispersed rather than a centralized authority having many elements which combine, interact with,
and check each other; these elements together contributing by a process of mutual support, mutual checking, and redressing of errors or
exaggerations to the many-sided fullness of the authority which Christ
has committed to His Church" (pp. 84-85). Noteworthy also in this
statement of 1981 is the particular responsibility attributed to the
episcopate (clause 4), the assertion that this responsibility is to be
shared collegially with the leaders of the other Churches (clause 5),
and the role that "criticism and response" are expected to play in the
exercise of authority (clause 7).

1.   The Anglican Communion accepts and endeavours to practise
the theology of dispersed authority as set out in the 1948 Lambeth
Conference document, The Anglican Communion ("The Meaning and
Unity of the Anglican Communion," pp. 84-86).
2.   Since that statement was written the Anglican Communion has
evolved two further institutions to meet the swift changing circumstances in different parts of the world: the Anglican Consultative
Council and the Primates' Meeting, within guidelines laid down by
the Lambeth Conference.
   Fundamentally these two institutions are consistent with the theology of dispersed authority, referred to above.
   The Primates' Meeting expressed that special responsibility characteristic of the episcopate. The A.C.C. reflects the responsibilities
characteristic of a synodically governed Church.

3.   In Christ's one holy, Catholic and Apostolic Church, every member has, in virtue of his or her own baptism, his or her special vocation and ministry.

4.   In the Anglican Church, the episcopate has a particular responsibility for teaching the faith, for encouraging, promoting and maintaining the proclamation in word and deed of the apostolic gospel by and in the whole Church.

5.   In a divided universal Church, the Anglican episcopate shares its peculiar responsibility with those called and chosen to exercise *episcopé* in the totality of Christ's Church. The Anglican episcopate acknowledges that it has a special obligation to consult with leaders of other Churches and thereby to practise collegiality in a divided Church.

6.   Anglicans recognise that all exercise of *episcopé* entails personal loyalty to Christ, commitment to the poor and outcast, willingness to suffer for him, and an open appeal to the common conscience of fellow human beings.

7.   In the continuing process of defining the *consensus fidelium*, Anglicans regard criticism and response as an essential element by which Authority is exercised and experienced and as playing a vital part in the work of the Holy Spirit in maintaining the Church in fidelity to the Apostolic Gospel.

Final Recommendations from the Anglican/Roman Catholic Leaders Conference

June 12, 1981

The ARC VII Statement of 1969 ended with a section dealing with the diffusion of information concerning the work of ecumenism and especially the promoting of organic unity between the Roman Catholic Church and the Anglican Communion. The ARC Twelve-Year Report elaborated this same theme in four of the five task forces it proposed. This conference dealt with the same issue, viz., coordination of effort to secure mutual planning and ease of communication throughout both Churches in matters related to Anglican-Roman Catholic relations.

United as sister Churches in the one authentic communion of the family of Christ, we rejoice in the gifts bestowed on us during our days of prayer, reflection and study together. From this experience we renew our full commitment to strengthening the existing bonds of Christian unity. In the spirit of love, we present the fruits of our working together to the Divine Shepherd of Unity and to our brothers and sisters in our two Churches.

1. We recommend that a Joint Commission be established to develop a standard pattern for pastoral ministry to ecumenical marriages between Anglicans and Roman Catholics to include:
   a. Premarital preparation
   b. Further developments in the canonical and liturgical provisions for such marriages
   c. Provision for ongoing ministry to the couples and their families. Once this pattern is approved, it is to be presented in joint clergy workshops.

2. In the event of the referral of the Final Report of ARCIC to U.S. Church bodies we recommend to the Presiding Bishop and the President of the NCCB/USCC that groups designated to consider this Report share in meetings with cognate groups of the other Church.

3. Since both Churches have a major concern for strengthening family life, and since the Roman Catholic Community has designated the 1980's as the Decade of the Family, we recommend that our Churches explore ways in which family resources and programs can be shared, with a special focus on couples in ARC marriages.

4. In the light of the successful completion of the Shared Reflection on the Episcopate by certain bishops of our two Churches, we recommend further meetings between bishops of our Churches for the purpose of:

    a. Spiritual sharing

    b. Fraternal growth in the exercise of the episcopal ministry in the Church today

5. We recommend that the two national organizations of diocesan ecumenical officers be asked to use their respective networks to gather information concerning communicating at the Holy Eucharist by members of our Churches in the other Church to determine the occasions, circumstances and motivation for this practice. The report would be submitted to both the BCEIA and the SCER.

6. We recommend a national conference for shared responsibility in the Church between the Committee for the Laity of the NCCB and the Education for Ministry unit of the Episcopal Church, to share experiences of lay life and participation in decision making in the Church today.

7. We recommend improved communication between our sister Churches at all levels, specifically through:

    a. Requesting a formal liaison between the Presiding Bishop, or his designate, and the President of the NCCB/USCC, or his designate

    b. Sharing specified minutes and reports of national and diocesan organizations with corresponding bodies in the other Church where common concerns are dealt with

    c. Preparing from the other Church official observers for the General Convention (and interim meetings of the House of Bishops) and the NCCB at meetings of both our Churches wherever possible, particularly at diocesan levels

    d. Developing a jointly sponsored popular pamphlet for parish distribution dealing with the emerging agreements between our Churches and helping readers to understand better the other Church as we grow in unity

8. So that we may give witness as sister Churches to our common mission in social justice, we recommend that a joint task force be established to study the ways by which together we can make a significant contribution in some specific area of social need, such as reform of the criminal justice system.

9. We recommend that opportunities systematically be sought to share the resources developed in our Churches to support those in ministry in our local parishes. Examples are conferences on spirituality, studies of the conditions affecting the exercise of ministry today, programs for the continuing education of the clergy, laity training programs, and joint lectionary study groups.

Episcopal Participants

Presiding Bishop John M. Allin
Bishop David Reed of Kentucky, Chair of SCER
Bishop Arthur A. Vogel of West Missouri, Co-chair of ARC
Bishop John E. Walker of Washington
Bishop Arthur E. Walmsley of Connecticut
William B. Lawson, President of EDEO
Kermit L. Lloyd, Director Chaplaincies, Pennsylvania Council
J. Robert Wright
Mother Mary Grace, Community of St. Mary
Charles Lawrence, President, House of Deputies
William A. Norgren, Ecumenical Officer
Clement W. Welsh, Warden, College of Preachers

Roman Catholic Participants

Archbishop John Roach of Minneapolis, President NCCB/USCC
Bishop James W. Malone of Youngstown, Vice-President
Archbishop John L. May of St. Louis
Bishop John S. Cummins of Oakland
Bishop Howard J. Hubbard of Albany
Bishop Ernest L. Unterkoefler of Charleston, S.C., Chair of BCEIA
Bishop Raymond W. Lessard of Savannah, Co-chair of ARC
Sister Clare Fitzgerald, President, Leadership Conference of Women
    Religious
Alan McCoy, President, Conference of Major Superiors of Men
Dolores Leckey, Executive Director, NCCB Committee for the Laity
Alex J. Brunett, President of NADEO
Herbert J. Ryan, SJ
John F. Hotchkin, Executive Director of NCCB Ecumenical Affairs

The Final Report

ANGLICAN-ROMAN CATHOLIC
INTERNATIONAL COMMISSION

Windsor, September 1981

Contents

Preface to the Final Report

The Report which follows is the outcome of work begun at Gazzada, Italy, on 9 January 1967. A Joint Preparatory Commission met there, in fulfilment of a joint decision by Pope Paul VI and Archbishop Michael Ramsey, expressed in a Common Declaration during their meeting in Rome in March 1966. Meeting three times in less than a year, that Commission produced a Report which registered considerable areas of Roman Catholic-Anglican agreement, pointed to per-

228

sisting historical differences and outlined a programme of 'growing together' which should include, though not be exhausted in, serious dialogue on these differences. It proclaimed penitence for the past, thankfulness for the graces of the present, urgency and resolve for a future in which our common aim would be the restoration of full organic unity.

That Report was endorsed in substance by a letter of Cardinal Bea in June 1968 and by the Lambeth Conference a few weeks later. In January 1970 the signatories of the present Report met first as "The Anglican—Roman Catholic International Commission." Eight members of the Preparatory Commission continued to serve on the new Commission.

The purpose of this Preface is to explain briefly the aim and methods of ARCIC as these have matured in the light of our own experience, of the developments—in some aspects rapid—within our own Churches in the twelve years of our experience, in response to criticisms we have received and having regard to other ecumenical dialogues.

From the beginning we were determined, in accordance with our mandate, and in the spirit of Phil. 3. 13, "forgetting what lies behind and straining forward to what lies ahead," to discover each other's faith as it is today and to appeal to history only for enlightenment, not as a way of perpetuating past controversy. In putting this resolve into practice we learned as we progressed. As early as 1970 our preliminary papers on our three main topics link each of them with "the Church," and this perspective was maintained and is reflected in what follows here: our work is introduced with a statement on the Church, building on the concept of *koinonia*. In the Statement *Eucharistic Doctrine* (Windsor 1971) we went so far as to claim "substantial agreement" which is consistent with "a variety of theological approaches within both our communions." The Preface to our Statement *Ministry and Ordination* (Canterbury 1973) expressed the belief "that in what we have said here both Anglicans and Roman Catholics will recognize their own faith."

It was in the first of our two Statements on Authority (*Authority in the Church I*, Venice 1976) that we spoke more fully and revealed a more developed awareness of our aims and methods. Because "it was precisely in the problem of papal primacy that our historical divisions found their unhappy origin," reference was made to the "distinction between the ideal and the actual which is important for the reading of our document and for the understanding of the method we have used" (Authority I, Preface). Acknowledging the growing convergence of method and outlook of theologians in our two traditions, we emphasized our avoidance of the emotive language of past polemics and our seeking to pursue *together* that restatement of doctrine which new times and conditions are, as we both recognize, regularly calling for (Authority I, para. 25). In concluding we felt already able to invite our authorities to consider whether our Statements expressed a unity at the level of faith sufficient to call for "closer sharing . . . in life, worship, and mission."

Some provisional response to this was forthcoming a few months later in the *Common Declaration* of Pope Paul VI and Archbishop Donald Coggan, made during the latter's visit to Rome in April 1977. Echoing our original statement of intent, "the restoration of complete communion in faith and sacramental life," Pope and Archbishop declared, "Our call to this is one with the sublime Christian vocation itself, which is a call to communion" (cf.1 John 1.3). This passage (*Common Declaration*, paras. 8-9) provides a striking endorsement of a central theme of our Statements, and insists that though our communion remains imperfect it "stands at the centre of our witness to the world." Our divisions hinder this witness, but they do not close all roads we may travel together." In other words, the *koinonia* which is the governing concept of what follows here is not a static concept— it demands movement forward, perfecting. We need to accept its implications.

This official encouragement has been echoed by many of our critics. We have seen all of them, encouraging or not, as reflecting the interest aroused by the dialogue and helping us to make ourselves clearer, as we have tried to do in the *Elucidations* (Salisbury 1979 and Windsor 1981).

Paragraph 24 of our Statement *Authority in the Church I* made it clear that, while we had reached a high degree of agreement on "authority in the Church and in particular on the basic principles of primacy," differences persisted concerning papal authority. A much closer examination of those differences has been our main task since then. The results of that work are embodied in the Statement *Authority in the Church II* (Windsor 1981) which is here presented for the first time. Though much of the material in this Final Report has been published earlier, we are confident that the Report will be read as a whole, and that particular sentences or passages will not be taken out of context.

We believe that growing numbers in both our communions accept that, in the words of the Second Vatican Council's *Decree on Ecumenism*, "There can be no ecumenism worthy of the name without interior conversion. For it is from newness of attitudes of mind, from self-denial and unstinted love, that desires of unity take their rise and develop in a mature way" (*Unitatis Redintegratio*, para. 7).

It would be wrong, however, to suggest that all the criticisms we have received over the twelve years of our work have been encouraging. We are aware of the limits of our work—that it is a service to the people of God, and needs to find acceptance among them.

But we have as much reason now as ever to echo the concluding lines of the *Common Declaration* of 1977:

> to be baptized into Christ is to be baptized into hope—"and hope does not disappoint us because God's love has been poured into our hearts through the Holy Spirit which has been given us" (Rom. 5.5). Christian hope manifests itself in prayer and action—in prudence but also in courage. We pledge ourselves and exhort the faithful of the Roman Catholic Church and of the Anglican Communion to live and work courageously in this hope of reconciliation and unity in our common Lord.

Introduction

1.   Our two communions have been separated for over 400 years. This separation, involving serious doctrinal differences, has been aggravated by theological polemics and mutual intolerance, which have reached into and affected many departments of life. Nevertheless, although our unity has been impaired through separation, it has not been destroyed. Many bonds still unite us: we confess the same faith in the one true God; we have received the same Spirit; we have been baptized with the same baptism; and we preach the same Christ.

2.   Controversy between our two communions has centred on the eucharist, on the meaning and function of ordained ministry, and on the nature and exercise of authority in the Church. Although we are not yet in full communion, what the Commission has done has convinced us that substantial agreement on these divisive issues is now possible.

3.   In producing these Statements, we have been concerned, not to evade the difficulties, but rather to avoid the controversial language in which they have often been discussed. We have taken seriously the issues that have divided us, and have sought solutions by re-examining our common inheritance, particularly the Scriptures.

4.   The subjects which we were required to consider as a result of the Report of the Joint Preparatory Commission all relate to the true nature of the Church. Fundamental to all our Statements is the concept of *koinonia* (communion). In the early Christian tradition, reflection on the experience of *koinonia* opened the way to the understanding of the mystery of the Church. Although *koinonia* is never equated with *Church* in the New Testament, it is the term that most aptly expresses the mystery underlying the various New Testament images of the Church. When, for example, the Church is called the people of the new covenant or the bride of Christ, the context is primarily that of communion. Although such images as the Temple, the new Jerusalem, or the royal priesthood may carry institutional overtones, their primary purpose is to depict the Church's experience as a partaking in the salvation of Christ. When the Church is described as the body of Christ, the household of God, or the holy nation, the emphasis is upon the relationships among its members as well as upon their relationship with Christ the Head.

5.   Union with God in Christ Jesus through the Spirit is the heart of Christian *koinonia*. Among the various ways in which the term *koinonia* is used in different New Testament contexts, we concentrate on that which signifies a relation between persons resulting from their participation in one and the same reality (cf. 1 John 1.3). The Son of God has taken to himself our human nature, and he has sent upon us his Spirit, who makes us so truly members of the body of Christ that we too are able to call God "Abba, Father" (Rom. 8.15; Gal. 4.6). Moreover, sharing in the same Holy Spirit, whereby we become members of the same body of Christ and adopted children of the same Father, we are also bound to one another in a completely new relationship. *Koinonia* with one another is entailed by our *koinonia* with God in Christ. This is the mystery of the Church.

6.   This theme of *koinonia* runs through our Statements. In them we present the eucharist as the effectual sign of *koinonia*, *episcope* as serving the *koinonia*, and primacy as a visible link and focus of *koinonia*.

In the Statement *Eucharistic Doctrine* the eucharist is seen as the sacrament of Christ, by which he builds up and nurtures his people in the *koinonia* of his body. By the eucharist all the baptized are brought into communion with the source of *koinonia*. He is the one who destroyed the walls dividing humanity (Eph. 2.14); he is the one who died to gather into unity all the children of God his Father (cf. John 11.52; 17.20ff).

In the Statement *Ministry and Ordination* it is made clear that *episcope* exists only to serve *koinonia*. The ordained minister presiding at the eucharist is a sign of Christ gathering his people and giving them his body and blood. The Gospel he preaches is the Gospel of unity. Through the ministry of word and sacrament the Holy Spirit is given for the building up of the body of Christ. It is the responsibility of those exercising *episcope* to enable all the people to use the gifts of the Spirit which they have received for the enrichment of the Church's common life. It is also their responsibility to keep the community under the law of Christ in mutual love and in concern for others; for the reconciled community of the Church has been given the ministry of reconciliation (2 Cor. 5.18).

In both Statements on authority the Commission, discussing primacy, sees it as a necessary link between all those exercising *episcope* within the *koinonia*. All ministers of the Gospel need to be in communion with one another, for the one Church is a communion of local churches. They also need to be united in the apostolic faith. Primacy, as a focus within the *koinonia*, is an assurance that what they teach and do is in accord with the faith of the apostles.

7. The Church as *koinonia* requires visible expression because it is intended to be the "sacrament" of God's saving work. A sacrament is both sign and instrument. The *koinonia* is a sign that God's purpose in Christ is being realized in the world by grace. It is also an instrument for the accomplishment of this purpose, inasmuch as it proclaims the truth of the Gospel and witnesses to it by its life, thus entering more deeply into the mystery of the Kingdom. The community thus announces what it is called to become.

8. The *koinonia* is grounded in the word of God preached, believed and obeyed. Through this word the saving work of God is proclaimed. In the fullness of time this salvation was realized in the person of Jesus, the Word of God incarnate. Jesus prepared his followers to receive through the Holy Spirit the fruit of his death and resurrection, the culmination of his life of obedience, and to become the heralds of salvation. In the New Testament it is clear that the community is established by a baptism inseparable from faith and conversion, that its mission is to proclaim the Gospel of God, and that its common life is sustained by the eucharist. This remains the pattern for the Christian Church. The Church is the community of those reconciled with God and with each other because it is the community of those who believe in Jesus Christ and are justified through God's grace. It is also the reconciling community, because it has been called to bring to all mankind, through the preaching of the Gospel, God's gracious offer of redemption.

9. Christ's will and prayer are that his disciples should be one. Those who have received the same word of God and have been baptized in the same Spirit cannot, without disobedience, acquiesce in a state of separation. Unity is of the essence of the Church, and since the Church is visible its unity also must be visible. Full visible communion between our two Churches cannot be achieved without mutual recognition of sacraments and ministry, together with the common acceptance of a universal primacy, at one with the episcopal college in the service of the *koinonia*.

Eucharistic Doctrine

Co-Chairmen's Preface

The following Agreed Statement evolved from the thinking and the discussion of the Anglican-Roman Catholic International Commission over the past two years. The result has been a conviction among members of the Commission that we have reached agreement on essential points of eucharistic doctrine. We are equally convinced ourselves that, though no attempt was made to present a fully comprehensive treatment of the subject, nothing essential has been omitted. The document, agreed upon at our third meeting, at Windsor, on 7 September 1971, has been presented to our official authorities, but obviously it cannot be ratified by them until such time as our respective Churches can evaluate its conclusions.

We would want to point out that the members of the Commission who subscribe to this Statement have been officially appointed and come from many countries, representing a wide variety of theological background. Our intention was to reach a consensus at the level of faith, so that all of us might be able to say, within the limits of the Statement: this is the Christian faith of the Eucharist.

H. R. McAdoo
Alan C. Clark

September 1971

The Statement (1971)

Introduction

1.   In the course of the Church's history several traditions have developed in expressing Christian understanding of the eucharist. (For example, various names have become customary as descriptions of the eucharist: Lord's supper, liturgy, holy mysteries, synaxis, mass, holy communion. The eucharist has become the most universally accepted term.) An important stage in progress towards organic unity is a substantial consensus on the purpose and meaning of the eucharist. Our intention has been to seek a deeper understanding of the reality of the eucharist which is consonant with biblical teaching and with the tradition of our common inheritance, and to express in this document the consensus we have reached.

2.   Through the life, death and resurrection of Jesus Christ God has reconciled men to himself, and in Christ he offers unity to all mankind. By his word God calls us into a new relationship with himself as our Father and with one another as his children—a relationship inaugurated by baptism into Christ through the Holy Spirit, nurtured and deepened through the eucharist, and expressed in a confession of one faith and a common life of loving service.

I. The Mystery of the Eucharist

3.   When his people are gathered at the eucharist to commemorate his saving acts for our redemption, Christ makes effective among us the eternal benefits of his victory and elicits and renews our response of faith, thanksgiving and self-surrender. Christ through the Holy Spirit in the eucharist builds up the life of the Church, strengthens its fellowship and furthers its mission. The identity of the Church as the body of Christ is both expressed and effectively proclaimed by

its being centred in, and partaking of, his body and blood. In the whole action of the eucharist, and in and by his sacramental presence given through bread and wine, the crucified and risen Lord, according to his promise, offers himself to his people.

4.   In the eucharist we proclaim the Lord's death until he comes. Receiving a foretaste of the kingdom to come, we look back with thanksgiving to what Christ has done for us, we greet him present among us, we look forward to his final appearing in the fullness of his kingdom when "The Son also himself (shall) be subject unto him that put all things under him, that God may be all in all" (1 Cor. 15.28). When we gather around the same table in this communal meal at the invitation of the same Lord and when we "partake of the one loaf," we are one in commitment not only to Christ and to one another, but also to the mission of the Church in the world.

II. The Eucharist and the Sacrifice of Christ

5.   Christ's redeeming death and resurrection took place once and for all in history. Christ's death on the cross, the culmination of his whole life of obedience, was the one, perfect and sufficient sacrifice for the sins of the world. There can be no repetition of or addition to what was then accomplished once for all by Christ. Any attempt to express a nexus between the sacrifice of Christ and the eucharist must not obscure this fundamental fact of the Christian faith.[1] Yet God has given the eucharist to his Church as a means through which the atoning work of Christ on the cross is proclaimed and made effective in the life of the Church. The notion of *memorial* as understood in the passover celebration at the time of Christ—i.e., the making effective in the present of an event in the past—has opened the way to a clearer understanding of the relationship between Christ's sacrifice and the eucharist. The eucharistic memorial is no mere calling to mind of a past event or of its significance, but the Church's effectual proclamation of God's mighty acts. Christ instituted the eucharist as a memorial *(anamnesis)* of the totality of God's reconciling action in him. In the eucharistic prayer the church continues to make a perpetual memorial of Christ's death, and his members, united with God and one another, give thanks for all his mercies, entreat the benefits of his passion on behalf of the whole Church, participate in these benefits and enter into the movement of his self-offering.

---

1. The early Church in expressing the meaning of Christ's death and resurrection often used the language of sacrifice. For the Hebrew *sacrifice* was a traditional means of communication with God. The passover, for example, was a communal meal; the day of atonement was essentially expiatory; and the covenant established communion between God and man.

III. The Presence of Christ

6. Communion with Christ in the Eucharist presupposes his true presence, effectually signified by the bread and wine which, in this mystery, become his body and blood.[2] The real presence of his body and blood can, however, only be understood within the context of the redemptive activity whereby he gives himself, and in himself reconciliation, peace and life, to his own. On the one hand the eucharistic gift springs out of the paschal mystery of Christ's death and resurrection, in which God's saving purpose has already been definitively realized. On the other hand, its purpose is to transmit the life of the crucified and risen Christ to his body, the Church, so that its members may be more fully united with Christ and with one another.

7. Christ is present and active, in various ways, in the entire eucharistic celebration. It is the same Lord who through the proclaimed word invites his people to his table, who through his minister presides at that table, and who gives himself sacramentally in the body and blood of his paschal sacrifice. It is the Lord present at the right hand of the Father, and therefore transcending the sacramental order, who thus offers to his Church, in the eucharistic signs, the special gift of himself.

8. The sacramental body and blood of the Saviour are present as an offering to the believer awaiting his welcome. When this offering is met by faith, a lifegiving encounter results. Through faith Christ's presence—which does not depend on the individual's faith in order to be the Lord's real gift of himself to his Church—becomes no longer just a presence *for* the believer, but also a presence *with* him. Thus, in considering the mystery of the eucharistic presence, we must recognize both the sacramental sign of Christ's presence and the personal relationship between Christ and the faithful which arises from that presence.

9. The Lord's words at the last supper, "Take and eat; this is my body," do not allow us to dissociate the gift of the presence and the act of sacramental eating. The elements are not mere signs; Christ's body and blood become really present and are really given. But they are really present and given in order that, receiving them, believers may be united in communion with Christ the Lord.

10. According to the traditional order of the liturgy the consecratory prayer *(anaphora)* leads to the communion of the faithful. Through

---

2. The word *transubstantiation* is commonly used in the Roman Catholic Church to indicate that God acting in the eucharist effects a change in the inner reality of the elements. The term should be seen as affirming the *fact* of Christ's presence and of the mysterious and radical change which takes place. In contemporary Roman Catholic theology it is not understood as explaining *how* the change takes place.

this prayer of thanksgiving, a word of faith addressed to the Father, the bread and wine become the body and blood of Christ by the action of the Holy Spirit, so that in communion we eat the flesh of Christ and drink his blood.

11. The Lord who thus comes to his people in the power of the Holy Spirit is the Lord of glory. In the eucharistic celebration we anticipate the joys of the age to come. By the transforming action of the Spirit of God, earthly bread and wine become the heavenly manna and the new wine, the eschatological banquet for the new man: elements of the first creation become pledges and first fruits of the new heaven and the new earth.

Conclusion

12. We believe that we have reached substantial agreement on the doctrine of the eucharist. Although we are all conditioned by the traditional ways in which we have expressed and practised our eucharistic faith, we are convinced that if there are any remaining points of disagreement they can be resolved on the principles here established. We acknowledge a variety of theological approaches within both our communions. But we have seen it as our task to find a way of advancing together beyond the doctrinal disagreements of the past. It is our hope that, in view of the agreement which we have reached on eucharistic faith, this doctrine will no longer constitute an obstacle to the unity we seek.

Elucidation (1979)

1. When each of the Agreed Statements was published, the Commission invited and has received comment and criticism. This *Elucidation* is an attempt to expand and explain to those who have responded some points raised in connection with *Eucharistic Doctrine* (Windsor 1971).

Substantial Agreement

2. The Commission was not asked to produce a comprehensive treatise on the eucharist, but only to examine differences which in the controversies of the past divided our two communions. The aim of the Commission has been to see whether we can today discover substantial agreement in faith on the eucharist. Questions have been asked about the meaning of *substantial* agreement. It means that the document represents not only the judgement of all its members— i.e., it is an agreement—but their unanimous agreement "on essential matters where it considers that doctrine admits no divergence" (Ministry, para. 17)—i.e., it is a substantial agreement. Members of the

Commission are united in their conviction "that if there are any remaining points of disagreement they can be resolved on the principles here established" (Eucharist, para. 12).

Comments and Criticisms

3.   The following comments and criticisms are representative of the many received and are considered by the Commission to be of particular importance.

In spite of the firm assertion made in the Agreed Statement of the "once for all" nature of Christ's sacrifice, some have still been anxious that the term *anamnesis* may conceal the reintroduction of the theory of a repeated immolation. Others have suspected that the word refers not only to the historical events of salvation but also to an eternal sacrifice in heaven. Others again have doubted whether *anamnesis* sufficiently implies the reality indicated by traditional sacrificial language concerning the eucharist. Moreover, the accuracy and adequacy of the Commission's exegesis of *anamnesis* have been questioned.

Some critics have been unhappy about the realistic language used in this Agreed Statement, and have questioned such words as *become* and *change*. Others have wondered whether the permanence of Christ's eucharistic presence has been sufficiently acknowledged, with a consequent request for a discussion of the reserved sacrament and devotions associated with it. Similarly there have been requests for clarification of the Commission's attitude to receptionism.

4.   Behind these criticisms there lies a profound but often unarticulated anxiety that the Commission has been using new theological language which evades unresolved differences. Related to this anxiety is the further question as to the nature of the agreement claimed by the Commission. Does the language of the Commission conceal an ambiguity (either intentional or unintentional) in language which enables members of the two churches to see their own faith in the Agreed Statement without having in fact reached a genuine consensus.

Anamnesis and Sacrifice

5.   The Commission has been criticized for its use of the term *anamnesis*. It chose the word used in New Testament accounts of the institution of the eucharist at the last supper:

"Do this as a memorial (*anamnesis*) of me" (1 Cor. 11.24-25; Luke 22.19: JB, NEB).

The word is also to be found in Justin Martyr in the second century. Recalling the last supper he writes

Jesus, taking bread and having given thanks, said "Do this for my memorial (*anamnesis*): This is my body"; and likewise, taking the cup, and giving thanks, he said, "This is my blood" (*First Apology* 66; cf. *Dialogue with Trypho* 117).

From this time onwards the term is found at the very heart of the eucharistic prayers of both East and West, not only in the institution narrative but also in the prayer which follows and elsewhere: cf. e.g. The Liturgy of St. John Chrysostom; Eucharistic Prayer I—The Roman Missal; The Order of the Administration of the Lord's Supper or Holy Communion—The Book of Common Prayer (1662); and Rites A and B of the Church of England Alternative Service Book (1980).

The word is also found in patristic and later theology. The Council of Trent in explaining the relation between the sacrifice of the cross and the eucharist uses the words *commemoratio* and *memoria* (Session 22, ch. 1); and in the Book of Common Prayer (1662) the Catechism states that the sacrament of the Lord's Supper was ordained "for the continual *remembrance* of the sacrifice of the death of Christ, and of the benefits which we receive thereby." The frequent use of the term in contemporary theology is illustrated by *One Baptism One Eucharist and a Mutually Recognized Ministry* (Faith and Order Commission Paper No. 73), as well as by the *General Instruction on the Roman Missal* (1970).

The Commission believes that the traditional understanding of sacramental reality, in which the once-for-all event of salvation becomes effective in the present through the action of the Holy Spirit, is well expressed by the word *anamnesis*. We accept this use of the word which seems to do full justice to the semitic background. Furthermore it enables us to affirm a strong conviction of sacramental realism and to reject mere symbolism. However the selection of this word by the Commission does not mean that our common eucharistic faith may not be expressed in other terms.

In the exposition of the Christian doctrine of redemption the word *sacrifice* has been used in two intimately associated ways. In the New Testament, sacrificial language refers primarily to the historical events of Christ's saving work for us. The tradition of the Church, as evidenced for example in its liturgies, used similar language to designate in the eucharistic celebration the *anamnesis* of this historical event. Therefore it is possible to say at the same time that there is only one unrepeatable sacrifice in the historical sense, but that the eucharist is a sacrifice in the sacramental sense, provided that it is clear that this is not a repetition of the historical sacrifice.

There is therefore one historical, unrepeatable sacrifice, offered once for all by Christ and accepted once for all by the Father. In the celebration of the memorial, Christ in the Holy Spirit unites his people with himself in a sacramental way so that the Church enters into the movement of his self-offering. In consequence, even though the Church is active in this celebration, this adds nothing to the efficacy of Christ's sacrifice upon the cross, because the action is itself the fruit of this sacrifice. The Church in celebrating the eucharist gives thanks for the gift of Christ's sacrifice and identifies itself with the will of Christ who has offered himself to the Father on behalf of all mankind.

Christ's Presence in the Eucharist

6.   Criticism has been evoked by the statement that the bread and wine become the body and blood of Christ in the eucharist (para. 10). The word *become* has been suspected of expressing a materialistic conception of Christ's presence, and this has seemed to some to be confirmed in the footnote on the word *transubstantiation* which also speaks of *change*. It is feared that this suggests that Christ's presence in the eucharist is confined to the elements, and that the Real Presence involves a physical change in them.

In order to respond to these comments the Commission recalls that the Statement affirmed that:

(a) It is the glorified Lord himself whom the community of the faithful encounters in the eucharistic celebration through the preaching of the word, in the fellowship of the Lord's supper, in the heart of the believer, and, in a sacramental way, through the gifts of his body and blood, already given on the cross for their salvation.

(b) His body and blood are given through the action of the Holy Spirit, appropriating bread and wine so that they become the food of the new creation already inaugurated by the coming of Christ (cf. paras. 7, 10, 11).

Becoming does not here imply material change. Nor does the liturgical use of the word imply that the bread and wine become Christ's body and blood in such a way that in the eucharistic celebration his presence is limited to the consecrated elements. It does not imply that Christ becomes present in the eucharist in the same manner that he was present in his earthly life. It does not imply that this *becoming* follows the physical laws of this world. What is here affirmed is a sacramental presence in which God uses realities of this world to convey the realities of the new creation: bread for this life becomes the bread of eternal life. Before the eucharistic prayer, to the question: "What is that?" the believer answers: "It is bread." After the eucharistic prayer, to the same question he answers: "It is truly the body of Christ, the Bread of Life."

In the sacramental order the realities of faith become present in visible and tangible signs, enabling Christians to avail themselves of the fruits of the once-for-all redemption. In the eucharist the human person encounters in faith the person of Christ in his sacramental body and blood. This is the sense in which the community, the body of Christ, by partaking of the sacramental body of the risen Lord, grows into the unity God intends for his Church. The ultimate change intended by God is the transformation of human beings into the likeness of Christ. The bread and wine *become* the sacramental body and blood of Christ in order that the Christian community may *become* more truly what it already is, the body of Christ.

Gift and Reception

7.   This transformation into the likeness of Christ requires that the eucharistic gifts be received in faith. In the mystery of the eucharist we discern not one but two complementary movements within an indissoluble unity: Christ giving his body and blood, and the communicants feeding upon them in their hearts by faith. Some traditions have placed a special emphasis on the association of Christ's presence with the consecrated elements; others have emphasized Christ's presence in the heart of the believer through reception by faith. In the past, acute difficulties have arisen when one or other of these emphases has become almost exclusive. In the opinion of the Commission neither emphasis is incompatible with eucharistic faith, provided that the complementary movement emphasized by the other position is not denied. Eucharistic doctrine must hold together these two movements since in the eucharist, the sacrament of the New Covenant, Christ gives himself to his people so that they may receive him through faith.

Reservation

8.   The practice of reserving the sacrament for reception after the congregation has dispersed is known to date back to the second century (cf. Justin Martyr, *First Apology*, 65 and 67). In so far as it maintains the complementary movements already referred to (as for example, when communion is taken to the sick) this practice clearly accords with the purpose of the institution of the eucharist. But later there developed a tendency to stress the veneration of Christ's presence in the consecrated elements. In some places this tendency became so pronounced that the original purpose of reservation was in danger of becoming totally obscured. If veneration is wholly dissociated from the eucharistic celebration of the community it contradicts the true doctrine of the eucharist.

Consideration of this question requires clarification of the understanding of the eucharist. Adoration in the celebration of the eucharist is first and foremost offered to the Father. It is to lead us to the Father that Christ unites us to himself through our receiving of his body and blood. The Christ whom we adore in the eucharist is Christ glorifying his Father. The movement of all our adoration is to the Father, through, with, and in Christ, in the power of the Spirit.

The whole eucharistic action is a continuous movement in which Christ offers himself in his sacramental body and blood to his people and in which they receive him in faith and thanksgiving. Consequently communion administered from the reserved sacrament to those unable to attend the eucharistic celebration is rightly understood as an extension of that celebration. Differences arise between those who would practise reservation for this reason only, and those who would also regard it as a means of eucharistic devotion. For the latter, adoration of Christ in the reserved sacrament should be regarded as an extension of eucharistic worship, even though it does not include immediate sacramental reception, which remains the primary purpose of reservation (cf. the Instruction *Eucharisticum Mysterium*, para. 49, of the Sacred Congregation of Rites (AAS 59, 1967)). Any dissociation of such devotion from this primary purpose, which is communion in Christ of all his members, is a distortion in eucharistic practice.

9.   In spite of this clarification, others still find any kind of adoration of Christ in the reserved sacrament unacceptable. They believe that it is in fact impossible in such a practice truly to hold together the two movements of which we have spoken: and that this devotion can hardly fail to produce such an emphasis upon the association of Christ's sacramental presence with the consecrated bread and wine as to suggest too static and localized a presence that disrupts the movement as well as the balance of the whole eucharistic action (cf. Article 28 of the Articles of Religion).

That there can be a divergence in matters of practice and in theological judgements relating to them, without destroying a common eucharistic faith, illustrates what we mean by *substantial* agreement. Differences of theology and practice may well coexist with a real consensus on the essentials of eucharistic faith—as in fact they do within each of our communions.

Other Issues

10. Concern has been expressed that we have said nothing about intercommunion, though claiming to have attained a substantial agreement on eucharistic faith. The reason is that we are agreed that a responsible judgment on this matter cannot be made on the basis of this Statement alone, because intercommunion also involves issues relating to authority and to the mutual recognition of ministry. There are other important issues, such as the eschatological dimension of the eucharist and its relation to contemporary questions of human liberation and social justice, which we have either not fully developed or not explicitly treated. These are matters which call for the common attention of our churches, but they are not a source of division between us and are therefore outside our mandate.

Ministry and Ordination

Co-Chairmen's Preface

At Windsor, in 1971, the Anglican-Roman Catholic International Commission was able to achieve an Agreed Statement on Eucharistic Doctrine. In accordance with the programme adopted at Venice in 1970, we have now, at our meeting in Canterbury in 1973, turned our attention to the doctrine of ministry, specifically to our understanding of the ordained ministry and its place in the life of the Church. The present document is the result of the work of this officially appointed Commission and is offered to our authorities for their consideration. At this stage it remains an agreed statement of the Commission and no more.

We acknowledge with gratitude our debt to the many studies and discussions which have treated the same material. While respecting the different forms that ministry has taken in other traditions, we hope that the clarification of our understanding expressed in the statement will be of service to them also.

We have submitted the statement, therefore, to our authorities and, with their authorization, we publish it as a document of the Commission with a view to its discussion. Even though there may be differences of emphasis within our two traditions, yet we believe that in what we have said here both Anglican and Roman Catholic will recognize their own faith.

H. R. McAdoo
Alan C. Clark

September 1973

The Statement (1973)

Introduction

1. Our intention has been to seek a deeper understanding of ministry which is consonant with biblical teaching and with the traditions of our common inheritance, and to express in this document the consensus we have reached.[1] This Statement is not designed to be an exhaustive treatment of ministry. It seeks to express our basic agreement in the doctrinal areas that have been the source of contro-

---

1. Cf. Eucharist, para. 1, which similarly speaks of a consensus reached with regard to the eucharist.

versy between us, in the wider context of our common convictions about the ministry.

2. Within the Roman Catholic Church and the Anglican Communion there exists a diversity of forms of ministerial service. Of more specific ways of service, while some are undertaken without particular initiative from official authority, others may receive a mandate from ecclesiastical authorities. The ordained ministry can only be rightly understood within this broader context of various ministries, all of which are the work of one and the same Spirit.

I. Ministry in the Life of the Church

3. The life and self-offering of Christ perfectly express what it is to serve God and man. All Christian ministry, whose purpose is always to build up the community (*koinonia*), flows and takes its shape from this source and model. The communion of men with God (and with each other) requires their reconciliation. This reconciliation, accomplished by the death and resurrection of Jesus Christ, is being realized in the life of the Church through the response of faith. While the Church is still in process of sanctification, its mission is nevertheless to be the instrument by which this reconciliation in Christ is proclaimed, his love manifested, and the means of salvation offered to men.

4. In the early Church the apostles exercised a ministry which remains of fundamental significance for the Church of all ages. It is difficult to deduce, from the New Testament use of "apostle" for the Twelve, Paul, and others, a precise portrait of an apostle, but two primary features of the original apostolate are clearly discernible: a special relationship with the historical Christ, and a commission from him to the Church and the world (Matt. 28.19; Mark 3.14). All Christian apostolate originates in the sending of the Son by the Father. The Church is apostolic not only because its faith and life must reflect the witness to Jesus Christ given in the early Church by the apostles, but also because it is charged to continue in the apostles' commission to communicate to the world what it has received. Within the whole history of mankind the Church is to be the community of reconciliation.

5. All ministries are used by the Holy Spirit for the building up of the Church to be this reconciling community for the glory of God and the salvation of men (Eph. 4.11-13). Within the New Testament ministerial actions are varied and functions not precisely defined. Explicit emphasis is given to the proclamation of the word and the preservation of apostolic doctrine, the care of the flock, and the example of Christian living. At least by the time of the Pastoral Epistles and 1 Peter, some ministerial functions are discernible in a more exact form. The evidence suggests that with the growth of the Church the importance of certain functions led to their being located in specific officers of the community. Since the Church is built up by the Holy Spirit primarily but not exclusively through these ministerial functions, some form of recognition and authorization is already required in the New Testament period for those who exercise them in the name of Christ. Here we can see elements which will remain at the heart of what today we call ordination.

6. The New Testament shows that ministerial office played an essential part in the life of the Church in the first century, and we believe that the provision of a ministry of this kind is part of God's design for his people. Normative principles governing the purpose and function of the ministry are already present in the New Testament documents (e.g., Mark 10.43-5; Acts 20.28; 1 Tim. 4.12-16; 1. Pet. 5.1-4). The early churches may well have had considerable diversity in the structure of pastoral ministry, though it is clear that some churches were headed by ministers who were called *episcopoi* and *presbyteroi*. While the first missionary churches were not a loose aggregation of autonomous communities, we have no evidence that "bishops" and "presbyters" were appointed everywhere in the primitive period. The terms "bishop" and "presbyter" could be applied to the same man or to men with identical or very similar functions. Just as the formation of the canon of the New Testament was a process incomplete until the second half of the second century, so also the full emergence of the threefold ministry of bishop, presbyter, and deacon required a longer period than the apostolic age. Thereafter this threefold structure became universal in the Church.

II. The Ordained Ministry

7. The Christian community exists to give glory to God through the fulfilment of the Father's purpose. All Christians are called to serve this purpose by their life of prayer and surrender to divine grace, and by their careful attention to the needs of all human beings. They should witness to God's compassion for all mankind and his concern for justice in the affairs of men. They should offer themselves to God in praise and worship, and devote their energies to bringing men into the fellowship of Christ's people, and so under his rule of love. The goal of the ordained ministry is to serve this priesthood of all the faithful. Like any human community the Church requires a focus of leadership and unity, which the Holy Spirit provides in the ordained ministry. This ministry assumes various patterns to meet the varying needs of those whom the Church is seeking to serve, and it is the role of the minister to co-ordinate the activities of the Church's fellowship and to promote what is necessary and useful for the Church's life and mission. He is to discern what is of the Spirit in the diversity of the Church's life and promote its unity.

8. In the New Testament a variety of images is used to describe the functions of this minister. He is servant, both of Christ and of the Church. As herald and ambassador he is an authoritative representative of Christ and proclaims his message of reconciliation. As teacher he explains and applies the word of God to the community. As shepherd he exercises pastoral care and guides the flock. He is a steward who may only provide for the household of God what belongs to Christ. He is to be an example both in holiness and in compassion.

9. An essential element in the ordained ministry is its responsibility for "oversight" *(episcope).* This responsibility involves fidelity to the apostolic faith, its embodiment in the life of the Church today, and its transmission to the Church of tomorrow. Presbyters are joined with the bishop in his oversight of the church and in the ministry of the word and the sacraments; they are given authority to preside at the eucharist and to pronounce absolution. Deacons, although not so empowered, are associated with bishops and presbyters in the ministry of word and sacrament, and assist in oversight.

10. Since the ordained ministers are ministers of the Gospel, every facet of their oversight is linked with the word of God. In the original mission and witness recorded in Holy Scripture lies the source and ground of their preaching and authority. By the preaching of the word they seek to bring those who are not Christians into the fellowship of Christ. The Christian message needs also to be unfolded to the faithful, in order to deepen their knowledge of God and their response of grateful faith. But a true faith calls for beliefs that are correct and lives that endorse the Gospel. So the ministers have to guide the community and to advise individuals with regard to the implications of commitment to Christ. Because God's concern is not only for the welfare of the Church but also for the whole of creation, they must also lead their communities in the service of humanity. Church and people have continually to be brought under the guidance of the apostolic faith. In all these ways a ministerial vocation implies a responsibility for the word of God supported by constant prayer (cf. Acts 6.4).

11. The part of the ministers in the celebration of the sacraments is one with their responsibility for ministry of the word. In both word and sacrament Christians meet the living Word of God. The responsibility of the ministers in the Christian community involves them in being not only the persons who normally administer baptism, but also those who admit converts to the communion of the faithful and restore those who have fallen away. Authority to pronounce God's forgiveness of sin, given to bishops and presbyters at their ordination, is exercised by them to bring Christians to a closer communion with God and with their fellow men through Christ and to assure them of God's continuing love and mercy.

12. To proclaim reconciliation in Christ and to manifest his reconciling love belong to the continuing mission of the Church. The central act of worship, the eucharist, is the memorial of that reconciliation and nourishes the Church's life for the fulfilment of its mission. Hence it is right that he who has oversight in the church and is the focus of its unity should preside at the celebration of the eucharist. Evidence as early as Ignatius shows that, at least in some churches, the man exercising this oversight presided at the eucharist and no other could do so without his consent (*Letter to the Smyrnaeans*, 8.1).

13. The priestly sacrifice of Jesus was unique, as is also his continuing High Priesthood. Despite the fact that in the New Testament ministers are never called "priests" (*hieros*),[2] Christians came to see the priestly role of Christ reflected in these ministers and used priestly terms in describing them. Because the eucharist is the memorial of the sacrifice of Christ, the action of the presiding minister in reciting again the words of Christ at the last supper and distributing to the assembly the holy gifts is seen to stand in a sacramental relation to what Christ himself did in offering his own sacrifice. So our two traditions commonly use priestly terms in speaking about the ordained ministry. Such language does not imply any negation of the once-for-all sacrifice of Christ by any addition or repetition. There is in the eucharist a memorial (*anamnesis*)[3] of the totality of God's reconciling action in Christ, who through his minister presides at the Lord's Supper and gives himself sacramentally. So it is because the eucharist is central in the Church's life that the essential nature of the Christian ministry, however this may be expressed, is most clearly seen in its celebration; for, in the eucharist, thanksgiving is offered to God, the gospel of salvation is proclaimed in word and sacrament, and the community is knit together as one body in Christ. Christian ministers are members of this redeemed community. Not only do they share through baptism in the priesthood of the people of God, but they are—particularly in presiding at the eucharist—representative of the whole Church in the fulfilment of its priestly vocation of self-offering to God as a living sacrifice (Rom. 12.1). Nevertheless their ministry is not an extension of the common Christian priesthood but belongs to another realm of the gifts of the Spirit. It exists to help the Church to be "a royal priesthood, a holy nation, God's own people, to declare the wonderful deeds of him who called [them] out of darkness into his marvellous light" (1 Pet. 2.9).

---

2. In the English language the word "priest" is used to translate two distinct Greek words, *hieros* which belongs to the cultic order and *presbyteros* which designates an elder in the community.
3. Cf. Eucharist, para. 5.

II. Vocation and Ordination

14. Ordination denotes entry into this apostolic and God-given ministry, which serves and signifies the unity of the local churches in themselves and with one another. Every individual act of ordination is therefore an expression of the continuing apostolicity and catholicity of the whole Church. Just as the original apostles did not choose themselves but were chosen and commissioned by Jesus, so those who are ordained are called by Christ in the Church and through the Church. Not only is their vocation from Christ but their qualification for exercising such a ministry is the gift of the Spirit: "our sufficiency is from God, who has qualified us to be ministers of a new covenant, not in a written code but in the Spirit" (2 Cor. 3.5-6). This is expressed in ordination, when the bishop prays God to grant the gift of the Holy Spirit and lays hands on the candidate as the outward sign of the gifts bestowed. Because ministry is in and for the community and because ordination is an act in which the whole Church of God is involved, this prayer and laying on of hands takes place within the context of the eucharist.

15. In this sacramental act,[4] the gift of God is bestowed upon the ministers, with the promise of divine grace for their work and for their sanctification; the ministry of Christ is presented to them as a model for their own; and the Spirit seals those whom he has chosen and consecrated. Just as Christ has united the Church inseparably with himself, and as God calls all the faithful to lifelong discipleship, so the gifts and calling of God to the ministers are irrevocable. For this reason, ordination is unrepeatable in both our churches.

16. Both presbyters and deacons are ordained by the bishop. In the ordination of a presbyter the presbyters present join the bishop in the laying on of hands, thus signifying the shared nature of the commission entrusted to them. In the ordination of a new bishop, other bishops lay hands on him, as they request the gift of the Spirit for his ministry and receive him into their ministerial fellowship. Because they are entrusted with the oversight of other churches, this participation in his ordination signifies that this new bishop and his church are within the communion of churches. Moreover, because they are representative of their churches in fidelity to the teaching and mission of the apostles and are members of the episcopal college, their par-

---

4. Anglican use of the word "sacrament" with reference to ordination is limited by the distinction drawn in the Thirty-nine Articles (Article 25) between the two "sacraments of the Gospel" and the "five commonly called sacraments." Article 25 does not deny these latter the name "sacrament," but differentiates between them and the "two sacraments ordained by Christ" described in the Catechism as "necessary to salvation" for all men.

ticipation also ensures the historical continuity of this church with the apostolic Church and of its bishop with the original apostolic ministry. The communion of the churches in mission, faith, and holiness, through time and space, is thus symbolized and maintained in the bishop. Here are comprised the essential features of what is meant in our two traditions by ordination in the apostolic succession.

Conclusion

17. We are fully aware of the issues raised by the judgement of the Roman Catholic Church on Anglican Orders. The development of the thinking in our two communions regarding the nature of the Church and of the ordained ministry, as represented in our Statement, has, we consider, put these issues in a new context. Agreement on the nature of ministry is prior to the consideration of the mutual recognition of ministries. What we have to say represents the consensus of the Commission on essential matters where it considers that doctrine admits no divergence. It will be clear that we have not yet broached the wide-ranging problems of authority which may arise in any discussion of ministry, nor the question of primacy. We are aware that present understanding of such matters remains an obstacle to the reconciliation of our churches in the one Communion we desire, and the Commission is now turning to the examination of the issues involved. Nevertheless we consider that our consensus, on questions where agreement is indispensable for unity, offers a positive contribution to the reconciliation of our churches and of their ministries.

Elucidation (1979)

Comments and Criticisms

1. After the publication of the Statement *Ministry and Ordination,* the Commission received comments and criticisms, among which it judged the following to be of special concern.

It has been suggested that in the discussion of ministry insufficient attention was given to the priesthood of the whole people of God, so that the document seemed to have too clerical an emphasis. In this connection it has also been said that the distinction between this priesthood of all the faithful and the priesthood of the ordained ministry was not clearly enough explained. Questions have also been raised about the Commission's treatment of the origins and historical development of the ordained ministry and its threefold form; about its comparison of that development with the emergence of the canon of Scripture; and about its views on the place of episcopacy within *episcope* as it is outlined in the Statement (para. 9).

Some have wondered whether the Statement adequately expressed the sacramental nature of the rite of ordination, others whether this aspect has been overemphasized. The Commission has been asked to consider the implications of the Statement for the question of the ordination of women. There have also been inquiries about the bearing of the Statement upon the problem of recognizing the validity of Anglican Orders.

Priesthood

2. In common Christian usage the term *priesthood* is employed in three distinct ways: the priesthood of Christ, the priesthood of the people of God, the priesthood of the ordained ministry.

The priesthood of Christ is unique. He is our High Priest who has reconciled mankind with the Father. All other priesthood derives from his and is wholly dependent upon it.

The priesthood of the whole people of God (1 Peter 2.5) is the consequence of incorporation by baptism into Christ. This priesthood of all the faithful (para. 7) is not a matter of disagreement between us. In a document primarily concerned with the ordained ministry, the Commission did not consider it necessary to develop the subject further than it has already done in the Statement. Here the ordained ministry is firmly placed in the context of the ministry of the whole Church and exists for the service of all the faithful.

The Statement (para. 13) explains that the ordained ministry is called priestly principally because it has a particular sacramental relationship with Christ as High Priest. At the eucharist Christ's people do what he commanded in memory of himself and Christ unites them sacramentally with himself in his self-offering. But in this action it is only the ordained minister who presides at the eucharist, in which, in the name of Christ and on behalf of his Church, he recites the narrative of the institution of the Last Supper, and invokes the Holy Spirit upon the gifts.

The word *priesthood* is used by way of analogy when it is applied to the people of God and to the ordained ministry. These are two distinct realities which relate, each in its own way, to the high priesthood of Christ, the unique priesthood of the new covenant, which is their source and model. These considerations should be borne in mind throughout para. 13, and in particular they indicate the significance of the statement that the ordained ministry "is not an extension of the common Christian priesthood but belongs to another realm of the gifts of the Spirit."

In this as in other cases the early Church found it necessary for its understanding and exposition of the faith to employ terminology in ways in which it was not used in the New Testament. Today in seeking to give an account of our faith both our communions, in the interpretation of the Scriptures, take cognisance of the Church's growing understanding of Christian truth (cf. Authority I, paras. 2, 3, and 15).

Sacramentality of Ordination

3.   The phrase "in this sacramental act" in para. 15 has caused anxiety on two different counts: that this phrase seems to give the sacrament of ordination the same status as the two "sacraments of the Gospel"; and that it does not adequately express the full sacramentality of ordination.

Both traditions agree that a sacramental rite is a visible sign through which the grace of God is given by the Holy Spirit in the Church. The rite of ordination is one of these sacramental rites. Those who are ordained by prayer and the laying on of hands receive their ministry from Christ through those designated in the Church to hand it on; together with the office they are given the grace needed for its fulfilment (cf. para. 14). Since New Testament times the Church has required such recognition and authorization for those who are to exercise the principal functions of *episcope* in the name of Christ. This is what both traditions mean by the sacramental rite of ordination.

Both traditions affirm the pre-eminence of baptism and the eucharist as sacraments "necessary to salvation." This does not diminish their understanding of the sacramental nature of ordination, as to which there is no significant disagreement between them.

Origins and Development of the Ordained Ministry

4.   Our treatment of the origins of the ordained ministry has been criticized. While the evidence leaves ground for differences of interpretation, it is enough for our purpose to recall that, from the beginning of the Christian Church, there existed *episcope* in the community, however its various responsibilities were distributed and described, and whatever the names given to those who exercise it (cf. paras. 8, 9, and especially 6). It is generally agreed that, within the first century, evidence of ordination such as we have described above is provided by the *First Epistle of Clement*, chapters 40-44, commonly dated 95 A.D. Some New Testament passages appear to imply the same conclusion, e.g., Acts 14.23. Early in the second century, the pattern of a threefold ministry centred on episcopacy was already discernible, and probably widely found (cf. the Epistles of Ignatius to the *Ephesians*, 4; *Magnesians*, 13; *Trallians*, 2; *Philadelphians*, 2; *Smyrnaeans*, 8). It was recognized that such ministry must be in continuity not only with the apostolic faith but also with the commission given to the apostles (cf. the *First Epistle of Clement*, 42).

Our intention in drawing a parallel between this emergence of the threefold ministry and the formation of the New Testament canon was to point to comparable processes of gradual development without determining whether the comparison could be carried further (cf. para. 6). The threefold ministry remained universal until the divisions of Western Christianity in the sixteenth century. However, both our communions have retained it.

We both maintain that *episcope* must be exercised by ministers ordained in the apostolic succession (cf. para. 16). Both our communions have retained and remained faithful to the threefold ministry centred on episcopacy as the form in which this *episcope* is to be exercised. Because our task was limited to examining relations between our two communions, we did not enter into the question whether there is any other form in which this *episcope* can be realized.

Ordination of Women

5.   Since the publication of the Statement there have been rapid developments with regard to the ordination of women. In those churches of the Anglican Communion where canonical ordinations of women have taken place, the bishops concerned believe that their action implies no departure from the traditional doctrine of the ordained ministry (as expounded, for instance, in the Statement). While the Commission realizes that the ordination of women has created for the Roman Catholic Church a new and grave obstacle to the reconciliation of our communions (cf. Letter of Pope Paul VI to Archbishop Donald Coggan, 23 March 1976, AAS 68), it believes that the principles upon which its doctrinal agreement rests are not affected by such ordinations; for it was concerned with the origin and nature of the ordained ministry and not with the question who can or cannot be ordained. Objections, however substantial, to the ordination of women are of a different kind from objections raised in the past against the validity of Anglican Orders in general.

Anglican Orders

6.   In answer to the questions concerning the significance of the Agreed Statements for the mutual recognition of ministry, the Commission has affirmed that a consensus has been reached that places the questions in a new context (cf. para. 17). It believes that our agreement on the essentials of eucharistic faith with regard to the sacramental presence of Christ and the sacrificial dimension of the eucharist, and on the nature and purpose of priesthood, ordination, and apostolic succession, is the new context in which the questions should now be discussed. This calls for a reappraisal of the verdict on Anglican Orders in *Apostolicae Curae* (1896).

Mutual recognition presupposes acceptance of the apostolicity of each other's ministry. The Commission believes that its agreements have demonstrated a consensus in faith on eucharist and ministry which has brought closer the possibility of such acceptance. It hopes that its own conviction will be shared by members of both our communions; but mutual recognition can only be achieved by the decision of our authorities. It has been our mandate to offer to them the basis upon which they may make this decision.

Authority in the Church I

Co-Chairmen's Preface

The Malta Report of the Anglican-Roman Catholic Joint Preparatory Commission (1968) outlined the large measure of agreement in faith which exists between the Roman Catholic Church and the churches of the Anglican Communion (para. 7). It then went on to note three specific areas of doctrinal disagreement. These were listed in the Report as matters for joint investigation. Accordingly the Anglican-Roman Catholic International Commission, proposed by the Report, was recommended to examine jointly "the question of intercommunion, and the related matters of Church and Ministry," and "the question of authority, its nature, exercise, and implications."

To our previous Agreed Statements on the Eucharist (Windsor 1971) and Ministry (Canterbury 1973) we now add an Agreed Statement on Authority in the Church (Venice 1976). The Commission thus submits its work to the authorities who appointed it and, with their permission, offers it to our churches.

The question of authority in the Church has long been recognized as crucial to the growth in unity of the Roman Catholic Church and the churches of the Anglican Communion. It was precisely in the problem of papal primacy that our historical divisions found their unhappy origin. Hence, however significant our consensus on the doctrine of the eucharist and of the ministry, unresolved questions on the nature and exercise of authority in the Church would hinder the growing experience of unity which is the pattern of our present relations.

The present Statement has, we believe, made a significant contribution to the resolution of these questions. Our consensus covers a very wide area; though we have not been able to resolve some of the difficulties of Anglicans concerning Roman Catholic belief relating to the office of the bishop of Rome, we hope and trust that our analysis has placed these problems in a proper perspective.

There is much in the document, as in our other documents, which presents the ideal of the Church as willed by Christ. History shows how the Church has often failed to achieve this ideal. An awareness of this distinction between the ideal and the actual is important both for the reading of the document and for the understanding of the method we have pursued.

The consensus we have reached, if it is to be accepted by our two communities, would have, we insist, important consequences. Common recognition of Roman primacy would bring changes not only to the Anglican Communion but also to the Roman Catholic Church. On both sides the readiness to learn, necessary to the achievement of such a wider *koinonia*, would demand humility and charity. The prospect should be met with faith, not fear. Communion with the see of Rome would bring to the churches of the Anglican Communion not only a wider *koinonia* but also a strengthening of the power to realize its traditional ideal of diversity in unity. Roman Catholics, on their side, would be enriched by the presence of a particular tradition of spirituality and scholarship, the lack of which has deprived the Roman Catholic Church of a precious element in the Christian heritage. The Roman Catholic Church has much to learn from the Anglican synodical tradition of involving the laity in the life and mission of the Church. We are convinced, therefore, that our degree of agreement, which argues for greater communion between our churches, can make a profound contribution to the witness of Christianity in our contemporary society.

It is in this light that we would wish to submit our conclusions to our respective authorities, believing that our work, indebted, as it is, to many sources outside the Commission as well as to its own labours, will be of service not only to ourselves but to Christians of other traditions in our common quest for the unity of Christ's Church.

H. R. McAdoo
Alan C. Clark

September 1976

The Statement (1976)

Introduction

1. The confession of Christ as Lord is the heart of the Christian faith. To him God has given all authority in heaven and on earth. As Lord of the Church he bestows the Holy Spirit to create a communion of men with God and with one another. To bring this *koinonia* to perfection is God's eternal purpose. The Church exists to serve the fulfilment of this purpose when God will be all in all.

I. Christian Authority

2. Through the gift of the Spirit the apostolic community came to recognize in the words and deeds of Jesus the saving activity of God

and their mission to proclaim to all men the good news of salvation. Therefore they preached Jesus through whom God has spoken finally to men. Assisted by the Holy Spirit they transmitted what they had heard and seen of the life and words of Jesus and their interpretation of his redemptive work. Consequently the inspired documents in which this is related came to be accepted by the Church as a normative record of the authentic foundation of the faith. To these the Church has recourse for the inspiration of its life and mission; to these the Church refers its teaching and practice. Through these written words the authority of the Word of God is conveyed. Entrusted with these documents, the Christian community is enabled by the Holy Spirit to live out the Gospel and so to be led into all truth. It is therefore given the capacity to assess its faith and life and to speak to the world in the name of Christ. Shared commitment and belief create a common mind in determining how the Gospel should be interpreted and obeyed. By reference to this common faith each person tests the truth of his own belief.

3.   The Spirit of the risen Lord, who indwells the Christian community, continues to maintain the people of God in obedience to the Father's will. He safeguards their faithfulness to the revelation of Jesus Christ and equips them for their mission in the world. By this action of the Holy Spirit the authority of the Lord is active in the Church. Through incorporation into Christ and obedience to him Christians are made open to one another and assume mutual obligations. Since the Lordship of Christ is universal, the community also bears a responsibility towards all mankind, which demands participation in all that promotes the good of society and responsiveness to every form of human need. The common life in the body of Christ equips the community and each of its members with what they need to fulfil this responsibility: they are enabled so to live that the authority of Christ will be mediated through them. This is Christian authority: when Christians so act and speak, men perceive the authoritative word of Christ.

II. Authority in the Church

4.   The Church is a community which consciously seeks to submit to Jesus Christ. By sharing in the life of the Spirit all find within the *koinonia* the means to be faithful to the revelation of their Lord. Some respond more fully to his call; by the inner quality of their life they win a respect which allows them to speak in Christ's name with authority.

5.   The Holy Spirit also gives to some individuals and communities special gifts for the benefit of the Church, which entitle them to speak and be heeded (e.g. Eph. 4.11, 12; 1 Cor. 12.4-11).

Among these gifts of the Spirit for the edification of the Church is the *episcope* of the ordained ministry. There are some whom the Holy Spirit commissions through ordination for service to the whole community. They exercise their authority in fulfilling ministerial functions related to "the apostles' teaching and fellowship, to the breaking of bread and the prayers" (Acts 2.42). This pastoral authority belongs primarily to the bishop, who is responsible for preserving and promoting the integrity of the *koinonia* in order to further the Church's response to the Lordship of Christ and its commitment to mission. Since the bishop has general oversight of the community, he can require the compliance necessary to maintain faith and charity in its daily life. He does not, however, act alone. All those who have ministerial authority must recognize their mutual responsibility and interdependence. This service of the Church, officially entrusted only to ordained ministers, is intrinsic to the Church's structure according to the mandate given by Christ and recognized by the community. This is yet another form of authority.

6.   The perception of God's will for his Church does not belong only to the ordained ministry but is shared by all its members. All who live faithfully within the *koinonia* may become sensitive to the leading of the Spirit and be brought towards a deeper understanding of the Gospel and of its implications in diverse cultures and changing situations. Ordained ministers commissioned to discern these insights and give authoritative expression to them, are part of the community, sharing its quest for understanding the Gospel in obedience to Christ and receptive to the needs and concerns of all.

The community, for its part, must respond to and assess the insights and teaching of the ordained ministers. Through this continuing process of discernment and response, in which the faith is expressed and the Gospel is pastorally applied, the Holy Spirit declares the authority of the Lord Jesus Christ, and the faithful may live freely under the discipline of the Gospel.

7.   It is by such means as these that the Holy Spirit keeps the Church under the Lordship of Christ, who, taking full account of human weakness, has promised never to abandon his people. The authorities in the Church cannot adequately reflect Christ's authority because they are still subject to the limitations and sinfulness of human nature. Awareness of this inadequacy is a continual summons to reform.

III. Authority in the Communion of the Churches

8.   The *koinonia* is realized not only in the local Christian communities, but also in the communion of these communities with one another. The unity of local communities under one bishop constitutes what is commonly meant in our two communions by "a local church," though the expression is sometimes used in other ways. Each local church is rooted in the witness of the apostles and entrusted with the apostolic mission. Faithful to the Gospel, celebrating the one eucharist and dedicated to the service of the same Lord, it is the Church of Christ. In spite of diversities each local church recognizes its own essential features in the others and its true identity with them. The authoritative action and proclamation of the people of God to the world therefore are not simply the responsibilities of each church acting separately, but of all the local churches together. The spiritual gifts of one may be an inspiration to the others. Since each bishop must ensure that the local community is distinctively Christian he has to make it aware of the universal communion of which it is part. The bishop expresses this unity of his church with the others: this is symbolized by the participation of several bishops in his ordination.

9.   Ever since the Council of Jerusalem (Acts 15) the churches have realized the need to express and strengthen the *koinonia* by coming together to discuss matters of mutual concern and to meet contemporary challenges. Such gatherings may be either regional or worldwide. Through such meetings the Church, determined to be obedient to Christ and faithful to its vocation, formulates its rule of faith and orders its life. In all these councils, whether of bishops only, or of bishops, clergy, and laity, decisions are authoritative when they express the common faith and mind of the Church. The decisions of what has traditionally been called an "ecumenical council" are binding upon the whole Church; those of a regional council or synod bind only the churches it represents. Such decrees are to be received by the local churches as expressing the mind of the Church. This exercise of authority, far from being an imposition, is designed to strengthen the life and mission of the local churches and of their members.

10.   Early in the history of the Church a function of oversight of the other bishops of their regions was assigned to bishops of prominent sees. Concern to keep the churches faithful to the will of Christ was among the considerations which contributed to this development. This practice has continued to the present day. This form of *episcope* is a service to the Church carried out in co-responsibility with all the bishops of the region; for every bishop receives at ordination both responsibility for his local church and the obligation to maintain it in living awareness and practical service of the other churches. The Church of God is found in each of them and in their *koinonia*.

11.   The purpose of *koinonia* is the realization of the will of Christ: "Father, keep them in thy name, which thou hast given me, that they may be one, even as we are one. . . . so that the world may believe that thou hast sent me" (John 17.11, 21). The bishop of a principal see should seek the fulfilment of this will of Christ in the churches of his region. It is his duty to assist the bishops to promote in their churches right teaching, holiness of life, brotherly unity, and the Church's mission to the world. When he perceives a serious defi-

ciency in the life or mission of one of the churches he is bound, if necessary, to call the local bishop's attention to it and to offer assistance. There will also be occasions when he has to assist other bishops to reach a common mind with regard to their shared needs and difficulties. Sharing together and active mutual concern are indispensable to the churches' effective witness to Christ.

12. It is within the context of this historical development that the see of Rome, whose prominence was associated with the death there of Peter and Paul, eventually became the principal centre in matters concerning the Church universal.

The importance of the bishop of Rome among his brother bishops, as explained by analogy with the position of Peter among the apostles, was interpreted as Christ's will for his Church.

On the basis of this analogy the First Vatican Council affirmed that this service was necessary to the unity of the whole Church. Far from overriding the authority of the bishops in their own dioceses, this service was explicitly intended to support them in their ministry of oversight. The Second Vatican Council placed this service in the wider context of the shared responsibility of all the bishops. The teaching of these councils shows that communion with the bishop of Rome does not imply submission to an authority which would stifle the distinctive features of the local churches. The purpose of this episcopal function of the bishop of Rome is to promote Christian fellowship in faithfulness to the teaching of the apostles.

The theological interpretation of this primacy and the administrative structures through which it has been exercised have varied considerably through the centuries. Neither theory nor practice, however, has ever fully reflected these ideals. Sometimes functions assumed by the see of Rome were not necessarily linked to the primacy; sometimes the conduct of the occupant of this see has been unworthy of his office; sometimes the image of this office has been obscured by interpretations placed upon it; and sometimes external pressures have made its proper exercise almost impossible. Yet the primacy, rightly understood, implies that the bishop of Rome exercises his oversight in order to guard and promote the faithfulness of all the churches to Christ and one another. Communion with him is intended as a safeguard of the catholicity of each local church, and as a sign of the communion of all the churches.

IV. Authority in Matters of Faith

13. A local church cannot be truly faithful to Christ if it does not desire to foster universal communion, the embodiment of that unity for which Christ prayed. This communion is founded on faith in Jesus Christ, the incarnate Son of God, crucified, risen, ascended, and now living through his Spirit in the Church. Every local church must therefore ever seek a deeper understanding and clearer expression of this common faith, both of which are threatened when churches are isolated by division.

14. The Church's purpose in its proclamation is to lead mankind to accept God's saving work in Christ, an acceptance which not only requires intellectual assent but also demands the response of the whole person. In order to clarify and transmit what is believed and to build up and safeguard the Christian life, the Church has found the formulation of creeds, conciliar definitions, and other statements of belief indispensable. But these are always instrumental to the truth which they are intended to convey.

15. The Church's life and work are shaped by its historical origins, by its subsequent experience, and by its endeavour to make the relevance of the Gospel plain to every generation. Through reflection upon the word, through the proclamation of the Gospel, through baptism, through worship, especially the eucharist, the people of God are moved to the living remembrance of Jesus Christ and of the experience and witness of the apostolic community. This remembrance supports and guides them in their search for language which will effectively communicate the meaning of the Gospel.

All generations and cultures must be helped to understand that the good news of salvation is also for them. It is not enough for the Church simply to repeat the original apostolic words. It has also prophetically to translate them in order that the hearers in their situation may understand and respond to them. All such restatement must be consonant with the apostolic witness recorded in the Scriptures; for in this witness the preaching and teaching of ministers, and statements of local and universal councils, have to find their ground and consistency. Although these clarifications are conditioned by the circumstances which prompted them, some of their perceptions may be of lasting value. In this process the Church itself may come to see more clearly the implications of the Gospel. This is why the Church has endorsed certain formulas as authentic expressions of its witness, whose significance transcends the setting in which they were first formulated. This is not to claim that these formulas are the only possible, or even the most exact, way of expressing the faith, or that they can never be improved. Even when a doctrinal definition is regarded by the Christian community as part of its permanent teaching, this does not exclude subsequent restatement. Although the categories of thought and the mode of expression may be superseded, restatement always builds upon, and does not contradict, the truth intended by the original definition.

16. Local councils held from the second century determined the limits of the New Testament, and gave to the Church a canon which has remained normative. The action of a council in making such a decision on so momentous a matter implies an assurance that the Lord himself is present when his people assemble in his name (Matt. 18.20), and that a council may say, "it has seemed good to the Holy Spirit and to us" (Acts 15.28). The conciliar mode of authority exercised in the matter of the canon has also been applied to questions of discipline and of fundamental doctrine. When decisions (as at Nicaea in 325) affect the entire Church and deal with controverted matters which have been widely and seriously debated, it is important to establish criteria for the recognition and reception of conciliar definitions and disciplinary decisions. A substantial part in the process of reception is played by the subject matter of the definitions and by the response of the faithful. This process is often gradual, as the decisions come to be seen in perspective through the Spirit's continuing guidance of the whole Church.

17. Among the complex historical factors which contributed to the recognition of conciliar decisions considerable weight attached to their confirmation by the principal sees, and in particular by the see of Rome. At an early period other local churches actively sought the support and approbation of the church in Rome; and in course of time the agreement of the Roman see was regarded as necessary to the general acceptance of synodal decisions in major matters of more than regional concern, and also, eventually, to their canonical validity. By their agreement or disagreement the local church of Rome and its bishop fulfilled their responsibility towards other local churches and their bishops for maintaining the whole Church in the truth. In addition the bishop of Rome was also led to intervene in controversies relating to matters of faith—in most cases in response to appeals made to him, but sometimes on his own initiative.

18. In its mission to proclaim and safeguard the Gospel the Church has the obligation and the competence to make declarations in matters of faith. This mission involves the whole people of God, among whom some may rediscover or perceive more clearly than others certain aspects of the saving truth. At times there result conflict and debate. Customs, accepted positions, beliefs, formulations, and practices, as well as innovations and re-interpretations, may be shown to be inadequate, mistaken, or even inconsistent with the Gospel. When conflict endangers unity or threatens to distort the Gospel the Church must have effective means for resolving it.

In both our traditions the appeal to Scripture, to the creeds, to the Fathers, and to the definitions of the councils of the early Church is regarded as basic and normative.[1] But the bishops have a special responsibility for promoting truth and discerning error, and the interaction of bishop and people in its exercise is a safeguard of Christian

---

1. This is emphasized in the Anglican tradition. Cf. the Lambeth Conferences of 1948 and 1968.

life and fidelity. The teaching of the faith and the ordering of life in the Christian community require a daily exercise of this responsibility; but there is no guarantee that those who have an everyday responsibility will—any more than other members—invariably be free from errors of judgement, will never tolerate abuses, and will never distort the truth. Yet, in Christian hope, we are confident that such failures cannot destroy the Church's ability to proclaim the Gospel and to show forth the Christian life; for we believe that Christ will not desert his Church and that the Holy Spirit will lead it into all truth. That is why the Church, in spite of its failures, can be described as indefectible.

V. Conciliar and Primatial Authority

19. In times of crisis or when fundamental matters of faith are in question, the Church can make judgements, consonant with Scripture, which are authoritative. When the Church meets in ecumenical council its decisions on fundamental matters of faith exclude what is erroneous. Through the Holy Spirit the Church commits itself to these judgements, recognizing that, being faithful to Scripture and consistent with Tradition, they are by the same Spirit protected from error. They do not add to the truth but, although not exhaustive, they clarify the Church's understanding of it. In discharging this responsibility bishops share in a special gift of Christ to his Church. Whatever further clarification or interpretation may be propounded by the Church, the truth expressed will always be confessed. This binding authority does not belong to every conciliar decree, but only to those which formulate the central truths of salvation. This authority is ascribed in both our traditions to decisions of the ecumenical councils of the first centuries.[2]

20. The bishops are collectively responsible for defending and interpreting the apostolic faith. The primacy accorded to a bishop implies that, after consulting his fellow bishops, he may speak in their name and express their mind. The recognition of his position by the faithful creates an expectation that on occasion he will take an initiative in speaking for the Church. Primatial statements are only one way by which the Holy Spirit keeps the people of God faithful to the truth of the Gospel.

21. If primacy is to be a genuine expression of *episcope* it will foster the *koinonia* by helping the bishops in their task of apostolic leadership both in their local church and in the Church universal. Primacy fulfils

---

2. Since our historical divisions, the Roman Catholic Church has continued the practice of holding general councils of its bishops, some of which it has designated as ecumenical. The churches of the Anglican Communion have developed other forms of conciliarity.

its purpose by helping the churches to listen to one another, to grow in love and unity, and to strive together towards the fullness of Christian life and witness; it respects and promotes Christian freedom and spontaneity; it does not seek uniformity where diversity is legitimate, or centralize administration to the detriment of local churches.

A primate exercises his ministry not in isolation but in collegial association with his brother bishops. His intervention in the affairs of a local church should not be made in such a way as to usurp the responsibility of its bishop.

22. Although primacy and conciliarity are complementary elements of *episcope* it has often happened that one has been emphasized at the expense of the other, even to the point of serious imbalance. When churches have been separated from one another, this danger has been increased. The *koinonia* of the churches requires that a proper balance be preserved between the two with the responsible participation of the whole people of God.

23. If God's will for the unity in love and truth of the whole Christian community is to be fulfilled, this general pattern of the complementary primatial and conciliar aspects of *episcope* serving the *koinonia* of the churches needs to be realized at the universal level. The only see which makes any claim to universal primacy and which has exercised and still exercises such *episcope* is the see of Rome, the city where Peter and Paul died.

It seems appropriate that in any future union a universal primacy such as has been described should be held by that see.

VI. Problems and Prospects

24. What we have written here amounts to a consensus on authority in the Church and, in particular, on the basic principles of primacy. This consensus is of fundamental importance. While it does not wholly resolve all the problems associated with papal primacy, it provides us with a solid basis for confronting them. It is when we move from these basic principles to particular claims of papal primacy and to its exercise that problems arise, the gravity of which will be variously judged:

(a) Claims on behalf of the Roman see as commonly presented in the past have put a greater weight on the Petrine texts (Matt. 16.18, 19; Luke 22.31, 32; John 21.15-17) than they are generally thought to be able to bear. However, many Roman Catholic scholars do not now feel it necessary to stand by former exegesis of these texts in every respect.

(b) The First Vatican Council of 1870 uses the language of "divine right" of the successors of Peter. This language has no clear interpretation in modern Roman Catholic theology. If it is understood as affirming that the universal primacy of the bishop of Rome is

part of God's design for the universal *koinonia* then it need not
be a matter of disagreement. But if it were further implied that
as long as a church is not in communion with the bishop of Rome,
it is regarded by the Roman Catholic Church as less than fully a
church, a difficulty would remain: for some this difficulty would
be removed by simply restoring communion, but to others the
implication would itself be an obstacle to entering into communion with Rome.

(c) Anglicans find grave difficulty in the affirmation that the pope
can be infallible in his teaching. It must, however, be borne in
mind that the doctrine of infallibility[3] is hedged round by very
rigorous conditions laid down at the First Vatican Council. These
conditions preclude the idea that the pope is an inspired oracle
communicating fresh revelation, or that he can speak indepen-
dently of his fellow bishops and the Church, or on matters not
concerning faith or morals. For the Roman Catholic Church the
pope's dogmatic definitions, which, fulfilling the criteria of infallibility, are preserved from error, do no more but no less than
express the mind of the Church on issues concerning the divine
revelation. Even so, special difficulties are created by the recent
Marian dogmas, because Anglicans doubt the appropriateness,
or even the possibility, of defining them as essential to the faith
of believers.

(d) The claim that the pope possesses universal immediate jurisdiction, the limits of which are not clearly specified, is a source
of anxiety to Anglicans who fear that the way is thus open to its
illegitimate or uncontrolled use. Nevertheless, the First Vatican
Council intended that the papal primacy should be exercised only
to maintain and never to erode the structures of the local churches.
The Roman Catholic Church is today seeking to replace the juridical outlook of the nineteenth century by a more pastoral
understanding of authority in the Church.

25. In spite of the difficulties just mentioned, we believe that this
Statement on Authority in the Church represents a significant convergence with far-reaching consequences. For a considerable period
theologians in our two traditions, without compromising their respective allegiances, have worked on common problems with the same
methods. In the process they have come to see old problems in new
horizons and have experienced a theological convergence which has
often taken them by surprise.

---

3. "Infallibility" is a technical term which does not bear precisely the same
meaning as the word does in common usage. Its theological sense is
seen in paras. 15 and 19 above.

In our three Agreed Statements we have endeavoured to get behind the opposed and entrenched positions of past controversies. We have tried to reassess what are the real issues to be resolved. We have often deliberately avoided the vocabulary of past polemics, not with any intention of evading the real difficulties that provoked them, but because the emotive associations of such language have often obscured the truth. For the future relations between our churches the doctrinal convergence which we have experienced offers hope that remaining difficulties can be resolved.

Conclusion

26. The Malta Report of 1968 envisaged the coming together of the Roman Catholic Church and the churches of the Anglican Communion in terms of "unity by stages." We have reached agreements on the doctrines of the eucharist, ministry, and, apart from the qualifications of para. 24, authority. Doctrinal agreements reached by theological commissions cannot, however, by themselves achieve the goal of Christian unity. Accordingly, we submit our Statements to our respective authorities to consider whether or not they are judged to express on these central subjects a unity at the level of faith which not only justifies but requires action to bring about a closer sharing between our two communions in life, worship, and mission.

Elucidation (1981)

Comments and Criticisms

1.   After the publication of the first Statement on Authority the Commission received comments and criticisms. Some of the questions raised, such as the request for a clarification of the relation between infallibility and indefectibility, find an answer in the second Statement on Authority. Another question, concerning our understanding of *koinonia*, is answered in the Introduction to this Final Report, where we show how the concept underlies all our Statements.

Behind many reactions to the Statement is a degree of uneasiness as to whether sufficient attention is paid to the primary authority of Scripture, with the result that certain developments are given an authority comparable to that of Scripture. Serious questions have also been asked about councils and reception, and some commentators have claimed that what the Statement says about the protection of an ecumenical council from error is in conflict with Article 21 of the Anglican Articles of Religion. It has been suggested that the treatment of the place and authority of the laity in the Church is inadequate. There have also been requests for a clarification of the nature of ministerial authority and of jurisdiction. Some questions have been asked about the status of regional primacies—for example, the patriarchal office as exercised in the Eastern churches. Finally, a recurring question has been whether the Commission is suggesting that a universal primacy is a theological necessity simply because one has existed or been claimed.

In what follows the Commission attempts to address itself to these problems and to elucidate the Statement as it bears on each of them. In seeking to answer the criticisms that have been received we have sometimes thought it necessary to go further and elucidate the basic issues that underlie them. In all that we say we take for granted two fundamental principles—that Christian faith depends on divine revelation and that the Holy Spirit guides the Church in the understanding and transmission of revealed truth.

The Place of Scripture

2.   Our documents have been criticized for failing to give an adequate account of the primary authority of Scripture in the Church, thereby making it possible for us to treat certain developments as possessing an authority comparable to that of Scripture itself. Our description of "the inspired documents . . . as a normative record of the authentic foundation of the faith" (para. 2) has been felt to be an inadequate statement of the truth.

The basis of our approach to Scripture is the affirmation that Christ is God's final word to man—his eternal Word made flesh. He is the culmination of the diverse ways in which God has spoken since the beginning (Heb. 1.1-3). In him God's saving and revealing purpose is fully and definitively realized.

The patriarchs and the prophets received and spoke the word of God in the Spirit. By the power of the same Spirit the Word of God became flesh and accomplished his ministry. At Pentecost the same Spirit was given to the disciples to enable them to recall and interpret what Jesus did and taught, and so to proclaim the Gospel in truth and power.

The person and work of Jesus Christ, preached by the apostles and set forth and interpreted in the New Testament writings, through the inspiration of the Holy Spirit, are the primary norm for Christian faith and life. Jesus, as the Word of God, sums up in himself the whole of God's self-disclosure. The Church's essential task, therefore, in the exercise of its teaching office, is to unfold the full extent and implications of the mystery of Christ, under the guidance of the Spirit of the risen Lord.

No endeavour of the Church to express the truth can add to the revelation already given. Moreover, since the Scriptures are the uniquely inspired witness to divine revelation, the Church's expression of that revelation must be tested by its consonance with Scripture. This does not mean simply repeating the words of Scripture, but also both delving into their deeper significance and unravelling their implications for Christian belief and practice. It is impossible to do this without resorting to current language and thought. Consequently the teaching of the Church will often be expressed in words that are different from the original text of Scripture without being alien to its meaning. For instance, at the First Ecumenical Council the Church felt constrained to speak of the Son of God as "of one substance with the Father" in order to expound the mystery of Christ. What was understood by the term "of one substance" at this time was believed to express the content of Christian faith concerning Christ, even though the actual term is never used in the apostolic writings. This combination of permanence in the revealed truth and continuous exploration of its meaning is what is meant by Christian tradition. Some of the results of this reflection, which bear upon essential matters of faith, have come to be recognized as the authentic expression of Christian doctrine and therefore part of the "deposit of faith."

Tradition has been viewed in different ways. One approach is primarily concerned never to go beyond the bounds of Scripture. Under the guidance of the Spirit undiscovered riches and truths are sought in the Scriptures in order to illuminate the faith according to the needs of each generation. This is not slavery to the text of Scripture. It is an unfolding of the riches of the original revelation. Another approach, while different, does not necessarily contradict the former. In the conviction that the Holy Spirit is seeking to guide the Church into the fullness of truth, it draws upon everything in human experience and thought which will give to the content of the revelation its fullest expression and widest application. It is primarily concerned with the growth of the seed of God's word from age to age. This does not imply any denial of the uniqueness of the revelation. Because these two attitudes contain differing emphases, conflict may arise, even though in both cases the Church is seeking the fullness of revelation. The seal upon the truthfulness of the conclusions that result from this search will be the reception by the whole Church, since neither approach is immune from the possibility of error.

Councils and Reception

3. The Commission has been said to contradict Article 21 of the Articles of Religion in its affirmation that the decisions of what have traditionally been called ecumenical councils "exclude what is erroneous." The Commission is very far from implying that general councils cannot err and is well aware that they "sometimes have erred"; for example the Councils of Ariminum and of Seleucia of 359 A.D. Article 21 in fact affirms that general councils have authority only when their judgments "may be declared that they be taken out of

Holy Scripture." According to the argument of the Statement also, only those judgments of general councils are guaranteed to "exclude what is erroneous" or are "protected from error" which have as their content "fundamental matters of faith," which "formulate the central truths of salvation" and which are "faithful to Scripture and consistent with Tradition. They do not add to the truth but, although not exhaustive, they clarify the Church's understanding of it" (para. 19).

The Commission has also been asked to say whether reception by the whole people of God is part of the process which gives authority to the decisions of ecumenical councils.

By "reception" we mean the fact that the people of God acknowledge such a decision or statement because they recognize in it the apostolic faith. They accept it because they discern a harmony between what is proposed to them and the *sensus fidelium* of the whole Church. As an example, the creed which we call Nicene has been received by the Church because in it the Church has recognized the apostolic faith. Reception does not create truth nor legitimize the decision: it is the final indication that such a decision has fulfilled the necessary conditions for it to be a true expression of faith. In this acceptance the whole Church is involved in a continuous process of discernment and response (cf. para. 6).

The Commission therefore avoids two extreme positions. On the one hand it rejects the view that a definition has no authority until it is accepted by the whole Church or even derives its authority solely from that acceptance. Equally, the Commission denies that a council is so evidently self-sufficient that its definitions owe nothing to reception.

The Place of the Laity

4.   The Commission has been accused of an overemphasis upon the ordained ministry to the neglect of the laity.

In guarding and developing communion, every member has a part to play. Baptism gives everyone in the Church the right, and consequently the ability, to carry out his particular function in the body. The recognition of this fundamental right is of great importance. In different ways, even if sometimes hesitantly, our two Churches have sought to integrate in decision-making those who are not ordained.

The reason why the Statement spoke at length about the structure and the exercise of the authority of the ordained ministry was that this was the area where most difficulties appeared to exist. There was no devaluing of the proper and active role of the laity. For instance, we said that the Holy Spirit gives to some individuals and communities special gifts for the benefit of the Church (para. 5), that all the members of the Church share in the discovery of God's will (para. 6), that the *sensus fidelium* is a vital element in the comprehension of

God's truth (para. 18), and that all bear witness to God's compassion for mankind and his concern for justice in the world (Ministry, para. 7).

The Authority of the Ordained Ministry

5.   We have been asked to clarify the meaning of what some of our critics call "hierarchical authority"—an expression we did not use. Here we are dealing with a form of authority which is inherent in the visible structure of the Church. By this we mean the authority attached to those ordained to exercise *episcope* in the Church. The Holy Spirit gives to each person power to fulfil his particular function within the body of Christ. Accordingly, those exercising *episcope* receive the grace appropriate to their calling and those for whom it is exercised must recognize and accept their God-given authority.

Both Anglicans and Roman Catholics, however, have criticized the emphasis we placed on a bishop's authority in certain circumstances to require compliance.

The specific oversight of the ordained ministry is exercised and acknowledged when a minister preaches the Gospel, presides at the eucharist, and seeks as pastor to lead the community truly to discern God's word and its relevance to their lives. When this responsibility laid upon a bishop (or other ordained minister under the direction of a bishop) requires him to declare a person to be in error in respect of doctrine or conduct, even to the point of exclusion from eucharistic communion, he is acting for the sake of the integrity of the community's faith and life. Both our communions have always recognized this need for disciplinary action on exceptional occasions as part of the authority given by Christ to his ministers, however difficult it may be in practice to take such action. This is what we meant by saying that the bishop "can require the compliance necessary to maintain faith and charity in its daily life" (para. 5). At the same time the authority of the ordained minister is not held in isolation, but is shared with other ministers and the rest of the community. All the ministers, whatever their role in the body of Christ, are involved in responsibility for preserving the integrity of the community.

Jurisdiction

6.   Critics have asked for clarification on two matters.

First, what do we mean by jurisdiction? We understand jurisdiction as the authority or power (*potestas*) necessary for the effective fulfilment of an office. Its exercise and limits are determined by what that office involves (cf. Authority II, paras. 16-22).

In both our communions we find dioceses comprising a number of parishes, and groups of dioceses at the provincial, national or international level. All of these are under the oversight of a special *episcope* exercised by ministers with a shared responsibility for the overall care of the Church. Every form of jurisdiction given to those exercising such an *episcope* is to serve and strengthen both the *koinonia* in the community and that between different Christian communities.

Secondly, it has been questioned whether we imply that jurisdiction attached to different levels of *episcope*—even within the same order of ministry—is always to be exercised in an identical way. Critics give the example of the relation and possible conflict between metropolitans and local bishops. We believe that the problem is not basically that of jurisdiction but of the complementarity and harmonious working of these differing forms of *episcope* in the one body of Christ. Jurisdiction, being the power necessary for the fulfilment of an office, varies according to the specific functions of each form of *episcope*. That is why the use of this juridical vocabulary does not mean that we attribute to all those exercising *episcope* at different levels exactly the same canonical power (cf. Authority II, para. 16).

Regional Primacy

7.   Concern has been voiced that the Commission's treatment of regional primacy is inadequate. In particular, reference has been made to the ancient tradition of patriarchates.

The Commission did not ignore this tradition in its treatment of the origins of primacy (cf. para. 10). It avoided specific terms such as "metropolitan" and "patriarch," but in speaking of bishops with a special responsibility of oversight in their regions, the Commission intended to point to the reality behind the historical terms used for this form of episcopal co-responsibility in both east and west. It also pointed to the contemporary development and importance of new forms of regional primacy in both our traditions, e.g., the elective presidencies of Roman Catholic episcopal conferences and certain elective primacies in the Anglican Communion.

Primacy and History

8.   It has been alleged that the Commission commends the primacy of the Roman see solely on the basis of history. But the Commission's argument is more than historical (cf. para. 23).

According to Christian doctrine the unity in truth of the Christian community demands visible expression. We agree that such visible expression is the will of God and that the maintenance of visible unity at the universal level includes the *episcope* of a universal primate. This is a doctrinal statement. But the way *episcope* is realized concretely in ecclesial life (the balance fluctuating between conciliarity and primacy) will depend upon contingent historical factors and upon development under the guidance of the Holy Spirit.

Though it is possible to conceive a universal primacy located else-where than in the city of Rome, the original witness of Peter and Paul and the continuing exercise of a universal *episcope* by the see of Rome present a unique presumption in its favour (cf. Authority II, paras. 6-9). Therefore, while to locate a universal primacy in the see of Rome is an affirmation at a different level from the assertion of the necessity for a universal primacy, it cannot be dissociated from the providential action of the Holy Spirit.

The design of God through the Holy Spirit has, we believe, been to preserve at once the fruitful diversity within the *koinonia* of local churches and the unity in essentials which must mark the universal *koinonia*. The history of our separation has underlined and continues to underline the necessity for this proper theological balance, which has often been distorted or destroyed by human failings or other historical factors (cf. para. 22).

The Commission does not therefore say that what has evolved historically or what is currently practised by the Roman see is nec-essarily normative: it maintains only that visible unity requires the realization of a "general pattern of the complementary primatial and conciliar aspects of *episcope*" in the service of the universal "*koinonia* of the churches" (para. 23). Indeed much Anglican objection has been directed against the manner of the exercise and particular claims of the Roman primacy rather than against universal primacy as such.

Anglicanism has never rejected the principle and practice of pri-macy. New reflection upon it has been stimulated by the evolving role of the archbishop of Canterbury within the Anglican Commun-ion. The development of this form of primacy arose precisely from the need for a service of unity in the faith in an expanding communion of Churches. It finds expression in the Lambeth Conferences con-voked by successive archbishops of Canterbury which originated with requests from overseas provinces for guidance in matters of faith. This illustrates a particular relationship between conciliarity and pri-macy in the Anglican Communion.

The Commission has already pointed to the possibilities of mutual benefit and reform which should arise from a shared recognition of one universal primacy which does not inhibit conciliarity—a "pros-pect (which) should be met with faith, not fear" (Co-Chairmen's Pre-face). Anglicans sometimes fear the prospect of over-centralization, Roman Catholics the prospect of doctrinal incoherence. Faith, ban-ishing fear, might see simply the prospect of the right balance between a primacy serving the unity and a conciliarity maintaining the just diversity of the *koinonia* of all the churches.

Authority in the Church II

The Statement (1981)

Introduction

1.   In our conclusion to our first Statement on Authority in the Church we affirmed that we had reached "a consensus on authority in the Church and, in particular, on the basic principles of primacy," which we asserted to be of "fundamental importance" (para. 24). Nevertheless we showed that four outstanding problems related to this subject required further study since, if they remained unresolved, they would appear to constitute serious obstacles to our growing together towards full communion. The four difficulties were the interpretation of the Petrine texts, the meaning of the language of "divine right," the affirmation of papal infallibility, and the nature of the jurisdiction ascribed to the bishop of Rome as universal primate. After five years of further study we are able to present a fresh appraisal of their weight and implications.

Petrine Texts

2.   The position of Peter among the apostles has often been discussed in relation to the importance of the bishop of Rome among the bishops. This requires that we look at the data of the New Testament and what are commonly called the Petrine texts.
3.   While explicitly stressing God's will to root the Church in the apostolic witness and mandate, the New Testament attributes to Peter a special position among the Twelve. Whether the Petrine texts contain the authentic words of Jesus or not, they witness to an early tradition that Peter already held this place during Jesus' ministry. Individually the indications may seem to be inconclusive, but taken together they provide a general picture of his prominence. The most important are: the bestowal on Simon of the name Cephas, his being mentioned first among, the Twelve and in the smaller circle of the three (Peter, James and John), the faith which enabled him to confess Jesus' Messiahship (Matt. 16.16; Mark 8.29; Luke 9.20; and John 6.69), and the answer of Jesus (Matt. 16.18) in which he is called rock, the charge to strengthen his brethren (Luke 22.31-32) and to feed the sheep (John 21.16-17) and the special appearance to him of the risen Lord (e.g., Luke 24.34; 1 Cor. 15.5). Although the author of Acts underlined the apostolic authority of Paul in the latter part of his book, he focused in the first part on Peter's leadership. For instance, it is Peter who frequently speaks in the name of the apostolic community (Acts 3.15,10.41), he is the first to proclaim the Gospel to the

Jews and the first to open the Christian community to the Gentiles. Paul seems to have recognized this prominence of Peter among the apostles as well as the importance of James (Gal. 1.18-19). He appears also to have accepted the lead given by Peter at the Council of Jerusalem (Acts 15), even though he was prepared to oppose Peter when he held Peter to be at fault (Gal. 2.11).

4.   Responsibility for pastoral leadership was not restricted to Peter. The expression "binding and loosing," which is used for the explicit commission to Peter in Matt. 16.19, appears again in Matt. 18.18 in the promise made by Christ directly to all the disciples. Similarly the foundation upon which the Church is built is related to Peter in Matt. 16.18 and to the whole apostolic body elsewhere in the New Testament (e.g., Eph. 2.20). Even though Peter was the spokesman at Pentecost, the charge to proclaim the Gospel to all the world had previously been given by the risen Christ to the Eleven (Acts 1.2-8). Although Paul was not among the Twelve, he too was conspicuous for the leadership which he exercised with an authority received from the Lord himself, claiming to share with Peter and others parallel responsibility and apostolic authority (Gal. 2.7-8; 1 Cor. 9.1).

5.   In spite of being strongly rebuked by Christ and his dramatic failure in denying him, in the eyes of the New Testament writers Peter holds a position of special importance. This was not due to his own gifts and character although he had been the first to confess Christ's Messiahship. It was because of his particular calling by Christ (Luke 6.14; John 21.15-17). Yet while the distinctive features of Peter's ministry are stressed, this ministry is that of an apostle and does not isolate him from the ministry of the other apostles. In accordance with the teaching of Jesus that truly to lead is to serve and not to dominate others (Luke 22.24ff), Peter's role in strengthening the brethren (Luke 22.32) is a leadership of service. Peter, then, serves the Church by helping it to overcome threats to its unity (e.g., Acts 11.1-18), even if his weakness may require help or correction, as is clear from his rebuke by Paul (Gal. 2.11-14). These considerations help clarify the analogy that has been drawn between the role of Peter among the apostles and that of the bishop of Rome among his fellow bishops.

6.   The New Testament contains no explicit record of a transmission of Peter's leadership; nor is the transmission of apostolic authority in general very clear. Furthermore, the Petrine texts were subjected to differing interpretations as early as the time of the Church Fathers. Yet the church at Rome, the city in which Peter and Paul taught and were martyred, came to be recognized as possessing a unique responsibility among the churches: its bishop was seen to perform a special service in relation to the unity of the churches, and in relation to fidelity to the apostolic inheritance, thus exercising among his fellow bishops functions analogous to those ascribed to Peter, whose successor the bishop of Rome was claimed to be (cf. para. 12).

7.   Fathers and doctors of the Church gradually came to interpret the New Testament data as pointing in the same direction. This interpretation has been questioned, and it has been argued that it arose from an attempt to legitimize a development which had already occurred. Yet it is possible to think that a primacy of the bishop of Rome is not contrary to the New Testament and is part of God's purpose regarding the Church's unity and catholicity, while admitting that the New Testament texts offer no sufficient basis for this.

8.   Our two traditions agree that not everything said of the apostles as the witnesses to the resurrection and saving work of Christ (Acts 1.21-22) is transmitted to those chosen to continue their mission. The apostles are the foundations precisely because they are the unique, commissioned witnesses to the once-for-all saving work of Christ. Peter's role is never isolated from that of the apostolic group; what is true of the transmissibility of the mission of the apostolic group is true of Peter as a member of it. Consequently though the sentence, "On this rock I will build my church," is spoken to Peter, this does not imply that the same words can be applied to the bishop of Rome with an identical meaning. Even if Peter's role cannot be transmitted in its totality, however, this does not exclude the continuation of a ministry of unity guided by the Spirit among those who continue the apostolic mission.

9.   If the leadership of the bishop of Rome has been rejected by those who thought it was not faithful to the truth of the Gospel and hence not a true focus of unity, we nevertheless agree that a universal primacy will be needed in a reunited Church and should appropriately be the primacy of the bishop of Rome, as we have specified it (Authority I, para. 23). While the New Testament taken as a whole shows Peter playing a clear role of leadership it does not portray the Church's unity and universality exclusively in terms of Peter. The universal communion of the churches is a company of believers, united by faith in Christ, by the preaching of the word, and by participation in the sacraments assured to them by a pastoral ministry of apostolic order. In a reunited Church a ministry modelled on the role of Peter will be a sign and safeguard of such unity.

Jus Divinum

10.   The first Statement on Authority poses two questions with respect to the language of "divine right" applied by the First Vatican Council to the Roman primacy: What does the language actually mean? What implications does it have for the ecclesial status of non-Roman Catholic communions (Authority I, para. 24b)? Our purpose is to clarify the Roman Catholic position on these questions; to suggest a possible Anglican reaction to the Roman Catholic position; and to attempt a statement of consensus.

11. The Roman Catholic conviction concerning the place of the Roman primacy in God's plan for his Church has traditionally been expressed in the language of *jus divinum* (divine law or divine right). This term was used by the First Vatican Council to describe the primacy of the "successor in the chair of Peter" whom the Council recognized in the bishop of Rome. The First Vatican Council used the term *jure divino* to say that this primacy derives from Christ.[1] While there is no universally accepted interpretation of this language, all affirm that it means at least that this primacy expresses God's purpose for his Church. *Jus divinum* in this context need not be taken to imply that the universal primacy as a permanent institution was directly founded by Jesus during his life on earth. Neither does the term mean that the universal primate is a "source of the Church" as if Christ's salvation had to be channelled through him. Rather, he is to be the sign of the visible *koinonia* God wills for the Church and an instrument through which unity in diversity is realized. It is to a universal primate thus envisaged within the collegiality of the bishops and the *koinonia* of the whole Church that the qualification *jure divino* can be applied.

12. The doctrine that a universal primacy expresses the will of God does not entail the consequence that a Christian community out of communion with the see of Rome does not belong to the Church of God. Being in canonical communion with the bishop of Rome is not among the necessary elements by which a Christian community is recognized as a church. For example, the Roman Catholic Church has continued to recognize the Orthodox churches as churches in spite of division concerning the primacy (Vatican II, *Unitatis Redintegratio*, para. 14). The Second Vatican Council, while teaching that the Church of God subsists in the Roman Catholic Church, rejected the position that the Church of God is co-extensive with the Roman Catholic Church and is exclusively embodied in that Church. The Second Vatican Council allows it to be said that a church out of communion with the Roman see may lack nothing from the viewpoint of the Roman Catholic Church except that it does not belong to the visible manifestation of full Christian communion which is maintained in the Roman Catholic Church (*Lumen Gentium*, para 8; *Unitatis Redintegratio*, para. 13).

13. Relations between our two communions in the past have not encouraged reflection by Anglicans on the positive significance of the Roman primacy in the life of the universal Church. Nonetheless, from time to time Anglican theologians have affirmed that, in changed circumstances, it might be possible for the churches of the Anglican Communion to recognize the development of the Roman primacy as

---

1. *"ex ipsius Christi Domini institutione seu iure divino"* (*Pastor Aeternus*, ch. 2).

a gift of divine providence—in other words, as an effect of the guidance of the Holy Spirit in the Church. Given the above interpretation of the language of divine right in the First Vatican Council, it is reasonable to ask whether a gap really exists between the assertion of a primacy by divine right (*jure divino*) and the acknowledgement of its emergence by divine providence (*divina providentia*).

14. Anglicans have commonly supposed that the claim to divine right for the Roman primacy implied a denial that the churches of the Anglican Communion are churches. Consequently, they have concluded that any reconciliation with Rome would require a repudiation of their past history, life and experience—which in effect would be a betrayal of their own integrity. However, given recent developments in the Roman Catholic understanding of the status of other Christian churches, this particular difficulty may no longer be an obstacle to Anglican acceptance, as God's will for his Church, of a universal primacy of the bishop of Rome such as has been described in the first Statement on Authority (para. 23).

15. In the past, Roman Catholic teaching that the bishop of Rome is universal primate by divine right or law has been regarded by Anglicans as unacceptable. However, we believe that the primacy of the bishop of Rome can be affirmed as part of God's design for the universal *koinonia* in terms which are compatible with both our traditions. Given such a consensus, the language of divine right used by the First Vatican Council need no longer be seen as a matter of disagreement between us.

Jurisdiction

16. Jurisdiction in the Church may be defined as the authority or power (*potestas*) necessary for the exercise of an office. In both our communions it is given for the effective fulfilment of office and this fact determines its exercise and limits. It varies according to the specific functions of the *episcope* concerned. The jurisdictions associated with different levels of *episcope* (e.g., of primates, metropolitans and diocesan bishops) are not in all respects identical.

The use of the same juridical terms does not mean that exactly the same authority is attributed to all those exercising *episcope* at different levels. Where a metropolitan has jurisdiction in his province this jurisdiction is not merely the exercise in a broader context of that exercised by a bishop in his diocese: it is determined by the specific functions which he is required to discharge in relation to his fellow bishops.

17. Each bishop is entrusted with the pastoral authority needed for the exercise of his *episcope*. This authority is both required and limited by the bishop's task of teaching the faith through the proclamation and explanation of the word of God, of providing for the administration of the sacraments in his diocese and of maintaining his church in holiness and truth (cf. Authority I, para. 5). Hence decisions taken by the bishop in performing his task have an authority which the faithful in his diocese have a duty to accept. This authority of the bishop, usually called jurisdiction, involves the responsibility for making and implementing the decisions that are required by his office for the sake of the *koinonia*. It is not the arbitrary power of one man over the freedom of others, but a necessity if the bishop is to serve his flock as its shepherd (cf. Authority Elucidation, para. 5). So too, within the universal *koinonia* and the collegiality of the bishops, the universal primate exercises the jurisdiction necessary for the fulfilment of his functions, the chief of which is to serve the faith and unity of the whole Church.

18. Difficulties have arisen from the attribution of universal, ordinary and immediate jurisdiction to the bishop of Rome by the First Vatican Council. Misunderstanding of these technical terms has aggravated the difficulties. The jurisdiction of the bishop of Rome as universal primate is called ordinary and immediate (i.e., not mediated) because it is inherent in his office; it is called universal simply because it must enable him to serve the unity and harmony of the *koinonia* as a whole and in each of its parts.

The attribution of such jurisdiction to the bishop of Rome is a source of anxiety to Anglicans (Authority I, para. 24*d*) who fear, for example, that he could usurp the rights of a metropolitan in his province or of a bishop in his diocese; that a centralized authority might not always understand local conditions or respect legitimate cultural diversity; that rightful freedom of conscience, thought and action could be imperilled.

19. The universal primate should exercise, and be seen to exercise, his ministry not in isolation but in collegial association with his brother bishops (Authority I, paras. 21 and 23). This in no way reduces his own responsibility on occasion to speak and act for the whole Church. Concern for the universal Church is intrinsic to all episcopal office; a diocesan bishop is helped to make this concern a reality by the universal jurisdiction of the universal primate. But the universal primate is not the source from which diocesan bishops derive their authority, nor does his authority undermine that of the metropolitan or diocesan bishop. Primacy is not an autocratic power over the Church but a service in and to the Church which is a communion in faith and charity of local churches.

20. Although the scope of universal jurisdiction cannot be precisely defined canonically, there are moral limits to its exercise: they derive from the nature of the Church and of the universal primate's pastoral office. By virtue of his jurisdiction, given for the building up of the Church, the universal primate has the right in special cases to intervene in the affairs of a diocese and to receive appeals from the deci-

sion of a diocesan bishop. It is because the universal primate, in collegial association with his fellow bishops, has the task of safeguarding the faith and unity of the universal Church that the diocesan bishop is subject to his authority.

21. The purpose of the universal primate's jurisdiction is to enable him to further catholicity as well as unity and to foster and draw together the riches of the diverse traditions of the churches. Collegial and primatial responsibility for preserving the distinctive life of the local churches involves a proper respect for their customs and traditions, provided these do not contradict the faith or disrupt communion. The search for unity and concern for catholicity must not be divorced.

22. Even though these principles concerning the nature of jurisdiction be accepted as in line with the understanding which Anglicans and Roman Catholics share with regard to the Church's structure, there remain specific questions about their practical application in a united Church. Anglicans are entitled to assurance that acknowledgement of the universal primacy of the bishop of Rome would not involve the suppression of theological, liturgical and other traditions which they value or the imposition of wholly alien traditions. We believe that what has been said above provides grounds for such assurance. In this connection we recall the words of Paul VI in 1970: "There will be no seeking to lessen the legitimate prestige and the worthy patrimony of piety and usage proper to the Anglican Church . . ."[2]

Infallibility

23. It is Christ himself, the Way, the Truth and the Life, who entrusts the Gospel to us and gives to his Church teaching authority which claims our obedience. The Church as a whole, indwelt by the Spirit according to Christ's promise and looking to the testimony of the prophets, saints and martyrs of every generation, is witness, teacher and guardian of the truth (cf. Authority I, para. 18). The Church is confident that the Holy Spirit will effactually enable it to fulfil its mission so that it will neither lose its essential character nor fail to reach its goal.[3] We are agreed that doctrinal decisions made by legit-

---

2. "There will be no seeking to lessen the legitimate prestige and the worthy patrimony of piety and usage proper to the Anglican Church when the Roman Catholic Church—this humble 'Servant of the servants of God'—is able to embrace her ever beloved Sister in the one authentic communion of the family of Christ . . ." (AAS 62 (1970), p. 753).
3. This is the meaning of *indefectibility*, a term which does not speak of the Church's lack of defects but confesses that, despite all its many weaknesses and failures, Christ is faithful to his promise that the gates of hell shall not prevail against it.

imate authority must be consonant with the community's faith as grounded in Scripture and interpreted by the mind of the Church, and that no teaching authority can add new revelation to the original apostolic faith (cf. Authority I, paras. 2 and 18). We must then ask whether there is a special ministerial gift of discerning the truth and of teaching bestowed at crucial times on one person to enable him to speak authoritatively in the name of the Church in order to preserve the people of God in the truth.

24. Maintenance in the truth requires that at certain moments the Church can in a matter of essential doctrine make a decisive judgement which becomes part of its permanent witness.[4] Such a judgement makes it clear what the truth is, and strengthens the Church's confidence in proclaiming the Gospel. Obvious examples of such judgements are occasions when general councils define the faith. These judgements, by virtue of their foundation in revelation and their appropriateness to the need of the time, express a renewed unity in the truth to which they summon the whole Church.

25. The Church in all its members is involved in such a definition which clarifies and enriches their grasp of the truth. Their active reflection upon the definition in its turn clarifies its significance. Moreover, although it is not through reception by the people of God that a definition first acquires authority, the assent of the faithful is the ultimate indication that the Church's authoritative decision in a matter of faith has been truly preserved from error by the Holy Spirit. The Holy Spirit who maintains the Church in the truth will bring its members to receive the definition as true and to assimilate it if what has been declared genuinely expounds the revelation.

26. The Church exercises teaching authority through various instruments and agencies at various levels (cf. Authority I, paras. 9 and 18-22). When matters of faith are at stake decisions may be made by the Church in universal councils; we are agreed that these are authoritative (cf. Authority I, para. 19). We have also recognized the need in a united Church for a universal primate who, presiding over the *koinonia* can speak with authority in the name of the Church (cf. Authority I, para. 23). Through both these agencies the Church can make a decisive judgement in matters of faith, and so exclude error.

27. The purpose of this service cannot be to add to the content of revelation, but is to recall and emphasize some important truth; to expound the faith more lucidly; to expose error; to draw out implications not sufficiently recognized; and to show how Christian truth applies to contemporary issues. These statements would be intended

---

4. That this is in line with Anglican belief is clear from the Thirty-nine Articles (Article 20): "The Church hath . . . authority in Controversies of Faith."

to articulate, elucidate or define matters of faith which the community believes at least implicitly. The welfare of the *koinonia* does not require that all the statements of those who speak authoritatively on behalf of the Church should be considered permanent expressions of the truth. But situations may occur where serious divisions of opinion on crucial issues of pastoral urgency call for a more definitive judgement. Any such statement would be intended as an expression of the mind of the Church, understood not only in the context of its time and place but also in the light of the Church's whole experience and tradition. All such definitions are provoked by specific historical situations and are always made in terms of the understanding and framework of their age (cf. Authority I, para. 15). But in the continuing life of the Church they retain a lasting significance if they are safeguarding the substance of the faith.

The Church's teaching authority is a service to which the faithful look for guidance especially in times of uncertainty; but the assurance of the truthfulness of its teaching rests ultimately rather upon its fidelity to the Gospel than upon the character or office of the person by whom it is expressed. The Church's teaching is proclaimed because it is true; it is not true simply because it has been proclaimed. The value of such authoritative proclamation lies in the guidance that it gives to the faithful. However, neither general councils nor universal primates are invariably preserved from error even in official declarations (cf. Authority Elucidation, para. 3).

28. The Church's judgement is normally given through synodal decision, but at times a primate acting in communion with his fellow bishops may articulate the decision even apart from a synod. Although responsibility for preserving the Church from fundamental error belongs to the whole Church, it may be exercised on its behalf by a universal primate. The exercise of authority in the Church need not have the effect of stifling the freedom of the Spirit to inspire other agencies and individuals. In fact, there have been times in the history of the Church when both councils and universal primates have protected legitimate positions which have been under attack.

29. A service of preserving the Church from error has been performed by the bishop of Rome as universal primate both within and outside the synodal process. The judgement of Leo I, for example, in his letter received by the Council of Chalcedon, helped to maintain a balanced view of the two natures of Christ. This does not mean that other bishops are restricted to a merely consultative role, nor that every statement of the bishop of Rome instantly solves the immediate problem or decides the matter at issue for ever. To be a decisive discernment of the truth, the judgement of the bishop of Rome must satisfy rigorous conditions. He must speak explicitly as the focus within the *koinonia*; without being under duress from external pressures; having sought to discover the mind of his fellow bishops and of the Church as a whole; and with a clear intention to issue a binding decision upon a matter of faith or morals. Some of these conditions were laid down by the First Vatican Council.[5] When it is plain that all these conditions have been fulfilled, Roman Catholics conclude that the judgement is preserved from error and the proposition true. If the definition proposed for assent were not manifestly a legitimate interpretation of biblical faith and in line with orthodox tradition, Anglicans would think it a duty to reserve the reception of the definition for study and discussion.

30. This approach is illustrated by the reaction of many Anglicans to the Marian definitions, which are the only examples of such dogmas promulgated by the bishop of Rome apart from a synod since the separation of our two communions. Anglicans and Roman Catholics can agree in much of the truth that these two dogmas are designed to affirm. We agree that there can be but one mediator between God and man, Jesus Christ, and reject any interpretation of the role of Mary which obscures this affirmation. We agree in recognizing that Christian understanding of Mary is inseparably linked with the doctrines of Christ and of the Church. We agree in recognizing the grace and unique vocation of Mary, Mother of God Incarnate (*Theotokos*), in observing her festivals, and in according her honour in the communion of saints. We agree that she was prepared by divine grace to be the mother of our Redeemer, by whom she herself was redeemed and received into glory. We further agree in recognizing in Mary a model of holiness, obedience and faith for all Christians. We accept that it is possible to regard her as a prophetic figure of the Church of God before as well as after the Incarnation.[6] Nevertheless the dogmas of the Immaculate Conception and the Assumption raise a special

---

5. The phrase "*eiusmodi . . . definitiones ex sese, non autem ex consensu ecclesiae irreformabiles esse*": "such definitions are irreformable by themselves and not by reason of the agreement of the Church" (*Pastor Aeternus*, ch. 4) does not deny the importance of reception of doctrinal statements in the Roman Catholic Church. The phrase was used by the Council to rule out the opinion of those who maintained that such a statement becomes "irreformable" only subsequently when it is approved by the bishops. The term "irreformable" means that the truth expressed in the definition can no longer be questioned. "Irreformable" does not mean that the definition is the Church's last word on the matter and that the definition cannot be restated in other terms.
6. The affirmation of the Roman Catholic Church that Mary was conceived without original sin is based on recognition of her unique role within the mystery of the Incarnation. By being thus prepared to be the mother of our Redeemer, she also becomes a sign that the salvation won by Christ was operative among all mankind before his birth. The affirmation that her glory in heaven involves full participation in the fruits of salvation expresses and reinforces our faith that the life of the world to come has already broken into the life of our world. It is the conviction of Roman Catholics that the Marian dogmas formulate a faith consonant with Scripture.

problem for those Anglicans who do not consider that the precise definitions given by these dogmas are sufficiently supported by Scripture. For many Anglicans the teaching authority of the bishop of Rome, independent of a council, is not recommended by the fact that through it thèse Marian doctrines were proclaimed as dogmas binding on all the faithful. Anglicans would also ask whether, in any future union between our two Churches, they would be required to subscribe to such dogmatic statements. One consequence of our separation has been a tendency for Anglicans and Roman Catholics alike to exaggerate the importance of the Marian dogmas in themselves at the expense of other truths more closely related to the foundation of the Christian faith.

31. In spite of our agreement over the need of a universal primacy in a united Church, Anglicans do not accept the guaranteed possession of such a gift of divine assistance in judgement necessarily attached to the office of the bishop of Rome by virtue of which his formal decisions can be known to be wholly assured before their reception by the faithful. Nevertheless the problem about reception is inherently difficult. It would be incorrect to suggest that in controversies of faith no conciliar or papal definition possesses a right to attentive sympathy and acceptance until it has been examined by every individual Christian and subjected to the scrutiny of his private judgement. We agree that, without a special charism guarding the judgement of the universal primate, the Church would still possess means of receiving and ascertaining the truth of revelation. This is evident in the acknowledged gifts of grace and truth in churches not in full communion with the Roman see.

32. Roman Catholic tradition has used the term infallibility to describe guaranteed freedom from fundamental error in judgement.[7] We agree that this is a term applicable unconditionally only to God, and that to use it of a human being, even in highly restricted circumstances, can produce many misunderstandings. That is why in stating our belief in the preservation of the Church from error we have avoided using the term. We also recognize that the ascription to the bishop of Rome of infallibility under certain conditions has tended to lend exaggerated importance to all his statements.

33. We have already been able to agree that conciliarity and primacy are complementary (Authority I, paras. 22-23). We can now together affirm that the Church needs both a multiple, dispersed authority, with which all God's people are actively involved, and also a universal

---

7. In Roman Catholic doctrine, *infallibility* means only the preservation of the judgement from error for the maintenance of the Church in the truth, not positive inspiration or revelation. Moreover the infallibility ascribed to the bishop of Rome is a gift to be, in certain circumstances and under precise conditions, an organ of the infallibility of the Church.

primate as servant and focus of visible unity in truth and love. This does not mean that all differences have been eliminated; but if any Petrine function and office are exercised in the living Church of which a universal primate is called to serve as a visible focus, then it inheres in his office that he should have both a defined teaching responsibility and appropriate gifts of the Spirit to enable him to discharge it.

Contemporary discussions of conciliarity and primacy in both communions indicate that we are not dealing with positions destined to remain static. We suggest that some difficulties will not be wholly resolved until a practical initiative has been taken and our two Churches have lived together more visibly in the one *koinonia*.

Conclusion

This Final Report of the Anglican-Roman Catholic International Commission represents a significant stage in relations between the Anglican Communion and the Roman Catholic Church. The decision by our respective authorities, made as long ago as 1966, to enter into serious dialogue in order to resolve long-standing issues which have been at the origin of our separation, resulted in our concentration on three main areas of controversy: the doctrine of the eucharist, ministry and ordination, and the nature and exercise of authority in the Church.

This dialogue, however, has been directed not merely to the achievement of doctrinal agreement, which is central to our reconciliation, but to the far greater goal of organic unity. The convergence reflected in our Final Report would appear to call for the establishing of a new relationship between our Churches as a next stage in the journey towards Christian unity.

We understand but do not share the fears of those who think that such Statements constitute a threat to all that is distinctive and true in their own traditions. It is our hope to carry with us in the substance of our agreement not only Roman Catholics and Anglicans but all Christians, and that what we have done may contribute to the visible unity of all the people of God as well as to the reconciliation of our two Churches.

We are well aware of how much we owe to others and of how much we have left others still to do. Our agreement still needs to be tested, but in 1981 it has become abundantly clear that, under the Holy Spirit, our Churches have grown closer together in faith and charity. There are high expectations that significant initiatives will be boldly undertaken to deepen our reconciliation and lead us forward in the quest for the full communion to which we have been committed, in obedience to God, from the beginning of our dialogue.

Appendices

Meetings of the Commission

1. *The first meeting of the Anglican-Roman Catholic International Commission took place at St. George's House, Windsor Castle, 9-15 January 1970.* The Commission, following the Malta Report, examined eucharist, ministry and authority in relation to the overall concept of *koinonia*. Anglican and Roman Catholic position papers had been prepared in advance on all three subjects.

2. *The second meeting took place in Venice, 21-28 September 1970 at the Fondazione Cini on the Isola San Giorgio.* Preparatory papers on authority had been prepared by members in Oxford, a Roman Catholic position paper on ministry was presented from the USA and a working paper on the eucharist from the South African Anglican-Roman Catholic Commission. Working papers on Eucharist, Ministry and Authority were published from this meeting in *Theology* (February 1971), *Clergy Review* (February 1971), and *One in Christ* (2-3 1971) but only carried the authority of the respective sub-commissions which were responsible for them. Consideration was also given to questions of moral theology, and three consultants presented papers to the Commission. However, pressure of the main work of the Commission prevented them being pursued, and it was decided that from then on the Commission should concentrate on one subject at a time.

3. *The Commission returned to St. George's House, Windsor Castle, for its third meeting, 1-8 September 1971.* A collection of short papers on eucharistic sacrifice had been prepared for this meeting in Oxford. Anglican and Roman Catholic position papers on the real presence were offered from Canada and a sub-commission met at Poringland, Norwich, 12-16 April 1971, which prepared a draft statement on the eucharist. At Windsor the Commission worked in three sub-commissions on the Poringland draft, concentrating on the problems of presence and sacrifice. After redrafting, the Commission completed its *Agreed Statement on Eucharistic Doctrine* and it was published on 31 December 1971, with the permission of the authorities of the two Churches. Social and cultural factors were also considered at this meeting, and the Commission received a paper presented by a sociological consultant.

4. *The next meeting took place at the Villa Cagnola, Gazzada, Italy, 30 August-7 September 1972.* Short preparatory papers on ministry in the New Testament had been prepared in Oxford, and a Roman Catholic paper on *Sacerdotium* was offered from Canada. A number of papers, both Anglican and Roman Catholic, were written in the USA on bishops and priests, and a paper on the problem of orders was prepared in South Africa. A sub-commission met in Woodstock College,

New York, 22-26 May 1972 to consider all this preparatory material. At Gazzada the Commission produced two draft texts on ministry in the New Testament and on apostolicity.

5. *The fifth meeting took place in Canterbury, 28 August-6 September 1973 at St. Augustine's College.* In preparation for this meeting there had been joint work on apostolic succession in Oxford, on priesthood in Montreal and on ordination in South Africa. A sub-commission met at Poringland, Norwich, 11-15 June 1973 at which all the preparatory material was reviewed, including that from the previous full meeting, and a draft statement on ministry and ordination was offered to the full Commission. At Canterbury the Poringland draft was revised and elaborated and its major themes were accepted: ministries in the life of the Church (including ministry in the New Testament and early Church), the ordained ministry (including the use of priestly language) and ordination (including apostolic succession). The Statement *Ministry and Ordination* was then accepted. It was published on 13 December 1973, with the permission of the respective authorities, and included a historical appendix by the then Anglican Co-Secretary, the Revd. Colin Davey.

6. *At the Centro Mariapoli, Grottaferrata, Italy, 27 August-5 September 1974, the Commission reverted to the issue of authority.* Material on the authority of the Bible had been prepared in South Africa, on *koinonia* and ecclesiology in the USA and on the ecclesiology of Vatican II in Oxford. The English Anglican-Roman Catholic Commission also prepared material on indefectibility and infallibility. There were also important position papers by individual members of the Commission on schism, on magisterium in the early Church, on Vatican I, and on the *sensus fidelium*. The main work of the full Commission that year centred on the authority of Scripture and on the role of the *sensus fidelium*. On 3 September the Commission was received in audience by Pope Paul VI at Castelgandolfo.

7. *The next meeting of the Commission took place in Oxford at St. Stephen's House, 29 August-5 September 1975.* To prepare for this meeting a small sub-commission met at Poringland, Norwich, 11-15 December 1974 which revised drafts from the previous meeting. A further sub-commission met at the Royal Foundation of St. Katharine, Stepney, London, 22-26 June 1975 which continued the work of the Poringland meeting and offered the full Commission a draft text on the lordship of Christ, the authority of the Scriptures, the *sensus fidelium* and the authority conferred by holiness and by special gifts of the Spirit. The full Commission also had before it four important position papers: two Anglican papers on the exercise of authority in the Church and on the relation between truth and authority, and two Roman Catholic papers on the primacy of the bishop of Rome and on jurisdiction. The full Commission scrutinized the St. Katharine's draft but refrained from amending it at that stage. Instead it continued the logic of the

draft by dividing into two sub-commissions to deal with primacy in relation to unity, and infallibility and truth in relation to councils. On 3 September the Commission was joined by the Archbishop of Canterbury, Dr. Donald Coggan.

8. *The Commission returned to Venice for its eighth meeting, staying at the Casa Cardinale Piazza, Madonna dell' Orto, 24 August-2 September 1976.* A small sub-commission had again met at Poringland, Norwich, 9-12 February 1976. It put together the draft material on unity and truth from the two sub-commissions at the Oxford meeting. A larger sub-commission met later at Hengrave Hall, Bury St. Edmunds, 21-25 June 1976 and after revision of the Poringland material added new material on primacy, collegiality and conciliarity. The full Commission therefore had an extended draft statement on authority before it. Sub-commissions at Venice then revised the new material from Poringland and Hengrave, with separate attention to the question of the development of doctrine and decisions in matters of faith. The whole draft was revised, an important conclusion added, and the Commission finally accepted the *Agreed Statement on Authority in the Church*. It was published on 20 January 1977, with the permission of the two authorities.

9. *The next meeting was at Chichester Theological College, 30 August-8 September 1977.* It had been decided that this meeting should be devoted to responding to criticisms of the Agreed Statements and papers were prepared cataloguing both Anglican and Roman Catholic criticisms. At Chichester it was decided to elucidate the Statements rather than simply engage in debate and three sub-commissions began this task.

10. *Due to the death of Pope Paul VI the next meeting of the Commission did not take place till 12-20 January 1979 at Salisbury and Wells Theological College, Salisbury.* Meanwhile there had been a small sub-commission meeting at Damascus House, Mill Hill, London, 9-10 June 1978, which revised the Chichester material on the eucharist, and a large sub-commission met later in the year at All Saints' Pastoral Centre, London Colney, St. Albans, 4-7 September (during part of the time when the full Commission would have been meeting) and completed a draft text on ministry and ordination. At Salisbury, therefore, the Commission revised the two texts and agreed to its response to criticisms of the first two Statements. *Elucidations* was published on 7 June 1979.

11. *The Commission resumed its discussion of authority at the Casa Cardinale Piazza, Madonna dell' Orto, Venice, 28 August-6 September 1979.* It had before it preliminary work on the four serious problems left unresolved at the conclusion of *Authority in the Church I* from a sub-commission which had met at Verulam House, St. Albans a year earlier, 5-9 June 1978. It also had before it position papers by members which had been prepared in time for this sub-commission: a joint Anglican-Roman Catholic paper on the Petrine texts from the USA, an Anglican paper on the Spirit's abiding in the Church with a Roman

Catholic response, joint notes on the problem of *jus divinum*, and a substantial Roman Catholic paper on the jurisdiction of the bishop of Rome. Two drafters had also prepared material to continue the earlier Statement. The Commission itself divided into four sub-commissions at Venice and four tentative drafts on the above subjects emerged.

12. *The twelfth meeting again took place in Venice at the Casa Cardinale Piazza, 26 August-4 September 1980.* The drafts from the previous meeting were criticized and refined. Material on the Petrine texts, *jus divinum* and jurisdiction was all but completed, but the draft on infallibility was unfinished. On 4 September the Commission was received in audience by Pope John Paul II at Castelgandolfo.

13. *The final meeting of the Commission took place at St. George's House, Windsor Castle, 25 August-3 September 1981.* A draft introduction had been prepared over a year before by a sub-commission which had met at the Southwark Diocesan Training Centre, Wychcroft, Redhill, 7-11 January 1980. This draft expounded the Commission's ecclesiology. Work had also begun in the same year on a response to criticisms of the first Statement on Authority by a sub-commission at the Cenacle Retreat and Conference Centre, Burnham, Slough, 22-26 June 1980. At a large sub-commission in Liverpool at St. Katharine's College, 15-19 December 1980, the draft material on infallibility left unfinished at the previous full meeting in Venice was completed. The St. Katharine's sub-commission also began revising the response to criticisms on Authority drafted at Burnham. A final sub-commission met at St. Agnes' Retreat House, Bristol, 9-13 June 1981 and revised the introductory draft on the Church prepared at Wychcroft, stressing the Commission's use of *koinonia*, and completing the revision of the draft response to criticisms on authority. The final meeting at Windsor had therefore a full set of draft texts for scrutiny, criticism and revision. For the first part of the meeting the Commission worked in five sub-commissions on Petrine texts, *jus divinum*, jurisdiction, infallibility, and an authority elucidation. For the second part the Commission worked as a whole, except the infallibility sub-commission, putting together all the drafts, revising the Introduction, and accepting the Preface. Towards the close of the final meeting all the new texts were unanimously agreed. On 1 September the Commission was received at Lambeth Place by the Archbishop of Canterbury, Dr. Robert Runcie. The permission of both authorities was given for publication of the final Report in January 1982.

Members of the Commission

Anglican Delegates

The Most Revd. Henry McAdoo, Archbishop of Dublin (Co-Chairman)

The Rt. Revd. Felix Arnott, formerly Archbishop of Brisbane, now Anglican Chaplain in Venice

The Rt. Revd. John Moorman, formerly Bishop of Ripon

The Rt. Revd. Edward Knapp-Fisher, Archdeacon of Westminster

The Rt. Revd. Arthur A. Vogel, Bishop of West Missouri

The Revd. Professor Henry Chadwick, Regius Professor of Divinity, University of Cambridge

The Revd. Julian Charley, Rector, St. Peter's, Everton, and Warden of Shrewsbury House

The Revd. Canon Eugene R. Fairweather, Keble Professor of Divinity, Trinity College, University of Toronto

The Revd. Canon Howard Root, Director of the Anglican Centre in Rome

Consultants

The Revd. Canon John Halliburton, Principal, Chichester Theological College

The Revd. Dr. Harry Smythe, formerly Director of the Anglican Centre, Rome

Secretaries

The Revd. Colin Davey, Assistant Chaplain, Archbishop of Canterbury's Counsellors on Foreign Relations (*until July 1974*)

The Revd. Christopher Hill, Assistant Chaplain, Archbishop of Canterbury's Counsellors on Foreign Relations (*from August 1974*)

Roman Catholic Delegates

The Rt. Revd. Alan Clark, Bishop of East Anglia (Co-Chairman)

The Rt. Revd. Christopher Butler, OSB, Auxiliary Bishop of Westminster

The Revd. Fr. Barnabas Ahern, CP, Professor of Sacred Scripture, Rome

The Revd. Fr. Pierre Duprey, WF, Under Secretary, Vatican Secretariat for Promoting Christian Unity

The Revd. Dr. Herbert Ryan, SJ, Professor of Theology, Loyola Marymount University, Los Angeles

Professor John Scarisbrick, Professor of History, University of Warwick

The Revd. Fr. George H. Tavard, AA, Professor of Theology, Methodist Theological School, Delaware, Ohio

The Revd. Fr. Jean Tillard, OP, Professor of Dogmatic Theology, Dominican Faculty of Theology, Ottawa

The Revd. Dr. Edward Yarnold, SJ, Tutor in Theology, Campion Hall, Oxford

Secretary

The Rt. Revd. Mgr. William Purdy, Staff Member, Vatican Secretariat for Promoting Christian Unity

World Council of Churches Observer

The Revd. Dr. Günther Gassmann, President, Lutherisches Kirchenamt, Hannover

Unity without Absorption
Lecture on Anglican-Roman Catholic Relations

by the Lord Archbishop of Canterbury, Dr. Robert Runcie,
given at Croydon, England

11 March 1982

This address, delivered at Croydon on
March 11, 1982, set forth the basic ecumenical themes and goals that
have characterized Archbishop Runcie's primacy at Canterbury thus
far: the relation of the local to the universal; the Church as a communion of local churches ("degrees of communion, rather than degrees
of being the Church"); the importance of holding together creatively
the various ecumenical dialogues in which the Anglican Communion
is engaged. The archbishop here gives positive anticipation to the
Final Report of the Anglican-Roman Catholic International Commission, which, at this time, was soon to be released. This address was
delivered only hours after anti-Catholic demonstrators had forced the
primate to abandon a previously scheduled talk in Liverpool. For
further background, see the headline story of *The Church Times*
(London), March 19, 1982.

Theologically, I believe that Anglicanism has regained the patristic
view of the Church as a eucharistic communion of local churches held
together by the episcopate.

This significant observation has the more strength because it was
originally made to me not by an Anglican at all but the distinguished
Swiss ecumenical theologian, Lukas Vischer. He said that the Anglican tradition offered a return to the Patristic view:

> The emphasis is on the Church as a eucharistic communion. Jesus
> Christ is present wherever and whenever the eucharist is celebrated.
> The episcopal ministry is to be understood as a service within this
> eucharistic fellowship. It helps to secure the cohesion of each local
> church in its life and witness and, at the same time, to make possible
> the common life and witness of all local churches in a universal
> conciliar fellowship.

I do not think this insight, couched as it is in twentieth century
ecumenical terminology, would have been rejected by that "classical"

Anglican Richard Hooker. He held that the universal Church was to be found in the local Church in a way which did not make all depend upon a pyramidal structure with the Pope at the apex. Nor was he a congregationalist. In a characteristically quaint way he tries to hold together the local and the universal in the image of seas and the ocean:

> In which consideration, as the main body of the sea being one, yet within divers precincts hath divers names, so the Catholic Church is in like sort divided into a number of distinct Societies, every one of which is termed a Church within itself.

If there is something in the view that Anglicans have almost accidentally re-discovered something of the patristic conception of the communion of the Churches—and I do not think it without significance that we use the term Anglican Communion as the way we describe ourselves—then this gives us something precious to offer all the Churches from our own experience of unity within a family of Churches.

Nor would such a view of the Church be unknown or unwelcome amongst other Christians. As might be expected because of its patristic affinities such a view of the Church would be welcome among the Orthodox. This is an area of Christian dialogue I am fairly familiar with and the Anglican Orthodox Moscow Agreed Statement—I was then Co-Chairman of the Commission—actually has a section entitled "The Church as the Eucharistic Community." But such a view of the Church also lies behind much of the work of the Faith and Order Commission of the World Council of Churches. More and more the re-discovery of the liturgical-sacramental tradition within the great Protestant traditions has gone hand in hand with an openness to reconsider the historic episcopate—in the words of the Lambeth Appeal to all Christian People of 1920—as the one means of providing "a ministry acknowledged by every part of the Church." Behind these developments lies a sacramental view of the Church in which unity is expressed in terms of communion and universality is expressed through the episcopate. The work of the Faith and Order Commission deserves to be better known. At Lima only last January the Commission completed its revision of important texts on Baptism, Eucharist and Ministry. They will eventually come to all the Churches for reception and we ought to take them very seriously in the Church of England for they will provide a possible way round the impasse Anglicans reach when the time comes to make a decision on any bilateral ecumenical discussion such as ARCIC or the Covenanting Proposals. If all the Churches can find a way of accepting the work of the Faith and Order Commission—which includes Roman Catholics and Orthodox as full participants—then I think we shall be close to the convergence on the nature of the Church. Furthermore the

Faith and Order texts may strengthen the theological undergirding of the Covenanting Proposals which have seemed to some of their opponents to betray a search for coalition rather than doctrinal unity.

When we look at our dialogue with Rome such an understanding of the Church is again welcomed. The Church as *communio* is one of the basic themes which runs through the Vatican II decree *On the Mystery of the Church*.

The Final Report of the Anglican/Roman Catholic International Commission will contain an Introduction on its understanding of the Church when it is published later this month. In the various leaks that have so far occurred no-one has yet emphasized the significance of the Commission's view that the one Church is a communion of local churches. The implications of this view are immensely important for all Christians talking to Rome. Such a view rules out the monolithic institutional ecclesiology of the past and gives us all room to breathe. Instead of the single barque of Peter sailing the ocean of history we are now given the picture of a whole flotilla of vessels. Admittedly the flagship flies the Papal Arms but we must not underestimate the real change proposed.

Perhaps I can digress here to emphasize the status of the document soon to be published. The ARCIC Final Report remains a study document. On the one hand it is more than a piece of free enterprise on the part of a few enthusiasts—it is the work of an official joint Commission which has been working for eleven years. On the other hand it has not been accepted by either the Roman Catholic Church or the Churches of the Anglican Communion and no-one should leap to the conclusion that the Archbishop of Canterbury, still less the General Synod, is about to accept the Vatican I definitions of Papal jurisdiction and infallibility. What the Commission has tried to do is to get behind the phraseology of confrontation to whatever truths lie beyond particular doctrinal expressions—including those Roman Catholics customarily use of the Bishop of Rome. Whether or not it has been successful in its aim only the Churches can judge but no-one with an ecumenical feeling will blame the Commission for not resting content with the hurling of slogans.

But it has to be admitted that there are some ambiguities in the Anglican discussion with Rome. The Religious Affairs Correspondent of *The Times* put his finger on them in an article of last Monday when he suggested that the kind of primacy described by the Anglican/ Roman Catholic International Commission "does not yet exist." It is certainly true that from the outside some aspects of Curial centralization do not seem yet to be in harmony with the spirit of Vatican II. But if I say this I must also allow for Roman Catholic criticism that the Anglican Church does not always live up to the best of its official theory.

If there is what ecumenists call an "emerging consensus" on the church which is also deeply rooted in the historical Anglican experience of life in a communion of Churches, what are the implications?

Let me conclude by offering two observations. The first is concerned with one of the most difficult issues in ecclesiology—the question of schism. It is generally accepted that in the Early Church schism is always from the Church, never within it. And this has broadly speaking remained the position of both the Roman Catholic Church and the Orthodox Churches to this day. It has the consequent logical implication that there can only be one true Church. It has the merit of being the simplest possible understanding of the creedal affirmation of the oneness of the Church—I believe in *one* holy Catholic and Apostolic Church. The problem ecumenically is that once it is stated that there is only one Church conversation necessarily stops.

The other view, held by many Anglicans, and most other Christians, that schism is within the Church has the great merit of not denying the obvious gifts of grace in the separate Christian communities. But it too has an unacceptable implication: if all Churches are more or less equally short of approximating to the one Church Christ intended, then that Church does not exist today.

A view of the Church as a communion of Churches does not remove all the problems associated with either view but it is certainly easier for Roman Catholics and even the Orthodox to envisage degrees of communion than degrees of being the Church.

The other implication for our view of unity and the Church is that the Church understood as a communion of local churches not only allows diversity but actually makes it fundamental to its structure. We need to quietly repeat that unity does not mean absorption when we speak with Rome—and I elaborated this theme in Westminster Abbey a year ago. But perhaps Anglicans need to think whether we are not guilty of wanting the unity by absorption of the Free Churches? Whatever form of unity we eventually achieve with the Free Churches it must surely take account of the gifts they have to offer from their diversity. It is at least an open question as to whether mission is more effectively served by a uniformity of organisation, spirituality and worship. One of the reasons for this series of lectures is to be ecumenically prepared for the visit of Pope John Paul II when he visits this country next May. His predecessor Gregory the Great, who sent a reluctant Augustine to England, believed in the diversity of the Churches. He told St. Augustine to take anything that he had found either in the Roman Church or the Gallican Church, or any other Church, and incorporate them into the Church for the English. He would not therefore mind if I slightly adapted a famous saying of his about the proclamation of the Scriptures in the Church and applied it to a vision of the Church itself: "a place in which lambs may paddle and elephants may swim." May our ecumenical search for a deeper understanding of the mystery of the Church make the Church such a place, whether we be elephants or lambs.

Statements of Archbishop Runcie and Pope John Paul II at Canterbury

May 29, 1982

Archbishop Runcie's Address in Canterbury Cathedral

At the beginning of the ecumenical service in Canterbury Cathedral, Archbishop Robert Runcie addressed Pope John Paul II as follows:

Witamy Jego Swiatobliwosc, drogiego Brata w Chrystusie, w imie Pana naszego Jezusa Chrystusa.

We welcome you, Your Holiness, with words of friendship, for this is a service of celebration. But the present moment is full of pain for so many in the world. Millions are hungry and the sacred gift of life is counted cheap, while the nations of the world use some of their best resources and much of their store of human ingenuity in refining weapons of death. With so much to celebrate in life and so much to be done to combat life's enemies, disease and ignorance, energy is being wasted in conflict. Our minds inevitably turn to the conflict and tragic loss of life in the South Atlantic and we also remember the suffering of Your Holiness's own fellow countrymen in Poland.

But Christians do not accept hunger, disease and war as inevitable. The present moment is not empty of hope, but waits to be transformed by the power which comes from remembering our beginnings and by a power which comes from a lively vision of the future. Remembering our beginnings, celebrating our hope for the future, freeing ourselves from cynicism and despair in order to act in the present. It is this style of Christian living which gives shape to this service. Every Christian service contains this element of remembering the beginnings of our community when our Lord walked this earth.

At this season of the year we particularly remember the gift of the Holy Spirit at the first Pentecost, and the sending out of the Apostles to carry the faith of Jesus Christ to the furthest ends of the world. We recall one of the first missionary endeavours of the Roman Church and its efforts to recapture for Christ a Europe overwhelmed by the barbarians. In the year 597, in the words of the English historian the Venerable Bede, Your Holiness's great predecessor Gregory, prompted by divine inspiration sent a servant of God named Augustine and several more Godfearing monks with him to preach the word of God to the English race. Augustine became the first Archbishop of Canterbury and I rejoice that the successors of Gregory and Augustine stand here today in the church which is built on their partnership in the Gospel.

We shall trace and celebrate our beginnings in this service, by reaffirming our baptismal vows, made at the font at the beginning of the Christian life, and by saying together the Creed, an expression of the heart of our common Christian faith, composed in the era before our unhappy division. The emphasis then will be on the richness of what we share and upon the existing unity of the Christian Church, which transcends all political divisions and frontiers imposed on the human family.

One of the gifts which Christians have to make to the peace of the world is to live out the unity that has already been given to them in their common love of Christ. But our unity is not in the past only, but also in the future. We have a common vision which also breaks up the lazy prejudices and easy assumptions of the present. Our chapel here of the martyrs of the 20th century will be the focus for the celebration of a common vision. We believe even in a world like ours which exalts and applauds self-interest and derides self-sacrifice, that the blood of the martyrs shall create the holy places of the earth.

Our own century has seen the creation of ruthless tyrannies by the use of violence, and cynical disregard of truth. We believe that such energies founded on force and lies destroy themselves. The kingdom spoken of by our Lord Jesus Christ is built by self-sacrificing love which can even turn places of sorrow and suffering into signs of hope.

We think of Your Holiness's own fellow countryman, the priest Maximilian Kolbe, who died in place of another in the hell of Auschwitz. We remember with gratitude our own brother, Archbishop Janani Luwum in Uganda, who worked in the worst conditions for Christ's kingdom of love and justice, and whose death inspires us still and will mark the future more deeply than the lives of his oppressors. We remember all the martyrs of our century of martyrs who have confirmed Christ's Church in the conviction that even in the places of horror, the concentration camps, and prisons and slums of the world, nothing in all creation can separate us from the active and creative love of God in Christ Jesus our Lord.

If we remember that beginning in Christ Jesus our Lord, if we can face the suffering of travelling in his way, if we can lift our eyes beyond the historic quarrels which have tragically disfigured Christ's Church and wasted so much Christian energy, then we shall indeed enter into a faith worthy of celebration, because it is able to remake the world. Thanks be to God. Amen.

The Pope's Homily in Canterbury Cathedral

1. The passage which has just been read is taken from the Gospel according to John and contains the words of our Lord Jesus Christ on the eve of his Passion. While he was at supper with his disciples, he prayed: *"that they may all be one; even as thou, Father, art in me, and I in thee, that they also may be in us, so that the world may believe that thou hast sent me"* (Jn 17:21).

These words are marked in a particular way by the Paschal Mystery of our Saviour, by his Passion, death and Resurrection. Though pronounced once only, they *endure throughout all generations*. Christ prays unceasingly for the unity of his Church, because he loves her with the same love with which he loved the apostles and disciples who were with him at the Last Supper. "I do not pray for these only, but also for those who believe in me through their word" (Jn 17:20). Christ reveals a *divine perspective* in which the Father and the Son and the Holy Spirit are present. Present also is the most profound mystery of the Church: the unity in love which exists between the Father and the Son and the Holy Spirit penetrates to the heart of the people whom God has chosen to be his own, and is the source of *their* unity.

Christ's words resound in a special way *today in this hallowed Cathedral* which recalls the figure of the great missionary Saint Augustine whom Pope Gregory the Great sent forth so that through his words the sons and daughters of England might believe in Christ.

Dear brethren, all of us have become *particularly sensitive to these words* of the priestly prayer of Christ. The Church of our time is the Church which participates in a particular way in the prayer of Christ for unity and which seeks the ways of unity, *obedient to the Spirit* who speaks in the words of the Lord. We desire to be obedient, especially today, on this historic day which centuries and generations have awaited. We desire to be obedient to him whom Christ calls the Spirit of truth.

2. On *the feast of Pentecost* last year Catholics and Anglicans joined with Orthodox and Protestants, both in Rome and in Constantinople, in commemorating the First Council of Constantinople by professing their common faith in the Holy Spirit, the Lord and Giver of life. Once again on this vigil of the great feast of Pentecost, we are gathered in prayer to implore our heavenly Father to pour out anew the Holy Spirit, the Spirit of Christ, upon his Church. For it is the Church which, in the words of that Council's Creed, we profess to be the work par excellence of the Holy Spirit when we say "we believe in one, holy, catholic and apostolic church."

Today's Gospel passages have called attention in particular to two aspects of the gift of the Holy Spirit which Jesus invoked upon his disciples: he is *the Spirit of truth and the Spirit of unity*. On the first Pentecost day, the Holy Spirit descended on that small band of disciples to confirm them in the truth of God's salvation of the world through the death and Resurrection of his Son, and to unite them into the one Body of Christ, which is the Church. Thus we know that when we pray "that all may be one" as Jesus and his Father are one, it is precisely in order that "the world may believe" and by this faith be saved (cf. Jn 17:21). For our faith can be none other than the faith of Pentecost, the faith in which the Apostles were confirmed by the Spirit of truth. We believe that the Risen Lord has authority to save us from sin and the powers of darkness. We believe, too, that we are called to "become one body, one spirit in Christ" (Eucharistic Prayer III).

3.   In a few moments we shall renew our baptismal vows together. We intend to perform this ritual, which we share in common as Anglicans and Catholics, as a clear *testimony to the one sacrament of Baptism by which we have been joined to Christ*. At the same time we are humbly mindful that the faith of the Church to which we appeal is not without the marks of our separation. Together we shall renew our renunciation of sin in order to make it clear that we believe that Jesus Christ has overcome the powerful hold of Satan upon "the world" (Jn 14:17). We shall profess anew our intention to turn away from all that is evil and to turn towards God who is the author of all that is good and the source of all that is holy. As we again make our profession of faith in the triune God—Father, Son and Holy Spirit— we find great hope in the promise of Jesus: "The Counsellor, the Holy Spirit, whom the Father will send in my name, he will teach you all things, and bring to your remembrance all that I have said to you" (Jn 14:26). Christ's promise gives us confidence in *the power of this same Holy Spirit to heal the divisions introduced into the Church* in the course of the centuries since that first Pentecost day. In this way the renewal of our baptismal vows will become a pledge to do all in our power to cooperate with the grace of the Holy Spirit, who alone can lead us to the day when we will profess the fullness of our faith together.

4.   We can be *confident in addressing our prayer for unity* to the Holy Spirit today, for according to Christ's promise the Spirit, the Counsellor, will be with us for ever (cf. Jn 14:16). It was with confidence that Archbishop Fisher made bold to visit Pope John XXIII at the time of the Second Vatican Council, and that Archbishops Ramsey and Coggan came to visit Pope Paul VI. It is with no less confidence that I have responded to the promptings of the Holy Spirit to be with you today at Canterbury.

5.   My dear brothers and sisters of the Anglican Communion, "whom I love and long for" (Phil 4:1), how happy I am to be able to speak directly to you today in this great Cathedral! The building itself is an eloquent witness both to *our long years of common inheritance and to the sad years of division that followed*. Beneath this roof Saint Thomas Becket suffered martyrdom. Here too we recall Augustine and Dunstan and Anselm and all those monks who gave such diligent service in this church. The great events of salvation history are retold in the ancient stained glass windows above us. And we have venerated here the

manuscript of the Gospels sent from Rome to Canterbury thirteen hundred years ago. Encouraged by the witness of so many who have professed their faith in Jesus Christ through the centuries—often at the cost of their own lives—a sacrifice which even today is asked of not a few, as the new chapel we shall visit reminds us—I appeal to you in this holy place, all my fellow Christians, and especially the members of the Church of England and the members of the Anglican Communion throughout the world, to accept the commitment to which Archbishop Runcie and I pledge ourselves anew before you today. This commitment is that of *praying and working for reconciliation and ecclesial unity according to the mind and heart of our Saviour Jesus Christ.*

6.   On this first visit of a Pope to Canterbury, *I come to you in love— the love of Peter* to whom the Lord said, "I have prayed for you that your faith may not fail; and when you have turned again, strengthen your brethren" (Lk 22:32). I come to you also in the love of Gregory, who sent Saint Augustine to this place to give the Lord's flock a shepherd's care (cf. 1 Pt 5:2). Just as every minister of the Gospel must do, so today I echo the words of the Master: "I am among you as one who serves" (Lk 22:27). With me I bring to you, beloved brothers and sisters of the Anglican Communion, the hopes and the desires, the prayers and good will of all who are united with the Church of Rome, which from earliest times was said to "preside in love" (Ignatius, *Ad Rom.*, Proem.).

7.   In a few moments Archbishop Runcie will join me in signing a *Common Declaration*, in which we give recognition to the steps we have already taken along the path of unity, and state the plans we propose and the hopes we entertain for the next stage of our common pilgrimage. And yet these hopes and plans will come to nothing if our striving for unity is not *rooted in our union with God;* for Jesus said, "In that day you will know that I am in my Father, and you in me, and I in you. He who has my commandments and keeps them, he it is who loves me; and he who loves me will be loved by my Father, and I will love him and manifest myself to him" (Jn 14:20-21). This love of God is poured out upon us in the person of the Holy Spirit, the Spirit of truth and of unity. Let us open ourselves to his powerful love, as we pray that, speaking the truth in love, we may all grow up in every way into him who is the head, into our Lord Jesus Christ (cf. Eph 4:15). May the dialogue we have begun lead us to the day of full restoration of unity in faith and love.

8.   On the eve of his Passion, Jesus told his disciples: "If you love me, you will keep my commandments" (Jn 14:15). We have felt compelled to come together here today in obedience to the great commandment: *the commandment of love.* We wish to embrace it in its entirety, to live by it completely, and to experience the power of this commandment in conformity with the words of the Master: "I will pray to the Father, and he will give you another Counsellor, to be

with you for ever, even *the Spirit of truth,* whom the world cannot receive, because it neither sees him nor knows him; you know him, for he dwells with you, and will be in you" (Jn 14:16-17).

Love grows by means of truth, and truth draws near to man by means of love. Mindful of this, I lift up to the Lord this prayer: O Christ, may all that is part of today's encounter *be born* of the Spirit of truth and *be made fruitful* through love.

Behold before us: the past and the future!

Behold before us: the desires of so many hearts!

You, who are the Lord of history and the Lord of human hearts, be with us! Christ Jesus, eternal Son of God, be with us! Amen.

Common Declaration of Pope John Paul II and the Archbishop of Canterbury

May 29, 1982

1. In the Cathedral Church of Christ at Canterbury the Pope and the Archbishop of Canterbury have met on the eve of Pentecost to offer thanks to God for the progress that has been made in the work of reconciliation between our communions. Together with leaders of other Christian Churches and Communities we have listened to the Word of God; together we have recalled our one baptism and renewed the promises then made; together we have acknowledged the witness given by those whose faith has led them to surrender the precious gift of life itself in the service of others, both in the past and in modern times.

2. The bond of our common baptism into Christ led our predecessors to inaugurate a serious dialogue between our Churches, a dialogue founded on the Gospels and the ancient common traditions, a dialogue which has as its goal the unity for which Christ prayed to his Father "so that the world may know that thou has sent me and has loved them even as thou hast loved me" (Jn 17:23). In 1966, our predecessors Pope Paul VI and Archbishop Michael Ramsey made a Common Declaration announcing their intention to inaugurate a serious dialogue between the Roman Catholic Church and the Anglican Communion which would "include not only theological matters such as Scripture, Tradition and Liturgy, but also matters of practical difficulty felt on either side" (Common Declaration, par. 6). After this dialogue had already produced three statements on Eucharist, Ministry and Ordination, and Authority in the Church, Pope Paul VI and Archbishop Donald Coggan, in their Common Declaration in 1977, took the occasion to encourage the completion of the dialogue on these three important questions so that the Commission's conclusions might be evaluated by the respective Authorities through procedures appropriate to each Communion. The Anglican-Roman Catholic International Commission has now completed the task assigned to it with the publication of its Final Report, and as our two Communions proceed with the necessary evaluation, we join in thanking the members of the Commission for their dedication, scholarship and integrity in a long and demanding task undertaken for love of Christ and for the unity of his Church.

3. The completion of this Commission's work bids us look to the next stage of our common pilgrimage in faith and hope towards the unity for which we long. We are agreed that it is now time to set up

a new international Commission. Its task will be to continue the work already begun: to examine, especially in the light of our respective judgments on the Final Report, the outstanding doctrinal differences which still separate us, with a view towards their eventual resolution; to study all that hinders the mutual recognition of the ministries of our Communions; and to recommend what practical steps will be necessary when, on the basis of our unity in faith, we are able to proceed to the restoration of full communion. We are well aware that this new Commission's task will not be easy, but we are encouraged by our reliance on the grace of God and by all that we have seen of the power of that grace in the ecumenical movement of our time.

4.   While this necessary work of theological clarification continues, it must be accompanied by the zealous work and fervent prayer of Roman Catholics and Anglicans throughout the world as they seek to grow in mutual understanding, fraternal love and common witness to the Gospel. Once more, then, we call on the bishops, clergy and faithful people of both our Communions in every country, diocese and parish in which our faithful live side by side. We urge them all to pray for this work and to adopt every possible means of furthering it through their collaboration in deepening their allegiance to Christ and in witnessing to him before the world. Only by such collaboration and prayer can the memory of the past enmities be healed and our past antagonisms overcome.

5.   Our aim is not limited to the union of our two Communions alone, to the exclusion of other Christians, but rather extends to the fulfilment of God's will for the visible unity of all his people. Both in our present dialogue, and in those engaged in by other Christians among themselves and with us, we recognize in the agreements we are able to reach, as well as in the difficulties which we encounter, a renewed challenge to abandon ourselves completely to the truth of the Gospel. Hence we are happy to make this Declaration today in the welcome presence of so many fellow Christians whose Churches and Communities are already partners with us in prayer and work for the unity of all.

6.   With them we wish to serve the cause of peace, of human freedom and human dignity, so that God may indeed be glorified in all his creatures. With them we greet in the name of God all men of good will, both those who believe in him and those who are still searching for him.

7.   This holy place reminds us of the vision of Pope Gregory in sending St. Augustine as an apostle to England, full of zeal for the preaching of the Gospel and the shepherding of the flock. On this eve of Pentecost, we turn again in prayer to Jesus, the Good Shepherd, who promised to ask the Father to give us another Advocate to be with

us for ever, the Spirit of truth (cf. Jn 14:16), to lead us to the full unity to which he calls us. Confident in the power of this same Holy Spirit, we commit ourselves anew to the task of working for unity with firm faith, renewed hope and ever deeper love.

The Five-Year Report

A Reflective Review of Five Joint Studies Produced by the
EDEO/NADEO Study Committee 1978-1983

The Anglican-Roman Catholic ecumenical venture has been aided
beyond measure by the very existence, not to mention the work, of
several key organizations. In the United States, a key structure of
long standing is the National Workshop on Christian Unity. Out of
this annual occasion for Christian encounter and dialogue came the
two largest and most closely allied ecclesiastical network organizations yet devised: the National Association of Diocesan Ecumenical
Officers (NADEO), and the Episcopal Diocesan Ecumenical Officers
(EDEO), its counterpart. Both organizations are based upon a design
of diocesan representation and participation and, therefore, enjoy a
kind of "grass roots" character and strength. For this reason alone,
they could be considered key organizations.

Among other essential organizations, and working at a very dif-
ferent level, were the official dialogue groups of ARCIC and ARC. It
is the stimulating document *Where Are We: A Challenge for the Future?
A Twelve-Year Report from ARC/USA* which encouraged NADEO and
EDEO at the April, 1978, Workshop on Christian Unity to create a
Standing Committee to respond to one of its challenges.

In its first publication a year later, the Standing Committee reflected
back upon the interaction of ARC, NADEO, and EDEO. Once again
at a Workshop gathering, they reported:

> One very practical suggestion of [the Twelve-Year] report was the
> exploration of ARC Covenants in the United States. The Episcopal
> and Roman Catholic Churches' two national associations of ecu-
> menical officers . . . felt that the existence of such covenants, pro-
> posed [by many] as an expression of the most effective grass roots
> models in the search for visible unity, also needed some evaluative
> consideration at this time. These same two associations felt that the
> ARC Twelve-Year Report had, creatively, called for this evaluation
> to be done jointly. In response [they] jointly established such a Task
> Force (Preface, *The Lived Experience*, April 1979).

The co-chairmen of the Standing Committee were selected on the
basis of their clear interest in Anglican-Roman Catholic relations, their
access to the resources of a major metropolitan area, and their record
of viable and recognized ecumenical programs. The Standing Committee membership was chosen, in part, on the basis of geographical
distribution. Paired members originally were drawn from the Great

Lakes region, the middle South, and the West Coast. Despite some change in composition, the integrity of this design has remained basically intact to the present.

Working as an EDEO/NADEO Standing Committee, to two Church bodies, necessitated the development of mutually agreed upon policies and procedures to ensure a successful collaboration. Early decisions established that the studies and reports were not to be primarily theological nor canonical in nature, but experiential and pastoral. It was also decided that, despite the suggestions to widen the investigations to include other Christian bodies, the studies would focus only upon the ARC enterprise. And finally, mindful of the sense of anticipated oneness which grows in ecumenical groups who live and work together, the members resolved that they would follow the letter of all ARC guidelines regarding *communio in sacris*, thus preserving, also, the integrity of their work.

As to procedure, it was decided that the investigations would be conducted both through questionnaires directed, where possible, to persons identified by a broad spectrum of diocesan ecumenical officers and also through on-site follow-up visits to carefully selected locations. For example, the second report is the on-site follow-up to the first. Reports three and four are based upon both procedures. All data was then made available to every member of the Standing Committee, which then met at various retreat centers to write each report as, more or less, a committee of the whole. Where possible, the Standing Committee sought respondents to each report, thus providing a springboard to critical analysis within the context of the publication itself. Finally, all research materials would be kept on file and available, within the bounds of confidentiality, to qualified researchers. It was also decided that the Standing Committee's published reports would be distributed to all NADEO and EDEO members, to the bishops and agencies of both Churches, and would then be available for purchase.

Since its creation in 1978, the EDEO/NADEO Standing Committee has developed four studies: (I) *The Lived Experience: A Survey of U.S. ARC Covenants*, April 25, 1979 (Second Printing, March 15, 1981); (II) *Tale of Three Cities: Ogden, Louisville, Tidewater: A Study of U.S. ARC Covenants*, March 11, 1980; (III) *ARC Marriages: A Study of U.S. Couples Living Episcopal-Roman Catholic Marriages*, May 5, 1981; and (IV) *Pastoral Care for ARC Couples: Models for Ministry to Engaged and Married Couples*, April 21, 1982.

Each topic was a direct outgrowth of the preceding year's study and each was authorized and assigned by the parent bodies on that same annual basis. The Standing Committee has never functioned as an organizational bureaucracy.

The second report provided the on-site investigation indicated by the data in the first report, as mentioned. Ogden, Louisville, and

Tidewater stood out as examples of viable covenants. From these, it was probably the Tidewater "tale" which pointed most clearly to the need for a focus upon ARC marriages, both in terms of their successes and their frustrations, i.e. report number three.

The fourth report sought ways of responding to those ARC marriages (and ministering to the ARC marriage to come) by seeking to address both the glory and the pain of those personal covenants with practical and tested models.

The fifth report, entitled (V) *Pastoral Perspective on Baptism in ARC Families*, will be presented to the parent bodies meeting at the Annual Workshop on Christian Unity in Louisville, Kentucky, in May, 1983. In it, the Standing Committee explores, again from a pastoral perspective, the matter of baptism (and infant baptism in particular) as it is experienced and understood in ARC families. The report poses fundamental questions about the nature of baptism and discusses the notion of "ecumenical baptism," the benefits of joint baptismal instruction and its relationship to Confirmation, Intercommunion, and "religious identity." Data for the report was submitted by couples selected from previous resource groups along with group responses from Ogden, Tidewater, and Detroit covenanted parishes.

The members of the Standing Committee have indeed been gratified by the enthusiasm and appreciation with which their work has been received. An outstanding example of that reception is the fact that the third report was placed on the agendas of the 1981 Workshop on Christian Unity held in Boston; and of the ARC Leadership Conference which took place later that same year in Washington, D.C. Growing interest is further reflected in the fact that the first report is now in its second printing and that orders for the publication have been received from as far away as Australia, Great Britain, New Zealand, and South Africa.

In retrospect, what, exactly, has been learned from the efforts of the EDEO/NADEO Standing Committee? The reports indicate that there is "good news" and "bad news." Under the heading of the good, it can be reported with some substantial support that many positive, creative things are taking place across the country in the ARC enterprise. The Standing Committee's findings indicate greater understanding, increasing enthusiasm, and, often, a very deep commitment on the part of the laity of both Churches to the quest for Anglican-Roman Catholic unity. We have encountered many healthy ecumenical cells in the Body of Christ!

The Standing Committee members were often told, also, of the very great need for organizations and endeavors of this kind to seek out and report on ecumenism in this way, lending support and encouragement to those who may not know how to begin, or, having begun, how to carry on in the face of disappointment or even obstruction. A word commonly used to describe the reports is *stimulating*.

Response to the studies, both in process and after publication, indicated great joy over the fact that an agency of the Church was listening to and passing along the hopes and the concerns of "simple parishioners."

But there is also the bad. In the matter of covenants, the studies show that there is often not enough preparation leading to the formal declaration of a covenant. All covenants seem to be fragile; and where the preparation is hasty, the chances for continual life and success of the covenant are further reduced. In the case of ARC marriages, the well-received third report reflected a history of insensitivity on the part of many of the clergy toward ARC couples in their preparation for marriage and in their life situation which followed. The couples' frustration was further increased by their concern for an appropriate religious education for their children, for which the two Churches do not yet seem to have a workable solution. Also, the data would seem to suggest strongly that the laity are moving more rapidly than the clergy in the direction indicated by the Twelve-Year Report and other ARC and ARCIC studies.

Within the framework circumscribed by the Standing Committee's five reports, there remains a great deal of work yet to be done. The reports have touched upon—but have not addressed—such matters as intercommunion, confirmation, the question of traditional religious identity in ecumenical life situations, continuing follow-up to the ARC marriage studies including a response to, and evaluation of, *Pastoral Care for ARC Couples*, an updated look at the continuing challenge presented by viable covenant ventures.

Finally, the Standing Committee has never received a systematic and direct response to its work from the parent bodies of NADEO and EDEO, or from any level of ecclesiastical authority. Such a response could well open up new areas for internal dialogue, advancing the ecumenical movement by causing each Church to clarify its own understanding and intentions. These unresolved items necessitate a look to the future. This *Five-Year Report* concludes, therefore, with yet another challenge to the National Association of Diocesan Ecumenical Officers and the Episcopal Diocesan Ecumenical Officers, meeting at the 1983 Workshop on Christian Unity in Louisville.

Recommendations

The Standing Committee members respectfully suggest that the parent bodies adopt a resolution to discharge the present Committee from further duties and to create a new Standing Committee. This Committee would have the responsibility of eliciting from the general membership of EDEO and NADEO its new agenda, specifying both the nature and the method of the work to be undertaken.

Appreciation

The 1978-1983 EDEO/NADEO Standing Committee members wish to thank the two associations for their support during these five years of collaboration. The members further express their deep gratitude to all the persons who cooperated in the several studies, both as resource persons and as respondents. And finally, the Standing Committee members thank those several devoted assistants, elsewhere identified, who made possible the smooth preparation of our final copy for printing and distribution.

EDEO/NADEO Standing Committee

The Rev. Canon Harold Hultgren, D.D.
The Rev. Msgr. Royale M. Vadakin, Co-Chairmen
The Rev. Alex Brunett
The Rev. Vincent Butler
The Rev. Ernest Falardeau, SSS
The Rev. George Kilcourse
The Rev. Dennis Odekirk

Images of God: Reflections on Christian Anthropology

The 1977 ARC Twelve-Year Report had
suggested four areas for further theological investigation. From the
four, ARC selected the potentially most divisive one. In the hope of
providing at least a more irenic context in which to discuss the cluster
of issues connected with the sexual differentiation of the human
species, the ARC members devoted five years of intensive research
to *Reflections on Christian Anthropology*. The final draft of the text was
prepared by Fathers Charles P. Price and Herbert J. Ryan, SJ, and
Sister Sara Butler, MSBT. It was approved by ARC at Columbus,
Ohio, on February 25, 1982. The final editing of the draft was
completed in July 1983.

Introduction

1.   For the past four years, ARC-USA has given its attention to Christian anthropology. We have tried to explore together a large theological context within which several subjects of deep concern to our two
churches may profitably be considered: the church's teaching about
human sexuality and Christian marriage; the role of Mary in the life,
devotion and theology of the church; and the admission of women
to the ordained ministry. The following paper indicates the range of
this theological exploration and some of the agreements and disagreements which we have discovered. As in many other matters,
our disagreements do not always follow along lines of church membership.

I. Jesus as the Image of God

A. *Jesus Shows Us What God Is Like*

2.   There is unanimous and complete agreement among us, based
on a common interpretation of New Testament texts and acceptance
of the decisions of the early ecumenical councils, that the only ade-

quate "image" of God is Jesus Christ. One has only to recall such New Testament passages as Colossians 1:15, "He is the image *(eikon)* of the invisible God, the first-born of all creation," and Hebrews 1:3, "He reflects the glory of God and bears the very stamp of his nature, upholding the universe by his word of power."

3.   Although God is a mystery which the human mind can never penetrate, God in his mystery has revealed himself to us in a unique and ultimate manner in his Word made flesh, Jesus Christ. Our ability to speak of God and apprehend what he has done in Christ, however, is based upon the fact of creation. God was revealing himself in the act of creation, which occurred before Jesus Christ, and even before human beings, appeared in the evolving universe. The use of that creation is the only way we, a part of it, can refer to God.

4.   The work of God in Christ and the new dispensation offered to the world by the Father in his Son is best appreciated in terms of creation and recreation. Redemption in Christ is recreation in him, a new type of total dependence upon him; in this sense, new life in Christ can only be understood on the basis of the first creation which the Son came to restore and lead beyond itself by the power of his Spirit.

5.   The new creation, although it is more than nature, can only be referred to in terms of the natural order God first created; in fact, Christians believe that the Word of God, the agent of the new creation, is also the means by which God first created the universe. The Epistle to the Hebrews, in the verse preceding the one we have already quoted, speaks of the Son as he through whom the world was created (1:2), and the Gospel of John refers to the Word who became flesh in Jesus as the one through whom "all things were made" (1:2).

6.   Creation and recreation are the key to each other in the Christian life, and so it is that the methodology we have employed in this study has found it necessary, on the one hand, to use nature as a key to understanding who God is and what he does in Christ, and, on the other hand, to use recreation in Christ as the key to understanding the purpose of the first creation, which preceded it in time.

7.   Theological anthropology is a central concern to our churches because it provides and probes concepts, images and symbols from creation for receiving and appropriating, expressing and communicating our understanding of the God in whom we believe.

8.   God is infinite. Our finite minds can have no comprehensive knowledge of him, but Christians believe that Jesus, the incarnate Word of God, indicates to us in human terms who God is and what God is.

9.   Our churches together affirm the Christology of the Chalcedonian definition: "at once complete in Godhead and complete in manhood, truly God and truly man (the word used was *anthropos* (human), not *aner* (male), . . . begotten, for us men and for our salvation, of Mary

the Virgin, the God-bearer *(theotokos)*; one and the same Christ, Son, Lord, only-begotten, recognized in two natures without confusion, without change, without division, without separation." Thus Jesus Christ is simultaneously one in being with the Father as regards his Godhead, and one in being with us as regards his humanity. He is, therefore, described, as we have seen, as the image of the invisible God.

10. Jesus' whole life of self-giving leads to his sacrificial death on the cross and indicates the unfathomable depth of the love of God. It is through Jesus the Christ, truly divine and truly human, that God the Father and God the Holy Spirit are revealed. God is shown to be a communion of divine persons, mysteriously related in infinite, personal, self-giving love.

11. Our churches together affirm that God is triune. Both subscribe to the definitions of Christian faith set forth by the first ecumenical councils: in the one God, who is love, there are three persons, of one substance, uncreated, and eternal—the Father, the Son and the Holy Spirit (cf. *Quicumque Vult*).

12. Jesus is truly human, truly endowed with human consciousness, intellect and will. He has the same type of appetites and feelings, and goes through the same processes of thinking and willing, that we do as we exercise our freedom, responsibility and rationality in the world. Image of the mysterious God, Jesus as truly human also reveals what human beings are called to be and do, namely, to love God with one's whole heart and mind and soul and to love one's neighbor as oneself; to show such great love as to lay down one's life for one's friend. Jesus' resurrection, the newness of life granted him after his sacrificial death on the cross, reveals the power of such love to bring all human beings into that communion with God which is their eternal destiny.

13. Because God incarnate as Jesus was truly human, he was committed to all aspects of the created order, limiting as they are. He was a male. He belonged to a particular family; he spoke a particular language. Joseph followed a particular trade, which Jesus also followed (Mk. 6:3). Jesus belonged to Israel, and was heir to Israel's religious tradition.

14. Are these particularities relevant to the image of God in him? Although we may affirm things about God on the basis of our knowledge of Jesus, those affirmations must be subject to careful and critical evaluation to determine their theological significance. One source of disagreement among us, not strictly according to church allegiance, is caused by different opinions regarding the relevance of sexuality in the revelation of God in Christ in general, and regarding the theological significance of Jesus maleness in particular.

II. Human Sexuality as Significant for the Imaging of God

A. Images of God: Male and Female

15. Since human beings are made in the image of God, and are sexual, the question presents itself: Is God imaged forth more adequately in one sex rather than the other? We find in the biblical evidences a clear preponderance of masculine over feminine imagery for God. In the Old Testament, God is depicted, for example, as shepherd, king, father and husband: as shepherd, true guardian of Israel (Gn. 49:24), gatherer of stray sheep, who leads them to their own pasture, binds up their wounds, watches over and feeds them as he guides them toward messianic restoration (Ez. 34:11-12); as king, ruler of Israel (Nm. 23:21), leader of all nations (Ps. 22:29), creator (Ps. 74:12) and savior of Israel (Is. 33:22); as a father who loves his child, Israel (Hos. 11:1), provides for him (Ex. 4:22f; Dt. 1:31), has compassion on him and forgives him (Is. 64:8; Jer. 31:20; Ps. 103:13f); as a husband who rejoices in his bride (Is. 62:5) and longs for the affection of his wayward wife (Is. 54:5-8). Some understand this imagery to depend in large part upon the patriarchal structure of the social order in ancient Israel.

16. There are also passages in the Old Testament where God's actions and attitudes in relation to Israel are depicted in feminine images. God's mother-love for his child is faithful and unconditional: God knows what it is to carry a child in the womb, to cry out in labor, to give birth (Is. 46:3-4; Dt. 32:18; Is. 42:13-14); God's attachment to his child is just as strong as any nursing mother's (Is 49:14-15); her tender compassion (Jer. 31:20) moves her to carry her child at her breast and comfort him (Is. 66:12-13), and to stand by her child all the days of its life. The psalmist envisions God as mother (Ps. 131:1-2), as midwife (Ps. 22:9f) and as mistress of a household (Ps. 123:2), an image echoed in the Wisdom literature (Prov. 9:1-6). God's Wisdom, personified, is feminine (Wis. 7:25-8:1). Wisdom shares in the divine attributes, and appeals to the faithful disciple to embrace her as bride and mother (Prov. 4:6-8, Sir. 15:2; Wis. 8:2); she can satisfy the heart's desire.

17. In the New Testament, the reference to God as Father predominates. God is uniquely the Father of Jesus Christ (Mt. 11:27 and par.). This name, "Father," becomes synonymous with God in the fourth Gospel. Jesus teaches his disciples to address God as Father in prayer (Mt. 6:9-13, Lk. 11:2-4), following his own example (Mt. 11:25f; Mk. 14:36; Jn. 11:41f, 12:27f, and ch. 17). In and through Christ we become God's adopted children, able in the power of the Spirit to share in his relationship with the Father (Gal. 4:6; Rom. 8:15f). Jesus, the incarnate Word of God, is a male. The maternal love of God for Israel, however, is recalled in Jesus' lament over Jerusalem: He longs to gather her children as a hen gathers her chicks under her wings (Mt. 23:27).

18. Female imagery of God, Christ and the Holy Spirit appears in certain strands of patristic and medieval theological reflection and piety. The Wisdom texts of the Old Testament are brought forward and interpreted as describing an eternal aspect of God in feminine terms; these are at times associated with the Word and at times with the Holy Spirit. Greek theology in Byzantium pursued this line of thought and dedicated many churches to the divine Sophia. The Holy Spirit is hymned as "mother" by St. Ephrem, and Christ is praised as "mother" by Clement of Alexandria and later by St. Anselm and Dame Julian of Norwich. In the medieval West, mystics and theologians exhibit great freedom in applying masculine and feminine names to God. The maternal imagery of bearing, birthing, nursing, nurturing, comforting and so on, carries forward in the spiritual writings of this period a rich expression of divine-human intimacy. Christ himself was sometimes depicted as feminine and motherly (often drawing on the mother-hen passage); giving us birth from his pierced side, feeding us on his own flesh and blood, embracing us tenderly as his beloved children. Christian religious experience and theological reflection, then, have discovered a full range of human characteristics, male and female, in the sacred humanity of Jesus.

19. The unseen God, however, is beyond sexuality. Our attempts to speak of God necessarily rely on analogy and symbolism. Nor can human images and symbols for God avoid having either a masculine or feminine character. But, of course, God is neither male nor female; rather as creator, God virtually includes the perfections of both sexes, as well as those of all creatures.

B. Sexual Union and the Imaging of God

20. The decisive statement affirming that both male and female image God, and that they image him equally, is to be found in the book of Genesis: "God created man in his own image, in the image of God he created him; male and female he created them" (Gn. 1:27). This text helps us to realize that the image of God resides not simply in the solitary human being, but even more in human beings in interpersonal relationships. For human beings by nature seek their fulfillment not just in sexual union, but in ever wider forms of community. Sexual relationship is thus a pointer to such wider community.

21. But it is not only as individuals that male and female human beings image God: The division of humankind into two sexes creates a framework for interrelationships that image self-giving in God. As embodied persons we exist either as women or men. Sexuality is a given, irreducible mode of being in the world. Our bodies are not merely the somatic envelopes of our spirits, nor are they purely instrumental. Rather, we exist as a substantial unity of body and spirit. And we are saved in our bodied existence. Whereas sexuality is manifested in bodily differences, it is erroneous to equate sexuality with its genital expression.

22. Taking marital union as that which is meant to express self-donation in love, this nuptial relationship then becomes a paradigm for the relationship between God and ourselves, as well as for other experiences of human relatedness. For one thing, it highlights the dimension of "otherness" which is often described in terms of sexual duality or complementarity. Men and women fulfill complementary functions in regard to procreation and the steps leading to it. This pro-creative complementarity does not in itself imply superiority or inferiority, domination or subservience. On the contrary, it underlines the call to communion and images identity-in-difference in a human way. The value of the sexual relation as a paradigm lies, in fact, in this remarkable and unexpected quality: that precisely through the intense and exclusive relation of husband and wife comes an equally intense and profound relation to the child, the other.

23. If the relationship of male and female is thus taken as a paradigm, it follows that all forms of human community should be structured as open communions, open beyond themselves *because* of the close bonds which tie the members together. Humans who belong together by birth, by culture, by language, by historical and geographical heritage, by shared tastes and purposes, will be joined in such a way that their union will always remain open to the wider human community, and ultimately to the universality of humanity in time and space.

C. Jesus Christ as Both Image of God and Model of True Humanity

24. Jesus Christ is the uniquely given mode of true humanity to appear in human history. He alone is Second Adam. Both male and female find representative expression in him, and in him there can be no difference between male and female being in the image of God. The Synod of Douzy (860) declared *et Eva ipsa est Adam*. Thus "Eve herself is indeed human (Man)," which reflects the belief that in Christ male and female are profoundly identical in their humanity. This identity was established in the creation. Human disobedience, however, disrupted this communion with God; and under the conditions of human life distorted by sin, the identity has been rendered imperfect, a fact symbolized by the different curses pronounced on Adam and Eve. Everywhere in history the relation between male and female labors under some degree of alienation. But in Christ, Christians believe that the relation of all persons to God has been restored, and in that redemptive act all are reconciled to each other. In the situation of redeemed humanity in the kingdom of God, and in the church which anticipates that perfection, male and female are once more identical in their capacity to be images of God. "There is neither Jew nor Greek, there is neither slave nor free, there is neither male nor female; for you are all one in Christ Jesus" (Gal. 3:28).

D. Sexuality Belongs to the Order of Creation

25. The creation account in Genesis shows that the embodiment of human persons as male or female is part of God's design. Though the human person shares the condition of sexuality with most other material life-forms, human sexuality is of a different order. The creating and nurturing activity of the living God can be reflected and symbolized by sexuality in any part of the created order. Human sexuality, however, whether male or female, is that of a free and responsible creature capable of self-possession and deliberate self-donation in love. The fact of human sexuality, therefore, opens human beings to the possibility of entering into loving communal relationships which reflect the communion of divine self-giving love in God.
26. Yet the Genesis account vividly tells us of the entrance of sin into human life and the consequent distortion of the imaging of God in the human person. We find, as a result of sin, that persons, instead of being open to the other in self-donating love, become self-centered, self-seeking and self-absorbed. They become incapable of either giving or receiving the very love they were created to image. Instead, they experience sexual disorder, a drive either to dominate others or to be subservient to others. Coercive power tends to replace love as the strongest cohesive force in human community.
27. History testifies to much destructive inequity between men and women and to the evolution of roles in a way that undermines the dignity of both sexes. An example would be the responsibilities prescribed for women which even in the industrial democracies isolated women from the process of political enfranchisement and placed women in a position of legal inferiority to men until the success of the suffrage movement. The result of this legal treatment of women contributes even today to their being treated as inferior. Although such roles frequently come to be described as normative, one cannot rightly appeal to Christian theology to justify them.

E. Reconstitution of the Divine Image in Christ

28. The fundamental Christian assertion is that in the person of Jesus of Nazareth, the incarnate Son of God, crucified and risen, the divine image has appeared in history in an unbroken and undistorted form.

In Jesus Christ, the church sees in the midst of a sinful and alienated world what humanity was created to be and what God is truly like. Following St. Paul, we call him the Second Adam. At the incarnation, the new Adam and the new Eve appeared in history. In Jesus Christ, born of the Virgin Mary, the human enterprise begins afresh. The new creation has begun.

29. Jesus did not embody the image of God within a covenant of marriage, but rather by his whole—though single—life of sacrificial, self-giving love, culminating in his death for the world. Celibate love is, therefore, shown capable of revealing God's love without detracting from the witness given by marital love.

30. The doctrine of the image of God was developed during the first centuries of the church in light of Christian teaching about the triune God. Whereas for many this early development, especially in the West after Augustine, saw the Trinity imaged in the intrapersonal unity of the human person (memory, intellect and will), much contemporary trinitarian theology adds to this psychological analogy the comparison of the intra-trinitarian relationships with the ontological unity achieved in a loving community of persons. This communitarian analogy presupposes that the unity of the divine persons is not unlike the unity of a loving community in which each exists for the other and by reason of their mutual interrelationships.

31. The Spirit of God, present in our historical existence, working in and through the human spirit, calls each human person into a communion of love with the triune God. This relationship of the Holy Spirit to each human spirit may reconstitute in love each person's relation to self, and the person's communion with others and with the whole creation. "When we cry, 'Abba! Father!' it is the Spirit himself bearing witness with our spirit that we are children of God, and if children, then heirs, heirs of God and fellow heirs with Christ." (Rom 8:15-16, cf. Rom 5:5).

32. In other words, in the course of our present life, where the effects of sin have not been completely overcome, this basic human capacity for communion given by God in creation can be actualized, Christians believe, only by the work of the Holy Spirit. By grace, through faith, we are taken up into the relationship between the Son and the Father, and also into the mission of the Son's self-giving love for the world.

33. Jesus Christ is the one mediator of this love. He overcomes sin, death, and the law, through his dying and rising. Jesus' complete self-giving exposes as sin every act which obscures God's love. Love overcomes sin by forgiveness and by turning a person's self-centered affections to God's world. Love overcomes death, as the resurrection of Christ proclaims, and introduces the faithful to victorious participation in his resurrection.

34. Jesus represents the dawning of the epoch of the resurrection into human history. This introduces new possibilities for the imaging of God. Human sexuality points to an individual's need for others that finds its fulfillment in acts of mutual self-giving and in the openness of two—man and woman—standing side by side facing a third, the child. Besides this familial relationship, human beings are called to friendship, acquaintance and comradeship with other persons in daily social life, resulting in the joy that arises from human associations. Jesus reveals openness in all his relationships in which he gave as well as received joy, warmth and affection. Jesus' openness fulfills and transcends the openness to which human sexuality points. He had both male and female disciples; his freedom and friendship with the women of his company were unusual for his place and time. With the "12" apostles his relationship was transforming. Moreover, he characteristically reached out beyond his chosen disciples to help and heal the poor, the sick, the outcast. An immediate consequence of the cross and resurrection, the very result of his whole life of self-giving, was a model set before the whole world by the preaching and example of the apostolic community.

35. The significance of a relationship to Jesus which has the quality of *agape* is expressed powerfully in the fourth Gospel: "No longer do I call you servants . . . but I have called you friends" (Jn. 15:15). The Johannine phrase, "Greater love has no man than this, that a man lay down his life for his friends" (Jn. 15:13), applies in the first instance to Jesus whose death on the cross and glorious resurrection are both the cause and pattern of truly Christian friendship.

36. Christian marriage constitutes a special case of such friendship. The depth of the union of persons achieved through a sexual relationship is increased and transformed by the love which "bears all things, believes all things, hopes all things, endures all things" (I Cor. 13:7). Such a union in Christ is called in Ephesians the *una caro* (one flesh) which symbolized the relationship between Christ and the church: "This is a great mystery, and I take it to mean Christ and the church" (Eph. 5:32).

37. But friendship in the more general case provides a second set of images of God in relation to creation, as powerful in their way as the image of a man and woman bound together in sexual union and in the covenant of marriage. Marriage might be said to symbolize for the church the exclusive and radical commitment of God to those whom God calls into covenant through Christ. Friendship in the wider sense, and even other forms of human community, when transformed by the *agape* of Christ, may be said to symbolize the fact that in the kingdom of heaven, where "they neither marry nor are given in marriage" (Mt. 22:30), all persons are to be united to each other and to God by the self-donating love offered in the cross of Christ. In the church, where the kingdom of God both is already and is not yet, both sets of images are important for our understanding of God.

38. This vision of the kingdom of heaven introduces an eschatological perspective. In that consummation, all persons, male and female, are to be in so full and deep a relationship with one another as now is found on earth especially in marriage.

39. Since in human experience marital union is the means to a deep relationship, some would propose that, even in the present age, for each person some relationship besides marriage may include marital intimacy. In this context, something should be said about homosexuality.

40. There is a widely recognized distinction between homosexual orientation and genital homosexual acts. Homosexual persons, because they are human persons, are individually in the image of God. Where this has been forgotten, homosexual persons have suffered hurt and injustice in society and even exclusion from open participation in the life of the Christian community. Mitigation of this situation is urgently needed.

41. Both our churches teach that genital homosexual acts, like heterosexual genital acts outside of marriage, are morally wrong. Therefore a homosexual union, no matter how close or how evidently characterized by loyalty and self-giving love, does not constitute *una caro* (one flesh) or provide an image of God. Thus a homosexual relationship cannot be sanctified by the sacrament of marriage.

III. The Image of God in the Ecclesial Communion

A. The Church as "Sacrament" of Unity

42. The church is sacramental. It is an effective sign and instrument of communion with God and of the unity of humankind (*LG* 1 and 8). This vocation of the ecclesial community has two dimensions: first, the church itself is to be "a people made one with the unity of the Father, the Son and the Holy Spirit" (St. Cyprian, *De Orat. Dom.*, 23), and, second, it has the mission of restoring all people to this same unity (*BCP* 855).

43. The source and center of this ecclesial community is Jesus Christ, the Word made flesh, in the power of the Spirit. The action which most fully sacramentalizes the unity of the baptized is the eucharistic liturgy; at the table of the Lord all are made one body, one spirit with him in the one bread and the common cup. In this meal, the gift of Christ's life on the altar of the cross, the ultimate expression of self-donating love, is effectively proclaimed (Windsor 5). It is the power of this love which establishes the bonds of communion.

B. Baptism Establishes Equality in Christ

44. Through baptism the Holy Spirit conforms individual men and women to Christ in the mystery of his death and resurrection. The image of God, obscured by pride and disobedience, is restored in the waters of baptism. The newly baptized are reborn in Christ by the Spirit and truly put on Christ. Those who become members of one body by baptism all share in a common dignity, regardless of race, nationality, social condition or sex. In Christ there is neither Jew nor Greek, slave nor free, male nor female (Gal. 3:28). All have the same grace of adoption and the same vocation to holiness. Our churches agree that men and women are equal before God, and therefore equal in dignity and equal in rights before each other. We set behind us patterns of discrimination based on the supposition that women are inferior to men and therefore may not be granted the same fundamental personal rights as men (GS 29).

45. Even when there is a commitment to equality between men and women, there remains a tension whenever the principle of equality is applied to concrete situations. Part of the tension is due to the fact that in our churches several lines of thought co-exist without being fully harmonized. These often work at cross purposes and are not always clearly identified. One may briefly describe three such anthropologies, though there may well be more.

46. Some would choose to emphasize the complementary roles of men and women in society and in the church. These roles are understood to extend beyond those involved in marital union and the procreation of children. The notion of complementarity affects not only physical functions but the whole of the male or female personality. The advancement of women is approved and encouraged as long as their special nature is properly safeguarded. In church and society, equality is not identity, they urge, even if it is granted that in Christ and in the eyes of God, male and female are profoundly identical in constituting the image of God. The goal in the life of the church and the world is "effective complementarity, so that men and women bring their proper riches and dynamism to the building of a world, not leveled and uniform, but harmonious and unified, according to the design of the creator" (Paul VI, in "Women: Disciples and Co-Workers," *Origins* 4, May 1, 1975, p. 718). Different social roles, in this view, are not incompatible with equal dignity.

47. Others, on the basis of the same principle of baptismal equality, wish to state that physical characteristics aside, the elements of maleness and femaleness are by no means obvious, and their identification by no means straightforward. The diversity which is attested when the complementary dimensions of male and female are mentioned is also found within a "whole" person of either sex, who is usually discovered to display wide ranges of "masculine" and "feminine" characteristics in varying proportions. Therefore the division of roles in society and the church is not properly made on the basis of a complementarity between male and female. The effort to do this may in fact preclude the obedience of a man or a woman to a genuine vocation. This group, too, would affirm that in society and in the church, equality is not identity, even if equality implies identity in constituting the image of God. The world can best become the harmonious and unified whole according to the design of the creator by providing for both women and men the social and ecclesial freedom to offer themselves to any call from God.

48. It is also possible, and one may find grounds for this in some interpretations of the biblical and patristic traditions, to see maleness and femaleness as general ways of being fully human. Being determined more by culture than by nature, these ways may be interchangeable. They vary from place to place and they have changed through time. The freedom that comes from the Gospel both contributes to the emancipation of Christians from the cultural stereotypes of their milieu, and makes it possible for them to submit to such stereotypes if they so wish. In any case, the mutual relationship between male and female is not one of complementarity and it is not adequately described as equality or "unitariness"; it is rather a supplementarity. Each, being already fully human, receives from the other a supplement of humanity.

C. Christian Vocations

49. In accord with the new commandment given us by the Lord, "Love one another as I have loved you" (Jn. 15:12), commitment to the love of God and neighbor is at the heart of every Christian's calling. From the first centuries of Christian life, the pagans observed: "These Christians, see how they love one another" (Tertullian, *Apol.* 39).

50. The call to love of neighbor is not restricted to the Christian community, but extends into the social and political structures of the workplace. Christians, by reason of their baptismal commitment of faith and charity, profoundly nourished at the table of the eucharist, are sent forth in mission to proclaim the Gospel and to bring gospel values to bear on the daily events of family and civic life and on the larger world of work, politics, science, the arts, the media, the international order and so on. This transformation of the social order is the task of all Christians, especially lay persons, who by the witness of an integrally Christian life sanctify the world from within.

51. *The single life.* Jesus, while remaining single, perfectly fulfilled his Father's will in all things. The church needs to esteem the single life as a possible vocation in its own right, and regard it not as a rejection of marriage but as a grace-filled state by which the human person may image forth the divine love. The witness to this love offered by single persons, or by groups of single persons who share a common life, has been accepted by the church as a fruitful imaging of the trinitarian life of self-donating love (*LG* 41). In our age, Christians are rediscovering that there is a vocation to the single life. Many who respond to that vocation believe that they are called as individuals to find their community among those in the local church. Others respond to a call to join a community or association within the church which provides them support in this vocation.

Consecrated Virginity, Committed Celibacy and Religious Chastity

52. In our churches, chastity and virginity consecrated to God by vow, and celibacy for the sake of the kingdom (Mt. 19:22), are held in high esteem. Those called to this mode of imitation of Jesus experience their vocation as a special gift of grace. Their voluntary surrender of the great good of Christian marriage is a sign of preferential love for the Lord and the church, his body, an icon of the eschatological state in which there is no more marriage (Mt. 22:30). They especially symbolize for the church the extensive quality of Jesus' love which was open to all, complementing the symbol of intensive love provided by couples married in Christ. Commitment to the celibate life should free men and women to be available for loving service to the wider community. This state can be understood as a call to a nuptial relationship directly with Christ patterned on the love between Christ and the church described in Ephesians 5:32.

53. Both our churches interpret this eschatological witness as a counterpart and support to the incarnational witness of the love between married persons. These vocations are mutually enriching for the building up of the whole body of Christ in *agape*.

54. *Christian marriage.* Both our churches agree that matrimony is an "authentic sacramental means of grace" (*ARC 12-Year Report*). As such, Christian marriage is a way of salvation not only for the couple, but for the sake of the whole church. Both our churches agree that in marriage "the man and woman enter into a life-long union, make their vows before God and the church and receive the grace and blessing of God to help them fulfill their vows" (*BCP* 861).

55. It is our conviction that the life-giving and the love-making powers of the marital act are of equal dignity and value. Each aspect is an "authentic sacramental means of grace" (*ARC 12-Year Report*). And, although there are serious differences in formal teaching and pastoral practice between our churches regarding artificial contraception and divorce, the Anglican-Roman Catholic Special Commission on the Theology of Marriage and Its Application to Mixed Marriages offers hope that they need not be divisive. What is of primary significance, however, is that both our churches perceive that marriage sacramentalizes the "nuptial meaning of the body" (John Paul II, *Original Unity of Man and Woman*, pp. 106-112). "The union of husband and wife in heart, body, and mind is intended by God for their mutual joy, for the help and comfort given one another in prosperity and adversity; and, when it is God's will, for the procreation of children and their nurture in the knowledge and love of the Lord" (*BCP* 423).

56. The Scriptures provide, among many, three points of comparison which help to illuminate the reality of sacramental marriage. One we have already noted (no. 22) is the teaching that male and female taken together constitute an image of God. In the "one flesh" (Gn. 3:22) of their nuptial relationship, they are an image of God. God, however, according to biblical revelation, has no consort. The only nuptial relationship of the God of Israel is with the people he has created and redeemed. The covenant relationship between God and Israel, then, is likened to the bond of marriage between man and woman. God is pictured as the husband of a desert bride, the chosen people (Is. 54:5; Ezk. 16:8-14). The covenant pledge, "I will be their God and they will be my people" (Jer. 31:33), suggests the marriage vow. The new covenant is described as God's generous restoration of the marriage relationship which has been violated by Israel's "adultery" with the gods of the nations (Hos. 2:14-16; 19-23; Is. 62:3-5). Finally, the New Testament brings forward this symbolism by presenting Christ as the bridegroom of the church (2 Cor. 11:2; Rev. 19:4; 12:2-9). The nuptial relationship which characterizes the union of Christ and the church is set forth as a model in the exhortation to married Christians found in the letter to the Ephesians, 5:21-33. In particular, husbands are urged to love their wives in the manner in which Christ gave himself for his bride, the church (Eph. 5:25).

57. *Holy orders.* The distinctive witness of all ministry in the church, that of the baptized as well as that of the ordained, that of the married as well as that of the single, is "to represent Christ and his church" (*BCP*, pp. 855-856). Holy orders images Christ in keeping with the functions and charisms of the bishop (pastor), the priest (presbyter, or elder), the deacon (servant).

58. In the New Testament, Christ's ministry is identified as that of *episkope;* he is "the shepherd and bishop *(episkopos)* of your souls" (1 Pt. 2:25). Subsequently the office of bishop in both our communions has been identified as the normative pastoral office, with emphasis on responsible guidance and care. (Cf. *Canterbury Statement*, paras. 6, 9, 16).

59. As the mediator of the new covenant (Heb. 9:15), Christ is called archpriest (9:11). He presents God to us and us to God. As holy orders developed in the church, those who presided over the eucharist also came to be called priests, since they were perceived to officiate at the offering which participated in (and therefore was) Christ's priestly offering. They image to the church in many contexts Christ's mediatorial work.

60. We are reminded that both our churches see the whole church as called to participate in Christ's priestly offering and, as stated by Canterbury (no. 13), "Christian ministers are . . . particularly in presiding at the eucharist—representatives of the whole church in the

fulfillment of its priestly vocation of self-offering to God as a living sacrifice (Rom. 12:1). Nevertheless their (ordained) ministry is not an extension of the common Christian priesthood but belongs to another realm of the gifts of the Spirit."

61. Christ's ministry is also identified in the New Testament as that of servant or deacon: He "came not to be served, but to serve" (Mk. 10:45). The ministry of deacon was subsequently identified with Christ's servant role, an identification made as early as Ignatius of Antioch (Trallians 3.1). The function of the deacon is primarily to exercise a helping ministry, both in the liturgy and in the world.

62. Our churches differ over the admission of women to holy orders. In particular, we are divided on the question of their admission to the priesthood and episcopacy. (It appears that Roman Catholics have not formally ruled out for women the possibility of ordination to the diaconate.) Together we subscribe to the Canterbury Statement in its assertion: "Because the eucharist is the memorial of the sacrifice of Christ, the action of the presiding minister in reciting again the words of Christ at the last supper and distributing to the assembly the holy gifts is seen to stand in a sacramental relation to what Christ himself did in offering his own sacrifice" (no. 13).

Furthermore, we accept the elucidation on this passage which explains that "it is only the ordained minister who presides at the eucharist, in which, in the name of Christ and on behalf of his church, he recites the narrative of the institution of the last supper and invokes the Holy Spirit upon the gifts" (*Final Report*, p. 41). Our churches disagree, however, on whether a woman may be ordained to "stand in sacramental relation to Christ himself" in the special case of eucharistic presidency.

63. Recently, the Sacred Congregation for the Doctrine of the Faith, with the authorization of Pope Paul VI, reviewed this question and reaffirmed what the congregation sees as the unbroken tradition of the church, namely, that "the church, in fidelity to the example of the Lord, does not consider herself authorized to admit women to priestly ordination" (*Declaration on the Question of Admission of Women to the Ministerial Priesthood*, p. 4). The church's constant tradition is taken to be based on the example of the Lord and the apostles; this tradition is supported by an appeal (considered a "theological reflection," not demonstrative proof) to the "profound fittingness" of reserving priestly ordination to men.

64. In the eucharistic liturgy, the declaration states, the priest acts *in persona Christi*, that is, he takes the role of Christ in the eucharist "to the point of being his very image when he pronounces the words of consecration" (p. 12). Sacramental signification, according to the Vatican declaration, requires that there be a "natural resemblance" between the sign (priest) and the one signified (Christ). The declaration draws the conclusion that only a man may take the role of Christ in the eucharist, for in this capacity the priest is the image of Christ who was and remains a man.

65. The declaration considers the fact that the incarnation took place "according to the male sex" (p. 12) to be harmonious with the whole economy of salvation and especially with the nuptial imagery surrounding the mystery of the covenant. Christ loved the church and gave himself up for her (Eph. 5:25), sealing the new covenant in his blood. The priest, who acts *in persona Christi* in the sacramental celebration of this mystery, is a sign, therefore, of Christ as author of the new covenant, bridegroom and head of the church. On such grounds, the maleness of the celebrating priest seems appropriate.

66. Not all Episcopalians support the ordination of women to the priesthood. Even those who do would not wish to deny that there are allusions to the nuptial mystery in the celebration of the eucharist. But, they would argue, such an allusion is not explicit in the New Testament; and it does not seem to them that it should apply to the celebrant of the eucharist, at least in such a way as to necessitate the restriction of holy orders to men. These Episcopalians, in other words, do not maintain as the declaration does, the necessity of a natural resemblance between the maleness of the priest and maleness of Jesus. The church as a whole, including all its members, lay and ordained, male and female, is the bride of Christ; Christ, the risen and exalted Lord, is the bridegroom. The priest, these Episcopalians hold, is an image of Christ by virtue of what he or she is and does as a person baptized and ordained with power of the Spirit, not by virtue of male sexuality. Ordination to priesthood confers the power to represent Christ in all aspects of his mediatorial function, as Christ represented the church to God and God to the church. Ordination includes power to celebrate the sacraments. Episcopalians who defend the ordination of women therefore find no solid theological reasons to exclude women from the priesthood.

67. Furthermore, they believe that the priesthood should be able to claim all human gifts in its service, and thus stands to gain from the admission of women. Moreover, they believe that the ordination of women serves to protect the doctrine of God and Christology from an imbalance which diminishes Christian revelation and keeps women essentially unequal as members of the church. Male and female images of both Christ and God are found in Christian tradition, holding out rich possibilities for our contemporary understanding of the human as encompassing both male and female characteristics.

68. For both our churches, we believe that further studies are needed in the nature of representational imagery, especially as it applies to the eucharist and the ordained ministry. Moreover it is debated whether issues related to the eucharist and the ordained ministry are doctrinal or disciplinary. Increasing numbers in both our churches feel that our teachings are in fact compatible and that our differences need not separate us. (Cf. *Final Report*, pp. 1-45; *ARC-DOC IV*, "ARC Response to the Vatican Declaration on the Question of the Admission of Women to the Ministerial Priesthood"; *Decree on Ecumenism*, nos. 11 and 4 "on the hierarchy of truths").

D. The Communion of Saints

69. Holiness is the transparent radiancy of the image of God. But what does it mean to say that the church is holy? The church is holy because the Holy Spirit dwells within it and the church has been endowed with the sacramental means of grace. Through these means, the Holy Spirit enables the church fittingly to worship the triune God and to express in praise, blessing and thanksgiving its homage for the gift of creation and God's wondrous compassion of salvation. Christ, as head of the body which is his church, unceasingly intercedes with the Father for the whole human family, while the church and its members offer in the spirit their intercessions for their brothers and sisters through Christ, that God's will may be done on earth as it is in heaven. Both our traditions profess their belief in this communion of saints, the Spirit-led movement of perpetual prayer offered to the Father through Christ by his body which is the church. Moreover, the church is a proper home of the human imaging present in the culture of each period of history.

70. The Virgin Mary, the *Theotokos*, was perceived during the patristic era and by the theological tradition common to our two communions to be so unique a realization of holiness that she is considered to be the prototype of redeemed humanity. The doctrine of the immaculate conception reflects the faith that all of God's gifts are given "in the beginning," that is, that the divine initiative of grace does not come about because of our disposition to receive it but purely out of God's free and loving gift. God's grace, poured out on believers at baptism, is required for the Christian to respond to God's call. Mary responded fully: "Behold the servant of the Lord, be it done to me according to your word" (Lk. 1:38). Yet, as far as we know, Mary was not baptized. The Roman Catholic Church teaches that Mary, like us, needed God's grace to respond, but, unlike us, always possessed that grace. It is this reality to which the dogma of the immaculate conception refers. Mary is described in Luke's Gospel as "highly favored one" (commonly translated as "full of grace") because she is to be, as Jesus' mother, the Mother of God. The doctrine of Mary's perpetual virginity signifies that she has been chosen by God to give herself totally to God. The doctrine of the assumption signifies that it is the totality of her being which is taken up into God by grace and that she is "a sign of certain hope and comfort to the pilgrim people of God" (*LG* 68).

71. Mary has played a far less prominent role in Anglican piety and theology than in Roman Catholic. To be sure, Episcopalians recognize in her not only one who is "blessed among women" (Lk. 1:42), the "highly favored one" (Lk. 1:28), but also one who has been exalted in heaven above angels and archangels. "O, higher than the cherubim, more glorious than the seraphim . . . Thou, bearer of the eternal Word, most gracious, magnify the Lord," runs one of the most popular hymns in the Episcopal hymnal. As noted, Episcopalians, with the Council of Ephesus, acknowledge her as *Theotokos*.

72. Nevertheless, the English Reformation largely eliminated Marian piety, and it is unfamiliar to and thought to be unnecessary by many Episcopalians. In particular, the Marian doctrines of immaculate conception and assumption mentioned in the foregoing discussion, which received dogmatic definition during the time of separation of our two churches, could not easily be accepted as requirements necessary to faith. "One consequence of our separation has been a tendency for Anglicans and Roman Catholics alike to exaggerate the importance of Marian dogmas in themselves at the expense of other truths more closely related to the foundation of the Christian faith" (*Final Report*, p. 96).

73. Although the language would be unfamiliar, some Episcopalians could, without contradicting their accepted formularies, speak of the immaculate conception as Mary's vocation and election by God to be the mother of the Messiah, citing Jeremiah's account of God's calling on him to be a prophet, "Before I formed you in the womb, I knew you" (Jer. 1:5). Similarly they could entertain as a possible teaching that Mary has been taken up totally into God's presence by grace, witness the typology of Enoch (Gn. 5:24) or Elijah (II Kgs. 2:11), although the biblical basis for such a claim seems lacking in Mary's case, and its necessity therefore questionable.

74. It is plain that further discussion of these points is required before full understanding is achieved, but we think that a significant beginning has been made possible by the anthropological considerations made in this paper.

75. Both our churches have come to revere the Lord's mother and the other saints who form one ecclesial communion with us, and who give us examples of how we are to witness to Christ. We are grateful to the triune God who gives them to us as heroes and heroines of our faith. "He speaks to us in them and offers us a sign of the kingdom, to which we are powerfully attracted, so great a cloud of witnesses is there given (Cf. Heb. 12:1) and such a witness to the truth of the Gospel" (*LG* 50). Through the anointing of the Spirit, they have realized to the fullest degree what it means to be human by their transformation in Christ, and help confirm our hope of reaching full maturity in eternal life. Veneration (*dulia*) of them is essentially different from the worship (*latria*) due to God alone. Devotion to the saints is always for the sake of God's glory. "Every authentic witness of love, indeed, offered by us to those who are in heaven tends to and terminates in Christ, 'the crown of all the saints,' and through him in God who is wonderful in his saints and is glorified in them" (*LG* 50).

76. The intercessory role of the saints, especially that of Mary, need not obscure or diminish the unique mediatorship of our risen Lord, but may show its power. It should not interfere with the immediate union of the faithful with Christ, but foster it, since even intercessory prayers, whose form is always "pray *for* us," are directed to the Father. And all Christian prayer is directed to the Father through Christ, the one true mediator, in the Holy Spirit.

77. Veneration is a broader concept in the Roman Catholic Church than it is in the Anglican Communion. Anglicans may be found occasionally to use the language of veneration; but it is much more usual for them to speak of praising and thanking God *for* his saints and *with* his saints. It is more customary for them to speak of remembering his saints with honor and respect than of venerating them. The Roman Catholic Church does not worship the saints but directs prayers to the Father in the Spirit, with Christ, surrounded by his saints, who reflect his image in themselves. As we have said, holiness is the transparent radiancy of the image of God.

We conclude by suggesting that in the foregoing treatment of theological anthropology we have offered a context in which to approach many of the difficult questions that confront our two churches. We hope that our studies and this report offer a reasonable approach within which each church can better understand the different teachings and practice of the other as regards human sexuality, Christian marriage, the ordination of women to the ministerial priesthood, Marian doctrines and devotions, and the communion of saints, and by which further studies of our teachings on these questions can be conducted in more profitable and less polemical ways.

Members of ARC during the writing of
Images of God: Reflections on Christian Anthropology

Episcopal Members:

The Rt. Rev. Arthur A. Vogel, Chairman
Dr. V. Nelle Bellamy
The Rev. Prof. Charles P. Price
The Rt. Rev. David Reed
Prof. Henry B. Veatch
The Rt. Rev. William Weinhauer
The Rev. Prof. J. Robert Wright
The Rev. William A. Norgren (staff)

Roman Catholic Members:

The Most Rev. Raymond W. Lessard, Chairman
The Most Rev. William H. Keeler
Sr. Sara Butler, MSBT
The V. Rev. Frederick M. Jelly, OP
The Rev. Allan Laubenthal
The Rev. Herbert J. Ryan, SJ
The Rev. George Tavard
The Rev. Joseph W. Witmer (staff)

The Fellowship of St. Gregory and St. Augustine

The Fellowship of St. Gregory and St. Augustine[1] is an international communion of prayer, work and study dedicated to the organic reunion in diversity of the Anglican and Roman Catholic Churches.

The Fellowship is co-sponsored by the Camaldolese Order (Roman Catholic), the Order of the Holy Cross (Anglican), the Order of St. Helena (Anglican), and the Camaldolese Nuns' Communities (Roman Catholic).

Membership is open to all Christians who are interested in working for the goals of the Fellowship.

Besides individual membership, the Fellowship welcomes group memberships, especially of religious and parish communities with existing or potential Anglican-Roman Catholic covenant relationships.

The Fellowship sets for itself a threefold task and commitment:

1. *Prayer.* Believing that our coming reunion will be primarily a work of the Father through the Spirit of Christ, the Fellowship is dedicated to a patient but persistent prayer, both to petition such communion and to experience its fruits in anticipation through the unity of our prayers. Nourished by the monastic prayer of the sponsoring and other affiliated religious orders, this personal and shared prayer should be disseminated among the clergy and faithful everywhere.

2. *Work.* God works through the mediation of men and women, and the monastic tradition stresses, besides prayer, the complementary principle of work; the ecumenical effort cannot remain an inner-directed, ecclesial concern only, because the human family impatiently awaits a united Christian mission and service. Thus the Fellowship seeks to promote carefully studied joint ventures in the area of pastoral, catechetical and social work.

3. *Study.* Such prayer and work, if they are to bear their full fruit, must be nourished by careful and deep study of our distinctive historical, spiritual and theological heritages, of our underlying communion, and of the consequent ecumenical possibilities for the present and the future of "unity without absorption." Both the monastic

---

1. For further information about the Fellowship of St. Gregory and St. Augustine, or to obtain a subscription to the Fellowship Newsletter *Cross and Dove*, write: % Incarnation Priory, 1601 Oxford Street, Berkeley, CA 94709.

and parish experiences, which are profoundly interrelated, predate our separation. We believe that the biblical and patristic roots of these experiences offer an important area of study to understand better our future unity in diversity.

The Fellowship thus seeks to be a source of spiritual, pastoral and theological support for already existing Anglican and Roman Catholic organizations interested in the reunion of these two "sister churches." The visits of the Archbishops of Canterbury with the Popes in these recent years and their joint statements, and the theological documents of the Anglican-Roman Catholic International Commission, represent a key point of reference for the Fellowship, which seeks to disseminate to the faithful everywhere a fuller knowledge of these events and documents. We expect that specific programs for the promotion of the union of our churches will emerge out of the growing life of the Fellowship.

Thus the biblical-patristic-monastic values of communion (*koinonia*), of friendship love (*agape*), constitute the substance and scope of the Fellowship. Because these are permanent, indeed eschatological values, the Fellowship foresees, even after our hoped-for union is a blessed fact, a continuing task of deepening and guaranteeing the bonds of that communion by the same threefold commitment to prayer, work and study.

Index

95, 108, 109, 123, 128,
155, 158, 190, 201, 208,
221, 230, 258, 274, 291,
297
Anglican observers at   62
as promise of renewed
    Christianity   36
Decree on Ecumenism   16
Documents of   34
Secretariat for Promoting Christian
    Unity   12, 16, 62, 63, 64,
    68, 102, 132, 133, 134, 179
self-donation in love   314
separation, formal   120
of the Anglican from the
    Catholic Church   54
serious dialogue   8
service   144-146
commitment to   144
of humanity   246
varieties of among
    Churches   152
services of reconciliation   40
noneucharistic   10
sex roles, changing   171
sexual union and imaging of
    God   312-313
sexuality   308
belonging to order of
    creation   314
relevance in revelation of God
    in Christ   310
significant for imaging of
    God   311-317
shared ministry of the word   173
understandings   150
sin, forgiveness of   246
single life, the   319-320
sister Churches   161
Sistine Chapel   154-159
social community   30
justice   226
order, transformation as task of
    Christians   319
structure   170
solutions, practical   113
speakers for conferences   41
Spirit [see Holy Spirit]
spiritual calling of the
    Church   139
hunger   24
life   170
nature of relationships   66
relation   68-69
renewal   30

spirituality   173
stable ideology   215
Statement of Faith and Order of the
    Episcopal Church
    (1948)   34
students, temporary exchange
    of   9, 16
study of heritages   328
biblical and patristic roots
    of   329
monastic and parish experiences
    of   328-329
supernatural kinship   31
suspicion and mistrust, occasions
    of   105
synod of bishops   69
of Douzy   313
of the Anglican
    Communion   222
or regional council   257
Synoptic Gospels   80
tradition   87

teaching authority, exercised by
    Church   278
technology, positive and negative
    effects of   143
terminology   250
differences in   58
texts, internationally agreed   79
thankfulness   7
theologians, agreement of   8
growing convergence of method
    and outlook   229
task proper to   65
theological agreement   1
anthropology   326
approaches, variety of   237
commissions, doctrinal
    agreements by   264
convergences   158
dialogue   49
differences   175
discourse   58
discussion   48
education, co-operation in   19
exploration   149
expressions, variety of   60
interpretation of primacy of see
    of Rome   258
issues   171
joint research, necessity of   69
language, ambiguity of   59
methodology   161

About the Editors

Joseph W. Witmer, Associate Director of the Bishops' Committee for Ecumenical and Interreligious Affairs of the National Conference of Catholic Bishops, staffs the Anglican-Roman Catholic dialogue in the United States of America.

J. Robert Wright, Theological Consultant to the Ecumenical Office of the Episcopal Church, is a member of the Anglican-Roman Catholic International Commission and Professor of Church History at the General Theological Seminary in New York City. His academic specialty is Anglo-Papal relations of the Middle Ages, in which he took his doctorate at Oxford, and he has published substantial works.

Editors' Note: At the beginning of many entries in this publication, introductory notes were prepared by Herbert J. Ryan, SJ, and J. Robert Wright, both long-time members of ARC-USA.

For a full bibliography of the Anglican-Roman Catholic dialogue, at both national and international levels, see *A Bibliography of Interchurch and Interconfessional Theological Dialogue*, edited by J. F. Puglisi and S. J. Voicu (Rome: Centro Pro Unione, 1984).

Design
Mack Rowe Visual Communications, Ltd.; Alexandria, Va.

Typography
VIP Systems, Inc.; Alexandria, Va.

Typeface
Palatino and Palatino Bold